The world is parallel.

If we want to write programs that behave as other objects behave in
the real world, then these programs will have a concurrent structure.

Use a language that was designed for writing concurrent applications,
and development becomes a lot easier.

Erlang programs model how we think and interact.

► **Joe Armstrong**

Programming Erlang
Software for a Concurrent World

Programming Erlang
Software for a Concurrent World

Joe Armstrong

The Pragmatic Bookshelf
Raleigh, North Carolina   Dallas, Texas

Pragmatic Bookshelf

Many of the designations used by manufacturers and sellers to distinguish their products are claimed as trademarks. Where those designations appear in this book, and The Pragmatic Programmers, LLC was aware of a trademark claim, the designations have been printed in initial capital letters or in all capitals. The Pragmatic Starter Kit, The Pragmatic Programmer, Pragmatic Programming, Pragmatic Bookshelf and the linking *g* device are trademarks of The Pragmatic Programmers, LLC.

Every precaution was taken in the preparation of this book. However, the publisher assumes no responsibility for errors or omissions, or for damages that may result from the use of information (including program listings) contained herein.

Our Pragmatic courses, workshops, and other products can help you and your team create better software and have more fun. For more information, as well as the latest Pragmatic titles, please visit us at

http://www.pragmaticprogrammer.com

Copyright © 2007 armstrongonsoftware.

All rights reserved.

No part of this publication may be reproduced, stored in a retrieval system, or transmitted, in any form, or by any means, electronic, mechanical, photocopying, recording, or otherwise, without the prior consent of the publisher.

Printed in the United States of America.

ISBN-10: 1-9343560-0-X
ISBN-13: 978-1-934356-00-5
Printed on acid-free paper with 50% recycled, 15% post-consumer content.
P2.0 printing, August, 2007
Version: 2007-8-8

Contents

Chapter 1

Begin

Oh no! Not another programming language! Do I have to learn yet another one? Aren't there enough already?

I can understand your reaction. There are loads of programming languages, so why should you learn another?

Here are five reasons why you should learn Erlang:

- You want to write programs that run faster when you run them on a multicore computer.
- You want to write fault-tolerant applications that can be modified without taking them out of service.
- You've heard about "functional programming" and you're wondering whether the techniques really work.
- You want to use a language that has been battle tested in real large-scale industrial products that has great libraries and an active user community.
- You don't want to wear your fingers out by typing lots of lines of code.

Can we do these things? In Section 20.3, *Running SMP Erlang*, on page 370, we'll look at some programs that have linear speed-ups when we run them on a thirty-two-core computer. In Chapter 18, *Making a System with OTP*, we'll look at how to make highly reliable systems that have been in round-the-clock operation for years. In Section 16.1, *The Road to the Generic Server*, on page 286, we'll talk about techniques for writing servers where the software can be upgraded without taking the server out of service.

In many places we'll be extolling the virtues of functional programming. Functional programming forbids code with side effects. Side effects and concurrency don't mix. You can have sequential code with side effects, or you can have code and concurrency that is free from side effects. You have to choose. There is no middle way.

Erlang is a language where concurrency belongs to the programming language and not the operating system. Erlang makes parallel programming easy by modeling the world as sets of parallel processes that can interact only by exchanging messages. In the Erlang world, there are parallel processes but no locks, no synchronized methods, and no possibility of shared memory corruption, since there is no shared memory.

Erlang programs can be made from thousands to millions of extremely lightweight processes that can run on a single processor, can run on a multicore processor, or can run on a network of processors.

1.1 Road Map

- Chapter 2, *Getting Started*, on page 7 is a quick "jump in and swim around" chapter.
- Chapter 3, *Sequential Programming*, on page 33 is the first of two chapters on sequential programming. It introduces the ideas of pattern matching and of nondestructive assignments.
- Chapter 4, *Exceptions*, on page 67 is about exception handling. No program is error free. This chapter is about detecting and handling errors in sequential Erlang programs.
- Chapter 5, *Advanced Sequential Programming*, on page 77 is the second chapter on sequential Erlang programming. It takes up some advanced topics and fills in the remaining details of sequential programming.
- Chapter 6, *Compiling and Running Your Program*, on page 109 talks about the different ways of compiling and running your program.
- In Chapter 7, *Concurrency*, on page 129, we change gears. This is a nontechnical chapter. What are the ideas behind our way of programming? How do we view the world?
- Chapter 8, *Concurrent Programming*, on page 133 is about concurrency. How do we create parallel processes in Erlang? How do processes communicate? How fast can we create parallel processes?

- Chapter 9, *Errors in Concurrent Programs*, on page 151 talks about errors in parallel programs. What happens when a process fails? How can we detect process failure, and what can we do about it?

- Chapter 10, *Distributed Programming*, on page 167 takes up distributed programming. Here we'll write several small distributed programs and show how to run them on a cluster of Erlang nodes or on free-standing hosts using a form of socket-based distribution.

- Chapter 11, *IRC Lite*, on page 183 is a pure application chapter. We tie together the themes of concurrency and socket-based distribution with our first nontrivial application: a mini IRC-like client and server program.

- Chapter 12, *Interfacing Techniques*, on page 205 is all about interfacing Erlang to foreign-language code.

- Chapter 13, *Programming with Files*, on page 219 has numerous examples of programming with files.

- Chapter 14, *Programming with Sockets*, on page 239 shows you how to program with sockets. We'll look at how to build sequential and parallel servers in Erlang. We finish this chapter with the second sizable application: a SHOUTcast server. This is a streaming media server, which can be used to stream MP3 data using the SHOUTcast protocol.

- Chapter 15, *ETS and DETS: Large Data Storage Mechanisms*, on page 267 describes the low-level modules ets and dets. ets is a module for very fast, destructive, in-memory hash table operations, and dets is designed for low-level disk storage.

- Chapter 16, *OTP Introduction*, on page 285 is an introduction to OTP. OTP is a set of Erlang libraries and operating procedures for building industrial-scale applications in Erlang. This chapter introduces the idea of a behavior (a central concept in OTP). Using behaviors, we can concentrate on the functional behavior of a component, while allowing the behavior framework to solve the nonfunctional aspects of the problem. The framework might, for example, take care of making the application fault tolerant or scalable, whereas the behavioral callback concentrates on the specific aspects of the problem. The chapter starts with a general discussion on how to build your own behaviors and then moves to describing the gen_server behavior that is part of the Erlang standard libraries.

- Chapter 17, *Mnesia: The Erlang Database*, on page 307 talks about the Erlang database management system (DBMS) Mnesia. Mnesia is an integrated DBMS with extremely fast, soft real-time response times. It can be configured to replicate its data over several physically separated nodes to provide fault-tolerant operation.

- Chapter 18, *Making a System with OTP*, on page 329 is the second of the OTP chapters. It deals with the practical aspects of sewing together an OTP application. Real applications have a lot of small messy details. They must be started and stopped in a consistent manner. If they crash or if subcomponents crash, they must be restarted. We need error logs so that if they do crash, we can figure out what happened after the event. This chapter has all the nitty-gritty details of making a fully blown OTP application.

- Chapter 19, *Multicore Prelude*, on page 359 is a short introduction to why Erlang is suited for programming multicore computers. We talk in general terms about shared memory and message passing concurrency and why we strongly believe that languages with no mutable state and concurrency are ideally suited to programming multicore computers.

- Chapter 20, *Programming Multicore CPUs*, on page 361 is about programming multicore computers. We talk about the techniques for ensuring that an Erlang program will run efficiently on multicore computers. We introduce a number of abstractions for speeding up sequential programs on multicore computers. Finally we perform some measurements and develop our third major program, a full-text search engine. To write this, we first implement a function called mapreduce—this is a higher-order function for parallelizing a computation over a set of processing elements.

- Appendix A, on page 385, describes the type system used to document Erlang functions.

- Appendix B, on page 391, describes how to set up Erlang on the Windows operating system (and how to configure emacs on all operating systems).

- Appendix C, on page 395, has a catalog of Erlang resources.

- Appendix D, on page 399, describes lib_chan, which is a library for programming socket-based distribution.

- Appendix E, on page 415, looks at techniques for analyzing, profiling, debugging, and tracing your code.

- Appendix F, on page 435, has one-line summaries of the most used modules in the Erlang standard libraries.

1.2 Begin Again

Once upon a time a programmer came across a book describing a funny programming language. It had an unfamiliar syntax, equal didn't mean equals, and variables weren't allowed to vary. Worse, it wasn't even object-oriented. The programs were, well, different....

Not only were the programs different, but the whole approach to programming was different. The author kept on and on about concurrency and distribution and fault tolerance and about a method of programming called concurrency-oriented programming—whatever that might mean.

But some of the examples looked like fun. That evening the programmer looked at the example chat program. It was pretty small and easy to understand, even if the syntax was a bit strange. Surely it couldn't be that easy.

The basic program was simple, and with a few more lines of code, file sharing and encrypted conversations became possible. The programmer started typing....

What's This All About?

It's about concurrency. It's about distribution. It's about fault tolerance. It's about functional programming. It's about programming a distributed concurrent system without locks and mutexes but using only pure message passing. It's about speeding up your programs on multicore CPUs. It's about writing distributed applications that allow people to interact with each other. It's about design methods and behaviors for writing fault-tolerant and distributed systems. It's about modeling concurrency and mapping those models onto computer programs, a process I call *concurrency-oriented programming*.

I had fun writing this book. I hope you have fun reading it.

Now go read the book, write some code, and have fun.

1.3 Acknowledgments

Many people have helped in the preparation of this book, and I'd like to thank them all here.

First, Dave Thomas, my editor: Dave has been teaching me to write and subjecting me to a barrage of never-ending questions. Why this? Why that? When I started the book, Dave said my writing style was like "standing on a rock preaching." He said, "I want you to talk to people, not preach." The book is better for it. Thanks, Dave.

Next, I've had a little committee of language experts at my back. They helped me decide what to leave out. They also helped me clarify some of the bits that are difficult to explain. Thanks here (in no particular order) to Björn Gustavsson, Robert Virding, Kostis Sagonas, Kenneth Lundin, Richard Carlsson, and Ulf Wiger.

Thanks also to Claes Vikström who provided valuable advice on Mnesia, to Rickard Green on SMP Erlang, and to Hans Nilsson for the stemming algorithm used in the text-indexing program.

Sean Hinde and Ulf Wiger helped me understand how to use various OTP internals, and Serge Aleynikov explained active sockets to me so that I could understand.

Helen Taylor (my wife) has proofread several chapters and provided hundreds of cups of tea at appropriate moments. What's more, she put up with my rather obsessive behavior for the last seven months. Thanks also to Thomas and Claire; and thanks to Bach and Handel, Zorro and Daisy, and Doris, who have helped me stay sane, have purred when stroked, and have gotten me to the right addresses.

Finally, to all the readers of the beta book who filled in errata requests: I have cursed you and praised you. When the first beta went out, I was unprepared for the entire book to be read in two days and for you to shred every page with your comments. But the process has resulted in a much better book than I had imagined. When (as happened several times) dozens of people said, "I don't understand this page," then I was forced to think again and rewrite the material concerned. Thanks for your help, everybody.

Joe Armstrong
May 2007

Chapter 2

Getting Started

2.1 Overview

As with every learning experience, you'll pass through a number of stages on your way to Erlang mastery. Let's look at the stages we cover in this book and the things you'll experience along the way.

Stage 1: I'm Not Sure...

As a beginner, you'll learn how to start the system, run commands in the shell, compile simple programs, and become familiar with Erlang. (Erlang is a small language, so this won't take you long.)

Let's break this down into smaller chunks. As a beginner, you'll do the following:

- Make sure you have a working Erlang system on your computer.
- Learn to start and stop the Erlang shell.
- Discover how to enter expressions into the shell, evaluate them, and understand the results.
- See how to create and modify programs using your favorite text editor.
- Experiment with compiling and running your programs in the shell.

Stage 2: I'm Comfortable with Erlang

By now you'll have a working knowledge of the language. If you run into language problems, you'll have the background to make sense of Chapter 5, *Advanced Sequential Programming*, on page 77.

At this stage you'll be familiar with Erlang, so we'll move on to more interesting topics:

- You'll pick up more advanced uses of the shell. The shell can do a lot more than we let on when you were first learning it. (For example, you can recall and edit previous expressions. This is covered in Section 6.5, *Command Editing in the Erlang Shell*, on page 121.)
- You'll start learning the libraries (called *modules* in Erlang). Most of the programs I write can be written using five modules: lists, io, file, dict, and gen_tcp; therefore, we'll be using these modules a lot throughout the book.
- As your programs get bigger, you'll need to learn how to automate compiling and running them. The tool of choice for this is make. We'll see how to control the process by writing a makefile. This is covered in Section 6.4, *Automating Compilation with Makefiles*, on page 118.
- The bigger world of Erlang programming uses an extensive library collection called OTP.[1] As you gain experience with Erlang, you'll find that knowing OTP will save you lots of time. After all, why reinvent the wheel if someone has already written the functionality you need? We'll learn the major OTP *behaviors*, in particular gen_server. This is covered in Section 16.2, *Getting Started with gen_server*, on page 295.
- One of the main uses of Erlang is writing distributed programs, so now is the time to start experimenting. You can start with the examples in Chapter 10, *Distributed Programming*, on page 167, and you can extend them in any way you want.

Stage 2.5: I May Learn Some Optional Stuff

You don't have to read every chapter in this book the first time through.

Unlike most of the languages you have probably met before, Erlang is a concurrent programming language—this makes it particularly suited for writing distributed programs and for programming modern multi-core and SMP[2] computers. Most Erlang programs will just run faster when run on a multicore or SMP machine.

Erlang programming involves using a programming paradigm that I call *concurrency-oriented programming* (COP).

---

1. Open Telecom Platform.
2. Symmetric multiprocessing.

When you use COP, you break down problems and identify the natural concurrency in their solutions. This is an essential first step in writing any concurrent program.

Stage 3: I'm an Erlang Master

By now you've mastered the language and can write some useful distributed programs. But to achieve true mastery, you need to learn even more:

- Mnesia. The Erlang distribution comes complete with a built-in fast, replicated database called Mnesia. It was originally designed for telecom applications where performance and fault tolerance are essential. Today it is used for a wide range of nontelecom applications.
- Interfacing to code written in other programming languages, and using *linked-in drivers*. This is covered in Section 12.4, *Linked-in Drivers*, on page 214.
- Full use of the OTP behaviors-building supervision trees, start scripts, and so on. This is covered in Chapter 18, *Making a System with OTP*, on page 329.
- How to run and optimize your programs for a *multicore* computer. This is covered in Chapter 20, *Programming Multicore CPUs*, on page 361.

The Most Important Lesson

There's one rule you need to remember throughout this book: programming is fun. And I personally think programming distributed applications such as chat programs or instant messaging applications is a lot more fun than programming conventional sequential applications. What you can do on one computer is limited, but what you can do with networks of computers becomes unlimited. Erlang provides an ideal environment for experimenting with networked applications and for building production-quality systems.

To help you get started with this, I've mixed some real-world applications in among the technical chapters. You should be able to take these applications as starting points for your own experiments. Take them, modify them, and deploy them in ways that I hadn't imagined, and I'll be very happy.

2.2 Installing Erlang

Before you can do anything, you have to make sure you have a functioning version of Erlang on your system. Go to a command prompt, and type erl:

```
$ erl
Erlang (BEAM) emulator version 5.5.2 [source] ... [kernel-poll:false]

Eshell V5.5.2  (abort with ^G)
1>
```

On a Windows system, the command erl works only if you have installed Erlang and changed the PATH environment variable to refer to the program. Assuming you've installed the program in the standard way, you'll invoke Erlang through the Start > All Programs > Erlang OTP menu. In Appendix B, on page 391, I'll describe how I've rigged Erlang to run with MinGW and MSYS.

Note: I'll show the banner (the bit that says "Erlang (BEAM) ... (abort with ^G)") only occasionally. This information is useful only if you want to report a bug. I'm just showing it here so you won't get worried if you see it and wonder what it is. I'll leave it out in most of the examples unless it's particularly relevant.

If you see the shell banner, then Erlang is installed on your system. Exit from it (press Ctrl+G, followed by the letter q, and then hit Enter or Return).[3] Now you can skip ahead to Section 2.3, *The Code in This Book*, on page 12.

If instead you get an error saying erl is an unknown command, you'll need to install Erlang on your box. And that means you'll need to make a decision—do you want to use a prebuilt binary distribution, use a packaged distribution (on OS X), build Erlang from the sources, or use the Comprehensive Erlang Archive Network (CEAN)?

Binary Distributions

Binary distributions of Erlang are available for Windows and for Linux-based operating systems. The instructions for installing a binary system are highly system dependent. So, we'll go through these system by system.

---

3. Or give the command q() in the shell.

Windows

You'll find a list of the releases at http://www.erlang.org/download.html. Choose the entry for the latest version, and click the link for the Windows binary—this points to a Windows executable. Click the link, and follow the instructions. This is a standard Windows install, so you shouldn't have any problems.

Linux

Binary packages exist for Debian-based systems. On a Debian-based system, issue the following command:

```
> apt-get install erlang
```

Installing on Mac OS X

As a Mac user, you can install a prebuilt version of Erlang using the MacPorts system, or you can build Erlang from source. Using MacPorts is marginally easier, and it will handle updates over time. However, MacPorts can also be somewhat behind the times when it comes to Erlang releases. During the initial writing up this book, for example, the MacPorts version of Erlang was two releases behind the then current version. For this reason, I recommend you just bite the bullet and install Erlang from source, as described in the next section. To do this, you'll need to make sure you have the developer tools installed (they're on the DVD of software that came with your machine).

Building Erlang from Source

The alternative to a binary installation is to build Erlang from the sources. There is no particular advantage in doing this for Windows systems since each new release comes complete with Windows binaries and all the sources. But for Mac and Linux platforms, there can be some delay between the release of a new Erlang distribution and the availability of a binary installation package. For any Unix-like OS, the installation instructions are the same:

1. Fetch the latest Erlang sources.[4] The source will be in a file with a name such as otp_src_R11B-4.tar.gz (this file contains the fourth maintenance release of version 11 of Erlang).

---

4. From http://www.erlang.org/download.html.

2. Unpack, configure, make, and install as follows:

```
$ tar -xzf otp_src_R11B-4.tar.gz
$ cd otp_src_R11B-4
$ ./configure
$ make
$ sudo make install
```

Note: You can use the command ./configure --help to review the available configuration options before building the system.

Use CEAN

The Comprehensive Erlang Archive Network (CEAN) is an attempt to gather all the major Erlang applications in one place with a common installer. The advantage of using CEAN is that it manages not only the basic Erlang system but a large number of packages written in Erlang. This means that as well as being able to keep your basic Erlang installation up-to-date, you'll be able to maintain your packages as well.

CEAN has precompiled binaries for a large number of operating systems and processor architectures. To install a system using CEAN, go to http://cean.process-one.net/download/, and follow the instructions. (Note that some readers have reported that CEAN might not install the Erlang compiler. If this happens to you, then start the Erlang shell and give the command cean:install(compiler). This will install the compiler.)

2.3 The Code in This Book

Most of the code snippets we show come from full-length, running examples, which you can download.[5] To help you find your way, if a code listing in this book can be found in the download, there'll be a bar above the snippet (just like the one here):

```
shop1.erl
```
```
-module(shop1).
-export([total/1]).

total([{What, N}|T]) -> shop:cost(What) * N + total(T);
total([])            -> 0.
```

This bar contains the path to the code within the download. If you're reading the PDF version of this book and your PDF viewer supports hyperlinks, you can click the bar, and the code should appear in a browser window.

---

5. From http://pragmaticprogrammer.com/titles/jaerlang/code.html.

2.4 Starting the Shell

Now let's get started. We can interact with Erlang using an interactive tool called *the shell*. Once we've started the shell, we can type expressions, and the shell will display their values.

If you've installed Erlang on your system (as described in Section 2.2, *Installing Erlang*, on page 10), then the Erlang shell, erl, will also be installed. To run it, open a conventional operating system command shell (cmd on Windows or a shell such as bash on Unix-based systems). At the command prompt, start the Erlang shell by typing erl:

❶
```
$ erl
Erlang (BEAM) emulator version 5.5.1 [source] [async-threads:0] [hipe]

Eshell V5.5.1  (abort with ^G)
```
❷ `1> % I'm going to enter some expressions in the shell ..`
❸ `1> 20 + 30.`
❹ `50`
❺ `2>`

Let's look at what we just did:

❶ This is the Unix command to start the Erlang shell. The shell responds with a banner telling you which version of Erlang you are running.

❷ The shell printed the prompt 1>, and then we typed a comment. The percent (%) character indicates the start of a comment. All the text from the percent sign to the end of line is treated as a comment and is ignored by the shell and the Erlang compiler.

❸ The shell repeated the prompt 1> since we hadn't entered a complete command. At this point we entered the expression 20 + 30, followed by a period and a carriage return. (Beginners often forget to enter the period. Without it, Erlang won't know that we've finished our expression, and we won't see the result displayed.)

❹ The shell evaluated the expression and printed the result (50, in this case).

❺ The shell printed out another prompt, this time for command number 2 (because the command number increases each time a new command is entered).

Have you tried running the shell on your system? If not, please stop and try it now. If you just read the text without typing in the commands, you might think that you understand what is happening, but you will not have transferred this knowledge from your brain to your fingertips—programming is not a spectator sport. Just like any form of athletics, you have to practice a lot.

Enter the expressions in the examples exactly as they appear in the text, and then try experimenting with the examples and changing them a bit. If they don't work, stop and ask yourself what went wrong. Even an experienced Erlang programmer will spend a lot of time interacting with the shell.

As you get more experienced, you'll learn that the shell is a really powerful tool. Previous shell commands can be recalled (with Ctrl+P and Ctrl+N) and edited (with emacs-like editing commands). This is covered in Section 6.5, *Command Editing in the Erlang Shell*, on page 121. Best of all, when you start writing distributed programs, you will find that you can attach a shell to a running Erlang system on a different Erlang node in a cluster or even make a secure shell (ssh) connection directly to an Erlang system running on a remote computer. Using this, you can interact with any program on any node in a system of Erlang nodes.

Warning: You can't type everything you read in this book into the shell. In particular, you can't type the code that's listed in the Erlang program files into the shell. The syntactic forms in an .erl file are *not* expressions and are not understood by the shell. The shell can evaluate only Erlang expressions and doesn't understand anything else. In particular, you can't type module annotations into the shell; these are things that start with a hyphen (such as -module, -export, and so on).

The remainder of this chapter is in the form of a number of short dialogues with the Erlang shell. A lot of the time I won't explain all the details of what is going on, since this would interrupt the flow of the text. In Section 5.4, *Miscellaneous Short Topics*, on page 89, I'll fill in the details.

2.5 Simple Integer Arithmetic

Let's evaluate some arithmetic expressions:

```
1> 2 + 3 * 4.
14
2> (2 + 3) * 4.
20
```

Important: You'll see that this dialogue starts at command number 1 (that is the shell printed, 1>). This means we have started a new Erlang

Is the Shell Not Responding?

If the shell didn't respond after you typed a command, then you might have forgotten to end the command with a period followed by carriage return (called *dot-whitespace*).

Another thing that might have gone wrong is that you've started to type something that is quoted (that is, starts with a single or double quote mark) but have not yet typed a matching closing quote mark that should be the same as the open quote mark.

If any of these happen, then the best thing to do is type an extra closing quote, followed by dot-whitespace.

If things go really wrong and the system won't respond at all, then just press Ctrl+C (on Windows, Ctrl+Break). You'll see the following output:

```
BREAK: (a)bort (c)ontinue (p)roc info (i)nfo (l)oaded
       (v)ersion (k)ill (D)b-tables (d)istribution
```

Now just press a to abort the current Erlang session.

Advanced: You can start and stop multiple shells. See Section 6.7, *The Shell Isn't Responding*, on page 124 for details.

shell. Every time you see a dialogue that starts with 1>, you'll have to start a new shell if you want to *exactly* reproduce the examples in the book. When an example starts with a prompt number that is greater than 1, this means the shell session is continued from the previous examples so you don't have to start a new shell.

Note: If you're going to type these examples into the shell as you read the text (which is *absolutely* the best way to learn), then you might like to take a quick peek at Section 6.5, *Command Editing in the Erlang Shell*, on page 121.

You'll see that Erlang follows the normal rules for arithmetic expressions, so 2 + 3 * 4 means 2 + (3 * 4) and not (2 + 3) * 4.

Erlang uses arbitrary-sized integers for performing integer arithmetic. In Erlang, integer arithmetic is exact, so you don't have to worry about arithmetic overflows or not being able to represent an integer in a certain word size.

Variable Notation

Often we will want to talk about the values of particular variables. For this I'll use the notation Var ↦ Value, so, for example, A ↦ 42 means that the variable A has the value 42. When there are several variables, I'll write {A ↦ 42, B ↦ true ... }, meaning that A is 42, B is true, and so on.

Why not try it? You can impress your friends by calculating with very large numbers:

```
3> 123456789 * 987654321 * 112233445566778899 * 998877665544332211.
13669560260321809985966198898925761696613427909935341
```

You can enter integers in a number of ways.[6] Here's an expression that uses base 16 and base 32 notation:

```
4> 16#cafe * 32#sugar.
1577682511434
```

2.6 Variables

How can you store the result of a command so that you can use it later? That's what variables are for. Here's an example:

```
1> X = 123456789.
123456789
```

What's happening here? First, we assign a value to the variable X; then, the shell prints the value of the variable.

Note: All variable names *must* start with an uppercase letter.

If you want to see the value of a variable, just enter the variable name:

```
2> X.
123456789
```

Now that X has a value, you can use it:

```
3> X*X*X*X.
232305722798259244150093798251441
```

---

6. See Section 5.4, *Integers*, on page 102.

Single Assignment Is Like Algebra

When I went to school, my math teacher said, "If there's an *X* in several different parts in the same equation, then all the *X*s mean the same thing." That's how we can solve equations: if we know that X+Y=10 and X-Y=2, then *X* will be 6 and *Y* will be 4 in both equations.

But when I learned my first programming language, we were shown stuff like this:

X = X + 1

Everyone protested, saying "you can't do that!" But the teacher said we were wrong, and we had to unlearn what we learned in math class. X isn't a math variable: it's like a pigeon hole/little box....

In Erlang, variables are just like they are in math. When you associate a value with a variable, you're making an assertion—a statement of fact. This variable has that value. And that's that.

However, if you try to assign a different value to the variable X, you'll get a somewhat brutal error message:

```
4> X = 1234.
=ERROR REPORT==== 11-Sep-2006::20:32:49 ===
Error in process <0.31.0> with exit value:
  {{badmatch,1234},[{erl_eval,expr,3}]}

** exited: {{badmatch,1234},[{erl_eval,expr,3}]} **
```

What on Earth is going on here? Well, to explain it, I'm going to have to shatter two assumptions you have about the simple statement X = 1234:

- First, X is not a variable, at least not in the sense that you're used to in languages such as Java and C.
- Second, = is not an assignment operator.

This is probably one of the trickiest areas when you're new to Erlang, so let's spend a couple of pages digging deeper.

Variables That Don't Vary

Erlang has *single assignment variables*. As the name suggests, single assignment variables can be given a value only once. If you try to change the value of a variable once it has been set, then you'll get an error (in fact, you'll get the badmatch error we just saw). A variable that has had a value assigned to it is called a *bound* variable; otherwise, it is called an *unbound* variable. All variables start off unbound.

When Erlang sees a statement such as X = 1234, it binds the variable X to the value 1234. Before being bound, X could take any value: it's just an empty hole waiting to be filled. However, once it gets a value, it holds on to it forever.

At this point, you're probably wondering why we use the name variable. This is for two reasons:

- They are variables, but their value can be changed only once (that is, they change from being unbound to having a value).
- They look like variables in conventional programming languages, so when we see a line of code that starts like this:

  X = ...

  then our brains say, "Aha, I know what this is; X is a variable, and = is an assignment operator." And our brains are almost right: X is almost a variable, and = is almost an assignment operator.

  Note: The use of ellipses (...) in Erlang code examples just means "code I'm not showing."

In fact, = is a pattern matching operator, which behaves like assignment when X is an unbound variable.

Finally, the *scope* of a variable is the lexical unit in which it is defined. So if X is used inside a single function clause, its value does not "escape" to outside the clause. There are no such things as global or private variables shared by different clauses in the same function. If X occurs in many different functions, then all the values of X are different.

Pattern Matching

In most languages, = denotes an assignment statement. In Erlang, however, = denotes a *pattern matching* operation. Lhs = Rhs really means this: evaluate the right side (Rhs), and then match the result against the pattern on the left side (Lhs).

Now a variable, such as X, is a simple form of pattern. As we said earlier, variables can be given a value only once. The *first* time we say X = SomeExpression, Erlang says to itself, "What can I do to make this statement true?" Because X doesn't yet have a value, it can bind X to the value of SomeExpression, the statement becomes valid, and everyone is happy.

Then, if at a later stage we say X = AnotherExpression, then this will succeed only if SomeExpression and AnotherExpression are identical. Here's an example of this:

```
Line 1    1> X = (2+4).
   -      6
   -      2> Y = 10.
   -      10
   5      3> X = 6.
   -      6
   -      4> X = Y.
   -      =ERROR REPORT==== 27-Oct-2006::17:25:25 ===
   -      Error in process <0.32.0> with exit value:
  10         {{badmatch,10},[{erl_eval,expr,3}]}
   -      5> Y = 10.
   -      10
   -      6> Y = 4.
   -      =ERROR REPORT==== 27-Oct-2006::17:25:46 ===
  15      Error in process <0.37.0> with exit value:
   -         {{badmatch,4},[{erl_eval,expr,3}]}
   -      7> Y = X.
   -      =ERROR REPORT==== 27-Oct-2006::17:25:57 ===
   -      Error in process <0.40.0> with exit value:
  20         {{badmatch,6},[{erl_eval,expr,3}]}
```

Here's what happened: In line 1 the system evaluated the expression 2+4, and the answer was 6. So after this line, the shell has the following set of bindings: {X ↦ 6}. After line 3 has been evaluated, we have the bindings {X ↦ 6, Y ↦ 10}.

Now we come to line 5. Just before we evaluate the expression, we know that X ↦ 6, so the match X = 6 succeeds.

When we say X = Y in line 7, our bindings are {X ↦ 6, Y ↦ 10}, and therefore the match fails and an error message is printed.

Expressions 4 to 7 either succeed or fail depending upon the values of X and Y. Now is a good time to stare hard at these and make sure you really understand them before going any further.

At this stage it may seem that I am belaboring the point. All the patterns to the left of the "=" are just variables, either bound or unbound, but as we'll see later, we can make arbitrarily complex patterns and match them with the "=" operator. I'll be returning to this theme after we have introduced tuples and lists, which are used for storing compound data items.

Why Does Single Assignment Make My Programs Better?

In Erlang a variable is just a reference to a value—in the Erlang implementation, a bound variable is represented by a pointer to an area of storage that contains the value. This value cannot be changed.

The fact that we cannot change a variable is extremely important and is unlike the behavior of variables in imperative languages such as C or Java.

Let's see what can happen when you're allowed to change a variable. Let's define a variable X as follows:

```
1> X = 23.
23
```

Now we can use X in computations:

```
2> Y = 4 * X + 3.
95
```

Now suppose we could *change* the value of X (horrors):

```
3> X = 19.
```

Fortunately, Erlang doesn't allow this. The shell complains like crazy and says this:

```
=ERROR REPORT==== 27-Oct-2006::13:36:24 ===
Error in process <0.31.0> with exit value:
  {{badmatch,19},[{erl_eval,expr,3}]}
```

This just means that X cannot be 19 since we've already said it was 23.

But just suppose we could do this; then the value of Y would be wrong in the sense that we can no longer interpret statement 2 as an equation. Moreover, if X could change its value at many different points in the program and something goes wrong, it might be difficult saying which particular value of X had caused the failure and at exactly which point in the program it had acquired the wrong value.

In Erlang, variable values cannot be changed after they have been set. This simplifies debugging. To understand why this is true, we must ask ourselves what an error is and how an error makes itself known.

One rather common way that you discover that your program is incorrect is that a variable has an unexpected value. If this is the case, then you have to discover exactly the point in your program where the variable acquired the incorrect value. If this variable changed values many

> ### Absence of Side Effects Means We Can Parallelize Our Programs
>
> The technical term for memory areas that can be modified is *mutable state*. Erlang is a functional programming language and has immutable state.
>
> Much later in the book we'll look at how to program multicore CPUs. When it comes to programming multicore CPUs, the consequences of having immutable state are enormous.
>
> If you use a conventional programming language such as C or Java to program a multicore CPU, then you will have to contend with the problem of *shared memory*. In order not to corrupt shared memory, the memory has to be locked while it is accessed. Programs that access shared memory must not crash while they are manipulating the shared memory.
>
> In Erlang, there is no mutable state, there is no shared memory, and there are no locks. This makes it easy to parallelize our programs.

times and at many different points in your program, then finding out exactly which of these changes was incorrect can be extremely difficult.

In Erlang there is no such problem. A variable can be set only once and thereafter never changed. So once we know which variable is incorrect, we can *immediately* infer the place in the program where the variable became bound, and this must be where the error occurred.

At this point you might be wondering how it's possible to program *without* variables. How can you express something like X = X + 1 in Erlang? The answer is easy. Invent a new variable whose name hasn't been used before (say X1), and write X1 = X + 1.

2.7 Floating-Point Numbers

Let's try doing some arithmetic with floating-point numbers:

```
1> 5/3.
1.66667
2> 4/2.
2.00000
3> 5 div 3.
1
```

```
4> 5 rem 3.
2
5> 4 div 2.
2
6> Pi = 3.14159.
3.14159
7> R = 5.
5
8> Pi * R * R.
78.5397
```

Don't get confused here. In line 1 the number at the end of the line is the integer 3. The period signifies the end of the expression and is not a decimal point. If I had wanted a floating-point number here, I'd have written 3.0.

"/" always returns a float; thus, 4/2 evaluates to 2.0000 (in the shell). N div M and N rem M are used for integer division and remainder; thus, 5 div 3 is 1, and 5 rem 3 is 2.

Floating-point numbers must have a decimal point followed by at least one decimal digit. When you divide two integers with "/", the result is automatically converted to a floating-point number.

2.8 Atoms

In Erlang, atoms are used to represent different non-numerical constant values.

If you're used to enumerated types in C or Java, then you will already have used something very similar to atoms whether you realize it or not.

C programmers will be familiar with the convention of using symbolic constants to make their programs self-documenting. A typical C program will define a set of global constants in an include file that consists of a large number of constant definitions; for example, there might be a file glob.h containing this:

```
#define OP_READ 1
#define OP_WRITE 2
#define OP_SEEK 3
...
#define RET_SUCCESS 223
...
```

Typical C code using such symbolic constants might read as follows:

```
#include "glob.h"
int ret;
ret = file_operation(OP_READ, buff);
if( ret == RET_SUCCESS ) { ... }
```

In a C program the values of these constants are not interesting; they're interesting here only because they are all different and they can be compared for equality.

The Erlang equivalent of this program might look like this:

```
Ret = file_operation(op_read, Buff),
if
    Ret == ret_success ->
        ...
```

In Erlang, atoms are global, and this is achieved without the use of macro definitions or include files.

Suppose you want to write a program that manipulates days of the week. How would you represent a day in Erlang? Of course, you'd use one of the atoms monday, tuesday, ...

Atoms start with lowercase letters, followed by a sequence of alphanumeric characters or the underscore (_) or at (@) sign.[7] For example: red, december, cat, meters, yards, joe@somehost, and a_long_name.

Atoms can also be quoted with a single quotation mark ('). Using the quoted form, we can create atoms that start with uppercase letters (which otherwise would be interpreted as variables) or that contain nonalphanumeric characters. For example: 'Monday', 'Tuesday', '+', '*', 'an atom with spaces'. You can even quote atoms that don't need to be quoted, so 'a' means exactly the same as a.

The value of an atom is just the atom. So if you give a command that is just an atom, the Erlang shell will print the value of that atom:

```
1> hello.
hello
```

It may seem slightly strange talking about the value of an atom or the value of an integer. But because Erlang is a functional programming language, every expression must have a value. This includes integers and atoms that are just extremely simple expressions.

---

7. You might find that a period (.) can also be used in atoms—this is an unsupported extension to Erlang.

2.9 Tuples

Suppose you want to group a fixed number of items into a single entity. For this you'd use a *tuple*. You can create a tuple by enclosing the values you want to represent in curly brackets and separating them with commas. So, for example, if you want to represent someone's name and height, you might use {joe, 1.82}. This is a tuple containing an atom and a floating-point number.

Tuples are similar to structs in C, with the difference that they are anonymous. In C a variable P of type point might be declared as follows:

```
struct point {
  int x;
  int y;
} P;
```

You'd access the fields in a C struct using the dot operator. So to set the x and y values in the point, you might say this:

```
P.x = 10; P.y = 45;
```

Erlang has no type declarations, so to create a "point," we might just write this:

```
P = {10, 45}
```

This creates a tuple and binds it to the variable P. Unlike C, the fields of a tuple have no names. Since the tuple itself just contains a couple of integers, we have to remember what it's being used for. To make it easier to remember what a tuple is being used for, it's common to use an atom as the first element of the tuple, which describes what the tuple represents. So we'd write {point, 10, 45} instead of {10, 45}, which makes the program a lot more understandable.[8]

Tuples can be nested. Suppose we want to represent some facts about a person—their name, height, foot size, and eye color. We could do this as follows:

```
1> Person = {person,
               {name, joe},
               {height, 1.82},
               {footsize, 42},
               {eyecolour, brown}}.
```

---

8. This way of tagging a tuple is not a language requirement but is a recommended style of programming.

Note how we used atoms both to identify the field and (in the case of name and eyecolour) to give the field a value.

Creating Tuples

Tuples are created automatically when we declare them and are destroyed when they can no longer be used. Erlang uses a garbage collector to reclaim all unused memory, so we don't have to worry about memory allocation.

If you use a variable in building a new tuple, then the new tuple will share the value of the data structure referenced by the variable. Here's an example:

```
2> F = {firstName, joe}.
{firstName,joe}
3> L = {lastName, armstrong}.
{lastName,armstrong}
4> P = {person, F, L}.
{person,{firstName,joe},{lastName,armstrong}}
```

If you try to create a data structure with an undefined variable, then you'll get an error. So in the next line, if we try to use the variable Q that is undefined, we'll get an error:

```
5> {true, Q, 23, Costs}.
** 1: variable 'Q' is unbound **
```

This just means that the variable Q is undefined.

Extracting Values from Tuples

Earlier, we said that =, which looks like an assignment statement, was not actually an assignment statement but was really a pattern matching operator. You might wonder why we were being so pedantic. Well, it turns out that pattern matching is fundamental to Erlang and that it's used for lots of different tasks. It's used for extracting values from data structures, and it's also used for flow of control within functions and for selecting which messages are to be processed in a parallel program when you send messages to a process.

If we want to extract some values from a tuple, we use the pattern matching operator =.

Let's go back to our tuple that represents a point:

```
1> Point = {point, 10, 45}.
{point, 10, 45}.
```

Supposing we want to extract the fields of Point into the two variables X and Y, we do this as follows:

```
2> {point, X, Y} = Point.
{point,10,45}
3> X.
10
4> Y.
45
```

In command 2, X is bound to 10 and Y to 45. The value of the expression Lhs = Rhs is defined to be Rhs, so the shell prints {point,10,45}.

As you can see, the tuples on both sides of the equal sign must have the same number of elements, and the corresponding elements on both sides must bind to the same value.

Now suppose you had entered something like this:

```
5> {point, C, C} = Point.
=ERROR REPORT==== 28-Oct-2006::17:17:00 ===
Error in process <0.32.0> with exit value:
{{badmatch,{point,10,45}},[{erl_eval,expr,3}]}
```

What happened? The pattern {point, C, C} does not match {point, 10, 45}, since C cannot be simultaneously 10 and 45. Therefore, the pattern matching fails,[9] and the system prints an error message.

If you have a complex tuple, then you can extract values from the tuple by writing a pattern that is the same shape (structure) as the tuple and that contains unbound variables at the places in the pattern where you want to extract values.[10]

To illustrate this, we'll first define a variable Person that contains a complex data structure:

```
1> Person={person,{name,{first,joe},{last,armstrong}},{footsize,42}}.
{person,{name,{first,joe},{last,armstrong}},{footsize,42}}
```

Now we'll write a pattern to extract the first name of the person:

```
2> {_,{_,{_,Who},_},_} = Person.
{person,{name,{first,joe},{last,armstrong}},{footsize,42}}
```

---

9. For readers familiar with Prolog: Erlang considers nonmatching a failure and does not backtrack.
10. This method of extracting variables using pattern matching is called *unification* and is used in many functional and logic programming languages.

And finally we'll print out the value of Who:

```
3> Who.
joe
```

Note that in the previous example we wrote _ as a placeholder for variables that we're not interested in. The symbol _ is called an *anonymous variable*. Unlike regular variables, several occurrences of _ in the same pattern don't have to bind to the same value.

2.10 Lists

We use lists to store variable numbers of things: things you want to buy at the store, the names of the planets, the results returned by your prime factors function, and so on.

We create a list by enclosing the list elements in square brackets and separating them with commas. Here's how we could create a shopping list:

```
1> ThingsToBuy = [{apples,10},{pears,6},{milk,3}].
[{apples,10},{pears,6},{milk,3}]
```

The individual elements of a list can be of any type, so, for example, we could write the following:

```
2> [1+7,hello,2-2,{cost, apple, 30-20},3].
[8,hello,0,{cost,apple,10},3]
```

Terminology

We call the first element of a list the *head* of the list. If you imagine removing the head from the list, what's left is called the *tail* of the list.

For example, if we have a list [1,2,3,4,5], then the head of the list is the integer 1, and the tail is the list [2,3,4,5]. Note that the head of a list can be anything, but the tail of a list is usually also a list.

Accessing the head of a list is a very efficient operation, so virtually all list-processing functions start by extracting the head of a list, doing something to the head of the list, and then processing the tail of the list.

Defining Lists

If T is a list, then [H|T] is also a list,[11] with head H and tail T. The vertical bar | separates the head of a list from its tail. [ ] is the empty list.

Whenever we construct a list using a [...|T] constructor, we should make sure that T is a list. If it is, then the new list will be "properly formed." If T is not a list, then the new list is said to be an "improper list." Most of the library functions assume that lists are properly formed and won't work for improper lists.

We can add more than one element to the beginning of T by writing [E1,E2,...,En|T]. For example:

```
3> ThingsToBuy1 = [{oranges,4},{newspaper,1}|ThingsToBuy].
[{oranges,4},{newspaper,1},{apples,10},{pears,6},{milk,3}]
```

Extracting Elements from a List

As with everything else, we can extract elements from a list with a pattern matching operation. If we have the nonempty list L, then the expression [X|Y] = L, where X and Y are unbound variables, will extract the head of the list into X and the tail of the list into Y.

So, we're in the shop, and we have our shopping list ThingsToBuy1—the first thing we do is unpack the list into its head and tail:

```
4> [Buy1|ThingsToBuy2] = ThingsToBuy1.
[{oranges,4},{newspaper,1},{apples,10},{pears,6},{milk,3}]
```

This succeeds with bindings

Buy1 ↦ {oranges,4}

and

ThingsToBuy2 ↦ [{newspaper,1}, {apples,10}, {pears,6}, {milk,3}].

We go and buy the oranges, and then we could extract the next couple of items:

```
5> [Buy2,Buy3|ThingsToBuy3] = ThingsToBuy2.
[{newspaper,1},{apples,10},{pears,6},{milk,3}]
```

This succeeds with Buy2 ↦ {newspaper,1}, Buy3 ↦ {apples,10}, and ThingsTo-Buy3 ↦ [{pears,6},{milk,3}].

---

11. Note for LISP programmers: [H|T] is a CONS cell with CAR H and CDR T. In a pattern, this syntax unpacks the CAR and CDR. In an expression, it constructs a CONS cell.

2.11 Strings

Strictly speaking, there are no strings in Erlang. *Strings* are really just lists of integers. Strings are enclosed in double quotation marks ("), so, for example, we can write this:

```
1> Name = "Hello".
"Hello"
```

Note: In some programming languages, strings can be quoted with either single or double quotes. In Erlang, you must use double quotes.

"Hello" is just shorthand for the list of integers that represent the individual characters in that string.

When the shell prints the value of a list it prints the list as a string, but only if all the integers in the list represent printable characters:

```
2> [1,2,3].
[1,2,3]
3> [83,117,114,112,114,105,115,101].
"Surprise"
4> [1,83,117,114,112,114,105,115,101].
[1,83,117,114,112,114,105,115,101].
```

In expression 2 the list [1,2,3] is printed without any conversion. This is because 1, 2, and 3 are not printable characters.

In expression 3 all the items in the list are printable characters, so the list is printed as a string.

Expression 4 is just like expression 3, except that the list starts with a 1, which is not a printable character. Because of this, the list is printed without conversion.

We don't need to know which integer represents a particular character. We can use the "dollar syntax" for this purpose. So, for example, $a is actually the integer that represents the character *a*, and so on.

```
5> I = $s.
115
6> [I-32,$u,$r,$p,$r,$i,$s,$e].
"Surprise"
```

Character Sets Used in Strings

The characters in a string represent Latin-1 (ISO-8859-1) character codes. For example, the string containing the Swedish name Håkan will be encoded as [72,229,107,97,110].

Note: If you enter [72,229,107,97,110] as a shell expression, you might not get what you expect:

```
1> [72,229,107,97,110].
"H\345kan"
```

What has happened to "Håkan"—where did he go? This actually has nothing to do with Erlang but with the locale and character code settings of your terminal.

As far as Erlang is concerned, a string is a just a list of integers in some encoding. If they happen to be printable Latin-1 codes, then they should be displayed correctly (if your terminal settings are correct).

2.12 Pattern Matching Again

To round off this chapter, we'll go back to pattern matching one more time.

The following table has some examples of patterns and terms.[12] The third column of the table, marked *Result*, shows whether the pattern matched the term and, if so, the variable bindings that were created. Look through these examples, and make sure you really understand them:

Pattern	Term	Result
{X,abc}	{123,abc}	*Succeeds* X ↦ 123
{X,Y,Z}	{222,def,"cat"}	*Succeeds* X ↦ 222, Y ↦ def, Z ↦ "cat"
{X,Y}	{333,ghi,"cat"}	*Fails*—the tuples have different shapes
X	true	*Succeeds* X ↦ true
{X,Y,X}	{{abc,12},42,{abc,12}}	*Succeeds* X ↦ {abc,12}, Y ↦ 42
{X,Y,X}	{{abc,12},42,true}	*Fails*—X cannot be both {abc,12} and true
[H|T]	[1,2,3,4,5]	*Succeeds* H ↦ 1, T ↦ [2,3,4,5]
[H|T]	"cat"	*Succeeds* H ↦ 99, T ↦ "at"
[A,B,C|T]	[a,b,c,d,e,f]	*Succeeds* A ↦ a, B ↦ b, C ↦ c, T ↦ [d,e,f]

If you're unsure about any of these, then try entering a Pattern = Term expression into the shell to see what happens.

---

12. A *term* is just an Erlang data structure.

For example:

```
1> {X, abc} = {123, abc}.
{123,abc}.
2> X.
123
3> f().
ok
4> {X,Y,Z} = {222,def,"cat"}.
{222,def,"cat"}.
5> X.
222
6> Y.
def
...
```

Note: The command f() tells the shell to *forget* any bindings it has. After this command, all variables become unbound, so the X in line 4 has nothing to do with the X in lines 1 and 2.

Now that we're comfortable with the basic data types and with the ideas of single assignment and pattern matching, so we can step up the tempo and see how to define functions and modules. Let's see how in the next chapter.

Chapter 3

Sequential Programming

In this chapter, we'll see how to write simple sequential Erlang programs. In the first section, we'll talk about modules and functions. We'll see how the ideas on pattern matching that we learned about in the previous chapter are used when we define functions.

Immediately after this, we'll return to the shopping list that we introduced in the previous chapter, and we'll write some code to work out the total cost of the items in the shopping list.

As we go along, we'll make incremental improvements to the programs we develop. That way you'll be able to see how the basic ideas evolve, and not just be presented with some finished program with no explanation as to how we got there. By understanding the steps involved, you'll get some ideas that you can apply to your own programs.

Along the way we'll be talking about higher-order functions (called *funs*) and how they can be used to create your own control abstractions. Finally, we'll talk about guards, records, **case** expressions, and **if** expressions.

So, let's get to work....

3.1 Modules

Modules are the basic unit of code in Erlang. All the functions we write are stored in modules. Modules are stored in files with .erl extensions.

Modules must be compiled before the code can be run. A compiled module has the extension .beam.[1]

Before we write our first module, we'll remind ourselves about pattern matching. All we're going to do is create a couple of data structures representing a rectangle and a circle. Then we're going to unpack these data structures and extract the sides from the rectangle and the radius from the circle. Here's how:

```
1> Rectangle = {rectangle, 10, 5}.
{rectangle, 10, 5}.
2> Circle = {circle, 2.4}.
{circle,2.40000}
3> {rectangle, Width, Ht} = Rectangle.
{rectangle,10,5}
4> Width.
10
5> Ht.
5
6> {circle, R} = Circle.
{circle,2.40000}
7> R.
2.40000
```

In lines 1 and 2 we *created* a rectangle and circle. In lines 3 and 6 we *unpacked* the fields of the rectangle and circle using pattern matching. In lines 4, 5, and 7 we printed the variable bindings that were created by the pattern matching expressions. After line 7 the variable bindings in the shell are {Width ↦ 10, Ht ↦ 5, R ↦ 2.4}.

Going from pattern matching in the shell to pattern matching in functions is an extremely small step. Let's start with a function called area that computes the areas of rectangles and circles. We'll put this in a module called geometry and store the module in the file called geometry.erl. The entire module looks like this:

`geometry.erl`

```
-module(geometry).
-export([area/1]).
area({rectangle, Width, Ht}) -> Width * Ht;
area({circle, R})            -> 3.14159 * R * R.
```

Don't worry about the **-module** and **-export** annotations (we'll talk about these later); for now I want you just to stare at the code for the area function.

---

[1] Beam is short for Bogdan's Erlang Abstract Machine; Bogumil (Bogdan) Hausman wrote an Erlang compiler in 1993 and designed a new instruction set for Erlang.

The function area consists of two *clauses*. The clauses are separated by a semicolon, and the final clause is terminated by dot-whitespace. Each clause has a *head* and a *body*; the head consists of a function name followed by a pattern (in parentheses), and the body consists of a sequence of expressions,[2] which are evaluated if the pattern in the head is successfully matched against the calling arguments. The patterns are matched in the order they appear in the function definition.

Note that the patterns such as {rectangle, Width, Ht} have become part of the area function definition. Each pattern corresponds to exactly one clause. Let's look at the first clause of the area function:

```
area({rectangle, Width, Ht}) -> Width * Ht;
```

This is a rule for computing the area of a rectangle. When we call geometry:area({rectangle, 10, 5}), the earlier pattern matches with bindings {Width ↦ 10, Ht ↦ 5}. Following the match, the code following the arrow -> is evaluated. This is just Width * Ht, which is 10*5, or 50.

Now we'll compile and run it:

```
1> c(geometry).
{ok,geometry}
2> geometry:area({rectangle, 10, 5}).
50
3> geometry:area({circle, 1.4}).
6.15752
```

So what happened here? In line 1 we give the command c(geometry), which compiles the code in the file geometry.erl. The compiler returns {ok,geometry}, which means that the compilation succeeded and that the module geometry has been compiled and loaded. In lines 2 and 3 we call the functions in the geometry module. Note how we need to include the module name together with the function name in order to identify exactly which function we want to call.

Extending the Program

Now suppose we want to extend our program by adding a square to our geometric objects. We could write this:

```
area({rectangle, Width, Ht}) -> Width * Ht;
area({circle, R})            -> 3.14159 * R * R;
area({square, X})            -> X * X.
```

---

2. See Section 5.4, *Expressions and Expression Sequences*, on page 97.

or even this:

```
area({rectangle, Width, Ht}) -> Width * Ht;
area({square, X})            -> X * X;
area({circle, R})            -> 3.14159 * R * R.
```

In this case, the order of the clauses doesn't matter; the program means the same no matter how the clauses are ordered. This is because the patterns in the clause are mutually exclusive. This makes writing and extending programs very easy—we just add more patterns. In general, though, clause order does matter. When a function is entered, the clauses are pattern matched against the calling arguments in the order they are presented in the file.

Before going any further, you should note the following about the way the *area* function is written:

- The function *area* consists of several different clauses. When we call the function, execution starts in the first clause that matches the call arguments.

- Our function does not handle the case where none of the patterns match—our program will fail with a runtime error. This is deliberate.

Many programming languages, such as C, have only one entry point per function. If we had written this in C, the code might look like this:

```
enum ShapeType { Rectangle, Circle, Square };

struct Shape {
    enum ShapeType kind;
    union {
        struct { int width, height; } rectangleData;
        struct { int radius; }        circleData;
        struct { int side;}           squareData;
    } shapeData;
};

double area(struct Shape* s) {
    if( s->kind == Rectangle ) {
      int width, ht;
      width = s->shapeData.rectangleData.width;
      ht    = s->shapeData.rectangleData.ht;
      return width * ht;
    } else if ( s->kind == Circle ) {
      ...
```

Where Has My Code Gone?

If you download the code examples in this book or want to write your own examples, you have to make sure that when you run the compiler from the shell, you are in the right directory so that the system can find your code.

If you are running on a system with a command shell, then you should change directories to the directory where your code is before trying to compile the example code.

If you're running on Windows with the standard Erlang distribution, you will need to change directories to where you have stored your code. Two commands in the Erlang shell can help you get to the right directory. If you're lost, pwd() prints the current working directory. cd(Dir) changes the current working directory to Dir. You should use forward slashes in the directory name; for example:

```
1> cd("c:/work").
c:/work
```

Tip for Windows users: Create a file called C:/Program Files/erl5.4.12/bin/.erlang (you might have to change this if your installation details vary).

Add the following to the file:

```
io:format("consulting .erlang in ~p~n",
        [element(2,file:get_cwd())]).
%% Edit to the directory where you store your code
c:cd("c:/work").
io:format("Now in:~p~n", [element(2,file:get_cwd())]).
```

Now when you start Erlang, it will automatically change directory to C:/work.

The C code performs what is essentially a pattern matching operation on the argument to the function; only the programmer has to write the pattern matching code and make sure that it is correct.

In the Erlang equivalent, we merely write the patterns, and the Erlang compiler generates optimal pattern matching code, which selects the correct entry point for the program.

We can see what the equivalent code would look like in Java:[3]

```java
abstract class Shape {
    abstract double area();
}

class Circle extends Shape {
    final double radius;
    Circle(double radius) { this.radius = radius; }
    double area() { return Math.PI * radius*radius; }
}

class Rectangle extends Shape {
    final double ht;
    final double width;

    Rectangle(double width, double height) {
        this.ht = height;
        this.width  = width;
    }

    double area() { return width * ht; }
}

class Square extends Shape {
    final double side;

    Square(double side) {
        this.side = side;
    }

    double area() { return side * side; }
}
```

If you compare the Erlang code with Java code, you'll see that in the Java program the code for area is in three different places. In the Erlang program, all the code for area is in the same place.

---

3. Adapted from http://java.sun.com/developer/Books/shiftintojava/page1.html.

3.2 Back to Shopping

Recall that we had a shopping list that looked like this:

```
[{oranges,4},{newspaper,1},{apples,10},{pears,6},{milk,3}]
```

Now suppose that we'd like to know what our shopping costs. To work this out, we need to know how much each item in the shopping list costs. Let's assume that this information is computed in a module called shop. Start your favorite text editor, and enter the following into a file called shop.erl.

`shop.erl`

```
-module(shop).
-export([cost/1]).

cost(oranges)   -> 5;
cost(newspaper) -> 8;
cost(apples)    -> 2;
cost(pears)     -> 9;
cost(milk)      -> 7.
```

The function cost/1[4] is made up from five *clauses*. The head of each clause contains a pattern (in this case a very simple pattern that is just an atom). When we evaluate shop:cost(X), then the system will try to match X against each of the patterns in these clauses. If a match is found, the code to the right of the -> is evaluated.

The cost/1 function must also be *exported* from the module; this is necessary if we want to call it from outside the module.[5]

Let's test this. We'll compile and run the program in the Erlang shell:

```
1> c(shop).
{ok,shop}
2> shop:cost(apples).
2
3> shop:cost(oranges).
5
4> shop:cost(socks).
=ERROR REPORT==== 30-Oct-2006::20:45:10 ===
Error in process <0.34.0> with exit value:
        {function_clause,[{shop,cost,[socks]},
        {erl_eval,do_apply,5},
        {shell,exprs,6},
        {shell,eval_loop,3}]}
```

---

4. The notation Name/N means a function called Name with N arguments; N is called the *arity* of the function.

5. You can also say -**compile**(**export_all**), which exports all the functions in the module.

In line 1 we compiled the module in the file shop.erl. In lines 2 and 3, we asked how much apples and oranges cost (results, 2 and 5 units[6]). In line 4 we asked what socks cost, but no clause matched, so we got a pattern matching error, and the system printed an error message.[7]

Back to the shopping list. Suppose we have a shopping list like this:

```
1> Buy = [{oranges,4}, {newspaper,1}, {apples,10}, {pears,6}, {milk,3}].
[{oranges,4},{newspaper,1},{apples,10},{pears,6},{milk,3}]
```

And say we want to calculate the total value of all the items in the list. One way we do this might be as follows:

`shop1.erl`

```
-module(shop1).
-export([total/1]).

total([{What, N}|T]) -> shop:cost(What) * N + total(T);
total([])            -> 0.
```

Let's experiment with this:

```
2> c(shop1).
{ok,shop1}
3> shop1:total([]).
0
```

Why is this 0? It's because the second clause of total/1 says that total([]) -> 0:

```
4> shop1:total([{milk,3}]).
21
```

The function call total([{milk,3}]) matches the clause total([{What,N}|T]} with T = [].[8] After the match, the bindings of the variables are {What ↦ milk, N ↦ 3, T ↦ []}. Then the body of the function (shop:cost(What) * N + total(T)) is entered. All the variables in the body are replaced by the values in the bindings. So, the value of the body is now the expression shop:cost(milk) * 3 + total([]).

shop:cost(milk) is 7, and total([]) is 0; thus, the value of the body is 7*3+0 = 21.

What about a more complex argument?

```
5> shop1:total([{pears,6},{milk,3}]).
75
```

---

6. We're not really interested in the units here, just that the return values are numbers.
7. The "function_clause" part of the error message means that the function call failed because no clause matched the arguments.
8. This is because [X] is just shorthand for [X|[]].

Where Do I Put Those Semicolons?

We use three types of punctuation in Erlang.

Commas (,) separate arguments in function calls, data constructors, and patterns.

Periods (.) (followed by whitespace) separate entire functions and expressions in the shell.

Semicolons (;) separate *clauses*. We find clauses in several contexts: in function definitions and in **case**, **if**, **try..catch** and **receive** expressions.

Whenever we see sets of patterns followed by expressions, we'll see semicolons as separators:

```
Pattern1 ->
    Expressions1;
Pattern2 ->
    Expressions2;
...
```

This time the first clause of total matches with the bindings {What ↦ pears, N ↦ 6, T ↦ [{milk,3}]}. The result is shop:cost(pears) * 6 + total([{milk,3}]), which is 9 * 6 + total([{milk,3}]).

But we worked out before that total([{milk,3}]) was 21, so the final result is 9*6 + 21 = 75.

Finally:

```
6> shop1:total(Buy).
123
```

Before we leave this section, we should take a more detailed look at the function total. total(L) works by a case analysis of the argument L. There are two possible cases; L is a nonempty list, or L is an empty list. We write one clause for each possible case, like this:

```
total([Head|Tail]) ->
   some_function_of(Head)  + total(Tail);
total([]) ->
   0.
```

In our case, Head was a pattern {What,N}. When the first clause matches a nonempty list, it picks out the head from the list, does something with the head, and then calls itself to process the tail of the list. The second clause matches when the list has been reduced to an empty list ([]).

The function total/1 actually did two different things. First it looked up the prices of each of the elements in the list, and then it summed all the prices. We can rewrite total in a way that separates looking up the values of the individual items and summing the values. The resulting code will be clearer and easier to understand. To do this we'll write two small list-processing functions called sum and map. But before we talk about these, we have to introduce the idea of funs. After this, we'll write sum and map and then an improved version of total.

3.3 Functions with the Same Name and Different Arity

The *arity* of a function is the number of arguments that the function has. In Erlang, two functions with the same name and different arity in the same module represent *entirely* different functions. They have *nothing* to do with each other apart from a coincidental use of the same name.

By convention Erlang programmers often use functions with the same name and different arities as auxiliary functions. Here's an example:

`lib_misc.erl`

```
sum(L) -> sum(L, 0).

sum([], N)    -> N;
sum([H|T], N) -> sum(T, H+N).
```

The function sum(L) sums the elements of a list L. It makes use of an auxiliary routine called sum/2, but this could have been called anything. You could have called the auxilliary routine hedgehog/2, and the meaning of the program would be the same. sum/2 is a better choice of name, though, since it gives the reader of your program a clue as to what's going on and since you don't have to invent a new name (which is always difficult).

3.4 Funs

funs are "anonymous" functions. They are called this because they have no name. Let's experiment a bit. First we'll define a fun and assign it to the variable Z:

```
1> Z = fun(X) -> 2*X end.
#Fun<erl_eval.6.56006484>
```

When we define a fun, the Erlang shell prints #Fun<...> where the ... is some weird number. Don't worry about this now.

There's only one thing we can do with a fun, and that is to apply it to an argument, like this:

```
2> Z(2).
4
```

Z wasn't a very good name for the fun; a better name would be Double, which describes what the fun does:

```
3> Double = Z.
#Fun<erl_eval.6.10732646>
4> Double(4).
8
```

Funs can have any number of arguments. We can write a function to compute the hypotenuse of a right-angled triangle, like this:

```
5> Hypot = fun(X, Y) -> math:sqrt(X*X + Y*Y) end.
#Fun<erl_eval.12.115169474>
6> Hypot(3,4).
5.00000
```

If the number of arguments is incorrect, you'll get an error:

```
7> Hypot(3).
** exited: {{badarity,{#Fun<erl_eval.12.115169474>,[3]}},
           [{erl_eval,expr,3}]} **
```

Why is this error called badarity? Remember that *arity* is the number of arguments a function accepts. badarity means that Erlang couldn't find a function with the given name (Hypot in this case) that took the number of parameters we passed—our function takes two parameters, and we passed just one.

Funs can have several different clauses. Here's a function that converts temperatures between Fahrenheit and Centigrade:

```
8> TempConvert = fun({c,C}) -> {f, 32 + C*9/5};
8>                   ({f,F}) -> {c, (F-32)*5/9}
8>              end.
#Fun<erl_eval.6.56006484>
9> TempConvert({c,100}).
{f,212.000}
10> TempConvert({f,212}).
{c,100.000}
11> TempConvert({c,0}).
{f,32.0000}
```

Note: The expression in line 8 spans several lines. As we enter this expression, the shell repeats the prompt "8>" every time we enter a new line. This means the expression is incomplete and the shell wants more input.

Erlang is a functional programming language. Among other things this means that funs can be used as the arguments to functions and that functions (or funs) can return funs.

Functions that return funs, or functions that can accept funs as their arguments, are called *higher-order functions*. We'll see a few examples of these in the next sections.

Now all of this might not sound very exciting since we haven't seen what we can do with funs. So far, the code in a fun looks just like regular function code in a module, but nothing could be further from the truth. Higher-order functions are the very essence of functional programming languages—they breathe fire into the belly of the code. Once you've learned to use them, you'll love them. We'll see a lot more of them in the future.

Functions That Have Funs As Their Arguments

The module lists, which is in the standard libraries, exports several functions whose arguments are funs. The most useful of all these is lists:map(F, L). This is a function that returns a list made by applying the fun F to every element in the list L:

```
12> L = [1,2,3,4].
[1,2,3,4]
13> lists:map(Double, L).
[2,4,6,8].
```

Another useful function is lists:filter(P, L), which returns a new list of all the elements E in L such that P(E) is true.

Let's define a function Even(X) that is true if X is an even number:

```
14> Even = fun(X) -> (X rem 2) =:= 0 end.
#Fun<erl_eval.6.56006484>
```

Here X rem 2 computes the remainder after X has been divided by 2, and =:= is a test for equality. Now we can test Even, and then we can use it as an argument to map and filter:

```
15> Even(8).
true
16> Even(7).
false
17> lists:map(Even, [1,2,3,4,5,6,8]).
[false,true,false,true,false,true,true]
18> lists:filter(Even, [1,2,3,4,5,6,8]).
[2,4,6,8]
```

We call operations such as map and filter that do something to an entire list in one function call as *list-at-a-time* operations. Using list-at-a-time operations makes our programs small and easy to understand; they are easy to understand because we can regard each operation on the entire list as a single conceptual step in our program. Otherwise, we have to think of each individual operation on the elements of the list as single steps in our program.

Functions That Return Funs

Not only can funs be used as arguments to functions (such as map and filter), but functions can also *return* funs.

Here's an example—suppose I have a list of something, say fruit:

```
1> Fruit = [apple,pear,orange].
[apple,pear,orange]
```

Now I can define a function MakeTest(L) that turns a list of things (L) into a test function that checks whether its argument is in the list L:

```
2> MakeTest = fun(L) -> (fun(X) -> lists:member(X, L) end) end.
#Fun<erl_eval.6.56006484>
3> IsFruit = MakeTest(Fruit).
#Fun<erl_eval.6.56006484>
```

lists:member(X, L) returns true if X is a member of the list L; otherwise, it returns false. Now that we have built a test function, we can try it:

```
4> IsFruit(pear).
true
5> IsFruit(apple).
true
6> IsFruit(dog).
false
```

We can also use it as an argument to lists:filter/2:

```
7> lists:filter(IsFruit, [dog,orange,cat,apple,bear]).
[orange,apple]
```

The notation for funs that return funs takes a little getting used to, so let's dissect the notation to make what's going on a little clearer. A function that returns a "normal" value looks like this:

```
1> Double = fun(X) -> ( 2 * X ) end.
#Fun<erl_eval.6.56006484>
2> Double(5).
10
```

The code inside the parentheses (in other words, 2 * X) is clearly the "return value" of the function. Now let's try putting a *fun* inside the parentheses. Remember the thing inside the parentheses *is* the return value:

```
3> Mult = fun(Times) -> ( fun(X) -> X * Times end ) end.
#Fun<erl_eval.6.56006484>
```

The fun inside the parentheses is fun(X) -> X * Times end; this is just a function of X, but where does Times come from? Answer: This is just the argument of the "outer" fun.

Evaluating Mult(3) *returns* fun(X) -> X * 3 end, which is the body of the inner fun with Times substituted with 3. Now we can test this:

```
4> Triple = Mult(3).
#Fun<erl_eval.6.56006484>
5> Triple(5).
15
```

So, Mult is a *generalization* of Double. Instead of computing a value, *it returns a function, which when called will compute the required value.*

Defining Your Own Control Abstractions

Wait a moment—have you noticed something? So far, we haven't seen any **if** statements, **switch** statements, **for** statements, or **while** statements, and yet this doesn't seem to matter. Everything is written using pattern matching and higher-order functions. So far we haven't needed any additional control structures.

If we want additional control structures, we have a powerful glue that we can use to make our own control structures. Let's give an example of this: Erlang has no **for** loop, so let's make one:

lib_misc.erl

```
for(Max, Max, F) -> [F(Max)];
for(I, Max, F)   -> [F(I)|for(I+1, Max, F)].
```

So, for example, evaluating for(1,10,F) creates the list [F(1), F(2), ..., F(10)].

How does the pattern matching in the for loop work? The first clause in for matches only when the first and second arguments to for are the same. So if we call for(10,10,F), then the first clause will match binding Max to 10, and the result will be the list [F(10)]. If we call for(1,10,F), the first clause cannot match since Max cannot match both 1 and 10 at the same time. In this case, the second clause matches with bindings I ↦ 1 and Max ↦ 10; the value of the function is then [F(I)|for(I+1,10,F)] with I substituted by 1 and Max substituted by 10, which is just[F(1)|for(2,10,F)].

When Do We Use Higher-Order Functions?

As we have seen, when we use higher-order functions, we can create our own new control abstractions, we can pass functions as arguments, and we can write functions that return funs. In practice, not all these techniques get used often:

- Virtually all the modules that I write use functions like lists:map/2—this is so common that I almost consider map to be part of the Erlang language. Calling functions such as map and filter and partition in the module lists is extremely common.

- I sometimes create my own control abstractions. This is far less common than calling the higher-order functions in the standard library modules. This might happen a few times in a large module.

- Writing functions that return funs is something I do very infrequently. If I were to write a hundred modules, perhaps only one or two modules might use this programming technique. Programs with functions that return funs can be difficult to debug; on the other hand, we can use functions that return funs to implement things such as lazy evaluation, and we can easily write reentrant parsers and parser combinators that are functions that return parsers.

Now we have a simple for loop.[9] We can use it to make a list of the integers from 1 to 10:

```
1> lib_misc:for(1,10,fun(I) -> I end).
[1,2,3,4,5,6,7,8,9,10]
```

Or we can use to compute the squares of the integers from 1 to 10:

```
2> lib_misc:for(1,10,fun(I) -> I*I end).
[1,4,9,16,25,36,49,64,81,100]
```

As you become more experienced, you'll find that being able to create your own control structures can dramatically decrease the size of your programs and sometimes make them a lot clearer. This is because you can create exactly the right control structures that are needed to solve your problem and because you are not restricted by a small and fixed set of control structures that came with your programming language.

---

9. This is not quite the same as a for loop in an imperative language, but it is sufficient for our purposes.

Common Errors

Some readers have mistakenly typed into the shell fragments of code contained in the source code listings. These are not valid shell commands, and you'll get some very strange error message if you try to do this. So be warned: don't do this.

If you accidentally choose a module name that collides with one of the system modules, then when you compile your module, you'll get a strange message saying that you can't load a module that resides in a sticky directory. Just rename the module, and delete any beam file that you might have made when compiling your module.

3.5 Simple List Processing

Now that we've introduced funs, we can get back to writing sum and map, which we'll need for our improved version of total (which I'm sure you haven't forgotten about!).

We'll start with sum, which computes the sum of the elements in a list:

`mylists.erl`

```
❶   sum([H|T]) -> H + sum(T);
❷   sum([])    -> 0.
```

Note that the order of the two clauses in sum is unimportant. This is because the first clause matches a nonempty list and the second an empty list, and these two cases are mutually exclusive. We can test sum as follows:

```
1> c(mylists). %% <-- Last time I do this
{ok, mylists}
2> L = [1,3,10].
[1,3,10]
3> mylists:sum(L).
14
```

Line 1 compiled the module mylists. From now on, I'll often omit the command to compile the module, and you'll have to remember to do this yourself. It's pretty easy to understand how this works. Let's trace the execution:

1. sum([1,3,10])
2. sum([1,3,10]) = 1 + sum([3,10]) (by ❶)
3. = 1 + 3 + sum([10]) (by ❶)

4. = 1 + 3 + 10 + sum([]) (by ❶)
5. = 1 + 3 + 10 + 0 (by ❷)
6. = 14

Finally, let's look at map/2, which we met earlier. Here's how it's defined:

`mylists.erl`

```
❶ map(_, [])     -> [];
❷ map(F, [H|T]) -> [F(H)|map(F, T)].
```

❶ The first clause says what to do with an empty list. Mapping any function over the elements of an empty list (there are none!) just produces an empty list.

❷ The second clause is a rule for what to do with a list with a head H and tail T. That's easy. Just build a new list whose head is F(H) and whose tail is map(F, T).

Note: The definition of map/2 is copied from the standard library module lists to mylists. You can do anything you like to the code in mylists.erl. Do not under any circumstance try to make your own module called lists unless you know *exactly* what you're doing.

We can run map using a couple of functions that double and square the elements in a list, as follows:

```
1> L = [1,2,3,4,5].
[1,2,3,4,5].
2> mylists:map(fun(X) -> 2*X end, L).
[2,4,6,8,10]
3> mylists:map(fun(X) -> X*X end, L).
[1,4,9,16,25]
```

Have we said the final word on map? Well, no, not really! Later, we'll show an even shorter version of map written using list comprehensions, and in Section 20.2, *Parallelizing Sequential Code*, on page 366, we'll show how we can compute all the elements of the map *in parallel* (which will speed up our program on a multicore computer)—but this is jumping too far ahead. Now that we know about sum and map, we can rewrite total using these two functions:

`shop2.erl`

```
-module(shop2).
-export([total/1]).
-import(lists, [map/2, sum/1]).

total(L) ->
    sum(map(fun({What, N}) -> shop:cost(What) * N end, L)).
```

How I Write Programs

When I'm writing a program, my approach is to "write a bit" and then "test a bit." I start with a small module with few functions, and then I compile it and test it with a few commands in the shell. Once I'm happy with it, I write a few more functions, compile them, test them, and so on.

Often I haven't really decided what sort of data structures I'll need in my program, and as I run small examples, I can see whether the data structures I have chosen are appropriate.

I tend to "grow" programs rather than think them out completely before writing them. This way I don't tend to make large mistakes before I discover that things have gone wrong. Above all, it's fun, I get immediate feedback, and I see whether my ideas work as soon as I have typed in the program.

Once I've figured out how to do something in the shell, I usually then go and write a makefile and some code that reproduces what I've learned in the shell.

We can see how this function works by looking at the steps involved:

```
1> Buy = [{oranges,4},{newspaper,1},{apples,10},{pears,6},{milk,3}].
[{oranges,4},{newspaper,1},{apples,10},{pears,6},{milk,3}]
2> L1=lists:map(fun({What,N}) -> shop:cost(What) * N end, Buy).
[20,8,20,54,21]
3> lists:sum(L1).
123
```

Note also the use of the **-import** and **-export** declarations in the module:

- The declaration -import(lists, [map/2, sum/1]). means the function map/2 is *imported* from the module lists, and so on. This means we can write map(Fun, ...) instead of lists:map(Fun, ...). cost/1 was not declared in an import declaration, so we had to use the "fully qualified" name shop:cost.

- The declaration -export([total/1]) means the function total/1 can be called from outside the module shop2. Only functions that are exported from a module can be called from outside the module.

By this time you might think that our total function cannot be further improved, but you'd be wrong. Further improvement is possible. To do so, we'll use a list comprehension.

3.6   List Comprehensions

List comprehensions are expressions that create lists without having to use funs, maps, or filters. This makes our programs even shorter and easier to understand.

We'll start with an example. Suppose we have a list L:

```
1> L = [1,2,3,4,5].
[1,2,3,4,5]
```

And suppose we want to double every element in the list. We've done this before, but I'll remind you:

```
2> lists:map(fun(X) -> 2*X end, L).
[2,4,6,8,10]
```

But there's a much easier way that uses a list comprehension:

```
4> [2*X || X <- L ].
[2,4,6,8,10]
```

The notation [F(X) || X <- L] means "the list of F(X) where X is taken from the list L." Thus, [2*X || X <- L] means "the list of 2*X where X is taken from the list L."

To see how to use a list comprehension, we can enter a few expressions in the shell to see what happens. We start by defining Buy:

```
1> Buy=[{oranges,4},{newspaper,1},{apples,10},{pears,6},{milk,3}].
[{oranges,4},{newspaper,1},{apples,10},{pears,6},{milk,3}].
```

Now let's double the number of every item in the original list:

```
2> [{Name, 2*Number} || {Name, Number} <- Buy].
[{oranges,8},{newspaper,2},{apples,20},{pears,12},{milk,6}]
```

Note that the tuple {Name, Number} to the right side of the (||) sign is a *pattern* that matches each of the elements in the list Buy. The tuple to the left side, {Name, 2*Number}, is a *constructor*.

Suppose we want to compute the total cost of all the elements in the original list; we could do this as follows. First replace the name of every item in the list with its price:

```
3> [{shop:cost(A), B} || {A, B} <- Buy].
[{5,4},{8,1},{2,10},{9,6},{7,3}]
```

Now multiply the numbers together:

```
4> [shop:cost(A) *  B || {A, B} <- Buy].
[20,8,20,54,21]
```

Then sum them:

```
5> lists:sum([shop:cost(A) * B || {A, B} <- Buy]).
123
```

Finally, if we wanted to make this into a function, we'd write the following:

```
total(L) ->
    lists:sum([shop:cost(A) * B || {A, B} <- L]).
```

List comprehensions will make your code really short and easy to read. Just for fun we can use them to give an even shorter definition of map:

```
map(F, L) -> [F(X) || X <- L].
```

The most general form of a list comprehension is an expression of the following form:

```
[X || Qualifier1, Qualifier2, ...]
```

X is an arbitrary expression, and each qualifier is either a generator or a filter.

- Generators are written as Pattern <- ListExpr where ListExpr must be an expression that evaluates to a list of terms.

- Filters are either predicates (functions that return true or false) or boolean expressions.

Note that the generator part of a list comprehension works like a filter, so, for example:

```
1> [ X || {a, X} <- [{a,1},{b,2},{c,3},{a,4},hello,"wow"]].
[1,4]
```

We'll finish the section on list comprehensions with a few little examples:

Quicksort

Here's how to write a sort algorithm[10] using two list comprehensions:

`lib_misc.erl`

```
qsort([]) -> [];
qsort([Pivot|T]) ->
        qsort([X || X <- T, X < Pivot])
        ++ [Pivot] ++
        qsort([X || X <- T, X >= Pivot]).
```

---

10. This code is shown for its elegance rather than its efficiency. Using ++ in this way is not generally considered good programming practice.

(where ++ is the infix append operator):

```
1> L=[23,6,2,9,27,400,78,45,61,82,14].
[23,6,2,9,27,400,78,45,61,82,14]
2> lib_misc:qsort(L).
[2,6,9,14,23,27,45,61,78,82,400]
```

To see how this works, we'll step through the execution. We start with a list L and call qsort(L). This matches the second clause of qsort:

```
3>  [Pivot|T] = L.
[23,6,2,9,27,400,78,45,61,82,14]
```

with bindings Pivot ↦ 23 and T ↦ [6,2,9,27,400,78,45,61,82,14].

Now we split T into two lists, one with all the elements in T that are less than Pivot, and the other with all the elements greater than or equal to Pivot:

```
4> Smaller = [X || X <- T, X < Pivot].
[6,2,9,14]
5> Bigger  = [X || X <- T, X >= Pivot].
[27,400,78,45,61,82]
```

Now we sort Smaller and Bigger and combine them with Pivot:

```
qsort( [6,2,9,14] ) ++ [23] ++ qsort( [27,400,78,45,61,82] )
= [2,6,9,14] ++ [23] ++ [27,45,61,78,82,400]
= [2,6,9,14,23,27,45,61,78,82,400]
```

Pythagorean Triplets

Pythagorean triplets are sets of integers {A,B,C} such that $A^2 + B^2 = C^2$.

The function pythag(N) generates a list of all integers {A,B,C} such that $A^2 + B^2 = C^2$ and where the sum of the sides is less than or equal to N:

lib_misc.erl

```
pythag(N) ->
    [ {A,B,C} ||
        A <- lists:seq(1,N),
        B <- lists:seq(1,N),
        C <- lists:seq(1,N),
        A+B+C =< N,
        A*A+B*B =:= C*C
    ].
```

Just a few words of explanation: lists:seq(1, N) returns a list of all the integers from 1 to N. Thus, A <- lists:seq(1, N) means that A takes all possible values from 1 to N. So our program reads, "Take all values of A from 1 to N, all values of B from 1 to N, and all values of C from 1 to N such that A + B + C is less than or equal to N and A*A + B*B = C*C."

```
1> lib_misc:pythag(16).
[{3,4,5},{4,3,5}]
2> lib_misc:pythag(30).
[{3,4,5},{4,3,5},{5,12,13},{6,8,10},{8,6,10},{12,5,13}]
```

Anagrams

If you're interested in English-style crossword puzzles, you'll often find
yourself figuring out anagrams. Let's use Erlang to find all the permutations of a string using the beautiful little function perms where we
have the following:

`lib_misc.erl`

```
perms([]) -> [[]];
perms(L)  -> [[H|T] || H <- L, T <- perms(L--[H])].
```

```
1> lib_misc:perms("123").
["123","132","213","231","312","321"]
2> lib_misc:perms("cats").
["cats", "cast", "ctas", "ctsa", "csat", "csta", "acts", "acst",
"atcs", "atsc", "asct", "astc", "tcas", "tcsa", "tacs", "tasc",
"tsca", "tsac", "scat", "scta", "sact", "satc", "stca", "stac"]
```

X--Y is the list subtraction operator. It subtracts the elements in Y from
X; there's a more precise definition in Section 5.4, *List Operations ++
and* --, on page 99.

Just for once, I'm not going to explain how perms works, since the explanation would be many times longer than the program, so you can figure
this out for yourself! (But, here's a hint: To compute all permutations of
X123, compute all permutations of 123 [these are 123 132 213 231 312
321]. Now interleave the X at all possible positions in each permutation,
so adding X to 123 gives X123 1X23 12X3 123X, adding X to 132 gives
X132 1X32 13X2 132X, and so on. Apply these rules recursively.)

3.7 Arithmetic Expressions

All the possible arithmetic expressions are shown in Figure 3.1, on the
facing page. Each arithmetic operation has one or two arguments—
these arguments are shown in the table as Integer or Number (*Number*
means the argument can be an integer or a float).

Associated with each operator is a *priority*. The order of evaluation of a
complex arithmetic expression depends upon the priority of the operator: all operations with priority 1 operators are evaluated first, then all
operators with priority 2, and so on.

Op	Description	Argument Type	Priority
+ X	+ X	Number	1
- X	- X	Number	1
X * Y	X * Y	Number	2
X / Y	X / Y (floating-point division)	Number	2
bnot X	Bitwise not of X	Integer	2
X div Y	Integer division of X and Y	Integer	2
X rem Y	Integer remainder of X divided by Y	Integer	2
X band Y	Bitwise and of X and Y	Integer	2
X + Y	X + Y	Number	3
X - Y	X - Y	Number	3
X bor Y	Bitwise or of X and Y	Integer	3
X bxor Y	Bitwise xor of X and Y	Integer	3
X bsl N	Arithmetic bitshift left of X by N bits	Integer	3
X bsr N	Bitshift right of X by N bits	Integer	3

Figure 3.1: ARITHMETIC EXPRESSIONS

You can use parentheses to change the default order of evaluation—any parenthesized expressions are evaluated first. Operators with equal priorities are treated as left associative and are evaluated from left to right.

3.8 Guards

Guards are constructs that we can use to increase the power of pattern matching. Using guards, we can perform simple tests and comparisons on the variables in a pattern. Suppose we want to write a function max(X, Y) that computes the max of X and Y. We can write this using a guard as follows:

```
max(X, Y) when X > Y -> X;
max(X, Y) -> Y.
```

The first clause matches when X is greater than Y and the result is X.

If the first clause doesn't match, then the second clause is tried. The second clause always returns the second argument Y. Y must be greater than or equal to X; otherwise, the first clause would have matched.

You can use guards in the heads of function definitions where they are introduced by the **when** keyword, or you can use them at any place in the language where an expression is allowed. When they are used as expressions, they evaluate to one of the atoms true or false. If the guard evaluates to true, we say that the evaluation *succeeded*; otherwise, it *fails*.

Guard Sequences

A *guard sequence* is either a single guard or a series of guards, separated by semicolons (;). The guard sequence G1; G2; ...; Gn is true if at least one of the guards—G1, G2, ...—evaluates to true.

A *guard* is a series of *guard expressions*, separated by commas (,). The guard GuardExpr1, GuardExpr2, ..., GuardExprN is true if all the guard expressions—GuardExpr1, GuardExpr2, ...—evaluate to true.

The set of valid guard expressions is a subset of all valid Erlang expressions. The reason for restricting guard expressions to a subset of Erlang expressions is that we want to guarantee that evaluating a guard expression is free from side effects. Guards are an extension of pattern matching, and since pattern matching has no side effects, we don't want guard evaluation to have side effects.

In addition, guards cannot be user-defined boolean expressions, since we want to guarantee that they are side effect free and terminate.

The following syntactic forms are legal in a guard expression:

- The atom true

- Other constants (terms and bound variables); these all evaluate to false in a guard expression

- Calls to the guard predicates in Figure 3.2, on page 58 and to the BIFs[11] in Figure 3.3, on page 59.

- Term comparisons (Figure 5.3, on page 107)

- Arithmetic expressions (Figure 3.1, on the previous page)

- Boolean expressions (Section 5.4, *Boolean Expressions*, on page 94)

- Short-circuit boolean expressions (Section 5.4, *Short-Circuit Boolean Expressions*, on page 106)

When evaluating a guard expression, the precedence rules described in Section 5.4, *Operator Precedence*, on page 103 are used.

---

11. BIF is short for *built-in function* See Section 5.1, *BIFs*, on page 78.

Guard Examples

```
f(X,Y) when is_integer(X), X > Y, Y < 6 -> ...
```

This means "when X is an integer and X is greater than Y and Y is less than 6." The comma, which separates the test in the guard, means "and."

```
is_tuple(T), size(T) =:= 6, abs(element(3, T)) > 5
element(4, X) =:= hd(L)
...
```

The first line means T is a tuple of six elements, and the absolute value of the third element of T is greater than 5. The second line means that element 4 of the tuple X is identical to the head of the list L.

```
X =:= dog; X =:= cat
is_integer(X), X > Y ; abs(Y) < 23
...
```

The first guard means X is either a cat or a dog. The second guard either means that X is an integer and is greater than Y or means that the absolute value of Y is less than 23.

Here are some examples of guards using short-circuit boolean expressions:

```
A >= -1.0 andalso A+1 > B
is_atom(L) orelse (is_list(L) andalso length(L) > 2)
```

Advanced: The reason for allowing boolean expressions in guards is to make guards syntactically similar to other expressions. The reason for the orelse and andalso operators is that the boolean operators and/or were originally defined to evaluate both their arguments. In guards, there can be differences between (and and andalso) or between (or and orelse). For example, consider the following two guards:

```
f(X) when (X == 0) or (1/X > 2) ->
    ...

g(X) when (X == 0) orelse (1/X > 2) ->
    ...
```

The guard in f(X) fails when X is zero but succeeds in g(X).

In practice, few programs use complex guards, and simple (,) guards suffice for most programs.

Predicate	Meaning
is_atom(X)	X is an atom.
is_binary(X)	X is a binary.
is_constant(X)	X is a constant.
is_float(X)	X is a float.
is_function(X)	X is a fun.
is_function(X, N)	X is a fun with N arguments.
is_integer(X)	X is an integer.
is_list(X)	X is a list.
is_number(X)	X is an integer or a float.
is_pid(X)	X is a process identifier.
is_port(X)	X is a port.
is_reference(X)	X is a reference.
is_tuple(X)	X is a tuple.
is_record(X,Tag)	X is a record of type Tag.
is_record(X,Tag,N)	X is a record of type Tag and size N.

Figure 3.2: GUARD PREDICATES

Use of the True Guard

You might wonder why we need the true guard at all. The reason is that atom true can be used as a "catchall" guard at the end of an **if** expression, like this:

```
if
    Guard -> Expressions;
    Guard -> Expressions;
    ...
    true -> Expressions
end
```

if will be discussed in Section 3.10, *if Expressions*, on page 63.

Obsolete Guard Functions

If you come across some old Erlang code written a few years ago, the names of the guard tests were different. Old code used guard tests called atom(X), constant(X), float(X), integer(X), list(X), number(X), pid(X), port(X), reference(X), tuple(X), and binary(X). These tests have the same meaning as the modern tests named is_atom(X)... The use of old names in modern code is frowned upon.

Function	Meaning
abs(X)	Absolute value of X.
element(N, X)	Element N of X. Note X must be a tuple.
float(X)	Convert X, which must be a number, to a float.
hd(X)	The head of the list X.
length(X)	The length of the list X.
node()	The current node.
node(X)	The node on which X was created. X can be a process, an identifier, a reference, or a port.
round(X)	Converts X, which must be a number, to an integer.
self()	The process identifier of the current process.
size(X)	The size of X. X can be a tuple or a binary.
trunc(X)	Truncates X, which must be a number, to an integer.
tl(X)	The tail of the list X.

Figure 3.3: GUARD BUILT-IN FUNCTIONS

3.9 Records

When we program with tuples, we can run into a problem when the number of elements in a tuple becomes large. It becomes difficult to remember which element in the tuple means what. Records provide a method for associating a name with a particular element in a tuple, which solves this problem.

In a small tuple this is rarely a problem, so we often see programs that manipulate small tuples, and there is no confusion about what the different elements represent. Records are declared with the following syntax:

```
-record(Name, {
            %% the next two keys have default values
            key1 = Default1,
            key2 = Default2,
            ...
            %% The next line is equivalent to
            %% key3 = undefined
            key3,
            ...

        }).
```

Warning: **record** is not a shell command (use **rr** in the shell; see the description that comes later in this section). Record declarations can be used only in Erlang source code modules and *not* in the shell.

In the previous example, Name is the name of the record. key1, key2, and so on, are the names of the fields in the record; these must always be atoms. Each field in a record can have a default value that is used if no value for this particular field is specified when the record is created.

For example, suppose we want to manipulate a to-do list. We start by defining a todo record and storing it in a file (record definitions can be included in Erlang source code files or put in files with the extension .hrl, which are then included by Erlang source code files[12]).

`records.hrl`

```
-record(todo, {status=reminder,who=joe,text}).
```

Once a record has been defined, instances of the record can be created.

To do this in the shell, we have to read the record definitions into the shell before we can define a record. We use the shell function rr (short for *read records*) to do this:

```
1> rr("records.hrl").
[todo]
```

Creating and Updating Records

Now we're ready to define and manipulate records:

```
2> X=#todo{}.
#todo{status = reminder,who = joe,text = undefined}
3> X1 = #todo{status=urgent, text="Fix errata in book"}.
#todo{status = urgent,who = joe,text = "Fix errata in book"}
4> X2 = X1#todo{status=done}.
#todo{status = done,who = joe,text = "Fix errata in book"}
```

In lines 2 and 3 we *created* new records. The syntax #todo{key1=Val1, ..., keyN=ValN} is used to create a new record of type todo. The keys are all atoms and must be the same as those used in the record definition. If a key is omitted, then a default value is assumed for the value that comes from the value in the record definition.

In line 4 we *copied* an existing record. The syntax X1#todo{status=done} means create a copy of the X1 (which must be of type todo), changing the field value status to done. Remember this is a *copy* of the original record; the original record is not changed.

---

12. This is the only way to ensure that several Erlang modules use the same record definitions.

Extracting the Fields of a Record

As with everything else, we use pattern matching:

```
5> #todo{who=W, text=Txt} = X2.
#todo{status = done,who = joe,text = "Fix errata in book"}
6> W.
joe
7> Txt.
"Fix errata in book"
```

On the left side of the match operator (=), we write a record pattern with the unbound variables W and Txt. If the match succeeds, these variables get bound to the appropriate fields in the record. If we just want one field of a record, we can use the "dot syntax" to extract the field:

```
8> X2#todo.text.
"Fix errata in book"
```

Pattern Matching Records in Functions

We can write functions that pattern match on the fields of a record and that create new records. We usually write code like this:

```
clear_status(#todo{status=S, who=W} = R) ->
    %% Inside this function S and W are bound to the field
    %% values in the record
    %%
    %% R is the *entire* record
    R#todo{status=finished}
    %% ...
```

To match a record of a particular type, we might write the function definition:

```
do_something(X) when is_record(X, todo) ->
    %% ...
```

This clause matches when X is a record of type todo.

Records Are Tuples in Disguise

Records are just tuples. Now let's tell the shell to forget the definition of todo:

```
11> X2.
#todo{status = done,who = joe,text = "Fix errata in book"}
12> rf(todo).
ok
13> X2.
{todo,done,joe,"Fix errata in book"}
```

In line 12 we told the shell to forget the definition of the todo record. So now when we print X2, the shell displays X2 as a tuple. Internally there are only tuples. Records are a syntactic convenience so you can name the different elements in a tuple.

3.10 case and if Expressions

So far, we've used pattern matching for *everything*. This makes Erlang small and consistent. But sometimes defining separate function clauses for everything is rather inconvenient. When this happens, we can use **case** or **if** expressions.

case Expressions

case has the following syntax:

```
case Expression of
    Pattern1 [when Guard1] -> Expr_seq1;
    Pattern2 [when Guard2] -> Expr_seq2;
    ...
end
```

case is evaluated as follows. First, Expression is evaluated; assume this evaluates to Value. Thereafter, Value is matched in turn against Pattern1 (with the optional guard Guard1), Pattern2, and so on, until a match is found. As soon as a match is found, then the corresponding expression sequence is evaluated—the result of evaluating the expression sequence is the value of the case expression. If none of the patterns match, then an exception is raised.

Earlier, we used a function called filter(P, L); it returns a list of all those elements X in L for which P(X) is true. Now using pattern matching we could define filter as follows:

```
filter(P, [H|T]) ->  filter1(P(H), H, P, T);
filter(P, [])    ->  [].

filter1(true, H, P, T)  -> [H|filter(P, T)];
filter1(false, H, P, T) -> filter(P, T).
```

But this definition is rather ugly, so we have to invent an additional function (called filter1) and pass it all of the arguments of filter/2.

We can do this in a much clearer manner using the **case** construct, as follows:

```
filter(P, [H|T]) ->
    case P(H) of
        true  -> [H|filter(P, T)];
        false -> filter(P, T)
    end;
filter(P, []) ->
    [].
```

if Expressions

A second conditional primitive, **if**, is also provided. Here is the syntax:

```
if
  Guard1 ->
    Expr_seq1;
  Guard2 ->
    Expr_seq2;
  ...
end
```

This is evaluated as follows: First Guard1 is evaluated. If this evaluates to true, then the value of **if** is the value obtained by evaluating the expression sequence Expr_seq1. If Guard1 does not succeed, Guard2 is evaluated, and so on, until a guard succeeds. At least one of the guards in the if expression must evaluate to true; otherwise, an exception will be raised.

Often the final guard in an **if** expression is the atom true, which guarantees that the last form in the expression will be evaluated if all other guards have failed.

3.11 Building Lists in Natural Order

The most efficient way to build a list is to add the elements to the head of an existing list, so we often see code with this kind of pattern:

```
some_function([H|T], ..., Result, ...) ->
    H1 = ... H ...,
    some_function(T, ..., [H1|Result], ...);
some_function([], ..., Result, ...) ->
    {..., Result, ...}.
```

This code walks down a list extracting the head of the list H and computing some value based on this function (we can call this H1); it then adds H1 to the output list Result.

When the input list is exhausted, the final clause matches, and the output variable Result is returned from the function.

The elements in Result are in the opposite order to the elements in the original list, which may or may not be a problem, but if they are in the wrong order, they can easily be reversed in the final step.

The basic idea is fairly simple:

1. Always add elements to a list head.

2. Taking the elements from the head of an *InputList* and adding them head first to an *OutputList* results in the *OutputList* having the reverse order of the *InputList*.

3. If the order matters, then call lists:reverse/1, which is highly optimized.

4. Avoid going against these recommendations.

Note: Whenever you want to reverse a list, you should call lists:reverse and nothing else. If you look in the source code for the module lists, you'll find a definition of reverse. However, this definition is simply used for illustration. The compiler, when it finds a call to lists:reverse, calls a more efficient internal version of the function.

If you ever see code like this:

```
List ++ [H]
```

it should set alarm bells off in your brain—this is very inefficient and acceptable only if List is very short.

3.12 Accumulators

How can we get two lists out of a function? How can we write a function that splits a list of integers into two lists that contain the even and odd integers in the original list? Here's one way of doing it:

lib_misc.erl

```
odds_and_evens(L) ->
    Odds  = [X || X <- L, (X rem 2) =:= 1],
    Evens = [X || X <- L, (X rem 2) =:= 0],
    {Odds, Evens}.

5> lib_misc:odds_and_evens([1,2,3,4,5,6]).
{[1,3,5],[2,4,6]}
```

The problem with this code is that we traverse the list *twice*—this doesn't matter whether the list is short, but if the list is very long, it might be a problem.

To avoid traversing the list twice, we can recode this as follows:

`lib_misc.erl`

```
odds_and_evens_acc(L) ->
    odds_and_evens_acc(L, [], []).

odds_and_evens_acc([H|T], Odds, Evens) ->
    case (H rem 2) of
        1 -> odds_and_evens_acc(T, [H|Odds], Evens);
        0 -> odds_and_evens_acc(T, Odds, [H|Evens])
    end;
odds_and_evens_acc([], Odds, Evens) ->
    {Odds, Evens}.
```

Now this traverses the list only once, adding the odd and even arguments onto the appropriate output lists (which are called *accumulators*). This code also has an additional benefit, which is less obvious; the version with an accumulator is more *space efficient* than the version with the [H || filter(H)] type construction.

If we run this, we get *almost* the same result as before:

```
1> lib_misc:odds_and_evens_acc([1,2,3,4,5,6]).
{[5,3,1],[6,4,2]}
```

The difference is that the order of the elements in the odd and even lists is reversed. This is a consequence of the way that the list was constructed. If we want the list elements in the same order as they were in the original, all we have to do is reverse the lists in the final clause of the function by changing the second clause of odds_and_evens_acc to the following:

```
odds_and_evens_acc([], Odds, Evens) ->
    {lists:reverse(Odds), lists:reverse(Evens)}.
```

What We've Learned So Far

Now we can write Erlang modules and simple sequential Erlang code, and we have almost all the knowledge we need to write sequential Erlang programs.

The next chapter looks briefly at error handling. After this, we get back to sequential programming, looking at the remaining details that we've omitted up to now.

## Chapter 4

Exceptions

4.1 Exceptions

If you've been following along with the code in the previous chapter, you've probably seen some of Erlang's error reporting and handling at work. Before we dig deeper into sequential programming, let's take a brief detour and look at this in more detail. It may seem like a diversion, but if the eventual objective is to write robust distributed applications, a good understanding of how error handling works is essential.

Every time we call a function in Erlang, one of two things will happen: the function returns a value, or something goes wrong. We saw examples of this in the previous chapter. Remember the cost function?

`shop.erl`

```
cost(oranges)   -> 5;
cost(newspaper) -> 8;
cost(apples)    -> 2;
cost(pears)     -> 9;
cost(milk)      -> 7.
```

This is what happened when we ran it:

```
1> shop:cost(apples).
2
2> shop:cost(socks).
=ERROR REPORT==== 30-Oct-2006::20:45:10 ===
Error in process <0.34.0> with exit value:
        {function_clause,[{shop,cost,[socks]},
        {erl_eval,do_apply,5},
        {shell,exprs,6},
        {shell,eval_loop,3}]]}
```

When we called cost(socks), the function crashed. This happened because none of the clauses that define the function matched the calling arguments.

Calling cost(socks) is pure nonsense. There is no sensible value that the function can return, since the price of socks is undefined. In this case, instead of returning a value, the system *raises an exception*—this is the technical term for "crashing."

We don't try to repair the error because this is not possible. We don't know what socks cost, so we can't return a value. It is up to the *caller* of cost(socks) to decide what to do if the function crashes.

Exceptions are raised by the system when internal errors are encountered or explicitly in code by calling throw(Exception), exit(Exception). or erlang:error(Exception).

Erlang has two methods of *catching* an exception. One is to enclose the call to the function, which raised the exception within a **try...catch** expression. The other is to enclose the call in a **catch** expression.

4.2 Raising an Exception

Exceptions are raised automatically when the system encounters an error. Typical errors are pattern matching errors (no clauses in a function match) or calling BIFs with incorrectly typed arguments (for example, calling atom_to_list with an argument that is an integer).

We can also explicitly generate an error by calling one of the exception generating BIFs:

exit(Why)

> This is used when you really want to terminate the current process. If this exception is not caught, the message {'EXIT',Pid,Why} will be broadcast to all processes that are linked to the current process. We'll say a lot more about this in Section 9.1, *Linking Processes*, on page 151, so I won't dwell on the details here.

throw(Why)

> This is used to throw an exception that a caller might want to catch. In this case we *document* that our function might throw this exception. The user of this function has two alternatives: they can program for the common case and blissfully ignore exceptions, or they can enclose the call in a **try...catch** expression and handle the errors.

erlang:error(Why)

> This is used for denoting "crashing errors." That is, something rather nasty has happened that callers are not really expected to handle. This is on a par with internally generated errors.

Now let's try to catch these errors.

4.3 try...catch

If you're familiar with Java, then you'll have no difficulties understanding the **try...catch** expression. Java can trap an exception with the following syntax:

```
try {
    block
} catch (exception type identifier) {
    block
} catch (exception type identifier) {
    block
} ...
finally {
    block
}
```

Erlang has a remarkably similar construct, which looks like this:

```
try FuncOrExpressionSequence of
    Pattern1 [when Guard1] -> Expressions1;
    Pattern2 [when Guard2] -> Expressions2;
    ...
catch
    ExceptionType1: ExPattern1 [when ExGuard1] -> ExExpressions1;
    ExceptionType2: ExPattern2 [when ExGuard2] -> ExExpressions2;
    ...
after
    AfterExpressions
end
```

Notice the similarity between the **try...catch** expression and the **case** expression:

```
case Expression of
    Pattern1 [when Guard1] -> Expressions1;
    Pattern2 [when Guard2] -> Expressions2;
    ...
end
```

try...catch is like a **case** expression on steroids. It's basically a **case** expression with **catch** and **after** blocks at the end.

---

try...catch Has a Value

Remember, everything in Erlang is an expression, and all expressions have values. This means the expression **try...end** also has a value. So, we might write something like this:

```
f(...) ->
    ...
    X = try ... end,
    Y = g(X),
    ...
```

More often, we don't need the value of the **try...catch** expression. So, we just write this:

```
f(...) ->
    ...
    try ... end,
    ...
    ...
```

---

try...catch works as follows: First FuncOrExpessionSeq is evaluated. If this finishes without raising an exception, then the return value of the function is pattern matched against the patterns Pattern1 (with optional guard Guard1), Pattern2, and so on, until a match is found. If a match is found, then the value of the entire **try...catch** is found by evaluating the expression sequence following the matching pattern.

If an exception is raised within FuncOrExpressionSeq, then the catch patterns ExPattern1, and so on, are matched to find which sequence of expressions should be evaluated. ExceptionType is an atom (one of throw, exit, or error) that tells us how the exception was generated. If ExceptionType is omitted, then the value defaults to throw.

Note: Internal errors that are detected by the Erlang runtime system always have the tag error.

The code following the **after** keyword is used for cleaning up after FuncOrExpressionSeq. This code is guaranteed to be executed, even if an exception is raised. The code in the **after** section is run immediately after any code in Expressions in the **try** or **catch** section of the expression. The return value of AfterExpressions is lost.

If you're coming from Ruby, all of this should seem very familiar—in Ruby, we'd write a similar pattern:

```
begin
  ...
rescue
  ...
ensure
  ...
end
```

The keywords are different,[1] but the behavior is similar.

Shortcuts

We can omit several of the parts of a **try…catch** expression. This:

```
try F
catch
  ...
end
```

means the same as this:

```
try F of
  Val -> Val
catch
  ...
end
```

Also, the **after** section can be omitted.

Programming Idioms with try…catch

When we design applications, we often make sure that the code that catches an error can catch all the errors that a function can produce.

Here's a pair of functions that illustrates this. The first function generates all possible types of an exception:

`try_test.erl`

```
generate_exception(1) -> a;
generate_exception(2) -> throw(a);
generate_exception(3) -> exit(a);
generate_exception(4) -> {'EXIT', a};
generate_exception(5) -> erlang:error(a).
```

Now we'll write a wrapper function to call generate_exception in a **try… catch** expression.

---

1. And there is no retry expression in Erlang!

```
try_test.erl
```

```erlang
demo1() ->
    [catcher(I) || I <- [1,2,3,4,5]].

catcher(N) ->
    try generate_exception(N) of
        Val -> {N, normal, Val}
    catch
        throw:X -> {N, caught, thrown, X};
        exit:X  -> {N, caught, exited, X};
        error:X -> {N, caught, error, X}
    end.
```

Running this we obtain the following:

```erlang
> try_test:demo1().
[{1,normal,a},
 {2,caught,thrown,a},
 {3,caught,exited,a},
 {4,normal,{'EXIT',a}},
 {5,caught,error,a}]
```

This shows that we can trap and distinguish all the forms of exception that a function can raise.

4.4 catch

The other way to trap an exception is to use the primitive **catch**. When you catch an exception, it is converted into a tuple that describes the error. To demonstrate this, we can call generate_exception within a **catch** expression:

```
try_test.erl
```

```erlang
demo2() ->
    [{I, (catch generate_exception(I))} || I <- [1,2,3,4,5]].
```

Running this we obtain the following:

```erlang
2> try_test:demo2().
[{1,a},
 {2,a},
 {3,{'EXIT',a}},
 {4,{'EXIT',a}},
 {5,{'EXIT',{a,[{try_test,generate_exception,1},
               {try_test,'-demo2/0-fun-0-',1},
               {lists,map,2},
               {lists,map,2},
               {erl_eval,do_apply,5},
               {shell,exprs,6},
               {shell,eval_loop,3}]}}}]
```

If you compare this with the output from the **try...catch** section, you'll see that we lose a lot of precision in analyzing the cause of the problem.

4.5 Improving Error Messages

One use of erlang:error is to improve the quality of error messages. If we call math:sqrt(X) with a negative argument, we'll see the following:

```
1> math:sqrt(-1).
** exited: {badarith,[{math,sqrt,[-1]},
                      {erl_eval,do_apply,5},
                      {shell,exprs,6},
                      {shell,eval_loop,3}]} **
```

We can write a wrapper for this, which improves the error message:

`lib_misc.erl`
```
sqrt(X) when X < 0 ->
    erlang:error({squareRootNegativeArgument, X});
sqrt(X) ->
    math:sqrt(X).
```

```
2> lib_misc:sqrt(-1).
** exited: {{squareRootNegativeArgument,-1},
        [{lib_misc,sqrt,1},
         {erl_eval,do_apply,5},
         {shell,exprs,6},
         {shell,eval_loop,3}]} **
```

4.6 Programming Style with try...catch

How do you handle errors in practice? It depends....

Code Where Error Returns Are Common

If your function does not really have a "common case," you should probably return something like {ok, Value} or {error, Reason}, but remember that this forces all callers to do *something* with the return value. You then have to choose between two alternatives; you either write this:

```
...
case f(X) of
    {ok, Val} ->
        do_some_thing_with(Val);
    {error, Why} ->
        %% ... do something with the error ...
end,
...
```

which takes care of both return values, or write this:

```
...
{ok, Val} = f(X),
do_some_thing_with(Val);
...
```

which raises an exception if f(X) returns {error, ...}.

Code Where Errors Are Possible but Rare

Typically you should write code that is expected to handle errors as in this example:

```
try my_func(X)
catch
  throw:{thisError, X} -> ...
  throw:{someOtherError, X} -> ...
end
```

And the code that detects the errors should have matching **throws**:

```
my_func(X) ->
    case ... of
       ...
       ... ->
              ... throw({thisError, ...})
       ... ->
              ... throw({someOtherError, ...})
```

4.7 Catching Every Possible Exception

If we want to catch every possible error, we can use the following idiom (which uses the fact that _ matches anything):

```
try Expr
catch
   _:_ -> ... Code to handle all exceptions  ...
end
```

If we omit the tag and write this:

```
try Expr
catch
   _ -> ... Code to handle all exceptions  ...
end
```

then we *won't* catch all errors, since in this case the default tag throw is assumed.

4.8 Old- and New-Style Exception Handling

This section is for Erlang veterans only!

try...catch is a relatively new construct that was introduced to correct deficiencies in the **catch...throw** mechanism. If you're an old-timer who hasn't been reading the latest documentation (like me), then you'll automatically write code like this:

```
case (catch foo(...)) of
    {'EXIT', Why} ->
        ...
    Val ->
        ...
end
```

This is usually correct, but it's almost always better to write it as follows:

```
try foo(...) of
    Val -> ...
catch
    exit: Why ->
        ...
end
```

So, instead of writing case (catch ...) of ..., write try ... of ....

4.9 Stack Traces

When an exception is caught, we can find the latest stack trace by calling erlang:get_stacktrace(). Here's an example:

`try_test.erl`
```
demo3() ->
    try generate_exception(5)
    catch
      error:X ->
          {X, erlang:get_stacktrace()}
    end.

1> try_test:demo3().
{a,[{try_test,generate_exception,1},
    {try_test,demo3,0},
    {erl_eval,do_apply,5},
    {shell,exprs,6},
    {shell,eval_loop,3}]]}
```

The stack trace contains a list of the functions on the stack to which the current function will return if it returns. It's almost the same as the sequence of calls that got us to the current function, but any tail-recursive function calls[2] will be missing from the trace.

From the point of view of debugging our program, only the first few lines of the stack trace are interesting. The earlier stack trace tells us that the system crashed while evaluating the function generate_exception with one argument in the module try_test. try_test:generate_exception/1 was probably called by try_test:demo3() (we can't be sure about this because try_test:demo3() might have called some other function that made a tail-recursive call to try_test:generate_exception/1, in which case the stack trace won't have any record of the intermediate function).

---

2. See Section 8.9, *A Word About Tail Recursion*, on page 148.

## Chapter 5

Advanced Sequential Programming

By now we're well on our way to understanding sequential Erlang. Chapter 3, *Sequential Programming*, dealt with the basics of writing functions. This chapter covers the following:

- *BIFs*: Short for *built-in functions*, BIFs are functions that are part of the Erlang language. They look as if they might have been written in Erlang, but in fact they are implemented as primitive operations in the Erlang virtual machine.

- *Binaries*: This is a data type that we use to store raw chunks of memory in an efficient manner.

- *The bit syntax*: This is a pattern matching syntax used for packing and unpacking bit fields from binaries.

- *Miscellaneous topics*: This deals with a small number of topics needed to complete our mastery of sequential Erlang.

Once you have mastered this chapter, you'll know pretty much all there is to know about sequential Erlang, and you'll be ready to dive into the mysteries of concurrent programming.

5.1 BIFs

BIFs are functions that are built into Erlang. They usually do tasks that are impossible to program in Erlang. For example, it's impossible to turn a list into a tuple or to find the current time and date. To perform such an operation, we call a BIF.

For example, the BIF tuple_to_list/1 converts a tuple to a list, and time/0 returns the current time of day in hours, minutes, and seconds:

```
1> tuple_to_list({12,cat,"hello"}).
[12,cat,"hello"]
2> time().
{20,0,3}
```

All the BIFs behave as if they belong to the module erlang, though the most common BIFs (such as tuple_to_list) are *autoimported*, so we can call it by writing tuple_to_list(...) instead of erlang:tuple_to_list(...).

You'll find a full list of all BIFs in the erlang manual page in your Erlang distribution or online at http://www.erlang.org/doc/man/erlang.html.

5.2 Binaries

Use a data structure called a *binary* to store large quantities of raw data. Binaries store data in a much more space-efficient manner than in lists or tuples, and the runtime system is optimized for the efficient input and output of binaries.

Binaries are written and printed as sequences of integers or strings, enclosed in double less-than and greater-than brackets. For example:

```
1> <<5,10,20>>.
<<5,10,20>>
2> <<"hello">>.
<<"hello">>
```

When you use integers in a binary, each must be in the range 0 to 255. The binary <<"cat">> is shorthand for <<99,97,116>>; that is, the binary made up from the ASCII character codes of the characters in the string.

As with strings, if the content of a binary is a printable string, then the shell will print the binary as a string; otherwise, it will be printed as a sequence of integers.

We can build a binary and extract the elements of a binary using a BIF, or we can use the bit syntax (see Section 5.3, *The Bit Syntax*, on page 80). In this section, I'll talk only about the BIFs.

> ### @spec func(Arg1,..., Argn) -> Val
>
> What's all this @spec business?
>
> It's an example of the Erlang *type notation*, a documentation convention that the Erlang community uses for describing (among other things) the argument and return types of a function. It should be fairly self-explanatory, but for those who want the full details, turn to Appendix A, on page 385.

BIFs That Manipulate Binaries

The following BIFs manipulate binaries:

@spec list_to_binary(IoList) -> binary()

> list_to_binary returns a binary constructed from the integers and binaries in IoList. Here IoList is a list, whose elements are integers in 0..255, binaries, or IoLists:
>
> ```
> 1> Bin1 = <<1,2,3>>.
> <<1,2,3>>
> 2> Bin2 = <<4,5>>.
> <<4,5>>
> 3> Bin3 = <<6>>.
> <<6>>
> 4> list_to_binary([Bin1,1,[2,3,Bin2],4|Bin3]).
> <<1,2,3,1,2,3,4,5,4,6>>
> ```

@spec split_binary(Bin, Pos) -> {Bin1, Bin2}

> This splits the binary Bin into two parts at position Pos:
>
> ```
> 1> split_binary(<<1,2,3,4,5,6,7,8,9,10>>, 3).
> {<<1,2,3>>,<<4,5,6,7,8,9,10>>}
> ```

@spec term_to_binary(Term) -> Bin

> This converts any Erlang term into a binary.
>
> The binary produced by term_to_binary is stored in the so-called external term format. Terms that have been converted to binaries by using term_to_binary can be stored in files, sent in messages over a network, and so on, and the original term from which they were made can be reconstructed later. This is extremely useful for storing complex data structures in files or sending complex data structures to remote machines.

@spec binary_to_term(Bin) -> Term

> This is the inverse of term_to_binary:

```
1> B = term_to_binary({binaries,"are", useful}).
<<131,104,3,100,0,8,98,105,110,97,114,105,101,115,107,
0,3,97,114,101,100,0,6,117,115,101,102,117,108>>
2> binary_to_term(B).
{binaries,"are",useful}
```

@spec size(Bin) -> Int

> This returns the number of bytes in the binary.

```
1> size(<<1,2,3,4,5>>).
5
```

5.3 The Bit Syntax

The bit syntax is an extension to pattern matching used for extracting and packing individual bits or sequences of bits in binary data. When you're writing low-level code to pack and unpack binary data at a bit level, you'll find the bit syntax incredibly useful. The bit syntax was developed for protocol programming (something that Erlang excels at) and produces highly efficient code for packing and unpacking protocol data.

Suppose we have three variables—X, Y, and Z—that we want to pack into a 16-bit memory area in a variable M. X should take 3 bits in the result, Y should take 7 bits, and Z should take 6. In most languages this involves some messy low-level operations involving bit shifting and masking. In Erlang, you just write the following:

```
M = <<X:3, Y:7, Z:6>>
```

Easy!

The full bit syntax is slightly more complex, so we'll go through it in small steps. First we'll look at some simple code to pack and unpack RGB color data into 16-bit words. Then we'll dive into the details of bit syntax expressions. Finally we'll look at three examples taken from real-world code that uses the bit syntax.

Packing and Unpacking 16-bit Colors

We'll start with a very simple example. Suppose we want to represent a 16-bit RGB color. We decide to allocate 5 bits for the red channel, 6 bits for the green channel, and 5 bits for the blue channel.

(We use one more bit for the green channel because the human eye is more sensitive to green light.)

We can create a 16-bit memory area Mem containing a single RGB triplet as follows:

```
1> Red = 2.
2
2> Green = 61.
61
3> Blue = 20.
20
4> Mem = <<Red:5, Green:6, Blue:5>>.
<<23,180>>
```

Note in line 4 we created a 2-byte binary containing a 16-bit quantity. The shell prints this as <<23,180>>.

To pack the memory, we just wrote the expression <<Red:5, Green:6, Blue:5>>.

To unpack the word, we write a pattern:

```
5> <<R1:5, G1:6, B1:5>> = Mem.
<<23,180>>
6> R1.
2
7> G1.
61
8> B1.
20
```

Bit Syntax Expressions

Bit syntax expressions are of the following form:

```
<<>>
<<E1, E2, ..., En>>
```

Each element Ei specifies a single *segment* of the binary. Each element Ei can have one of four possible forms:

```
Ei = Value |
     Value:Size |
     Value/TypeSpecifierList |
     Value:Size/TypeSpecifierList
```

Whatever form you use, the total number of bits in the binary must be evenly divisible by 8. (This is because binaries contain bytes that take up 8 bits each, so there is no way of representing sequences of bits whose length is not a multiple of 8.)

When you construct a binary, Value must be a bound variable, a literal string, or an expression that evaluates to an integer, a float, or a binary. When used in a pattern matching operation, Value can be a bound or unbound variable, integer, literal string, float, or binary.

Size must be an expression that evaluates to an integer. In pattern matching, Size must be an integer or a bound variable whose value is an integer. Size cannot be an unbound variable.

The value of Size specifies the size of the segment in units (we discuss this later). The default value depends on the type (see below). For an integer it is 8, for a float it is 64, and for a binary it is the size of the binary. In pattern matching, this default value is valid only for the very last element. All other binary elements in the matching must have a size specification.

TypeSpecifierList is a hyphen-separated list of items of the form End-Sign-Type-Unit. Any of the previous items can be omitted, and the items can occur in any order. If an item is omitted, then a default value for the item is used.

The items in the specifier list can have the following values:

@type End = big | little | native
  (@type is also part of the Erlang type notation given in Appendix A).

  This specifies the endianess of the machine. native is determined at runtime, depending upon the CPU of your machine. The default is big. The only significance of this has to do with packing and unpacking integers from binaries. When packing and unpacking integers from binaries on different endian machines, you should take care to use the correct endianess.

  Tip: In the rare case that you really need to understand what's going on here, some experimentation may be necessary. To assure yourself that you are doing the right thing, try the following shell command:

```
1> {<<16#12345678:32/big>>,<<16#12345678:32/little>>,
      <<16#12345678:32/native>>,<<16#12345678:32>>}.
{<<18,52,86,120>>,<<120,86,52,18>>,
 <<120,86,52,18>>,<<18,52,86,120>>}
```

  The output shows you exactly how integers are packed in a binary using the bit syntax.

In case you're worried, term_to_binary and binary_to_term "do the right thing" when packing and unpacking integers. So, you can, for example, create a tuple containing integers on a big-endian machine. Then use term_to_binary to convert the term to a binary and send this to a little-endian machine. On the little-endian, you do binary_to_term, and all the integers in the tuple will have the correct values.

@type Sign = signed | unsigned

> This parameter is used only in pattern matching. The default is unsigned.

@type Type = integer | float | binary

> The default is integer.

@type Unit = 1 | 2 | ... 255

> The total size of the segment is Size x Unit bits long. The total segment size must be greater than or equal to zero and must be a multiple of 8.

> The default value of Unit depends upon Type and is 1 if Type is integer or float and 8 if Type is a binary.

If you've found the bit syntax description a bit daunting, don't panic. Getting the bit syntax patterns right *is* pretty tricky. The best way to approach this is to experiment in the shell with the patterns you need until you get it right and then cut and paste the result into your program. That's how I do it.

Advanced Bit Syntax Examples

Learning the bit syntax is difficult, but the benefits are enormous. This section has three examples from real life. All the code here is cut and paste from real-world programs. The examples are as follows:

- Finding the synchronization frame in MPEG data
- Unpacking COFF data
- Unpacking the header in an IPv4 datagram

Finding the Synchronization Frame in MPEG Data

Suppose we want to write a program that manipulates MPEG audio data. We might want to write a streaming media server in Erlang or extract the data tags that describe the content of an MPEG audio stream. To do this, we need to identify and synchronize with the data frames in an MPEG stream.

MPEG audio data is made up from a number of frames. Each frame has its own header followed by audio information—there is no file header, and in principle, you can cut an MPEG file into pieces and play any of the pieces. Any software that reads an MPEG stream is supposed to find the header frames and thereafter synchronize the MPEG data.

An MPEG header starts with an 11-bit *frame sync* consisting of eleven consecutive 1 bits followed by information that describes the data that follows:

```
AAAAAAAA AAABBCCD EEEEFFGH IIJJKLMM
```

AAAAAAAAAAA	The sync word (11 bits, all ones)
BB	2 bits is the MPEG Audio version ID
CC	2 bits is the layer description
D	1 bit, a protection bit

And so on...

The exact details of these bits need not concern us here. Basically, given knowledge of the values of A to M, we can compute the total length of an MPEG frame.

To find the sync point, we first assume that we are correctly positioned at the start of an MPEG frame. We use the information we find at that position to compute the length of the frame. We might be pointing at nonsense, in which case the length of the frame will be totally wrong. Assuming that we are at the start of a frame and given the length of the frame, then we can skip to the start of the next frame and see whether this is another MPEG header frame.

To find the sync point, we first assume that we are correctly positioned at the start of an MPEG header. We then try to compute the length of the frame. Then one of the following can happen:

- Our assumption was correct, so when we skip forward by the length of the frame, we will find another MPEG header.

- Our assumption was incorrect; either we are not positioned at a sequence of 11 consecutive 1 bits that marks the start of a header or the format of the word is incorrect so that we cannot compute the length of the frame.

- Our assumption was incorrect, but we are positioned at a couple of bytes of music data that happen to look like the start of a header. In this case, we can compute a frame length, but when we skip forward by this length, we cannot find a new header.

To be really sure, we look for three consecutive headers. The synchronization routine is as follows:

`mp3_sync.erl`

```erlang
find_sync(Bin, N) ->
    case is_header(N, Bin) of
        {ok, Len1, _} ->
            case is_header(N + Len1, Bin) of
                {ok, Len2, _} ->
                    case is_header(N + Len1 + Len2, Bin) of
                        {ok, _, _} ->
                            {ok, N};
                        error ->
                            find_sync(Bin, N+1)
                    end;
                error ->
                    find_sync(Bin, N+1)
            end;
        error ->
            find_sync(Bin, N+1)
    end.
```

find_sync tries to find three consecutive MPEG header frames. If byte N in Bin is the start of a header frame, then is_header(N, Bin) will return {ok, Length, Info}. If is_header returns error, then N cannot point to the start of a correct frame. We can do a quick test in the shell to make sure this works:

```erlang
1> {ok, Bin} = file:read_file("/home/joe/music/mymusic.mp3").
{ok,<<73,68,51,3,0,0,0,0,33,22,84,73,84,50,0,0,0,28, ...>>
2> mp3_sync:find_sync(Bin, 1).
{ok,4256}
```

This uses file:read_file to read the entire file into a binary (see Section 13.2, *Reading the Entire File into a Binary*, on page 224). Now for is_header:

`mp3_sync.erl`

```erlang
is_header(N, Bin) ->
    unpack_header(get_word(N, Bin)).

get_word(N, Bin) ->
    {_,<<C:4/binary,_/binary>>} = split_binary(Bin, N),
    C.

unpack_header(X) ->
    try decode_header(X)
    catch
        _:_ -> error
    end.
```

This is slightly more complicated. First we extract 32 bits of data to analyze (this is done by get_word); then we unpack the header using decode_header. Now decode_header is written to crash (by calling exit/1) if its argument is not at the start of a header. To catch any errors, we wrap the call to decode_header in a **try**...**catch** statement (read more about this in Section 4.1, *Exceptions*, on page 67). This will also catch any errors that might be caused by incorrect code in framelength/4. decode_header is where all the fun starts:

`mp3_sync.erl`

```erlang
decode_header(<<2#11111111111:11,B:2,C:2,_D:1,E:4,F:2,G:1,Bits:9>>) ->
    Vsn = case B of
            0 -> {2,5};
            1 -> exit(badVsn);
            2 -> 2;
            3 -> 1
        end,
    Layer = case C of
              0 -> exit(badLayer);
              1 -> 3;
              2 -> 2;
              3 -> 1
          end,
    %% Protection = D,
    BitRate = bitrate(Vsn, Layer, E) * 1000,
    SampleRate = samplerate(Vsn, F),
    Padding = G,
    FrameLength = framelength(Layer, BitRate, SampleRate, Padding),
    if
        FrameLength < 21 ->
            exit(frameSize);
        true ->
            {ok, FrameLength, {Layer,BitRate,SampleRate,Vsn,Bits}}
    end;
decode_header(_) ->
    exit(badHeader).
```

The magic lies in the amazing expression in the first line of the code.

```erlang
decode_header(<<2#11111111111:11,B:2,C:2,_D:1,E:4,F:2,G:1,Bits:9>>) ->
```

This pattern matches eleven consecutive 1 bits,[1] 2 bits into B, 2 bits into C, and so on. Note that the code exactly follows the bit-level specification of the MPEG header given earlier. More beautiful and direct code would be difficult to write. This code is beautiful. It's also highly efficient. The Erlang compiler turns the bit syntax patterns into highly optimized code that extracts the fields in an optimal manner.

---

1. 2#11111111111 is a base 2 integer.

Unpacking COFF Data

A few years ago I decided to write a program to make stand-alone Erlang programs that would run on Windows—I wanted to build a Windows executable on any machine that could run Erlang. Doing this involved understanding and manipulating the Microsoft Common Object File Format (COFF) formatted files. Finding out the details of COFF was pretty tricky, but various APIs for C++ programs were documented. The C++ programs used the type declarations DWORD, LONG, WORD, and BYTE (these type declarations will be familiar to programmers who have programmed Windows internals).

The data structures involved were documented, but only from a C or C++ programmer's point of view. The following is a typical C typedef:

```
typedef struct _IMAGE_RESOURCE_DIRECTORY {
    DWORD Characteristics;
    DWORD TimeDateStamp;
    WORD  MajorVersion;
    WORD  MinorVersion;
    WORD  NumberOfNamedEntries;
    WORD  NumberOfIdEntries;
} IMAGE_RESOURCE_DIRECTORY, *PIMAGE_RESOURCE_DIRECTORY;
```

To write my Erlang program, I first defined four macros that must be included in the Erlang source code file:

```
-define(DWORD, 32/unsigned-little-integer).
-define(LONG,  32/unsigned-little-integer).
-define(WORD,  16/unsigned-little-integer).
-define(BYTE,  8/unsigned-little-integer).
```

Note: Macros are explained in Section 5.4, *Macros*, on page 99. To expand these macros, we use the syntax ?DWORD, ?LONG, and so on. For example, the macro ?DWORD expands to the literal text 32/unsigned-little-integer.

These macros deliberately have the same names as their C counterparts. Armed with these macros, I could easily write some code to unpack image resource data into a binary:

```
unpack_image_resource_directory(Dir) ->
    <<Characteristics      : ?DWORD,
      TimeDateStamp        : ?DWORD,
      MajorVersion         : ?WORD,
      MinorVersion         : ?WORD,
      NumberOfNamedEntries : ?WORD,
      NumberOfIdEntries    : ?WORD, _/binary>> = Dir,
    ...
```

If you compare the C and Erlang code, you'll see that they are pretty similar. So by taking care with the names of the macros and the layout of the Erlang code, we can minimize the semantic gap between the C code and the Erlang code, something that makes our program easier to understand and less likely to have errors.

The next step was to unpack data in Characteristics, and so on.

Characteristics is a 32-bit word consisting of a collection of flags. Unpacking these using the bit syntax is extremely easy; we just write code like this:

```
<<ImageFileRelocsStripped:1, ImageFileExecutableImage:1, ...>> =
  <<Characteristics:32>>
```

The code <<Characteristics:32>> converted Characteristics, which was an integer, into a binary of size 32 bits. Then the following code unpacked the required bits into the variables ImageFileRelocsStripped, ImageFileExecutableImage, and so on:

```
<<ImageFileRelocsStripped:1, ImageFileExecutableImage:1, ...>> = ...
```

Again, I kept the same names as in the Windows API to keep the semantic gap between the specification and the Erlang program to a minimum.

Using these macros made unpacking data in the COFF format—well, I can't really use the word *easy*—but at least it was possible, and the code was reasonably understandable.

Unpacking the Header in an IPv4 Datagram

This example illustrates parsing an Internet Protocol version 4 (IPv4) datagram in a single pattern-matching operation:

```
-define(IP_VERSION, 4).
-define(IP_MIN_HDR_LEN, 5).

...
DgramSize = size(Dgram),
case Dgram of
  <<?IP_VERSION:4, HLen:4, SrvcType:8, TotLen:16,
    ID:16, Flgs:3, FragOff:13,
    TTL:8, Proto:8, HdrChkSum:16,
    SrcIP:32,
    DestIP:32, RestDgram/binary>> when HLen >= 5, 4*HLen =< DgramSize ->
        OptsLen = 4*(HLen - ?IP_MIN_HDR_LEN),
        <<Opts:OptsLen/binary,Data/binary>> = RestDgram,
        ...
```

This code matches an IP datagram in a single pattern-matching expression. The pattern is complex, spreading over three lines, and illustrates how data that does not fall on byte boundaries can easily be extracted (for example, the Flgs and FragOff fields that are 3 and 13 bits long, respectively). Having pattern matched the IP datagram, the header and data part of the datagram are extracted in a second pattern matching operation.

5.4 Miscellaneous Short Topics

We've now covered all the major topics in sequential Erlang. What remains are a number of small odds and ends that you have to know but that don't fit into any of the other topics. There's no particular logical order to these. The topics covered are as follows:

- *apply*: How to compute the value of a function from its name and arguments, when the function and module name are computed dynamically.
- *Attributes*: The syntax and meaning of the Erlang module attributes.
- *Block expressions*: Expressions using **begin** and **end**.
- *Boolean expressions*: All the boolean expressions.
- *Character set*: Which character set does Erlang use?
- *Comments*: Syntax of comments.
- *epp*: The Erlang preprocessor.
- *Escape sequences*: The syntax of the escape sequences used in strings and atoms.
- *Expressions and expression sequences*: What exactly is an expression?
- *Function references*: How to refer to functions.
- *Include files*: How to include files at compile time.
- *List operations*: ++ and - -.
- *Macros*: The Erlang macro processor.
- *Match operator in patterns*: How the match operator = can be used in patterns.
- *Numbers*: The syntax of numbers.
- *Operator precedence*: The priority and associativity of all the Erlang operators.
- *The process dictionary*: Each Erlang process has a local area of destructive storage, which can be useful sometimes.

- *References*: References are unique symbols.
- *Short-circuit boolean expressions*: Boolean expressions that are not fully evaluated.
- *Term comparisons*: All the term comparison operators and the lexical ordering of terms.
- *Underscore variables*: Variables that the compiler treats in a special way.

apply

The BIF apply(Mod, Func, [Arg1, Arg2, ..., ArgN]) applies the function Func in the module Mod to the arguments Arg1, Arg2, ... ArgN. It is equivalent to calling this:

```
Mod:Func(Arg1, Arg2, ..., ArgN)
```

apply lets you call a function in a module, passing it arguments. What makes it different from calling the function directly is that the module name and/or the function name can be computed dynamically.

All the Erlang BIFs can be called using apply by assuming that they belong to the module erlang. So, to build a dynamic call to a BIF, we might write the following:

```
1> apply(erlang, atom_to_list, [hello]).
"hello"
```

Warning: The use of apply should be avoided if possible. When the number of arguments to a function is known in advance, it is much better to use a call of the form M:F(Arg1, Arg2, ... ArgN) than apply. When calls to functions are built using apply, many analysis tools cannot work out what is happening, and certain compiler optimizations cannot be made. So, use apply sparingly and only when absolutely needed.

Attributes

Module attributes have the syntax -AtomTag(...)[2] and are used to define certain properties of a file. There are two types of module attributes: predefined and user-defined.

Predefined Module Attributes

The following module attributes have predefined meanings and must be placed before any function definitions.

---

2. -record(...) and -include(...) have a similar syntax but are not considered module attributes.

-module(modname).

> The module declaration. modname must be an atom. This attribute must be the first attribute in the file. Conventionally the code for modname should be stored in a file called modname.erl. If you do not do this, then automatic code loading will not work correctly; see Section E.4, *Dynamic Code Loading*, on page 431 for more details.

-import(Mod, [Name1/Arity1, Name2/Arity2,...]).

> Specify that the function Name1 with Arity1 arguments is to be imported from the module Mod.

> Once a function has been imported from a module, then calling the function can be achieved *without* specifying the module name. For example:

```erlang
-module(abc).
-import(lists, [map/2]).

f(L) ->
    L1 = map(fun(X) -> 2*X end, L),
    lists:sum(L1)
```

> The call to map needs no qualifying module name, whereas to call sum we need to include the module name in the function call.

-export([Name1/Arity1, Name2/Arity2, ...]).

> Export the functions Name1/Arity1, Name2/Arity2, and so on, from the current module. Note that only exported functions can be called from outside a module. For example:

abc.erl
```erlang
-module(abc).
-export([a/2, b/1]).

a(X, Y) -> c(X) + a(Y).
a(X) -> 2 * X.
b(X) -> X * X.
c(X) -> 3 * X.
```

> The export declaration means that only a/2 and b/1 can be called from outside the module abc. So, for example, calling abc:a(5) will result in an error because a/1 is not exported from the module.

```erlang
1> abc:a(1,2).
7
2> abc:b(12).
144
```

```
3> abc:a(5).
** exited: {undef,[{abc,a,[5]},
                   {erl_eval,do_apply,5},
                   {shell,exprs,6},
                   {shell,eval_loop,3}]} ="session">
```

-compile(Options).

Add Options to the list of compiler options. Options is a single compiler option or a list of compiler options (these are described in the manual page for the module compile).

Note: The compiler option **-compile(export_all)**. is often used while debugging programs. This exports all functions from the module without having to explicitly use the **-export** annotation.

-vsn(Version).

Specify a module version. Version is any literal term. The value of Version has no particular syntax or meaning, but it can be used by analysis programs or for documentation purposes.

User-Defined Attributes

The syntax of a user-defined module attribute is as follows:

```
-SomeTag(Value).
```

SomeTag must be an atom, and Value must be a literal term. The values of the module attributes are compiled into the module and can be extracted at runtime. Here's an example:

`attrs.erl`
```
-module(attrs).
-vsn(1234).
-author({joe,armstrong}).
-purpose("example of attributes").
-export([fac/1]).

fac(1) -> 1;
fac(N) -> N * fac(N-1).
```

```
1> attrs:module_info().
[{exports,[{fac,1},{module_info,0},{module_info,1}]},
 {imports,[]},
 {attributes,[{vsn,[1234]},
              {author,[{joe,armstrong}]},
              {purpose,"example of attributes"}]},
 {compile,[{options,[{cwd,"/home/joe/2006/book/JAERLANG/Book/code"},
                     {outdir,"/home/joe/2006/book/JAERLANG/Book/code"}]},
           {version,"4.4.3"},
           {time,{2007,2,21,19,23,48}},
           {source,"/home/joe/2006/book/JAERLANG/Book/code/attrs.erl"}]}]
```

```
2> attrs:module_info(attributes).
[{vsn,[1234]},{author,[{joe,armstrong}]},{purpose,"example of attributes"}]
3> beam_lib:chunks("attrs.beam",[attributes]).
{ok,{attrs,[{attributes,[{author,[{joe,armstrong}]},
                          {purpose,"example of attributes"},
                          {vsn,[1234]}]}]}}
```

The user-defined attributes contained in the source code file reappear as a subterm of {attributes, ...}. The tuple {compile, ...} contains information that was added by the compiler. The value {version,"4.4.3"} is the version of the compiler and should not be confused with the vsn tag defined in the module attributes. In the previous example, attrs:module_info() returns a property list of all the metadata associated with a compiled module. attrs:module_info(attributes)[3] returns a list of any attributes associated with the file.

Note that the functions module_info/0 and module_info/1 are automatically created every time a module is compiled.

The output of lines 2 and 3 is a bit difficult to read. To make life easier, we can write a little function that extracts a specific attribute and call it like this:

```
4> extract:attribute("attrs.beam", author).
[{joe,armstrong}]
```

The code to do this is easy:

`extract.erl`

```
-module(extract).
-export([attribute/2]).

attribute(File, Key) ->
    case beam_lib:chunks(File,[attributes]) of
        {ok, {_Module, [{attributes,L}]}} ->
            case lookup(Key, L) of
                {ok, Val} ->
                    Val;
                error ->
                    exit(badAttribute)
            end;
        _ ->
            exit(badFile)
    end.

lookup(Key, [{Key,Val}|_]) -> {ok, Val};
lookup(Key, [_|T])         -> lookup(Key, T);
lookup(_, [])              -> error.
```

---

3. Other arguments are exports, imports, and compile.

To run attrs:module_info, we have to load the beam code for the module attrs. The module beam_lib contains a number of functions for analyzing a module without loading the code. The example in extract.erl used beam_lib:chunks to extract the attribute data without loading the code for the module.

Block Expressions

```
begin
    Expr1,
    ...,
    ExprN
end
```

You can use block expressions to group a sequence of expressions, similar to a clause body. The value of a begin ... end block is the value of the last expression in the block.

Block expressions are used when the syntax requires a single expression but you want to have sequence of expressions at this point in the code.

Booleans

There is no distinct boolean type in Erlang; instead, the atoms true and false are given a special interpretation and are used to represent boolean literals.

Boolean Expressions

There are four possible boolean expressions:

- not B1: Logical not
- B1 and B2: Logical and
- B1 or B2: Logical or
- B1 xor B2: Logical xor

In all of these, B1 and B2 must be boolean literals or expressions that evaluate to booleans. Examples:

```
1> not true.
false.
2> true and false.
false
3> true or false.
true
4> (2 > 1) or (3 > 4).
true
```

Force Binary Functions to Return Booleans

Sometimes we write functions that return one of two possible atomic values. When this happens, it's good practice to make sure they return a boolean. It's also a good idea to name your functions to make it clear that they return a boolean.

For example, suppose we write a program that represents the state of some file. We might find ourselves writing a function file_state() that returns open or closed. When we write this function, we could think about renaming the function and letting it return a boolean. With a little thought we could rewrite our program to use a function called is_file_open() that returns true or false.

Why should we do this?

The answer is simple. There are a large number of functions in the standard libraries that work on functions that return booleans. So if we make sure all our functions that can return only one of two atomic values instead return booleans, then we'll be able to use them together with the standard library functions.

Character Set

Erlang source code files are assumed to be encoded in the ISO-8859-1 (Latin-1) character set. This means all Latin-1 printable characters can be used without using any escape sequences.

Internally Erlang has no character data type. Strings don't really exist but instead are represented by lists of integers. Unicode strings can be represented by lists of integers without any problems, though there is limited support for parsing and generating Unicode files from the Erlang lists of integers.

Comments

Comments in Erlang start with a percent character (%) and extend to the end of line. There are no block comments.

Note: You'll often see double percent characters (%%) in code examples. Double percent marks are recognized in the emacs erlang-mode and enable automatic indentation of commented lines.

```
% This is a comment
my_function(Arg1, Arg2) ->
    case f(Arg1) of
        {yes, X} ->   % it worked
           ..
```

epp

Before an Erlang module is compiled, it is automatically processed by the Erlang preprocessor epp. The preprocessor expands any macros that might be in the source file and inserts any necessary include files.

Ordinarily, you won't need to look at the output of the preprocessor, but in exceptional circumstances (for example, when debugging a faulty macro), you might want to save the output of the preprocessor. The output of the preprocessor can be saved in a file by giving the command compile:file(M, ['P']). This compiles any code in the file M.erl and produces a listing in the file M.P where all macros have been expanded and any necessary include files have been included.

Escape Sequences

Within strings and quoted atoms, you can use escape sequences to enter any nonprintable characters. All the possible escape sequences are shown in Figure 5.1, on the facing page.

Let's give some examples in the shell to show how these conventions work. (Note: ~w in a format string prints the list without any attempt to pretty print the result.)

```
%% Control characters
1> io:format("~w~n", ["\b\d\e\f\n\r\s\t\v"]).
[8,127,27,12,10,13,32,9,11]
ok
%% Octal characters in a string
3> io:format("~w~n", ["\123\12\1"]).
[83,10,1]
ok
%% Quotes and escapes in a string
4> io:format("~w~n", ["\'\"\\"]).
[39,34,92]
ok
%% Character codes
5> io:format("~w~n", ["\a\z\A\Z"]).
[97,122,65,90]
ok
```

Escape Sequence	Meaning	Integer Code
\b	Backspace	8
\d	Delete	127
\e	Escape	27
\f	Form feed	12
\n	New line	10
\r	Carriage return	13
\s	Space	32
\t	Tab	9
\v	Vertical tab	11
\NNN \NN \N	Octal characters (N is 0..7)	
\^a..\^z or \^A..\^Z	Ctrl+A to Ctrl+Z	1 to 26
\'	Single quote	39
\"	Double quote	34
\\	Backslash	92
\C	The ASCII code for C (C is a character)	(An integer)

Figure 5.1: ESCAPE SEQUENCES

Expressions and Expression Sequences

In Erlang, anything that can be evaluated to produce a value is called an *expression*. This means things such as **catch**, **if**, and **try...catch** are expressions. Things such as records and module attributes cannot be evaluated, so they are not expressions.

Expression sequences are sequences of expressions separated by commas. These are found all over the place immediately following an -> arrow. The value of the expression sequence E1, E2, ..., En is defined to be the value of the last expression in the sequence.[4] This is computed using any bindings created when computing the values of E1, E2, and so on.

Function References

Often we want to refer to a function that is defined in the current module or in some external module. You can use the following notation for this:

fun LocalFunc/Arity

> This is used to refer to the local function called LocalFunc with Arity arguments in the current module.

---

4. Equivalent to progn in LISP.

fun Mod:RemoteFunc/Arity

> This is used to refer to an external function called RemoteFunc with Arity arguments in the module Mod.

Here's an example of a function reference in the current module:

```
-module(x1).
-export([square/1, ...]).

square(X) -> X * X.
...
double(L) -> lists:map(fun square/1, L).
```

If we wanted to call a function in a remote module, we could refer to the function as in the following example:

```
-module(x2).


...
double(L) -> lists:map(fun x1:square/1, L).
```

fun x1:square/1 means the function square/1 in the module x1.

Include Files

Files can be included with the following syntax:

```
-include(Filename).
```

In Erlang, the convention is that include files have the extension .hrl. The FileName should contain an absolute or relative path so that the preprocessor can locate the appropriate file. Library header files can be included with the following syntax:

```
-include_lib(Name).
```

For example:

```
-include_lib("kernel/include/file.hrl").
```

In this case, the Erlang compiler will find the appropriate include files. (kernel, in the previous example, refers to the application that defines this header file.)

Include files usually contain record definitions. If many modules need to share common record definitions, then the common record definitions are put into include files that are included by all the modules that need these definitions.

List Operations ++ and - -

++ and -- are infix operators for list addition and subtraction.

A ++ B adds (that is, appends) A and B.

A -- B subtracts the list B from the list A. Subtraction means that every element in B is removed from A. Note that if some symbol X occurs only K times in B, then only the first K occurrence of X in A will be removed.

Examples:

```
1> [1,2,3] ++ [4,5,6].
[1,2,3,4,5,6]
2> [a,b,c,1,d,e,1,x,y,1] -- [1].
[a,b,c,d,e,1,x,y,1]
3> [a,b,c,1,d,e,1,x,y,1] -- [1,1].
[a,b,c,d,e,x,y,1]
4> [a,b,c,1,d,e,1,x,y,1] -- [1,1,1].
[a,b,c,d,e,x,y]
5> [a,b,c,1,d,e,1,x,y,1] -- [1,1,1,1].
[a,b,c,d,e,x,y]
```

++ in Patterns

++ can also be used in patterns. When matching strings, we can write patterns such as the following:

```
f("begin" ++ T) -> ...
f("end" ++ T) -> ...
...
```

The pattern in the first clause is expanded into [$b,$e,$g,$i,$n|T].

Macros

Erlang macros are written as shown here:

```
-define(Constant, Replacement).
-define(Func(Var1, Var2,.., Var), Replacement).
```

Macros are expanded by the Erlang preprocessor epp when an expression of the form ?MacroName is encountered. Variables occurring in the macro definition match complete forms in the corresponding site of the macro call.

```
-define(macro1(X, Y), {a, X, Y}).

foo(A) ->
    ?macro1(A+10, b)
```

That expands into this:

```
foo(A) ->
    {a,A+10,b}.
```

In addition, a number of predefined macros provide information about the current module. They are as follows:

- ?FILE expands to the current filename.
- ?MODULE expands to the current module name.
- ?LINE expands to the current line number.

Control Flow in Macros

Inside a macro definition, the following directives are supported. You can use them to direct the flow of control within a macro:

-undef(Macro).
> Undefines the macro; after this you cannot call the macro.

-ifdef(Macro).
> Evaluates the following lines only if Macro has been defined.

-ifndef(Macro).
> Evaluates the following lines only if Macro is undefined.

-else.
> Allowed after a **ifdef** or **ifndef** statement. If the condition was false, the statements following **else** are evaluated.

-endif.
> Marks the end of an **ifdef** or **ifndef** statement.

Conditional macros must be properly nested. They are conventionally grouped as follows:

```
-ifdef(debug).
-define(...).
-else.
-define(...).
-endif.
```

We can use these macros to define a TRACE macro. For example:

`m1.erl`

```
-module(m1).
-export([start/0]).

-ifdef(debug).
-define(TRACE(X), io:format("TRACE ~p:~p ~p~n",[?MODULE, ?LINE, X])).
-else.
-define(TRACE(X), void).
-endif.
```

```
start() -> loop(5).

loop(0) ->
    void;
loop(N) ->
    ?TRACE(N),
    loop(N-1).
```

Note: io:format(String, [Args]) prints the variables in [Args] in the Erlang shell according to the formatting information in String. The formatting codes are preceded by a (~) symbol. ~p is short for *pretty print*, and ~n produces a newline.[5]

To compile the code using the trace macro turned on and off, we can use an additional argument to c/2 as follows:

```
1> c(m1, {d, debug}).
{ok,m1}
2> m1:start().
TRACE m1:15  5
TRACE m1:15  4
TRACE m1:15  3
TRACE m1:15  2
TRACE m1:15  1
void
```

c(m1, Options) provides a way of passing options to the compiler. {d, debug} sets the debug flag to true so that it gets recognized in the -ifdef(debug) section of the macro definition.

When the macro is turned off, the trace macro just expands to the atom void. This choice of name has no significance; it's just a reminder to me that nobody is interested in the value of the macro.

Match Operator in Patterns

Let's suppose we have some code like this:

Line 1
```
func1([{tag1, A, B}|T]) ->
    ...
    ... f(..., {tag1, A, B}, ...)
    ...
```

In line 1, we pattern match the term {tag1, A, B}, and in line 3 we call f with an argument that is {tag1, A, B}. When we do this, the system rebuilds the term {tag1, A, B}. A much more efficient and less error prone

---

5. io:format understands an extremely large number of formatting options; for more information, see Section 13.3, *Write a List of Terms to a File*, on page 228.

way to do this is to assign the pattern to a temporary variable, Z, and pass this into f, like this:

```
func1([{tag1, A, B}=Z|T]) ->
    ...
    ... f(... Z, ...)
    ...
```

The match operator can be used at any point in the pattern, so if we have two terms that need rebuilding, such as in this code:

```
func1([{tag, {one, A}, B}|T]) ->
    ...
    ... f(..., {tag, {one,A}, B}, ...),
    ... g(..., {one, A}), ...)
    ...
```

then we could introduce two new variables, Z1 and Z2, and write the following:

```
func1([{tag, {one, A}=Z1, B}=Z2|T]) ->
    ..,.
    ... f(..., Z2, ...),
    ... g(..., Z1, ...),
    ...
```

Numbers

Numbers in Erlang are either integers or floats.

Integers

Integer arithmetic is exact, and the number of digits that can be represented in an integer is limited only by available memory.

Integers are written with one of three different syntaxes:

1. *Conventional syntax*: Here integers are written as you expect. For example, 12, 12375, and -23427 are all integers.

2. *Base K integers*: Integers in a number base other than ten are written with the syntax K#Digits; thus, we can write a number in binary as 2#00101010 or a number in hexadecimal as 16#af6bfa23. For bases greater than ten, the characters abc... (or ABC...) represent the numbers 10, 11, 12, and so on. The highest number base we can represent in this manner is base 36.

3. *$ syntax*: The syntax $C represents the integer code for the ASCII character C. Thus, $a is short for 97, $1 is short for 49, and so on.

   Immediately after the $ we can also use any of the escape sequences described in Figure 5.1, on page 97. Thus, $\n is 10, $\^c is 3, and so on.

Here are some examples of integers:

0 -65 2#010001110 -8#377 16#fe34 16#FE34 36#wow

(Their values are 0, -65, 142, -255, 65076, 65076, and 42368, respectively.)

Floats

A floating-point number has five parts: an optional sign, a whole number part, a decimal point, a fractional part, and an optional exponent part.

Here are some examples of floats:

1.0 3.14159 -2.3e+6 23.56E-27

After parsing, floating-point numbers are represented internally in IEEE 754 64-bit format. Real numbers in the range -10^{323} to 10^{308} can be represented by an Erlang float.

Operator Precedence

Figure 5.2 shows all the Erlang operators in order of descending priority together with their associativity. Operator precedence and associativity is used to determine the evaluation order in unparenthesized expressions.

Expression with higher priority (higher up in the table) are evaluated first, and then expressions with lower priority are evaluated. So, for example, to evaluate 3+4*5+6, we first evaluate the subexpression 4*5, since (*) is higher up in the table than (+). Now we evaluate 3+20+6. Since (+) is a left-associative operator, we interpret this as meaning (3+20)+6, so we evaluate 3+20 first yielding 23; finally we evaluate 23+6.

In its fully parenthesized form, 3+4*5+6 means ((3+(4*5))+6). As with all programming languages, it is better to use parentheses to denote scope than to rely upon the precedence rules.

Operators	Associativity
:	
#	
(unary) +, (unary) -, bnot, not	
/, *, div, rem, band, and	Left associative
+, -, bor, bxor, bsl, bsr, or, xor	Left associative
++, --	Right associative
==, /=, =<, <, >=, >, =:=, =/=	
andalso	
orelse	

Figure 5.2: OPERATOR PRECEDENCE

The Process Dictionary

Each process in Erlang has its own private data store called the *process dictionary*. The process dictionary is an associative array (in other languages this might be called a *map*, *hashmap*, or *hash table*) composed of a collection of keys and values. Each key has only one value.

The dictionary can be manipulated using the following BIFs:

@spec put(Key, Value) -> OldValue.

Add a Key, Value association to the process dictionary. The value of put is OldValue, which is the previous value associated with Key. If there was no previous value, the atom undefined is returned.

@spec get(Key) -> Value.

Look up the value of Key. If there is an association Key, Value association in the dictionary, return Value; otherwise, return the atom undefined

@spec get() -> [{Key,Value}].

Return the entire dictionary as a list of {Key,Value} tuples.

@spec get_keys(Value) -> [Key].

Return a list of keys that have the values Value in the dictionary.

@spec erase(Key) -> Value.

Return the value associated with Key or the atom undefined if there is no value associated with Key. Finally, erase the value associated with Key.

@spec erase() -> [{Key,Value}].

> Erase the entire process dictionary. The return value is a list of {Key,Value} tuples representing the state of the dictionary before it was erased.

For example:

```
1> erase().
[]
2> put(x, 20).
undefined
3> get(x).
20
4> get(y).
undefined
5> put(y, 40).
undefined
6> get(y).
40
7> get().
[{y,40},{x,20}]
8> erase(x).
20
9> get().
[{y,40}]
```

As you can see, variables in the process dictionary behave pretty much like conventional variables in imperative programming languages. If you use the process dictionary, your code will no longer be side effect free, and all the benefits of using nondestructive variables that we discussed in Section 2.6, *Variables That Don't Vary*, on page 17 do not apply. For this reason, you should use the process dictionary sparingly.

Note: I rarely use the process dictionary. Using the process dictionary can introduce subtle bugs into your program and make it difficult to debug. One form of usage that I do approve of is to use the processes dictionary to store "write-once" variables. If a key acquires a value exactly once and does not change the value, then storing it in the process dictionary is sometimes acceptable.

References

References are globally unique Erlang terms. They are created with the BIF erlang:make_ref(). References are useful for creating unique tags that can be included in data and then at a later stage compared for equality. For example, a bug-tracking system might add a reference to each new bug report in order to give it a unique identity.

Short-Circuit Boolean Expressions

Short-circuit boolean expressions are boolean expressions whose arguments are evaluated only when necessary.

There are two "short-circuit" boolean expressions:

Expr1 **orelse** Expr2
> This first evaluates Expr1. If Expr1 evaluates to true, Expr2 is not evaluated. If Expr1 evaluates to false, Expr2 is evaluated.

Expr1 **andalso** Expr2
> This first evaluates Expr1. If Expr1 evaluates to true, Expr2 is evaluated. If Expr1 evaluates to false, Expr2 is not evaluated.

Note: In the corresponding boolean expressions (A or B; A and B), both the arguments are always evaluated, even if the truth value of the expression can be determined by evaluating only the first expression.

Term Comparisons

There are eight possible term comparison operations, shown in Figure 5.3, on the facing page.

For the purposes of comparison, a total ordering is defined over all terms. This is defined so that the following is true:

number < atom < reference < fun < port < pid < tuple < list < binary

What does this mean? This means that, for example, a number (any number) is defined to be smaller than an atom (any atom), that a tuple is greater than an atom, and so on. (Note that for the purposes of ordering, ports and PIDs are included in this list. We'll talk about these later.)

Having a total order over all terms means we can sort lists of any type and build efficient data access routines based on the sort order of the keys.

All the term comparison operators, with the exception of =:= and =/=, behave in the following way if their arguments are numbers:

- If one argument is a integer and the other is a float, then the integer is converted to a float before the comparison is performed.

- If both arguments are integers or if both arguments are floats, then the arguments are used "as is," that is, without conversion.

You should also be really careful about using == (especially if you're a C or Java programmer). In 99 out of a 100 cases, you should be using =:=. == is useful *only* when comparing floats with integers. =:= is for testing

Operator	Meaning
X > Y	X is greater than Y.
X < Y	X is less than Y.
X =< Y	X is equal to or less than Y.
X >= Y	X is greater than or equal to Y.
X == Y	X is equal to Y.
X /= Y	X is not equal to Y.
X =:= Y	X is identical to Y.
X =/= Y	X is not identical to Y.

Figure 5.3: TERM COMPARISONS

whether two terms are *identical*.[6] If in doubt, use =:=, and be suspicious if you see ==. Note that a similar comment applies to using /= and =/=, where /= means "not equal to" and =/= means "not identical."

Note: In a lot of library and published code, you'll see == used when the operator should have been =:=. Fortunately, this kind of error does not often result in an incorrect program, since if the arguments to == do not contain any floats, then the behaviors of the two operators are the same.

You should also be aware that function clause matching always implies exact pattern matching, so if you define a fun F = fun(12) -> ... end, then trying to evaluate F(12.0) will fail.

Underscore Variables

There's one more thing to say about variables. The special syntax _Var-Name is used for a normal variable, not an anonymous variable. Normally the compiler will generate a warning if a variable is used only once in a clause since this is usually the sign of an error. If the variable is used only once but starts with an underscore, the warning message will not be generated.

Since _Var is a normal variable, very subtle bugs can be caused by forgetting this and using it as a "don't care" pattern. In a complicated pattern match, it can be difficult to spot that, for example, _Int is repeated when it shouldn't have been, causing the pattern match to fail.

---

6.   Identical means having the same value (like the Common Lisp EQUAL). Since values are immutable, this does not imply any notion of pointer identity.

There are two main uses of underscore variables:

- To name a variable that we don't intend to use. That is, writing open(File, _Mode) makes the program more readable than writing open(File, _).

- For debugging purposes. For example, suppose we write this:

```erlang
some_func(X) ->
    {P, Q} = some_other_func(X),
    io:format("Q = ~p~n", [Q]),
    P.
```

This compiles without an error message.

Now comment out the format statement:

```erlang
some_func(X) ->
    {P, Q} = some_other_func(X),
    %% io:format("Q = ~p~n", [Q]),
    P.
```

If we compile this, the compiler will issue a warning that the variable Q is not used.

If we rewrite the function like this:

```erlang
some_func(X) ->
    {P, _Q} = some_other_func(X),
    io:format("_Q = ~p~n", [_Q]),
    P.
```

then we can comment out the format statement, and the compiler will not complain.

Now we're actually through with sequential Erlang. We have not mentioned a few small topics, but we'll return to these as we run into them in the application chapters.

In the next chapter, we'll look at how to compile and run your programs in a variety of ways.

## Chapter 6

Compiling and Running Your Program

In the previous chapters, we didn't say much about compiling and running your programs—we just used the Erlang shell. This is fine for small examples, but as your programs become more complex, you'll want to automate the process to make life easier. That's where makefiles come in.

There are actually three different ways to run your programs. In this chapter, we'll look at all three so you can choose the best method for any particular occasion.

Sometimes things will go wrong: makefiles will fail, environment variables will be wrong, and your search paths will be incorrect. We'll help you deal with these issues by looking at what to do when things go wrong.

6.1 Starting and Stopping the Erlang Shell

On a Unix system (including Mac OS X), you start the Erlang shell from a command prompt:

```
$ erl
Erlang (BEAM) emulator version 5.5.1 [source] [async-threads:0] [hipe]

Eshell V5.5.1  (abort with ^G)
1>
```

On a Windows system, click the erl icon.

The easiest way to stop the system is just to press Ctrl+C (Windows Ctrl+Break) followed by A, as follows:

```
BREAK: (a)bort (c)ontinue (p)roc info (i)nfo (l)oaded
       (v)ersion (k)ill (D)b-tables (d)istribution
a
$
```

Instead, you can evaluate the expression erlang:halt() either in the shell or in a program.

erlang:halt() is a BIF that immediately stops the system, and it is the method I use most of the time. However, there is a slight disadvantage to this method of stopping the system. If you are running a large database application and simply halt the system, then the system will have to go through an error recovery process the next time you start the system, so you should try to stop the system in a controlled manner.

For a controlled shutdown, if the shell is responding to commands, you can type this:

```
1> q().
ok
$
```

This flushes all open files, stops the database (if running), and closes all OTP applications in an ordered manner. q() is a shell alias for the command init:stop().

If none of these methods works, read Section 6.6, *Getting Out of Trouble*, on page 122.

6.2 Modifying the Development Environment

When you start programming in Erlang, you'll probably put all your modules and files in the same directory and start Erlang from this directory. If you do this, then the Erlang loader will have no trouble finding your code. However, as your applications become more complex, you'll want to split them into manageable chunks and put the code into different directories. And when you include code from other projects, this external code will have its own directory structure.

Setting the Search Paths for Loading Code

The Erlang runtime system makes use of a code autoloading mechanism. For this to work correctly, you must set a number of search paths in order to find the correct version of your code.

The code-loading mechanism is actually programmed in Erlang—we'll talk more about it in Section E.4, *Dynamic Code Loading*, on page 431. Code loading is performed "on demand."

When the system tries to call a function in a module that has not been loaded, an exception occurs, and the system tries to find an object code file for the missing module. If the missing module is called myMissing-Module, then the code loader will search for a file called myMissingMod-ule.beam in all the directories that are in the current load path. The search stops at the first matching file, and the object code in this file is loaded into the system.

You can find the value of the current load path by starting an Erlang shell and giving the command code:get_path(). Here's an example:

```
code:get_path().
[".",
"/usr/local/lib/erlang/lib/kernel-2.11.3/ebin",
"/usr/local/lib/erlang/lib/stdlib-1.14.3/ebin",
"/usr/local/lib/erlang/lib/xmerl-1.1/ebin",
"/usr/local/lib/erlang/lib/webtool-0.8.3/ebin",
"/usr/local/lib/erlang/lib/typer-0.1.0/ebin",
"/usr/local/lib/erlang/lib/tv-2.1.3/ebin",
"/usr/local/lib/erlang/lib/tools-2.5.3/ebin",
"/usr/local/lib/erlang/lib/toolbar-1.3/ebin",
"/usr/local/lib/erlang/lib/syntax_tools-1.5.2/ebin",
...]
```

The two most common functions that we use to manipulate the load path are as follows:

@spec code:add_patha(Dir) => true | {error, bad_directory}
    Add a new directory, Dir, to the start of the load path.

@spec code:add_pathz(Dir) => true | {error, bad_directory}
    Add a new directory, Dir, to the end of the load path.

Usually it doesn't matter which you use. The only thing to watch out for is if using add_patha and add_pathz produces different results. If you suspect an incorrect module was loaded, you can call code:all_loaded() (which returns a list of all loaded module) or code:clash() to help you investigate what went wrong.

There are several other routines in the module code for manipulating the path, but you probably won't ever need to use them, unless you're doing some strange system programming.

The usual convention is to put these commands in a file called .erlang in your home directory. Alternatively, you can start Erlang with a command like this:

```
> erl -pa Dir1 -pa Dir2 ... -pz DirK1 -pz DirK2
```

The -pa Dir flag adds Dir to the beginning of the code search path, and -pz Dir adds the directory to the end of the code path.

Executing a Set of Commands When the System Is Started

We saw how you can set the load path in your .erlang file in your home directory. In fact, you can put any Erlang code in this file—when you start Erlang, it first reads and evaluates all the commands in this file.

Suppose my .erlang file is as follows:

```
io:format("Running Erlang~n").
code:add_patha(".").
code:add_pathz("/home/joe/2005/erl/lib/supported").
code:add_pathz("/home/joe/bin").
```

Then when I start the system, I'll see the following output:

```
$ erl
Erlang (BEAM) emulator version 5.5.1 [source] [async-threads:0] [hipe]

Running Erlang
Eshell V5.5.1  (abort with ^G)
1>
```

If there is a file called .erlang in the current directory when Erlang is started, then it will take precedence over the .erlang in your home directory. This way you can arrange that Erlang will behave in different ways depending upon where it is started. This can be useful for specialized applications. In this case, it's probably a good idea to include some print statements in the start-up file; otherwise, you might forget about the local start-up file, which could be very confusing.

Tip: In some systems, it's not clear where your home directory is, or it might not be where you think it is. To find out where Erlang thinks your home directory is, do the following:

```
1> init:get_argument(home).
{ok,[["/home/joe"]]}
```

From this we can infer that Erlang thinks that my home directory is /home/joe.

6.3 Different Ways to Run Your Program

Erlang programs are stored in modules. Once you have written your program, you have to compile it before you can run it. Alternatively, you can run your program directly without compiling it by running *escript*.

The next sections show how to compile and run a couple of programs in a number of ways. The programs are slightly different, and the ways in which we start and stop them differ.

The first program, hello.erl, just prints "Hello world." It's not responsible for starting or stopping the system, and it does not need to access any command-line arguments. By way of contrast, the second program, fac, needs to access the command-line arguments.

Here's our basic program. It writes the string containing "Hello world" followed by a newline (~n is interpreted as newline in the Erlang io and io_lib modules).

`hello.erl`

```erlang
-module(hello).
-export([start/0]).

start() ->
    io:format("Hello world~n").
```

Let's compile and run it three different ways.

Compile and Run in the Erlang Shell

```
$ erl
Erlang (BEAM) emulator version 5.5.1 [source] [async-threads:0] [hipe]

Eshell V5.5.1  (abort with ^G)
1> c(hello).
{ok,hello}
2> hello:start().
Hello world
ok
```

Compile and Run from the Command Prompt

```
$ erlc hello.erl
$ erl -noshell -s hello start -s init stop
Hello world
$
```

> ### Quick Scripting
>
> Often we want to be able to execute an arbitrary Erlang function from the OS command line. The -eval argument is very handy for quick scripting.
>
> Here's an example:
>
> ```
> erl -eval 'io:format("Memory: ~p~n", [erlang:memory(total)]).'\
>     -noshell -s init stop
> ```

Windows users: For this to work, you have to either set your PATH variable to include the directories containing the Erlang executables or give a fully qualified path (including the quote marks) to erlc and erl. For example:

```
"C:\Program Files\erl5.5.3\bin\erlc.exe" hello.erl
..
```

The first line, erlc hello.erl, compiles the file hello.erl, producing an object code file called hello.beam. The second command has three options:

-noshell

> Start Erlang without an interactive shell (so you don't get the Erlang "banner," which ordinarily greets you when you start the system).

-s hello start

> Run the function hello:start().
>
> *Note*: When using the -s Mod ... option, the Mod must have been compiled.

-s init stop

> When apply(hello, start, []) has finished, then the system evaluates the function init:stop().

The command erl -noshell ... can be put in a shell script, so typically we'd make a shell script to run our program that sets the path (with -pa *Directory*) and launches the program.

In our example, we used two -s .. commands. We can have as many functions as we like on the command line. Each -s ... command is evaluated with an apply statement, and when it has run to completion, the next command is evaluated.

Here's an example that launches hello.erl:

`hello.sh`

```
#!/bin/sh
erl -noshell -pa /home/joe/2006/book/JAERANG/Book/code\
            -s hello start -s init stop
```

Note: This script needs an absolute path that points to the directory containing the file hello.beam. So although this script works on my machine, you'll have to edit it to get it to run on your machine.

To run the shell script, we chmod the file (only once), and then we can run the script:

```
$ chmod u+x hello.sh
$ ./hello.sh
Hello world
$
```

Note: On Windows, the #! trick does not work. In a Windows environment, we create the batch file .bat, and we must use the full pathname to the Erlang executables if PATH is not set.

A typical Window batch file might be as follows:

`hello.bat`

```
"C:\Program Files\er15.5.3\bin\erl.exe" -noshell -s hello start -s init stop
```

Run As an Escript

Using escript you can run your programs directly as scripts—there's no need to compile them first.

Warning: escript is included in Erlang versions R11B-4 and onward. If you have an earlier version of Erlang, then you should upgrade to the latest version of Erlang.

To run *hello* as an escript, we create the following file:

`hello`

```
#!/usr/bin/env escript

main(_) ->
    io:format("Hello world\n").
```

Exporting Functions During Development

When you're developing code, it can be a bit of a pain to have to be continually adding and removing export declarations to your program just so that you can run the exported functions in the shell.

The special declaration -compile(export_all). tells the compiler to export every function in the module. Using this makes life much easier when you're developing code.

When you're finished developing the code, you should comment out the export_all declaration and add the appropriate export declarations. This is for two reasons. First, when you come to read your code later, you'll know that the only important functions are the exported functions, and all the other functions cannot be called from outside the module so you can change them in any way you like, provided the interfaces to the exported functions remain the same. Second, the compiler can produce much better code if it knows exactly which functions are exported from the module.

On a Unix system,[1] we can run this immediately and without compilation as follows:

```
$ chmod u+x hello
$ ./hello
Hello world
$
```

Note: The file mode for this file must be set to "executable" (on a Unix system, give the command chmod u+x File)—you have to do this only once, not every time you run the program.

Programs with Command-Line Arguments

"Hello world" had no arguments. Let's repeat the exercise with a program that computes factorials. It takes a single argument.

---

1. I don't know whether running escript is possible on Windows. If anybody knows how to do this, mail me, and I'll add some information to the book.

First, here's the code:

`fac.erl`

```
-module(fac).
-export([fac/1]).

fac(0) -> 1;
fac(N) -> N*fac(N-1).
```

We can compile fac.erl and run it in the Erlang shell like this:

```
$ erl
Erlang (BEAM) emulator version 5.5.1 [source] [async-threads:0] [hipe]

Eshell V5.5.1  (abort with ^G)
1> c(fac).
{ok,fac}
2> fac:fac(25).
15511210043330985984000000
```

If we want to be able to run this program from the command line, we'll need to modify it to take command-line arguments:

`fac1.erl`

```
-module(fac1).
-export([main/1]).

main([A]) ->
    I = list_to_integer(atom_to_list(A)),
    F = fac(I),
    io:format("factorial ~w = ~w~n",[I, F]),
    init:stop().

fac(0) -> 1;
fac(N) -> N*fac(N-1).
```

We can then compile and run it:

```
$ erlc fac1.erl
$ erl -noshell -s fac1 main 25
factorial 25 = 15511210043330985984000000
```

Note: The fact that the function is called main has no significance; it can be called anything. The important thing is that the function name and the name on the command line agree.

Finally, we can run it as an escript:

`factorial`

```
#!/usr/bin/env escript

main([A]) ->
    I = list_to_integer(A),
    F = fac(I),
    io:format("factorial ~w = ~w~n",[I, F]).

fac(0) -> 1;
fac(N) ->
    N * fac(N-1).
```

No compilation is necessary; just run it:

```
$ ./factorial 25
factorial 25 = 15511210043330985984000000
$
```

6.4 Automating Compilation with Makefiles

When I'm writing a large program, I like to automate as much as possible. There are two reasons for this. First, in the long run, it saves typing—typing the same old commands over and over again as I test and retest my program takes a lot of keystrokes, and I don't want to wear my fingers out.

Second, I often suspend what I'm working on and go work on some other project. It can be months before I return to a project that I have suspended, and when I return to the project, I've usually forgotten how to build the code in my project. make to the rescue!

make is *the* utility for automating my work—I use it for compiling and distributing my Erlang code. Most of my makefiles are extremely simple, and I have a simple template that solves most of my needs.

I'm not going to explain makefiles in general.[2] Instead, I'll show the form that I find useful for compiling Erlang programs. In particular, we'll look at the makefiles accompanying this book, so you'll be able to understand them and build your own makefiles.

---

2. See http://en.wikipedia.org/wiki/Make for a description of makefiles.

A Makefile Template

Here's the template that I base most of my makefiles on:

Makefile.template

```
# leave these lines alone
.SUFFIXES: .erl .beam .yrl

.erl.beam:
        erlc -W $<

.yrl.erl:
        erlc -W $<

ERL = erl -boot start_clean

# Here's a list of the erlang modules you want compiling
# If the modules don't fit onto one line add a \ character
# to the end of the line and continue on the next line

# Edit the lines below
MODS = module1 module2 \
        module3 ... special1 ...\
        ...
        moduleN

# The first target in any makefile is the default target.
# If you just type "make" then "make all" is assumed (because
#    "all" is the first target in this makefile)

all: compile

compile: ${MODS:%=%.beam} subdirs

## special compilation requirements are added here

special1.beam: special1.erl
        ${ERL} -Dflag1 -WO special1.erl

## run an application from the makefile

application1: compile
        ${ERL} -pa Dir1  -s application1 start Arg1 Arg2

# the subdirs target compiles any code in
# sub-directories

subdirs:
        cd dir1; make
        cd dir2; make
        ...
```

```
# remove all the code

clean:
        rm -rf *.beam erl_crash.dump
        cd dir1; make clean
        cd dir2; make clean
```

The makefile starts with some rules to compile Erlang modules and files with the extension .yrl (these are files containing parser definitions for the Erlang parser generator program[3]).

The important part is the line starting like this:

```
MODS = module1 module2
```

This is a list of all the Erlang modules that I want to compile.

Any module in the MODS list will be compiled with the Erlang command erlc *Mod*.erl. Some modules might need special treatment (for example the module special1 in the template file), so there is a separate rule to handle this.

Inside a makefile there are a number of *targets*. A target is a alphanumeric string starting in the first column and terminated by a colon (:). In the makefile template, all, compile, and special1.beam are all targets. To run the makefile, you give the shell command:

```
$ make [Target]
```

The argument Target is optional. If Target is omitted, then the first target in the file is assumed. In the previous example, the target all is assumed if no target is specified on the command line.

If I want to build all my software and run application1, then I'd give the command make application1. If I wanted this to be the default behavior, which happens when I just give the command make, then I'd move the lines defining the target application1 so that they were the first target in the makefile.

The target clean removes all compiled Erlang object code files and the file erl_crash.dump. The crash dump contains information that can help debug an application. See Section 6.10, *The Crash Dump*, on page 127 for details.

---

3. The Erlang parser generator is called yecc (an Erlang version of yacc, which is short for *yet another compiler compiler*); see the tutorial on the Internet at http://www.erlang.org/contrib/parser_tutorial-1.0.tgz.

Specializing the Makefile Template

I'm not a fan of clutter in my software, so what I usually do is start with the template makefile and remove all the lines that are not relevant to my application. This results in makefiles that are shorter and easier to read. Alternatively, you could have a common makefile that is included by all makefiles and that is parameterized by the variables in the makefiles.

Once I'm through with this process, I'll end up with a much simplified makefile, something like the following:

```
.SUFFIXES: .erl .beam

.erl.beam:
    erlc -W $<

ERL = erl -boot start_clean

MODS = module1 module2 module3

all: compile
    ${ERL} -pa '/home/joe/.../this/dir' -s module1 start

compile: ${MODS:%=%.beam}

clean:
    rm -rf *.beam erl_crash.dump
```

6.5 Command Editing in the Erlang Shell

The Erlang shell contains a built-in line editor. It understands a subset of the line-editing commands used in the popular emacs editor. Previous lines can be recalled and edited in a few keystrokes. The available commands are shown next (note that ^Key means you should press Ctrl+*Key*):

Command	Description
^A	Beginning of line.
^E	End of line.
^F or right arrow	Forward character.
^B or left arrow	Backward character.
^P or up arrow	Previous line.
^N or down arrow	Next line.
^T	Transpose last two characters.
Tab	Try to expand current module or function name.

6.6 Getting Out of Trouble

Erlang can sometimes be difficult to stop. Here are a number of possible reasons:

- The shell is not responding.
- The Ctrl+C handler has been disabled.
- Erlang has been started with the -detached flag so you may not be aware that it is running.
- Erlang has been started with the -heart Cmd option. This option causes an OS monitor process to be set up that watches over the Erlang OS process. If the Erlang OS process dies, then Cmd is evaluated. Often Cmd will simply restart the Erlang system. This is one of the tricks we use when making fault-tolerant nodes— if Erlang itself dies (which should never happen), it just gets restarted. The trick here is to find the heartbeat process (use ps on Unix-like systems and the Task Manager on Windows) and kill it before you kill the Erlang process.
- Something might have gone seriously wrong and left you with a detached zombie Erlang process.

6.7 When Things Go Wrong

This section lists some common problems (and their solutions).

Undefined (Missing) Code

If you try to run code in a module that the code loader cannot find (because the code search path was wrong), you'll be met with an undef error message. Here's an example:

```
1> glurk:oops(1,23).
** exited: {undef,[{glurk,oops,[1,23]},
                   {erl_eval,do_apply,5},
                   {shell,exprs,6},
                   {shell,eval_loop,3}]} **
```

Actually, there is no module called glurk, but that's not the issue here. The thing you should be concentrating on is the error message. The error message tells us that the system tried to call the function oops with arguments 1 and 23 in the module glurk. So, one of four things could have happened.

- There really is no module glurk—nowhere, not anywhere. This is probably because of a spelling mistake.

> **Has Anybody Seen My Semicolons?**
>
> If you forget the semicolons between the clauses in a function or put periods there instead, you'll be in trouble—real trouble.
>
> If you're defining a function foo/2 in line 1234 of the module bar and put a period instead of a semicolon, the compiler will say this:
>
> bar.erl:1234 function foo/2 already defined.
>
> Don't do it. Make sure your clauses are always separated by semicolons.

- There is a module glurk, but it hasn't been compiled. The system is looking for a file called glurk.beam somewhere in the code search path.
- There is a module glurk and it has been compiled, but the directory containing glurk.beam is not one of the directories in the code search path. To fix this, you'll have to change the search path. We'll see how to do this later.
- There are several different versions of glurk in the code load path, and we've chosen the wrong one. This is a rare error, but it can happen.

  If you suspect this has happened, you can run the code:clash() function, which reports all duplicated modules in the code search path.

My Makefile Doesn't Make

What can go wrong with a makefile? Well, lots, actually. But this isn't a book about makefiles, so I'll deal only with the most common errors. Here are the two most common errors that I get:

- *Blanks in the makefile*: Makefiles are extremely persnickety. Although you can't see them, each of the indented lines in the makefile (with the exception of continuation lines, where the *previous* line ends with a (\) character) should begin with a tab character. If there are any spaces there, make will get confused, and you'll start seeing errors.

- *Missing erlang file*: If one of the modules declared in Mods is missing, you'll get an error message. To illustrate this, assume that MODS contains a module name glurk but that there is no file called glurk.erl in the code directory. In this case, make will fail with the following message:

```
$ make
make: *** No rule to make target 'glurk.beam',
        needed by 'compile'.  Stop.
```

Alternatively, there is no missing module, but the module name is spelled incorrectly in the makefile.

The Shell Isn't Responding

If the shell is not responding to commands, then a number of things might have happened. The shell process itself might have crashed, or you might have issued a command that will never terminate. You might even have forgotten to type a closing quote mark or forgotten to type dot-carriage-return at the end of your command.

Regardless of the reason, you can interrupt the current shell by pressing Ctrl+G and proceeding as in the following example:

```
❶  1> receive foo -> true end.
   ^G
   User switch command
❷  --> h
   c [nn]    - connect to job
   i [nn]    - interrupt job
   k [nn]    - kill job
   j         - list all jobs
   s         - start local shell
   r [node]  - start remote shell
   q         - quit erlang
   ? | h     - this message
❸  --> j
   1* {shell,start,[init]}
❹  --> s
   --> j
   1  {shell,start,[init]}
   2* {shell,start,[]}
❺  --> c 2
   Eshell V5.5.1  (abort with ^G)
   1> init:stop().
   ok
   2> $
```

❶ Here I told the shell to receive a foo message. But since nobody ever sends the shell this message, the shell goes into an infinite wait. I press Ctrl+G.

❷ The system enters "shell JCL"[4] mode. Here I can never remember the commands, so I type h for help.

❸ I type j for a listing of all jobs. Job number 1 is marked with a star, which means it is the default shell. All the commands with an optional argument [nn] use the default shell unless a specific argument is supplied.

❹ I type s to start a new shell, followed by j again. This time I see there are two shells marked 1 and 2, and shell 2 has become the default shell.

❺ I type c 2, which connects me to the newly started shell 2, and then I stop the system.

As you can see, you can have many shells in operation and swap between them by pressing Ctrl+G and then the appropriate commands. You can even start a shell on a remote node with the r command.

6.8 Getting Help

On a Unix system, here is the code:

```
$ erl -man erl
NAME
erl - The Erlang Emulator

DESCRIPTION
The erl program starts the Erlang runtime system.
The exact details (e.g. whether erl is a script
or a program and which other programs it calls) are system-dependent.
...
```

You can also get help about individual modules as follows:

```
$ erl -man lists
MODULE
lists - List Processing Functions

DESCRIPTION
This module contains functions for list processing.
The functions are organized in two groups:
...
```

Note: On a Unix system, the manual pages are not installed by default. If the command erl -man ... does not work, then you need to install the

---

4. Job Control Language.

manual pages. All the manual pages are in a single compressed archive at http://www.erlang.org/download.html. The manual pages should be unpacked in the root of the Erlang installation directory (usually /usr/local/lib/erlang).

The documentation is also downloadable as a set of HTML files. On Windows the HTML documentation is installed by default and accessible through the Erlang section of the Start menu.

6.9 Tweaking the Environment

The Erlang shell has a number of built-in commands. You can see them all with the shell command help():

```
1> help().
** shell internal commands **
b()        -- display all variable bindings
e(N)       -- repeat the expression in query <N>
f()        -- forget all variable bindings
f(X)       -- forget the binding of variable X
h()        -- history
...
```

All these commands are defined in the module shell_default.

If you want to define your own commands, just create a module called user_default. For example:

`user_default.erl`

```
-module(user_default).

-compile(export_all).

hello() ->
    "Hello Joe how are you?".

away(Time) ->
    io:format("Joe is away and will be back in ~w minutes~n",
              [Time]).
```

Once this has been compiled and is placed somewhere in your load path, then you can call any of the functions in user_default without giving a module name:

```
1> hello().
"Hello Joe how are you?"
2> away(10).
Joe is away and will be back in 10 minutes
ok
```

6.10 The Crash Dump

If Erlang crashes, then it leaves behind a file called erl_crash.dump. The contents of this file might give you a clue as to what has gone wrong. To analyze the crash dump, there is a web-based crash analyzer. To start the analyzer, give the following command:

```
1> webtool:start().
WebTool is available at http://localhost:8888/
Or  http://127.0.0.1:8888/
{ok,<0.34.0>}
```

Then point your browser at http://localhost:8888/. You can then happily surf the error log.

Now we're through with the nuts-and-bolts stuff, so we can begin to look at concurrent programs. From now on, you'll be in unfamiliar territory, but this is where the fun really starts.

Chapter 7

Concurrency

We understand concurrency.

A deep understanding of concurrency is hardwired into our brains. We react to stimulation extremely quickly, using a part of the brain called the *amygdala*. Without this reaction, we would die. Conscious thought is just too slow; by the time the thought "hit the brakes" has formed itself, we have already done it.

While driving on a major road, we mentally track the positions of dozens, or perhaps hundreds, of cars. This is done without conscious thought. If we couldn't do this, we would probably be dead.

The world is parallel.

If we want to write programs that behave as other objects behave in the real world, then these programs will have a concurrent structure.

This is why we should program in a concurrent programming language.

And yet most often we program real-world applications in sequential programming languages. This is unnecessarily difficult.

Use a language that was designed for writing concurrent applications, and concurrent development becomes a lot easier.

Erlang programs model how we think and interact.

We don't have shared memory. I have my memory. You have yours. We have two brains, one each. They are not joined together. To change your memory, I send you a message: I talk, or I wave my arms.

You listen, you see, and your memory changes; however, without asking you a question or observing your response, I do not know that you have received my messages.

This is how it is with Erlang processes. Erlang processes have no shared memory. Each process has its own memory. To change the memory of some other process, you must send it a message and hope that it receives and understands the message.

To confirm that another process has received your message and changed its memory, you must ask it (by sending it a message). This is exactly how we interact.

Sue: *Hi Bill, my telephone number is 45 67 89 12.*

Sue: *Did you hear me?*

Bill: *Sure, your number is 45 67 89 12.*

These interaction patterns are well-known to us. From birth onward we learn to interact with the world by observing it and by sending it messages and observing the responses.

People function as independent entities who communicate by sending messages.

That's how Erlang processes work, and that's how we work, so it's very easy to understand an Erlang program.

An Erlang program is made up of dozens, thousands, or even hundreds of thousands of small processes. All these processes operate independently. They communicate with each other by sending messages. Each process has a private memory. They behave like a huge room of people all chattering away to each other.

This makes Erlang programs inherently easy to manage and scale. Suppose we have ten people (processes), and they have too much work to do. What can we do? Get more people. How can we manage these groups of people? It's easy—just shout instructions at them (broadcasting).

Erlang processes don't share memory, so there is no need to lock the memory while it is being used. Where there are locks, there are keys that can get lost. What happens when you lose your keys? You panic and don't know what to do. That's what happens in software systems when you lose your keys and your locks go wrong.

Distributed software systems with locks and keys always go wrong.

Erlang has no locks and no keys.

If somebody dies, other people will notice.

If I'm in a room and suddenly keel over and die, somebody will probably notice (well, at least I hope so). Erlang processes are just like people—they can on occasions die. Unlike people, when they die, they shout out in their last breath exactly what they have died from.

Imagine a room full of people. Suddenly one person keels over and dies. Just as they die, they say "I'm dying of a heart attack" or "I'm dying of an exploded gastric wobbledgog." That's what Erlang processes do. One process might die saying "I'm dying because I was asked to divide by zero." Another might say, "I'm dying because I was asked what the last element in an empty list was."

Now in our room full of people, we might imagine there are specially assigned people whose job it is to clear away the bodies. Let's imagine two people, Jane and John. If Jane dies, then John will fix any problems associated with Jane's death. If John dies, then Jane will fix the problems. Jane and John are linked together with an invisible agreement that says that if one of them dies, the other will fix up any problems caused by the death.

That's how error detection in Erlang works. Processes can be linked together. If one of the processes dies, the other process gets an error message saying why the first process dies.

That's basically it.

That's how Erlang programs work.

Here's what we've learned so far:

- Erlang programs are made of lots of processes. These processes can send messages to each other.

- These messages may or may not be received and understood. If you want to know whether a message was received and understood, you must send the process a message and wait for a reply.

- Pairs of processes can be linked together. If one of the processes in a linked pair dies, the other process in the pair will be sent a message containing the reason why the first process died.

This simple model of programming is part of a model I call *concurrency-oriented programming*.

In the next chapter, we'll start writing concurrent programs. We need to learn three new primitives: **spawn**, **send** (using the ! operator), and **receive**. Then we can write some simple concurrent programs.

When processes die, some other process notices if they are linked together. This is the subject of Chapter 9, *Errors in Concurrent Programs*, on page 151.

As you read the next two chapters, think of people in a room. The people are the processes. The people in the room have individual private memories; this is the state of a process. To change your memory, I talk to you, and you listen. This is sending and receiving messages. We have children; this is spawn. We die; this is a process exit.

Chapter 8

Concurrent Programming

In this chapter, we'll be talking about *processes*. These are small self-contained virtual machines that can evaluate Erlang functions.

I'm sure you've met processes before, but only in the context of operating systems.

In Erlang, processes belong to the programming language and NOT the operating system.

In Erlang:

- Creating and destroying processes is very fast.
- Sending messages between processes is very fast.
- Processes behave the same way on all operating systems.
- We can have very large numbers of processes.
- Processes share no memory and are completely independent.
- The only way for processes to interact is through message passing.

For these reasons Erlang is sometimes called a *pure message passing language*.

If you haven't programmed with processes before, you might have heard rumors that it is rather difficult. You've probably heard horror stories of memory violations, race conditions, shared-memory corruption, and the like. In Erlang, programming with processes is easy. It just needs three new primitives: **spawn**, **send**, and **receive**.

8.1 The Concurrency Primitives

Everything we've learned about sequential programming is still true for concurrent programming. All we have to do is to add the following primitives:

Pid = spawn(Fun)

Creates a new concurrent process that evaluates Fun. The new process runs in parallel with the caller. spawn returns a Pid (short for *process identifier*). You can use Pid to send messages to the process.

Pid ! Message

Sends Message to the process with identifier Pid. Message sending is asynchronous. The sender does not wait but continues with what it was doing. ! is called the *send* operator.

Pid ! M is defined to be M—the message sending primitive ! returns the message itself. Because of this, Pid1 ! Pid2 ! ... ! M means send the message M to all the processes Pid1, Pid2, and so on.

receive ... end

Receives a message that has been sent to a process. It has the following syntax:

```
receive
    Pattern1 [when Guard1] ->
        Expressions1;
    Pattern2 [when Guard2] ->
        Expressions2;
    ...
end
```

When a message arrives at the process, the system tries to match it against Pattern1 (with possible guard Guard1); if this succeeds, it evaluates Expressions1. If the first pattern does not match, it tries Pattern2, and so on. If none of the patterns matches, the message is saved for later processing, and the process waits for the next message. This is described in more detail in Section 8.6, *Selective Receive*, on page 145.

The patterns and guards used in a receive statement have exactly the same syntactic form and meaning as the patterns and guards that we use when we define a function.

8.2 A Simple Example

Remember how we wrote the area/1 function in Section 3.1, *Modules*, on page 33? Just to remind you, the code that defined the function looked like this:

`geometry.erl`

```erlang
area({rectangle, Width, Ht}) -> Width * Ht;
area({circle, R})            -> 3.14159 * R * R.
```

Now we'll rewrite the same function as a *process*:

`area_server0.erl`

```erlang
-module(area_server0).
-export([loop/0]).

loop() ->
    receive
        {rectangle, Width, Ht} ->
            io:format("Area of rectangle is ~p~n",[Width * Ht]),
            loop();
        {circle, R} ->
            io:format("Area of circle is ~p~n", [3.14159 * R * R]),
            loop();
        Other ->
            io:format("I don't know what the area of a ~p is ~n",[Other]),
            loop()
    end.
```

We can create a process that evaluates loop/0 in the shell:

```erlang
1> Pid = spawn(fun area_server0:loop/0).
<0.36.0>
2> Pid ! {rectangle, 6, 10}.
Area of rectangle is 60
{rectangle,6,10}
3> Pid ! {circle, 23}.
Area of circle is 1661.90
{circle,23}
4> Pid ! {triangle,2,4,5}.
I don't know what the area of a {triangle,2,4,5} is
{triangle,2,4,5}
```

What happened here? In line 1 we created a new parallel process. spawn(Fun) creates a parallel process that evaluates Fun; it returns Pid, which is printed as <0.36.0>.

In line 2 we sent a message to the process. This message matches the first pattern in the receive statement in loop/0:

```
loop() ->
    receive
        {rectangle, Width, Ht} ->
            io:format("Area of rectangle is ~p~n",[Width * Ht]),
            loop()
        ...
```

Having received a message, the process prints the area of the rectangle. Finally, the shell prints {rectangle, 6, 10}. This is because the value of Pid ! Msg is defined to be Msg. If we send the process a message that it doesn't understand, it prints a warning. This is performed by the Other ->... code in the **receive** statement.

8.3 Client-Server—An Introduction

Client-server architectures are central to Erlang. Traditionally, client-server architectures have involved a network that separates a client from a server. Most often there are multiple instances of the client and a single server. The word *server* often conjures up a mental image of some rather heavyweight software running on a specialized machine.

In our case, a much lighter-weight mechanism is involved. The client and server in a client-server architecture are separate processes, and normal Erlang message passing is used for communication between the client and the server. Both client and server can run on the same machine or on two different machines.

The words *client* and *server* refer to the roles that these two processes have; the client always initiates a computation by sending a *request* to the server. The server computes a reply and sends a *response* to the client.

Let's write our first client-server application. We'll start by making some small changes to the program we wrote in the previous section.

In the previous program, all that we needed was to send a request to a process that received and printed that request. Now, what we want to do is send a response to the process that sent the original request. The trouble is we do not know to whom to send the response. To send a response, the client has to include an address to which the server can reply. This is like sending a letter to somebody—if you want to get a reply, you had better include your address in the letter!

So, the sender must include a reply address. This can be done by changing this:

Pid ! {rectangle, 6, 10}

to the following:

Pid ! {self(),{rectangle, 6, 10}}

self() is the PID of the client process.

To respond to the request, we have to change the code that receives the requests from this:

```erlang
loop() ->
    receive
        {rectangle, Width, Ht} ->
            io:format("Area of rectangle is ~p~n",[Width * Ht]),
            loop()
        ...
```

to the following:

```erlang
loop() ->
    receive
        {From, {rectangle, Width, Ht}} ->
            From ! Width * Ht,
            loop();
        ...
```

Note how we now send the result of our calculation back to the process identified by the From parameter. Because the client set this parameter to its own process ID, it will receive the result.

The process that sends the initial request is usually called a *client*. The process that receives the request and sends a response is called a *server*.

Finally, we add a small utility function called rpc (short for *remote procedure call*) that encapsulates sending a request to a server and waiting for a response:

area_server1.erl

```erlang
rpc(Pid, Request) ->
    Pid ! {self(), Request},
    receive
        Response ->
            Response
    end.
```

Putting all of this together, we get the following:

`area_server1.erl`

```erlang
-module(area_server1).
-export([loop/0, rpc/2]).

rpc(Pid, Request) ->
    Pid ! {self(), Request},
    receive
        Response ->
            Response
    end.

loop() ->
    receive
        {From, {rectangle, Width, Ht}} ->
            From ! Width * Ht,
            loop();
        {From, {circle, R}} ->
            From !   3.14159 * R * R,
            loop();
        {From, Other} ->
            From ! {error,Other},
            loop()
    end.
```

We can experiment with this in the shell:

```erlang
1>  Pid = spawn(fun area_server1:loop/0).
<0.36.0>
2>  area_server1:rpc(Pid, {rectangle,6,8}).
48
3>  area_server1:rpc(Pid, {circle,6}).
113.097
4>  area_server1:rpc(Pid, socks).
{error,socks}
```

There's a slight problem with this code. In the function rpc/2, we send a request to the server and then wait for a response. *But we do not wait for a response from the server*; we wait for any message. If some other process sends the client a message while it is waiting for a response from the server, it will misinterpret this message as a response from the server. We can correct this by changing the form of the receive statement to this:

```erlang
loop() ->
    receive
        {From, ...} ->
            From ! {self(), ...}
            loop()
        ...
```

and by changing rpc to the following:

```
rpc(Pid, Request) ->
    Pid ! {self(), Request},
    receive
        {Pid, Response} ->
            Response
    end.
```

How does this work? When we have entered the rpc function, Pid is bound to some value, so in the pattern {Pid, Response}, Pid is bound, and Response is unbound. This pattern will match only a message containing a two-tuple[1] where the first element is Pid. All other messages will be queued. (**receive** provides what is called *selective receive*, which I'll describe after this section.)

With this change, we get the following:

`area_server2.erl`

```
-module(area_server2).
-export([loop/0, rpc/2]).

rpc(Pid, Request) ->
    Pid ! {self(), Request},
    receive
        {Pid, Response} ->
            Response
    end.

loop() ->
    receive
        {From, {rectangle, Width, Ht}} ->
            From ! {self(), Width * Ht},
            loop();
        {From, {circle, R}} ->
            From ! {self(), 3.14159 * R * R},
            loop();
        {From, Other} ->
            From ! {self(), {error,Other}},
            loop()
    end.
```

This works as expected:

```
1> Pid = spawn(fun area_server2:loop/0).
<0.37.0>
3> area_server2:rpc(Pid, {circle, 5}).
78.5397
```

---

1. N-tuple means a tuple of size N, so two-tuple is a tuple of size 2.

There's one final improvement we can make. We can *hide* the spawn and
rpc *inside* the module. This is good practice because we will be able to
change the internal details of the server without changing the client
code. Finally, we get this:

```
area_server_final.erl
-module(area_server_final).
-export([start/0, area/2]).

start() -> spawn(fun loop/0).

area(Pid, What) ->
    rpc(Pid, What).

rpc(Pid, Request) ->
    Pid ! {self(), Request},
    receive
        {Pid, Response} ->
            Response
    end.

loop() ->
    receive
        {From, {rectangle, Width, Ht}} ->
            From ! {self(), Width * Ht},
            loop();
        {From, {circle, R}} ->
            From ! {self(), 3.14159 * R * R},
            loop();
        {From, Other} ->
            From ! {self(), {error,Other}},
            loop()
    end.
```

To run this, we call the functions *start/0* and *area/2* (where before we
called spawn and rpc). These are better names that more accurately
describe what the server does:

```
1> Pid = area_server_final:start().
<0.36.0>
2> area_server_final:area(Pid, {rectangle, 10, 8}).
80
4> area_server_final:area(Pid, {circle, 4}).
50.2654
```

8.4 How Long Does It Take to Create a Process?

At this point, you might be worried about performance. After all, if we're
creating hundreds or thousands of Erlang processes, we must be pay-
ing some kind of penalty. Let's find out how much.

To investigate this, we'll time how long it takes to spawn a large number of processes. Here's the program:

`processes.erl`

```erlang
-module(processes).

-export([max/1]).

%% max(N)
%%    Create N processes then destroy them
%%    See how much time this takes

max(N) ->
    Max = erlang:system_info(process_limit),
    io:format("Maximum allowed processes:~p~n",[Max]),
    statistics(runtime),
    statistics(wall_clock),
    L = for(1, N, fun() -> spawn(fun() -> wait() end) end),
    {_, Time1} = statistics(runtime),
    {_, Time2} = statistics(wall_clock),
    lists:foreach(fun(Pid) -> Pid ! die end, L),
    U1 = Time1 * 1000 / N,
    U2 = Time2 * 1000 / N,
    io:format("Process spawn time=~p (~p) microseconds~n",
              [U1, U2]).

wait() ->
    receive
        die -> void
    end.

for(N, N, F) -> [F()];
for(I, N, F) -> [F()|for(I+1, N, F)].
```

Here are the results I obtained on the computer I'm using to write this book, a 2.40GHz Intel Celeron with 512MB of memory running Ubuntu Linux:

```
1> processes:max(20000).
Maximum allowed processes:32768
Process spawn time=3.50000 (9.20000) microseconds
ok
2> processes:max(40000).
Maximum allowed processes:32768
=ERROR REPORT==== 26-Nov-2006::14:47:24 ===
Too many processes
...
```

Spawning 20,000 processes took an average of 3.5 μs/process of CPU time and 9.2 μs of elapsed (wall-clock) time.

Note that I used the BIF erlang:system_info(process_limit) to find the maximum allowed number of processes. Note that some of these are reserved, so your program cannot actually use this number. When we exceed the system limit, the system crashes with an error report (command 2).

The system limit is set to 32,767 processes; to exceed this limit, you have to start the Erlang emulator with the +P flag as follows:

```
$ erl +P 500000
1> processes:max(50000).
Maximum allowed processes:500000
Process spawn time=4.60000 (10.8200) microseconds
ok
2> processes:max(200000).
Maximum allowed processes:500000
Process spawn time=4.10000 (10.2150) microseconds
3> processes:max(300000).
Maximum allowed processes:500000
Process spawn time=4.13333 (73.6533) microseconds
```

In the previous example, I set the system limit to half a million processes. We can see that the process spawn time is essentially constant between 50,000 to 200,000 processes. At 300,000 processes, the CPU time per spawn process remains constant, but the elapsed time increases by a factor of seven. I can also hear my disk chattering away. This is sure sign that the system is paging and that I don't have enough physical memory to handle 300,000 processes.

8.5 Receive with a Timeout

Sometimes a receive statement might wait forever for a message that never comes. This could be for a number of reasons. For example, there might be a logical error in our program, or the process that was going to send us a message might have crashed before it sent the message.

To avoid this problem, we can add a timeout to the receive statement. This sets a maximum time that the process will wait to receive a message. The syntax is as follows:

```
receive
    Pattern1 [when Guard1] ->
        Expressions1;
    Pattern2 [when Guard2] ->
        Expressions2;
    ...
after Time ->
    Expressions
end
```

If no matching message has arrived within Time milliseconds of entering the receive expression, then the process will stop waiting for a message and evaluate Expressions.

Receive with Just a Timeout

You can write a **receive** consisting of only a timeout. Using this, we can define a function sleep(T), which suspends the current process for T milliseconds.

`lib_misc.erl`

```
sleep(T) ->
    receive
    after T ->
        true
    end.
```

Receive with Timeout Value of Zero

A timeout value of 0 causes the body of the timeout to occur immediately, but before this happens, the system tries to match any patterns in the mailbox. We can use this to define a function flush_buffer, which entirely empties all messages in the mailbox of a process:

`lib_misc.erl`

```
flush_buffer() ->
    receive
        _Any ->
            flush_buffer()
    after 0 ->
        true
    end.
```

Without the timeout clause, flush_buffer would suspend forever and not return when the mailbox was empty. We can also use a zero timeout to implement a form of "priority receive," as follows:

`lib_misc.erl`

```
priority_receive() ->
    receive
        {alarm, X} ->
            {alarm, X}
    after 0 ->
        receive
            Any ->
                Any
        end
    end.
```

If there is *not* a message matching {alarm, X} in the mailbox, then priority_receive will receive the first message in the mailbox. If there is no message at all, it will suspend in the innermost receive and return the first message it receives. If there is a message matching {alarm, X}, then this message will be returned immediately. Remember that the **after** section is checked only after pattern matching has been performed on all the entries in the mailbox.

Without the after 0 statement, the alarm message would not be matched first.

Note: Using large mailboxes with priority receive is rather inefficient, so if you're going to use this technique, make sure your mailboxes are not too large.

receive with Timeout Value of Infinity

If the timeout value in a receive statement is the atom infinity, then the timeout will *never* trigger. This might be useful for programs where the timeout value is calculated outside the receive statement. Sometimes the calculation might want to return an actual timeout value, and other times it might want to have the receive wait forever.

Implementing a Timer

We can implement a simple timer using receive timeouts.

The function stimer:start(Time, Fun) will evaluate Fun (a function of zero arguments) after Time ms. It returns a handle (which is a PID), which can be used to cancel the timer if required.

`stimer.erl`
```
-module(stimer).
-export([start/2, cancel/1]).

start(Time, Fun) -> spawn(fun() -> timer(Time, Fun) end).

cancel(Pid) -> Pid ! cancel.

timer(Time, Fun) ->
    receive
        cancel ->
            void
    after Time ->
            Fun()
    end.
```

We can test this as follows:

```
1> Pid = stimer:start(5000, fun() -> io:format("timer event~n") end).
<0.42.0>
timer event
```

Here I waited more than five seconds so that the timer would trigger. Now I'll start a timer and cancel it before the timer period has expired:

```
2> Pid1 = stimer:start(25000, fun() -> io:format("timer event~n") end).
<0.49.0>
3> stimer:cancel(Pid1).
cancel
```

8.6 Selective Receive

So far we have glossed over exactly how **send** and **receive** work. **send** does not actually send a message to a process. Instead, **send** sends a message to the mailbox of the process, and **receive** tries to remove a message from the mailbox.

Each process in Erlang has an associated *mailbox*. When you send a message to the process, the message is put into the mailbox. The only time the mailbox is examined is when your program evaluates a **receive** statement:

```
receive
    Pattern1 [when Guard1] ->
        Expressions1;
    Pattern2 [when Guard1] ->
        Expressions1;
    ...
after
    Time ->
        ExpressionTimeout
end
```

receive works as follows:

1. When we enter a **receive** statement, we start a timer (but only if an **after** section is present in the expression).

2. Take the first message in the mailbox and try to match it against Pattern1, Pattern2, and so on. If the match succeeds, the message is removed from the mailbox, and the expressions following the pattern are evaluated.

3. If none of the patterns in the **receive** statement matches the first message in the mailbox, then the first message is removed from the mailbox and put into a "save queue." The second message

in the mailbox is then tried. This procedure is repeated until a matching message is found or until all the messages in the mailbox have been examined.

4. If none of the messages in the mailbox matches, then the process is suspended and will be rescheduled for execution the next time a new message is put in the mailbox. Note that when a new message arrives, the messages in the save queue are not rematched; only the new message is matched.

5. As soon as a message has been matched, then all messages that have been put into the save queue are reentered into the mailbox in the order in which they arrived at the process. If a timer was set, it is cleared.

6. If the timer elapses when we are waiting for a message, then evaluate the expressions ExpressionsTimeout and put any saved messages back into the mailbox in the order in which they arrived at the process.

8.7 Registered Processes

If we want to send a message to a process, then we need to know its PID. This is often inconvenient since the PID has to be sent to all processes in the system that want to communicate with this process. On the other hand, it is very *secure*; if you don't reveal the PID of a process, other processes cannot interact with it in any way.

Erlang has a method for *publishing* a process identifier so that any process in the system can communicate with this process. Such a process is called a *registered process*. There are four BIFs for managing registered processes:

register(AnAtom, Pid)

Register the process Pid with the name AnAtom. The registration fails if AnAtom has already been used to register a process.

unregister(AnAtom)

Remove any registrations associated with AnAtom.

Note: If a registered process dies it will be automatically unregistered.

whereis(AnAtom) -> Pid | undefined

Find out whether AnAtom is registered. Return the process identifier Pid, or return the atom undefined if no process is associated with AnAtom.

registered() -> [AnAtom::atom()]

Return a list of all registered processes in the system.

Using register, we can revise the example in Section 8.2, *A Simple Example*, on page 135, and we can try to register the name of the process that we created:

```
1> Pid = spawn(fun area_server0:loop/0).
<0.51.0>
2> register(area, Pid).
true
```

Once the name has been registered, we can send it a message like this:

```
3> area ! {rectangle, 4, 5}.
Area of rectangle is 20
{rectangle,4,5}
```

A Clock

We can use register to make a registered process that represents a clock:

clock.erl

```
-module(clock).
-export([start/2, stop/0]).

start(Time, Fun) ->
    register(clock, spawn(fun() -> tick(Time, Fun) end)).

stop() -> clock ! stop.

tick(Time, Fun) ->
    receive
        stop ->
            void
    after Time ->
            Fun(),
            tick(Time, Fun)
    end.
```

The clock will happily tick away until you stop it:

```
3> clock:start(5000, fun() -> io:format("TICK ~p~n",[erlang:now()]) end).
true
TICK {1164,553538,392266}
TICK {1164,553543,393084}
TICK {1164,553548,394083}
TICK {1164,553553,395064}
4> clock:stop().
stop
```

8.8 How Do We Write a Concurrent Program?

When I write a concurrent program, I almost always start with something like this:

`ctemplate.erl`

```
-module(ctemplate).
-compile(export_all).

start() ->
    spawn(fun() -> loop([]) end).

rpc(Pid, Request) ->
    Pid ! {self(), Request},
    receive
        {Pid, Response} ->
            Response
    end.

loop(X) ->
    receive
        Any ->
            io:format("Received:~p~n",[Any]),
            loop(X)
    end.
```

The receive loop is just any empty loop that receives and prints any message that I send to it. As I develop the program, I'll start sending messages to the processes. Because I start with no patterns in the receive loop that match these messages, I'll get a printout from the code at the bottom of the receive statement. When this happens, I add a matching pattern to the receive loop and rerun the program. This technique largely determines the order in which I write the program: I start with a small program and slowly grow it, testing it as I go along.

8.9 A Word About Tail Recursion

Take a look at the receive loop in the area server that we wrote earlier:

`area_server_final.erl`

```
loop() ->
    receive
        {From, {rectangle, Width, Ht}} ->
            From ! {self(), Width * Ht},
            loop();
        {From, {circle, R}} ->
            From ! {self(), 3.14159 * R * R},
            loop();
```

```
    {From, Other} ->
        From ! {self(), {error,Other}},
        loop()
end.
```

If you look carefully, you'll see that every time we receive a message, we process the message and then immediately call loop() again. Such a procedure is called *tail-recursive*. A tail-recursive function can be compiled so that the last function call in a sequence of statements can be replaced by a simple jump to the start of the function being called. This means that a tail-recursive function can loop forever without consuming stack space.

Suppose we wrote the following (incorrect) code:

```
Line 1  loop() ->
    -       {From, {rectangle, Width, Ht}} ->
    -           From ! {self(), Width * Ht},
    -           loop(),
    5           someOtherFunc();
    -       {From, {circle, R}} ->
    -           From ! {self(), 3.14159 * R * R},
    -           loop();
    -       ...
    10  end
```

In line 4, we call loop(), but the compiler must reason that "after I've called loop(), I have to return to here, since I have to call someOther-Func() in line 5." So, it pushes the address of someOtherFunc onto the stack and jumps to the start of loop. The problem with this is that loop() never returns; instead, it just loops forever. So, each time we pass line 4, another return address gets pushed onto the control stack, and eventually the system runs out of space.

Avoiding this is easy; if you write a function F that never returns (such as loop()), make sure that you never call anything *after* calling F, and don't use F in a list or tuple constructor.

8.10 Spawning with MFAs

Most programs we write use spawn(Fun) to create a new process. This is fine provided we don't want to dynamically upgrade our code. Sometimes we want to write code that can be upgraded as we run it. If we want to make sure that our code can be dynamically upgraded, then we have to use a different form of spawn.

```
spawn(Mod, FuncName, Args)
```
> This creates a new process. Args is a list of arguments of the form [Arg1, Args2, ..., ArgN]. The newly created process starts evaluating Mod:FuncName(Arg1, Arg2, ..., ArgN).

Spawning a function with an explicit module, function name, and argument list (called an MFA) is the proper way to ensure that our running processes will be correctly updated with new versions of the module code if it is compiled while it is being used. The dynamic code upgrade mechanism does not work with spawned funs. It works only with explicitly named MFAs. For more details, read Section E.4, *Dynamic Code Loading*, on page 431.

8.11 Problems

1. Write a function start(AnAtom, Fun) to register AnAtom as spawn(Fun). Make sure your program works correctly in the case when two parallel processes simultaneously evaluate start/2. In this case, you must guarantee that one of these processes succeeds and the other fails.

2. Write a ring benchmark. Create N processes in a ring. Send a message round the ring M times so that a total of N * M messages get sent. Time how long this takes for different values of N and M.

   Write a similar program in some other programming language you are familiar with. Compare the results. Write a blog, and publish the results on the Internet!

That's it—you can now write concurrent programs!

Next we'll look at error recovery and see how we can write fault-tolerant concurrent programs using three more concepts: links, signals, and trapping process exits. That's in the next chapter.

Chapter 9

Errors in Concurrent Programs

Earlier we saw how to trap errors in sequential programs. In this chapter, we'll extend the error handling mechanisms to take care of errors in concurrent programs.

This is the second and final stage in understanding how Erlang handles errors. To understand this, we need to introduce three new concepts: *links*, *exit signals*, and the idea of a *system process*.

9.1 Linking Processes

If a process in some way depends on another, then it may well want to keep an eye on the health of that second process. One way to do that is to use Erlang's link BIF. (The other is to use monitors, which are described in the erlang manual page).

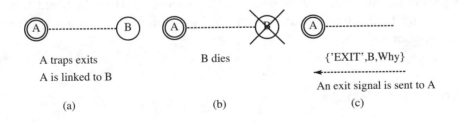

A traps exits
A is linked to B

B dies

{'EXIT',B,Why}

An exit signal is sent to A

(a)

(b)

(c)

Figure 9.1: EXIT SIGNALS AND LINKS

Figure 9.1, on the previous page, shows two processes, A and B. They are linked together (as shown by the dotted line in the diagram). The link was made when one of the processes called the BIF link(P), with P being the PID of the other process. Once linked, the two processes will implicitly monitor each other. If A dies, then B will be sent something called an *exit signal*. If B dies, then A receives the signal.

The mechanisms described in this chapter are completely general. They work on a single node, but they also work on sets of nodes in a distributed Erlang system. As we'll see later in Chapter 10, *Distributed Programming*, on page 167, we can spawn processes on remote nodes just as easily as we can spawn processes on the current node. All the link mechanisms that we talk about in the chapter work equally well in a distributed system.

What happens when a process receives an exit signal? If the receiver hasn't taken any special steps, the exit signal will cause it, too, to exit. However, a process can ask to trap these exit signals. When a process is in this state, it is called a *system process*. If a process linked to a system process exits for some reason, the system process is not automatically terminated. Instead, the system process receives an exit signal, which it can trap and process.

Part (a) of the diagram shows the processes linked together. A is a system process (shown by a double circle). In part (b), B dies, and in part (c), an exit signal is sent to A.

Later in the chapter, we'll go through all the details of exactly what happens when an exit signal arrives at a process. But before this, we'll start with a short example that shows how to use this mechanism to write a simple exit handler. The exit handler is a process that evaluates a particular function, when some other process crashes. The exit handler is in itself a useful building block for constructing more advanced abstractions.

9.2 An on_exit Handler

We want to perform some action when a process exits. We can write a function on_exit(Pid, Fun) that creates a link to the process Pid. If Pid dies with reason Why, then Fun(Why) is evaluated.

Here's the program:

lib_misc.erl

```
Line 1  on_exit(Pid, Fun) ->
            spawn(fun() ->
                        process_flag(trap_exit, true),
                        link(Pid),
    5                   receive
                            {'EXIT', Pid, Why} ->
                                Fun(Why)
                        end
                  end).
```

In line 3, the statement process_flag(trap_exit, true) turns the spawned process into a system process. link(Pid) (line 4) links the newly spawned process to Pid. Finally, when the process dies, an exit signal is received (line 6) and processed (line 7).

Note: When you read this code, you'll see we just used a variable Pid everywhere. This is the process identifier of the linked process. We can't use a variable name like LinkedPid to say this, because before we have evaluated link(Pid), it's not a linked process. When you see a message like {'EXIT', Pid, _}, this should alert you that Pid is a linked process and that it has just died.

To test this, we'll define a function F that waits for a single message X and then computes list_to_atom(X):

```
1> F = fun() ->
         receive
           X -> list_to_atom(X)
         end
       end.
#Fun<erl_eval.20.69967518>
```

We'll spawn this:

```
2> Pid = spawn(F).
<0.61.0>
```

And we'll set up an on_exit handler to monitor it:

```
3> lib_misc:on_exit(Pid,
                 fun(Why) ->
                        io:format(" ~p died with:~p~n",[Pid, Why])
                 end).
    <0.63.0>
```

If we send an atom to Pid, the process will die (because it tries to evaluate list_to_atom of a nonlist), and the on_exit handler will be called:

```
4> Pid ! hello.
hello
<0.61.0> died with:{badarg,[{erlang,list_to_atom,[hello]}]}
```

The function that is invoked when the process dies can, of course, perform any computation it likes: it can ignore the error, log the error, or restart the application. The choice is up to the programmer.

9.3 Remote Handling of Errors

Let's just stop and think for a moment about the previous example. It illustrates an extremely important part of the Erlang philosophy, namely, the *remote handling of errors.*

Because an Erlang system consists of large numbers of parallel processes, we are no longer forced to deal with errors in the process where the error occurs; we can deal with them in a different process. The process that deals with the error *doesn't even have to be on the same machine.* In distributed Erlang, described in the next chapter, we'll see that this simple mechanism even works across machine boundaries. This is very important, since if the entire machine has crashed, the program that fixes the error cannot be on the same machine.

9.4 The Details of Error Handling

Let's look again at the three concepts that underlie Erlang error handling:

Links

A *link* is something that defines an error propagation path between two processes. If two processes are linked together and one of the processes dies, then an *exit signal* will be sent to the other process.

The set of processes that are currently linked to a given process is called the *link set* of that process.

Exit signals

An *exit signal* is something generated by a process when the process dies. This signal is broadcast to all processes that are in the link set of the dying process. The exit signal contains an argument giving the reason why the process died. The reason can be any Erlang data term. This reason can be set explicitly by calling the primitive exit(Reason), or it is set implicitly when an error occurs. For example, if a program tries to divide a number by zero, then the exit reason will be the atom badarith.

When a process has successfully evaluated the function it was spawned with, it will die with the exit reason normal.

In addition, a process Pid1 can explicitly send an exit signal X to a process Pid2 by evaluating exit(Pid2, X). The process that sends the exit signal does not die; it resumes execution after it has sent the signal. Pid2 will receive a {'EXIT', Pid1, X} message (if it is trapping exits), exactly as if the originating process had died. Using this mechanism, Pid1 can "fake" its own death (this is deliberate).

System processes

When a process receives a non-normal exit signal, it too will die unless it is special kind of process called a *system process*. When a system process receives an exit signal Why from a process Pid, then the exit signal is converted to the message {'EXIT', Pid, Why} and added to the mailbox of the system process.

Calling the BIF process_flag(trap_exit, true) turns a normal process into a system process that can trap exits.

When an *exit signal* arrives at a process, then a number of different things might happen. What happens depends upon the state of the receiving process and upon the value of the exit signal and is determined by the following table:

trap_exit	Exit Signal	Action
true	kill	Die: Broadcast the exit signal killed to the link set.
true	X	Add {'EXIT', Pid, X} to the mailbox.
false	normal	Continue: Do-nothing signal vanishes.
false	kill	Die: Broadcast the exit signal killed to the link set.
false	X	Die: Broadcast the exit signal X to the link set.

If the reason is given as kill, then an *untrappable exit signal* will be sent. *An untrappable exit signal will always kill the process it is sent to, even if it is a system process.* This is used by the supervisor process in OTP to kill rogue processes. When a process receives a kill signal, it dies and broadcasts killed signals to the processes in its link set. This is a safety measure to avoid accidentally killing more of the system than you had intended.

The kill signal is intended to kill rogue processes. Think hard before using it.

Programming Idioms for Trapping Exits

Trapping exits is actually a lot easier than you might suspect from reading the preceding sections. Although it is possible to use the exit generation and trapping mechanisms in a number of ingenious ways, most programs use one of three simple idioms.

Idiom 1: I Don't Care If a Process I Create Crashes

Here the process that creates a parallel process that just uses **spawn**:

```
Pid = spawn(fun() -> ... end)
```

Nothing else. If the spawned process crashes, the current process continues.

Idiom 2: I Want to Die If a Process I Create Crashes

To be strict, we should say, "If the process I create crashes with a non-normal exit." To achieve this, the process that creates a parallel process uses **spawn_link** and must not have previously been set to trap exits. We just write this:

```
Pid = spawn_link(fun() -> ... end)
```

Then if the spawned process crashes with a non-normal exit, the current process will also crash.

Idiom 3: I Want to Handle Errors If a Process I Create Crashes

Here we use **spawn_link** and **trap_exits**. We code this as follows:

```
...
process_flag(trap_exit, true),
Pid = spawn_link(fun() -> ... end),
...
loop(...).

loop(State) ->
    receive
        {'EXIT', SomePid, Reason} ->
            %% do something with the error
            loop(State1);
        ...
    end
```

The process evaluating loop now traps exits and does not die if the processes it is linked to dies. It will see all exit signals (converted to messages) from dying processes,[1] and can take any action it wants when it detects process failures.

Trapping Exit Signals (Advanced)

You can skip this section on a first reading. Most of what you want to do will be correctly handled by one of the three idioms shown in the previous section. If you really want to know, read on. But be warned. It can be difficult to understand the precise details of these mechanisms. In most cases, you don't need to understand the mechanism since if you use one of the common program idioms (in the previous section) or the OTP libraries, then the system will "do the right thing" without you having to worry.

To really understand the details of error handling, we'll write a little program to illustrate how error handling and links interact. Our program starts as follows:

`edemo1.erl`
```erlang
-module(edemo1).
-export([start/2]).

start(Bool, M) ->
    A = spawn(fun() -> a() end),
    B = spawn(fun() -> b(A, Bool) end),
    C = spawn(fun() -> c(B, M) end),
    sleep(1000),
    status(b, B),
    status(c, C).
```

This starts three processes: A, B, and C. The idea is that A will be linked to B, and B will be linked to C. A will trap exits and watch for exits from B. B will trap exits if Bool is true, and C will die with exit reason M.

(You might by wondering about the sleep(1000) statement. This is to allow any messages that come when C dies to be printed before we check the status of the three processes. It doesn't change the logic of the program, but it does alter the printout order.)[2]

---

1. Apart from the signal generated by exit(Pid, kill)
2. Using sleep to synchronize processes is unsafe. It's OK in a short example, but for production-quality code, explicit synchronization should be performed.

The code for the A, B, and C processes is as follows:

`edemo1.erl`

```erlang
a() ->
    process_flag(trap_exit, true),
    wait(a).

b(A, Bool) ->
    process_flag(trap_exit, Bool),
    link(A),
    wait(b).

c(B, M) ->
    link(B),
    case M of
        {die, Reason} ->
            exit(Reason);
        {divide, N} ->
            1/N,
            wait(c);
        normal ->
            true
    end.
```

wait/1 just prints any message that it receives:

`edemo1.erl`

```erlang
wait(Prog) ->
    receive
        Any ->
            io:format("Process ~p received ~p~n",[Prog, Any]),
            wait(Prog)
    end.
```

And the remainder of the program is as follows:

`edemo1.erl`

```erlang
sleep(T) ->
    receive
    after T -> true
    end.

status(Name, Pid) ->
    case erlang:is_process_alive(Pid) of
        true ->
            io:format("process ~p (~p) is alive~n", [Name, Pid]);
        false ->
            io:format("process ~p (~p) is dead~n", [Name,Pid])
    end.
```

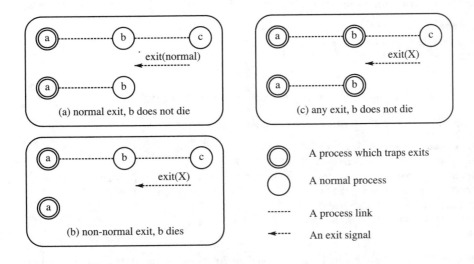

Figure 9.2: TRAPPING EXIT SIGNALS

Now we'll run the program, generating different exit signals in C and observing the effect in B. As we run the program, you might want to refer to Figure 9.2, which illustrates what happens when an exit signal comes from C. Each diagram shows which processes exist, whether they are system processes, and how they are linked together. The diagrams have two parts: the "before" part (at the top of each diagram) shows the processes before receiving an exit signal, and the "after" part (at the bottom of each diagram) shows the processes after the exit signal has been received by the middle process.

First suppose B is a normal process (that is, a process that has not evaluated process_flag(trap_exit, true)):

```
1> edemo1:start(false, {die, abc}).
Process a received {'EXIT',<0.44.0>,abc}
process b (<0.44.0>) is dead
process c (<0.45.0>) is dead
ok
```

When C evaluates exit(abc), process B dies (because it is not trapping exits). As it exits, B rebroadcasts the unmodified exit signal to all the processes in its link set. A (which *is* trapping exits) receives the exit signal and converts it to the error message {'EXIT',<0.44.0>,abc}. (Note that process <0.44.0> is process B, because it is process B that dies.)

Let's try another scenario. Here we tell C to die with the reason normal.[3]

```
2> edemo1:start(false, {die, normal}).
process b (<0.48.0>) is alive
process c (<0.49.0>) is dead
ok
```

B does not die, since it received an exit normal signal.

Now let's make C generate an arithmetic error:

```
3> edemo1:start(false, {divide,0}).
=ERROR REPORT==== 8-Dec-2006::11:12:47 ===
Error in process <0.53.0> with exit value: {badarith,[{edemo1,c,2}]}
Process a received {'EXIT',<0.52.0>,{badarith,[{edemo1,c,2}]}}
process b (<0.52.0>) is dead
process c (<0.53.0>) is dead
ok
```

When C tries to divide by zero, an error occurs, and the process dies with a {badarith,..} error. B receives this and dies, and the error is propagated to A.

Finally, we'll have C exit with a Reason of kill:

```
4> edemo1:start(false, {die,kill}).
Process a received {'EXIT',<0.56.0>,killed} <-- ** changed to killed **
process b (<0.56.0>) is dead
process c (<0.57.0>) is dead
ok
```

The exit reason kill causes B to die, and the error is propagated to the link set of B with reason killed. The behavior in these cases is illustrated in Figure 9.2, on the preceding page, boxes (a) and (b).

We can repeat these tests with B trapping exits. This is the situation depicted in box (c) of Figure 9.2, on the previous page:

```
5> edemo1:start(true, {die, abc}).
Process b received {'EXIT',<0.61.0>,abc}
process b (<0.60.0>) is alive
process c (<0.61.0>) is dead
ok
6> edemo1:start(true, {die, normal}).
Process b received {'EXIT',<0.65.0>,normal}
process b (<0.64.0>) is alive
process c (<0.65.0>) is dead
ok
```

---

3. When a process terminates normally, it has the same effect as if it had evaluated exit(normal).

```
7> edemo1:start(true, normal).
Process b received {'EXIT',<0.69.0>,normal}
process b (<0.68.0>) is alive
process c (<0.69.0>) is dead
8> edemo1:start(true, {die,kill}).
Process b received {'EXIT',<0.73.0>,kill}
process b (<0.72.0>) is alive
process c (<0.73.0>) is dead
ok
```

In all cases, B traps the error. B acts as a kind of "firewall," trapping all errors from C and not allowing them to propagate to A. We can test exit/2 with code/edemo2.erl. This program is similar to edemo1 with the exception of the function c/2, which now calls exit/2. It now reads as follows:

edemo2.erl

```
c(B, M) ->
    process_flag(trap_exit, true),
    link(B),
    exit(B, M),
    wait(c).
```

Running edemo2, we observe the following:

```
1> edemo2:start(false, abc).
Process c received {'EXIT',<0.81.0>,abc}
Process a received {'EXIT',<0.81.0>,abc}
process b (<0.81.0>) is dead
process c (<0.82.0>) is alive
ok
2> edemo2:start(false, normal).
process b (<0.85.0>) is alive
process c (<0.86.0>) is alive
ok
3> edemo2:start(false, kill).
Process c received {'EXIT',<0.97.0>,killed}
Process a received {'EXIT',<0.97.0>,killed}
process b (<0.97.0>) is dead
process c (<0.98.0>) is alive
ok
4> edemo2:start(true, abc).
Process b received {'EXIT',<0.102.0>,abc}
process b (<0.101.0>) is alive
process c (<0.102.0>) is alive
ok
5> edemo2:start(true, normal).
Process b received {'EXIT',<0.106.0>,normal}
process b (<0.105.0>) is alive
process c (<0.106.0>) is alive
ok
```

```
6> edemo2:start(true, kill).
Process c received {'EXIT',<0.109.0>,killed}
Process a received {'EXIT',<0.109.0>,killed}
process b (<0.109.0>) is dead
process c (<0.110.0>) is alive
ok
```

9.5   Error Handling Primitives

Here are the most common primitives for manipulating links and for trapping and sending exit signals:

@spec spawn_link(Fun) -> Pid

> This is exactly like spawn(Fun), but it also creates a link between the parent and child processes. (spawn_link is an atomic operation, which is not equivalent to spawn followed by link since the process might die between the spawn and the link.)

@spec process_flag(trap_exit, true)

> This turns the current process into a system process. A system process is a process that can receive and process error signals.

> *Note*: It is possible to set the trap_exit flag to false, after it has been set to true. This primitive should be used *only* to change a regular process into a system process and not the other way around.

@spec link(Pid) -> true

> Create a link to the process Pid if there is not already a link. Links are symmetric. If a process A evaluates link(B), then it will be linked to B. The net effect is the same as if B had evaluated link(A).

> If the process Pid does not exist, then an exit noproc exception is raised.

> If A is already linked to B and evaluates link(B) (or vice versa), the call is ignored.

@spec unlink(Pid) -> true

> This removes any link between the current process and the process Pid.

@spec exit(Why) -> none()

> This causes the current process to terminate with reason Why. If the clause that executes this statement is not within the scope of

> ## \\// Joe Asks. . .
> ### How Can We Make a Fault-Tolerant System?
>
> To make something fault tolerant, we need at least two computers. One computer does the job, and another computer watches the first computer and must be ready to take over at a moment's notice if the first computer fails.
>
> This is exactly how error recovery works in Erlang. One process does the job, and another process watches the first process and takes over if things go wrong. That's why we need to monitor processes and to know why things fail. The examples in this chapter show you how to do this.
>
> In distributed Erlang, the process that does the job and the processes that monitor the process that does the job can be placed on physically different machines. Using this technique, we can start designing fault-tolerant software.
>
> This pattern is common. We call it the *worker-supervisor* model, and an entire section of the OTP libraries is devoted to building *supervision trees* that use this idea.
>
> The basic language primitive that makes all this possible is the link primitive.
>
> Once you understand how link works and get yourself access to two computers, then you're well on your way to building your first fault-tolerant system.

a **catch** statement, then the current process will broadcast an exit signal, with argument Why to all processes to which it is currently linked.

@spec exit(Pid, Why) -> true

This sends an exit signal with reason Why to the process Pid.

@spec erlang:monitor(process, Item) -> MonitorRef

This sets up a monitor. Item is a PID or a registered name of a process. For details, see the erlang manual page.

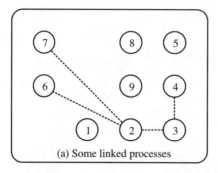 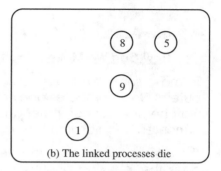

Figure 9.3: TRAPPING EXIT SIGNALS

9.6 Sets of Linked Processes

Suppose we have a large set of parallel processes that are involved in some computation and something goes wrong. How can we identify and kill all the processes that are involved?

The easiest way to do this is make sure that *all* the processes that you want to die as a group are linked together and do not trap exits. If any of the processes terminates with a non-**normal** exit reason, then all the processes in the group will die.

This behavior is illustrated in Figure 9.3. Box (a) represents a set of nine processes, where processes 2, 3, 4, 6, and 7 are linked together. If any of these processes dies with a non-normal exit, then the entire group of processes will die, resulting in box (b).

Sets of linked processes are used to structure software to make fault-tolerant systems. You can do this yourself in your own design, or you can use the library functions described in Section 18.5, *The Supervision Tree*, on page 345.

9.7 Monitors

Sometimes programming with links is tricky, because links are *symmetric*. If A dies, B will be sent an exit signal, and vice versa. To prevent a process from dying, we have to make it a system process, but we might not want to do this. In such occasions we can use a monitor.

A *monitor* is an asymmetric link. If process A monitors process B and B dies, A will be sent an exit signal. But if A dies, B will not be sent a signal. We can find full details of how to create a monitor in the erlang manual page.

9.8 A Keep-Alive Process

To wind up this chapter, we'll make a keep-alive process. The idea is to make a registered process that is always alive—if it dies for any reason, it will be immediately restarted.

We can use on_exit to program this:

`lib_misc.erl`

```
keep_alive(Name, Fun) ->
    register(Name, Pid = spawn(Fun)),
    on_exit(Pid, fun(_Why) -> keep_alive(Name, Fun) end).
```

This makes a registered process called Name that evaluates spawn(Fun). If the process dies for any reason, then it is restarted.

There is a rather subtle error in on_exit and keep_alive. I wonder if you've noticed it? When we say things such as this:

```
Pid = register(...),
on_exit(Pid, fun(X) -> ..),
```

there is a possibility the process dies in the gap *between* these two statements. If the process dies before on_exit gets evaluated, then no link will be created, and the on_exit process will not work as you expected. This could happen if two programs try to evaluate keep_alive at the same time and with the same value of Name. This is called a *race condition*—two bits of code (this bit) and the code section that performs the link operation inside on_exit are racing each other. If things go wrong here, your program might behave in an unexpected manner.

I'm not going to solve this problem here—I'll let you think about how to do this yourself. When you combine the Erlang primitives spawn, spawn_link, register, and so on, you must think carefully about possible race conditions. Write your code in such a way that race conditions cannot happen.

Fortunately, the OTP libraries have code for building servers, supervision trees, and so on. These libraries have been well tested and should not suffer from any race conditions. Use these libraries to build your applications.

We have now covered all the mechanisms for detecting and trapping errors in an Erlang program. In later chapters we'll be using these mechanisms to build reliable software systems that can recover from faults. Now we've finished with programming techniques aimed at single-processor systems.

The next chapter looks at simple distributed systems.

## Chapter 10

Distributed Programming

In this chapter, we'll introduce the libraries and Erlang primitives that we'll use to write distributed Erlang programs.*Distributed programs* are programs that are designed to run on networks of computers and that can coordinate their activities only by message passing.

There are number of reasons why we might want to write distributed applications. Here are some:

Performance

> We can make our programs go faster by arranging that different parts of the program are run in parallel on different machines.

Reliability

> We can make fault-tolerant systems by structuring the system to run on several machines. If one machine fails, we can continue on another machine.

Scalability

> As we scale up an application, sooner or later we will exhaust the capabilities of even the most powerful machine. At this stage we have to add more machines to add capacity. Adding a new machine should be a simple operation that does not require large changes to the application architecture.

Intrinsically distributed application

> Many applications are inherently distributed. If we write a multiuser game or chat system, different users will be scattered all over the globe. If we have a large number of users in a particular geographic location, we want to place the computation resources near the users.

Fun

> Most of the fun programs that I want to write are distributed. Many of these involve interaction with people and machines all over the world.

In this book we'll talk about two main models of distribution:

- *Distributed Erlang*: Provides a method for programming applications that run on a set of tightly coupled computers.[1] In distributed Erlang, programs are written to run on Erlang *nodes*. We can spawn a process on any node, and all the message passing and error handling primitives we talked about in previous chapters work as in the single node case.

  Distributed Erlang applications run in a *trusted* environment— since any node can perform any operation on any other Erlang node, a high degree of trust is involved. Typically distributed Erlang applications will be run on clusters on the same LAN and behind a firewall, though they can run in an open network.

- *Socket-based distribution*: Using TCP/IP sockets, we can write distributed applications that can run in an *untrusted* environment. The programming model is less powerful than that used in distributed Erlang but more secure. In Section 10.5, *Socket-Based Distribution*, on page 179, we'll see how to make applications using a simple socket-based distribution mechanism.

If you think back to the previous chapters, you'll recall that the basic unit that we construct programs from is the process. Writing a distributed Erlang program is easy; all we have to do is spawn our processes on the correct machines, and then everything works as before.

We are all used to writing sequential programs. Writing distributed programs is usually a lot more difficult. In this chapter, we'll look at a number of techniques for writing simple distributed programs. Even though the programs are simple, they are very useful.

We'll start with a number of small examples. To do this, we'll need to learn only two things; then we can make our first distributed program. We'll learn how to start an Erlang node and how to perform a remote procedure call on a remote Erlang node.

---

1. For example, machines on the same LAN dedicated to solving a particular problem.

When I develop a distributed application, I always work on the program in a specific order, which is as follows:

1. I write and test my program in a regular nondistributed Erlang session. This is what we've been doing up to now, so it presents no new challenges.

2. I test my program on two different Erlang nodes running *on the same computer.*

3. I test my program on two different Erlang nodes running *on two physically separated computers* either in the same local area network or anywhere on the Internet.

The final step can be problematic. If we run on machines within the same administrative domain, this is rarely a problem. But when the nodes involved belong to machines in different domains, we can run into problems with connectivity, and we have to ensure that our system firewalls and security settings are correctly configured.

In the next sections, we'll make a simple name server, going through these steps in order. Specifically, we will do the following:

- Stage 1: Write and test the name server in a regular undistributed Erlang system.

- Stage 2: Test the name server on two nodes on the same machine.

- Stage 3: Test the name server on two different nodes on two different machines on the same local area network.

- Stage 4: Test the name server on two different machines belonging to two different domains in two different countries.

10.1 The Name Server

A *name server* is a program that, given a name, returns a value associated with that name. We can also change the value associated with a particular name.

Our first name server is extremely simple. It is not fault tolerant, so all the data it stores will be lost if it crashes. The point of this exercise is not to make a fault-tolerant name server but to get started with distributed programming techniques.

Stage 1: A Simple Name Server

Our name server kvs is a simple Key ↦ Value, server. It has the following interface:

@spec kvs:start() -> true

> Start the server; this creates a server with the registered name kvs.

@spec kvs:store(Key, Value) -> true

> Associate Key with Value.

@spec kvs:lookup(Key) -> {ok, Value} | undefined

> Look up the value of Key, and return {ok, Value} if there is a value associated with Key; otherwise, return undefined.

The key-value server is implemented using the process dictionary get and put primitives, as follows:

`socket_dist/kvs.erl`

```erlang
-module(kvs).
-export([start/0, store/2, lookup/1]).

start() -> register(kvs, spawn(fun() -> loop() end)).

store(Key, Value) -> rpc({store, Key, Value}).

lookup(Key) -> rpc({lookup, Key}).

rpc(Q) ->
    kvs ! {self(), Q},
    receive
        {kvs, Reply} ->
            Reply
    end.

loop() ->
    receive
        {From, {store, Key, Value}} ->
            put(Key, {ok, Value}),
            From ! {kvs, true},
            loop();
        {From, {lookup, Key}} ->
            From ! {kvs, get(Key)},
            loop()
    end.
```

We'll start by testing the server locally to see that it works correctly:

```erlang
1> kvs:start().
true
2> kvs:store({location, joe}, "Stockholm").
true
```

```
3> kvs:store(weather, raining).
true
4> kvs:lookup(weather).
{ok,raining}
5> kvs:lookup({location, joe}).
{ok,"Stockholm"}
6> kvs:lookup({location, jane}).
undefined
```

So far, we get no unpleasant surprises.

Stage 2: Client on One Node, Server on Second Node but Same Host

Now we'll start two Erlang nodes on the *same* computer. To do this, we need to open two terminal windows and start two Erlang systems.

First, we fire up a terminal shell,[2] and start a distributed Erlang node in this shell called gandalf; then we start the server:

```
$ erl -sname gandalf
(gandalf@localhost) 1> kvs:start().
true
```

Windows note: The Windows name might not be localhost; if it is not localhost, then you will have to use the name that Windows returned in place of localhost in all subsequent commands.

The argument -sname gandalf means "start an Erlang node with name gandalf on the local host." Note how the Erlang shell prints the name of the Erlang node[3] before the command prompt.

Second, we start a *second* terminal session and start an Erlang node called bilbo. Then we can call the functions in kvs using the library module rpc. (Note that rpc is a standard Erlang library module, which is not the same as the rpc function we wrote earlier.)

```
$ erl -sname bilbo
(bilbo@localhost) 1> rpc:call(gandalf@localhost,
                             kvs,store, [weather, fine]).
true
(bilbo@localhost) 2> rpc:call(gandalf@localhost,
                             kvs,lookup,[weather]).
{ok,fine}
```

---

2. *Windows users*: Read Appendix B, on page 391. Once you have access to a shell window, the command erl -name Node should work. Remember to set your paths so you can find erl.exe (this should have a name something like C:\Program Files\erl5.4.4\bin\erl.exe.
3. The node name is of the form Name@Host. Name and Host are both atoms, so they will have to be quoted if they contain any nonatom characters.

Now it may not look like it, but we've actually performed our first-ever distributed computation! The server ran on the first node that we started, and the client ran on the second node.

The call to set the value of weather was made on the bilbo node; we can swap back to gandalf and check the value of the weather:

```
(gandalf@localhost)2> kvs:lookup(weather).
{ok,fine}
```

rpc:call(Node, Mod, Func, [Arg1, Arg2, ..., ArgN]) performs a *remote procedure call* on Node. The function to be called is Mod:Func(Arg1, Arg2, ..., ArgN).

As we can see, the program works as in the nondistributed Erlang case; now the only difference is that the client is running on one node and the server is running on a different node.

The next step is to run the client and the server on different machines.

Stage 3: Client and Server on Different Machines on the Same LAN

We're going to use two nodes. The first node is called gandalf on doris.myerl.example.com, and the second is called bilbo on george.myerl.example.com. Before we do this, we start two terminal windows[4] on the two different machines. We'll call these two windows *doris* and *george*. Once we've done this, we can easily enter commands on both machines.

Step 1: Start an Erlang node on doris:

```
doris $ erl -name gandalf -setcookie abc
(gandalf@doris.myerl.example.com) 1> kvs:start().
true
```

Step 2: Start an Erlang node on george, and send some commands to gandalf:

```
george $ erl -name bilbo -setcookie abc
(bilbo@george.myerl.example.com) 1> rpc:call(gandalf@doris.myerl.example.com,
                                          kvs,store,[weather,cold]).
true
(bilbo@george.myerl.example.com) 2> rpc:call(gandalf@doris.myerl.example.com,
                                          kvs,lookup,[weather]).
{ok,cold}
```

Things behave exactly as in the case with two different nodes on the same machine.

---

4. Using something like ssh.

Now for this to work, things are a slightly more complicated than in the case where we ran two nodes on the same computer. We have to take four steps:

1. Start Erlang with the -name parameter. When we have two nodes on the same machine, we use "short" names (as indicated by the -sname flag), but if they are on different networks, we use -name.

   We can also use -sname on two different machines when they are on the same subnet. Using -sname is also the only method that will work if no DNS service is available.

2. Ensure that both nodes have the same *cookie*. This is why both nodes were started with the command-line argument -setcookie abc. (We'll talk more about cookies later in this chapter.[5])

3. Make sure the fully qualified hostnames of the nodes concerned are resolvable by DNS. In my case, the domain name myerl. example.com is purely local to my home network and is resolved locally by adding an entry to /etc/hosts.

4. Make sure that both systems have the same version of the code[6] that we want to run. In our case, the same version of the code for kvs has to be available on both systems. There are several ways of doing this:

   a) In my setup at home, I have two physically separated computers with no shared file systems; here I physically copy kvs.erl to both machines and compile it before starting the programs.

   b) On my work computer we use workstations with a shared NFS disk. Here I merely start Erlang in the shared directory from two different workstations.

   c) Configure the code server to do this. I won't describe how to do this here. Have a look at the manual page for the module erl_prim_loader.

   d) Use the shell command nl(Mod). This loads the module Mod on all connected nodes.

---

5. When we ran two nodes on the *same* machine, both nodes could access the same cookie file, $HOME/.erlang.cookie, which is why we didn't have to add the cookie to the Erlang command line.
6. And the same version of Erlang. If you don't do this, you'll get serious and mysterious errors.

Note: For this to work, you have to make sure that all the nodes are connected. Nodes become connected when they first try to access each other. This happens the first time you evaluate any expression involving a remote node. The easiest way to do this is to evaluate net_adm:ping(Node) (see the manual page for net_adm for more details).

Stage 4: Client and Server on Different Hosts in the Internet

In principle, this is the same as in stage 3, but now we have to be much more concerned with security. When we run two nodes on the same LAN, we probably don't have to worry too much about security. In most organizations, the LAN is isolated from the Internet by a firewall. Behind the firewall we are free to allocate IP addresses in a haphazard manner and generally misconfigure our machines.

When we connect several machines in an Erlang cluster on the Internet, we can expect to run into problems with firewalls that do not permit incoming connections. We will have to correctly configure our firewalls to accept incoming connections. There is no way to do this in a generic manner, since every firewall is different.

To prepare your system for distributed Erlang, you will have to take the following steps:

1. Make sure that port 4369 is open for both TCP and UDP traffic. This port is used by a program called *epmd* (short for the Erlang Port Mapper Daemon).

2. Choose a port or range of ports to be used for distributed Erlang, and make sure these ports are open. If these ports are Min and Max (use Min = Max if you want to use only one port), then start Erlang with the following command:

```
$ erl -name ... -setcookie ... -kernel inet_dist_listen_min Min \
                               inet_dist_listen_max Max
```

10.2 The Distribution Primitives

The central concept in distributed Erlang is the node. A node is a self-contained Erlang system containing a complete virtual machine with its own address space and own set of processes.

Access to a single node or set of nodes is secured by a cookie system. Each node has a single cookie, and this cookie must be the same as the cookies of any nodes to which the node talks. To ensure this, all the nodes in a distributed Erlang system must have been started with the same magic cookie or have their cookie changed to the same value by evaluating erlang:set_cookie.

The set of connected nodes having the same cookie defines an Erlang cluster.

The BIFs that are used for writing distributed programs are as follows:[7]

@spec spawn(Node, Fun) -> Pid

> This works exactly like spawn(Fun), but the new process is spawned on Node.

@spec spawn(Node, Mod, Func, ArgList) -> Pid

> This works exactly like spawn(Mod, Func, ArgList), but the new process is spawned on Node. spawn(Mod, Func, Args) creates a new process that evaluates apply(Mod, Func, Args). It returns the PID of the new process.
>
> *Note*: This form of spawn is more robust than spawn(Node, Fun). spawn(Nod, Fun) can break when the distributed nodes are not running exactly the same version of a particular module.

@spec spawn_link(Node, Fun) -> Pid

> This works exactly like spawn_link(Fun), but the new process is spawned on Node.

@spec spawn_link(Node, Mod, Func, ArgList) -> Pid

> This works like spawn(Node, Mod, Func, ArgList), but the new process is linked to the current process.

@spec disconnect_node(Node) -> bool() | ignored

> This forcibly disconnects a node.

@spec monitor_node(Node, Flag) -> true

> If Flag is true, monitoring is turned on; if Flag is false, monitoring is turned off. If monitoring has been turned on, then the process that evaluated this BIF will be sent {nodeup, Node} and {nodedown, Node} messages if Node joins or leaves the set of connected Erlang nodes.

---

7. For a fuller description of these BIFs, see the manual page for the erlang module.

@spec node() -> Node

> This returns the name of the local node. nonode@nohost is returned if the node is not distributed.

@spec node(Arg) -> Node

> This returns the node where Arg is located. Arg can be a PID, a reference, or a port. If the local node is not distributed, nonode@nohost is returned.

@spec nodes() -> [Node]

> This returns a list of all other nodes in the network to which we are connected.

@spec is_alive() -> bool()

> This returns true if the local node is alive and can be part of a distributed system. Otherwise, it returns false.

In addition, send can be used to send messages to a locally registered process in a set of distributed Erlang nodes. The following syntax:

```
{RegName, Node} ! Msg
```

sends the message Msg to the registered process RegName on the node Node.

An Example of Remote Spawning

As a simple example, we can show how to spawn a process on a remote node. We'll start with the following program:

`dist_demo.erl`

```
-module(dist_demo).
-export([rpc/4, start/1]).

start(Node) ->
    spawn(Node, fun() -> loop() end).

rpc(Pid, M, F, A) ->
    Pid ! {rpc, self(), M, F, A},
    receive
        {Pid, Response} ->
            Response
    end.

loop() ->
    receive
        {rpc, Pid, M, F, A} ->
            Pid ! {self(), (catch apply(M, F, A))},
            loop()
    end.
```

Then we start two nodes; both nodes have to be able to load this code. If both nodes are on the same host, then this is not a problem. We merely start two Erlang nodes from the same directory. If the nodes are on two physically separated nodes with different file systems, then the program must be copied to all nodes and compiled before starting both the nodes (alternatively, the .beam file can be copied to all nodes). In the example, I'll assume we've done this.

On the host doris, we start a node named gandalf:

```
doris $ erl -name gandalf -setcookie abc
(gandalf@doris.myerl.example.com) 1>
```

And on the host george, we start a node named bilbo, remembering to use the same cookie:

```
george $ erl -name bilbo -setcookie abc
(bilbo@george.myerl.example.com) 1>
```

Now (on bilbo) we can spawn a process on the remote node (gandalf):

```
(bilbo@george.myerl.example.com) 1> Pid =
    dist_demo:start('gandalf@doris.myerl.example.com').
<5094.40.0>
```

Pid is now a process identifier of the process *on the remote node*, and we can call dist_demo:rpc/4 to perform a remote procedure call on the remote node:

```
(bilbo@george.myerl.example.com)2> dist_demo:rpc(Pid, erlang, node, []).
'gandalf@doris.myerl.example.com'
```

This evaluates erlang:node() *on the remote node* and returns the value.

10.3 Libraries for Distributed Programming

The previous section showed the BIFs that we can use for writing distributed programs. In fact, most Erlang programmers will never use these BIFs; instead, they will use a number of powerful libraries for distribution. The libraries are written using the distribution BIFs, but they hide a lot of the complexity from the programmer.

Two modules in the standard distribution cover most needs:

- rpc provides a number of remote procedure call services.

- global has functions for the registration of names and locks in a distributed system and for the maintenance of a fully connected network.

> **Read the Manual Pages for RPC**
>
> The module rpc contains a veritable cornucopia of functionality.

The single most useful function in the module rpc is the following function:

call(Node, Mod, Function, Args) -> Result | {badrpc, Reason}
> This evaluates apply(Mod, Function, Args) on Node and returns the result Result or {badrpc, Reason} if the call fails.

10.4 The Cookie Protection System

For two distributed Erlang nodes to communicate, they must have the same *magic cookie*. We can set the cookie in three ways:

- *Method 1*: Store the same cookie in the file $HOME/.erlang.cookie. This file contains a random string and is automatically created the first time Erlang is run on your machine.

  This file can be copied to all machines that we want to participate in a distributed Erlang session. Alternatively, we can explicitly set the value. For example, on a Linux system, we could give the following commands:

  ```
  $ cd
  $ cat > .erlang.cookie
  AFRTY12ESS3412735ASDF12378
  $ chmod 400 .erlang.cookie
  ```

  The chmod makes the .erlang.cookie file accessible only by the owner of the file.

- *Method 2*: When Erlang is started, we can use the command-line argument -setcookie C to set the magic cookie to C. For example:

  ```
  $ erl -setcookie AFRTY12ESS3412735ASDF12378 ...
  ```

- *Method 3*: The BIF erlang:set_cookie(node(), C) sets the cookie of the local node to the atom C.

Note: If your environment is insecure, then method 1 or 3 is better than method 2 since on a Unix system anybody can discover your cookie using the ps command.

In case you're wondering, cookies are never sent across the network in the clear. Cookies are used only for the initial authentication of a session. Distributed Erlang sessions are not encrypted but can be set up to run over encrypted channels. (Google the Erlang mailing list for up-to-date information on this.)

10.5 Socket-Based Distribution

In this section, we will write a simple program using socket-based distribution. As we have seen, distributed Erlang is fine for writing cluster applications where you can trust everybody involved but is less suitable in an open environment where not everyone can be trusted.

The main problem with distributed Erlang is that the client can decide to spawn *any* process on the server machine. So, to destroy your system, all you'd have to do is evaluate the following:

```
rpc:multicall(nodes(), os, cmd, ["cd /; rm -rf *"])
```

Distributed Erlang is useful in the situation where you own all the machines and want to control all the machines from a single machine. But this model of computation is not suited to the situation where different people own the individual machines and want to control exactly which software can be executed on their machines.

In these circumstances, we will use a restricted form of spawn where the owner of a particular machine has explicit control over what gets run on their machines.

lib_chan

lib_chan is a module that allows a user to explicitly control which processes are spawned on their machines. The implementation of lib_chan is rather complex, so I've taken it out of the normal chapter flow; you can find it in Appendix D, on page 399. The interface is as follows:

@spec start_server() -> true

> This starts a server on the local host. The behavior of the server is determined by the file $HOME/.erlang/lib_chan.conf.

@spec start_server(Conf) -> true

> This starts a server on the local host. The behavior of the server is determined by the file Conf.

> In both cases, the server configuration file contains a file of tuples of the following form:

{port, NNNN}

> This starts listening to port number NNNN.

{service, S, password, P, mfa, SomeMod, SomeFunc, SomeArgsS}

> This defines a service S protected by password P. If the service is started, then a process is created by spawning SomeMod: SomeFunc(MM, ArgsC, SomeArgsS) to handle messages from the client. Here MM is the PID of a proxy process that can be used to send messages to the client, and the argument ArgsC comes from the client connect call.

@spec connect(Host, Port, S, P, ArgsC) -> {ok, Pid} | {error, Why}

> Try to open the port Port on the host Host, and then try to activate the service S, which is protected with the password P. If the password is correct, {ok, Pid} will be returned, where Pid will be the process identifier of a proxy process that can be used to send messages to the server.

When a connection is established by the client calling connect/5, two proxy processes are spawned: one on the client side and the other on the server side. These proxy processes handle the conversion of Erlang messages to TCP packet data, trapping exits from the controlling processes, and socket closure.

This explanation might look complicated, but it will become a lot clearer when we use it.

The following is a complete example of how to use lib_chan together with the kvs service that we described earlier.

The Server Code

First, we write a configuration file:

```
{port, 1234}.
{service, nameServer, password, "ABXy45",
        mfa, mod_name_server, start_me_up, notUsed}.
```

This means we are going to offer a service called nameServer on port 1234 of our machine. The service is protected by the password ABXy45.

When a connection is created by the client calling:

connect(Host, 1234, nameServer, "ABXy45", nil)

the server will spawn mod_name_server:start_me_up(MM, nil, notUsed). MM is the PID of a proxy process that is used to talk to the client.

Important: At this stage, you should stare at the previous line of code and make sure you see where the arguments in the call come from:

- mod_name_server, start_me_up, and notUsed come from the configuration file.
- nil is the last argument in the connect call.

mod_name_server is as follows:

`socket_dist/mod_name_server.erl`
```erlang
-module(mod_name_server).
-export([start_me_up/3]).

start_me_up(MM, _ArgsC, _ArgS) ->
    loop(MM).

loop(MM) ->
    receive
        {chan, MM, {store, K, V}} ->
            kvs:store(K, V),
            loop(MM);
        {chan, MM, {lookup, K}} ->
            MM ! {send, kvs:lookup(K)},
            loop(MM);
        {chan_closed, MM} ->
            true
    end.
```

mod_name_server follows this protocol:

- If the client sends the server a message {send, X}, it will appear in mod_name_server as a message of the form {chan, MM, X} (MM is the PID of the server proxy process.)
- If the client terminates or the socket used in communication closes for any reason, then a message of the form {chan_closed, MM} will be received by the server.
- If the server wants to send a message X to the client, it does so by calling MM ! {send, X}.
- If the server wants to explicitly close the connection, it can do so by evaluating MM ! close.

This protocol is the middle-man protocol that is obeyed by both the client code and the server code. The socket middle-man code is explained in more detail in Section D.2, *lib_chan_mm: The Middle Man*, on page 403.

To test this code, we will first make sure that everything works on one machine.

Now we can start the name server (and the module kvs):

```
1> kvs:start().
true
2> lib_chan:start_server().
Starting a port server on 1234...
true
```

Now we can start a second Erlang session and test this from any client:

```
1> {ok, Pid} = lib_chan:connect("localhost", 1234, nameServer,
                                 "ABXy45", "").
{ok, <0.43.0>}
2> lib_chan:cast(Pid, {store, joe, "writing a book"}).
{send,{store,joe,"writing a book"}}
3> lib_chan:rpc(Pid, {lookup, joe}).
{ok,"writing a book"}
4> lib_chan:rpc(Pid, {lookup, jim}).
undefined
```

Having tested that this works on one machine, we go through the same steps we described earlier and perform similar tests on two physically separated machines.

Note that in this case, it is the owner of the remote machine who decides the contents of the configuration file. The configuration file specifies which applications are permitted on this machine and which port is to be used to communicate with these applications.

Chapter 11

IRC Lite

It's about time for an application. So far we have seen all the parts but not how to put the parts together. We've seen how to write sequential code, how to spawn processes, how to make registered processes, and so on. Now we'll assemble those concepts into something that works.

In this chapter, we'll develop a simple "IRC-like" program. We won't follow the actual IRC protocol. Instead, we'll invent our own totally different and incompatible protocols.[1] As far as a user is concerned, our program *is* an implementation of IRC, but underneath the implementation is a lot easier than might be expected, since we'll use Erlang messages as the basis for all interprocess messaging. This totally eliminates all message parsing and really simplifies the design.

Our program is also a *pure* Erlang program, which makes no use of the OTP libraries and minimal use of the standard libraries. So, for example, it has a complete self-contained client-server architecture and a form of error recovery based on explicit manipulation of links. The reason for not using the libraries is that I want to introduce you to one concept at a time and show what we can achieve with the language alone and minimal use of libraries. We'll write the code as a set of components. Each component is simple, but they fit together in a complex manner. We can make a lot of this complexity go away by using the OTP libraries, so later in the book we'll show better ways of organizing code based on the OTP generic libraries for building client-server and supervision trees.

---

1. This makes our lives easier and lets us concentrate on the application, rather than low-level protocol details.

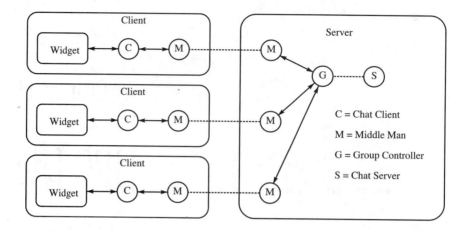

Figure 11.1: THE PROCESS STRUCTURE

Our application is built from five components; the structure of these components is shown in Figure 11.1. The figure shows three client nodes (assumed to be on different machines) and a single server node (on a different machine). These components perform the following functions:

The User Interface Widget

The user interface is a GUI widget that is used to send messages and display received messages. The messages are sent to the chat client.

The Chat Client

The chat client ("C" in the figure) manages messages from the chat widget and sends them to the group controller for the current group. It also receives messages from the group controller and sends them to the widget.

The Group Controller

The group controller ("G" in the figure) manages a single chat group. If a message is sent to the controller, it broadcasts the message to all members in the group. It keeps track of new members who join and leave the group and dies when there are no longer any members in the group.

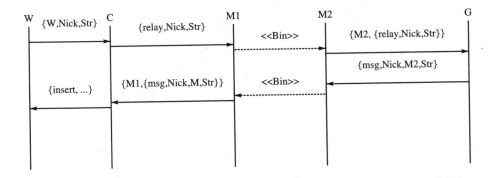

Figure 11.2: THE FLOW OF MESSAGES INVOLVED IN SENDING A MESSAGE

The Chat Server

The chat server ("S" in the figure) keeps track of the group controllers. The chat server is needed only when a new member tries to join a group. The chat server is a single process, whereas there is one group controller for every active group.

The Middle Men

The middle men ("M" in the figure) take care of the transport of data through the system. If a C process sends a message to M, it will arrive at G (see Figure 11.1, on the preceding page). The M process hides the low-level socket interface between the two machines. Essentially the M process "abstracts out" the physical boundary between the machines. This means the entire application can be built using Erlang message passing and is unconcerned with the details of the underlying communication infrastructure.

11.1 Message Sequence Diagrams

It's easy to lose track of what's happening when we have many parallel processes. To help us understand what's going on, we can draw a message sequence diagram (MSD) that shows the interaction between different processes.

The message sequence diagram in Figure 11.2 shows the sequence of messages that results from a user typing a line into the io widget message entry region. This results in a message to the chat controller (C),

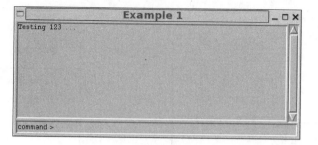

Figure 11.3: THE IO WIDGET

followed by a message to one of the middle men (M1); this goes via M2 to the group controller (G). The step between the middle men is a binary encoding of the Erlang messages involved.

The MSD gives a good overview of what's happening. If you stare hard at the MSD and the program code, you should be able to convince yourself that the code implements the message passing sequence described in the diagram.

When I'm designing a program like the chat system, I often cover the backs of lots of envelopes with MSDs—this helps me think about what's taking place. I'm not usually a fan of graphical design methods, but MSDs are useful for visualizing what's happening in a set of parallel processes that exchange messages to solve some particular problem.

We'll now look at the individual components.

11.2 The User Interface

The user interface is built using a simple io widget. This io widget is shown in Figure 11.3. The code for this widget is fairly long and is mostly concerned with accessing the windowing system using the standard gs library. Because we don't want to dive down that rabbit hole just yet, we won't show the code listing here (but you'll find it starting on page 201). The interface to the io widget is as follows:

@spec io_widget:start(Pid) -> Widget

Create a new io widget. Returns Widget, which is a PID that can be used to talk to the widget. When the user types anything in the entry section of the widget, a message of the form {Widget, State,

Parse} will be sent to the process that evaluated this function. State is a state variable stored in the widget that can be set by the user, and Parse is the result of parsing the input string with a user-defined parser.

@spec io_widget:set_title(Widget, Str)

> Set the title in the widget.

@spec io_widget:set_state(Widget, State)

> Set the state of the widget.

@spec io_widget:insert_str(Widget, Str)

> Insert a string into the main area of the widget.

@spec io_widget:set_handler(Widget, Fun)

> Set the widget parser to Fun (see later).

The io widget can generate the following messages:

{Widget, State, Parse}

> This message gets sent when the user enters a string in the lower command region of the widget. Parse is the result of parsing this string with the parser associated with the widget.

{Widget, destroyed}

> This message gets sent when the user destroys the io widget by killing the window.

Finally, the io widget is a programmable widget. It can be parameterized with a parser that is used to parse all messages that are entered in the entry box of the widget. Parsing is accomplished by calling a function Parse(Str). This function can be set by calling set_handler(Widget, Parse).

The default parser is the following function:

```
Parse = fun(Str) -> {str, Str} end
```

11.3 Client-Side Software

The client side of the chat program has three processes: the io widget (which we've talked about), the chat client (which interfaces the io widget to the middle man), and the middle-man process itself. In this section, we'll concentrate on the chat client.

The Chat Client

We start the chat client by calling start/0:

socket_dist/chat_client.erl

```
start() ->
    connect("localhost", 2223, "AsDT67aQ", "general", "joe").
```

This tries to connect to localhost port 2223 (this is hardwired for testing purposes). The function connect/5 simply creates a parallel process by spawning handler/5. The handler has to perform several tasks:

- It makes itself into a system process so that it can trap exits.
- It creates an io widget and sets up the prompt and title of the widget.
- It then spawns connection process (which tries to connect to the server).
- Finally, it waits for a connection event in disconnected/2.

The code for this is as follows:

socket_dist/chat_client.erl

```
connect(Host, Port, HostPsw, Group, Nick) ->
    spawn(fun() -> handler(Host, Port, HostPsw, Group, Nick) end).

handler(Host, Port, HostPsw, Group, Nick) ->
    process_flag(trap_exit, true),
    Widget = io_widget:start(self()),
    set_title(Widget, Nick),
    set_state(Widget, Nick),
    set_prompt(Widget, [Nick, " > "]),
    set_handler(Widget, fun parse_command/1),
    start_connector(Host, Port, HostPsw),
    disconnected(Widget, Group, Nick).
```

In the disconnected state, either the process will receive a {connected, MM}[2] message, in which case it sends a login message to the server and waits for a login response, or the widget might be destroyed, in which case everything is stopped. The connecting process sends periodic status messages to the chat client. These are just sent to the io widget to be displayed.

---

2. MM stands for *middle man*. This is a proxy process that can be used to communicate with the server.

`socket_dist/chat_client.erl`

```
disconnected(Widget, Group, Nick) ->
    receive
        {connected, MM} ->
            insert_str(Widget, "connected to server\nsending data\n"),
            lib_chan_mm:send(MM, {login, Group, Nick}),
            wait_login_response(Widget, MM);
        {Widget, destroyed} ->
            exit(died);
        {status, S} ->
            insert_str(Widget, to_str(S)),
            disconnected(Widget, Group, Nick);
        Other ->
            io:format("chat_client disconnected unexpected:~p~n",[Other]),
            disconnected(Widget, Group, Nick)
    end.
```

The {connected, MM} message should eventually come from the connection processes that was started by the call start_connector(Host, Port, HostPsw). This created a parallel process that periodically tries to connect to the IRC server.

`socket_dist/chat_client.erl`

```
start_connector(Host, Port, Pwd) ->
    S = self(),
    spawn_link(fun() -> try_to_connect(S, Host, Port, Pwd) end).

try_to_connect(Parent, Host, Port, Pwd) ->
    %% Parent is the Pid of the process that spawned this process
    case lib_chan:connect(Host, Port, chat, Pwd, []) of
        {error, _Why} ->
            Parent ! {status, {cannot, connect, Host, Port}},
            sleep(2000),
            try_to_connect(Parent, Host, Port, Pwd);
        {ok, MM} ->
            lib_chan_mm:controller(MM, Parent),
            Parent ! {connected, MM},
            exit(connectorFinished)
    end.
```

try_to_connect loops forever, trying every two seconds to connect to the server. If it cannot connect, it sends a status message to the chat client.

Note: In start_connector, we wrote this:

```
S = self(),
spawn_link(fun() -> try_to_connect(S, ...) end)
```

This is not the same as the following:

```
spawn_link(fun() -> try_to_connect(self(), ...) end)
```

The reason is that, in the first code fragment, self() is evaluated inside the parent process. In the second code fragment, self() is evaluated inside the spawned fun, so it returns the process identifier of the spawned process and not, as you might think, the PID of the current process. This is a common cause of error (and confusion).

If a connection is made, then it sends a {connected, MM} message to the chat client. When a connection message arrives, the client sends a login message to the server (both these events happened in disconnected/2) and waits for the reply in wait_login_response/2:

```
socket_dist/chat_client.erl
wait_login_response(Widget, MM) ->
    receive
        {chan, MM, ack} ->
            active(Widget, MM);
        Other ->
            io:format("chat_client login unexpected:~p~n",[Other]),
            wait_login_response(Widget, MM)
    end.
```

If all goes well, the process should receive an acknowledgment (ack) message. (In our case, this is the only possibility since the password was correct.) After receiving the acknowledgment message, this function calls active/2:

```
socket_dist/chat_client.erl
active(Widget, MM) ->
    receive
        {Widget, Nick, Str} ->
            lib_chan_mm:send(MM, {relay, Nick, Str}),
            active(Widget, MM);
        {chan, MM, {msg, From, Pid, Str}} ->
            insert_str(Widget, [From,"@",pid_to_list(Pid)," ", Str, "\n"]),
            active(Widget, MM);
        {'EXIT',Widget,windowDestroyed} ->
            lib_chan_mm:close(MM);
        {close, MM} ->
            exit(serverDied);
        Other ->
            io:format("chat_client active unexpected:~p~n",[Other]),
            active(Widget, MM)
    end.
```

active/2 just sends messages from the widget to the group (and vice versa) and monitors the connection with the group.

Apart from some module declarations and trivial formatting and parsing routines, this completes the chat client.

The full listing of the chat client starts on page 196.

11.4 Server-Side Software

The server-side software is more complex than the client-side software. For each chat client, there is a corresponding chat controller that interfaces the chat client to the chat server. There is a single chat server that knows about all the chat sessions that are in progress, and there are a number of group managers (one per chat group) that manage the individual chat groups.

The Chat Controller

The chat controller is a plug-in for lib_chan, the socket-based distribution kit. We met this in Section 10.5, *lib_chan*, on page 179. lib_chan needs a configuration file and a plug-in module.

The configuration file for the chat system is as follows:

`socket_dist/chat.conf`
```
{port, 2223}.
{service, chat, password,"AsDT67aQ",mfa,mod_chat_controller,start,[]}.
```

If you look back at the code in chat_client.erl, you'll see that the port number, service name, and password agree with the information in the configuration file.

The chat controller module is very simple:

`socket_dist/mod_chat_controller.erl`
```
-module(mod_chat_controller).
-export([start/3]).
-import(lib_chan_mm, [send/2]).

start(MM, _, _) ->
    process_flag(trap_exit, true),
    io:format("mod_chat_controller off we go ...~p~n",[MM]),
    loop(MM).
```

```
loop(MM) ->
    receive
        {chan, MM, Msg} ->
            chat_server ! {mm, MM, Msg},
            loop(MM);
        {'EXIT', MM, _Why} ->
            chat_server ! {mm_closed, MM};
        Other ->
            io:format("mod_chat_controller unexpected message =~p (MM=~p)~n",
                      [Other, MM]),
            loop(MM)
    end.
```

This code should receive only two messages. When the client connects, it will receive an arbitrary message, and it just sends it to the chat server. Otherwise, if the session is terminated for any reason, it will receive an exit message, and it then just tells the chat server that the client has died.

The Chat Server

The chat server is a registered process called (unsurprisingly) chat_server. Calling chat_server:start/0 starts and registers a server, and it starts lib_chan.

`socket_dist/chat_server.erl`

```
start() ->
    start_server(),
    lib_chan:start_server("chat.conf").

start_server() ->
    register(chat_server,
             spawn(fun() ->
                           process_flag(trap_exit, true),
                           Val= (catch server_loop([])),
                           io:format("Server terminated with:~p~n",[Val])
                   end)).
```

The server loop is simple. It waits for a {login, Group, Nick}[3] message from a middle man with PID Channel. If there is a chat group controller for this group, then it just sends the login message to the group controller; otherwise, it starts a new group controller.

---

3. Nick is the nickname of the user.

The chat server is the only process that knows the PIDs of all the group controllers, so when a new connection is made to the system, the chat server is contacted to find out the process identifier of the group controller.

The server itself is simple:

socket_dist/chat_server.erl

```
server_loop(L) ->
    receive
        {mm, Channel, {login, Group, Nick}} ->
            case lookup(Group, L) of
                {ok, Pid} ->
                    Pid ! {login, Channel, Nick},
                    server_loop(L);
                error ->
                    Pid = spawn_link(fun() ->
                                        chat_group:start(Channel, Nick)
                                end),
                    server_loop([{Group,Pid}|L])
            end;
        {mm_closed, _} ->
            server_loop(L);
        {'EXIT', Pid, allGone} ->
            L1 = remove_group(Pid, L),
            server_loop(L1);
        Msg ->
            io:format("Server received Msg=~p~n",
                    [Msg]),
            server_loop(L)
    end.
```

The code to manipulate the group lists involves some simple list-processing routines:

socket_dist/chat_server.erl

```
lookup(G, [{G,Pid}|_]) -> {ok, Pid};
lookup(G, [_|T])       -> lookup(G, T);
lookup(_,[])           -> error.

remove_group(Pid, [{G,Pid}|T]) -> io:format("~p removed~n",[G]), T;
remove_group(Pid, [H|T])       -> [H|remove_group(Pid, T)];
remove_group(_, [])            -> [].
```

The Group Manager

The group manager is now all that's left. The most important part of this is the dispatcher:

```
socket_dist/chat_group.erl
```

```erlang
group_controller([]) ->
    exit(allGone);
group_controller(L) ->
    receive
        {chan, C, {relay, Nick, Str}} ->
            foreach(fun({Pid,_}) -> send(Pid, {msg,Nick,C,Str}) end, L),
            group_controller(L);
        {login, C, Nick} ->
            controller(C, self()),
            send(C, ack),
            self() ! {chan, C, {relay, Nick, "I'm joining the group"}},
            group_controller([{C,Nick}|L]);
        {chan_closed, C} ->
            {Nick, L1} = delete(C, L, []),
            self() ! {chan, C, {relay, Nick, "I'm leaving the group"}},
            group_controller(L1);
        Any ->
            io:format("group controller received Msg=~p~n", [Any]),
            group_controller(L)
    end.
```

The argument L in group_controller(L) is {Pid, Nick} list of Nicks and middle man PID.

When the group manager receives a {relay,Nick,Str} message, it merely broadcasts it to all the processes in the group. If a {login, C, Nick} message arrives, it adds a {C,Nick} tuple to the broadcast list. The *important* point to note is the call to lib_chan_mm:controller/2. This call sets the controlling process of the middle man to the group controller, which means that *all messages sent to the socket that is controlled by the middle man will be sent to the group controller*—this is probably the key to understanding how all of this code works.

All that remains is the code that starts the group server:

```
socket_dist/chat_group.erl
```

```erlang
-module(chat_group).
-import(lib_chan_mm, [send/2, controller/2]).
-import(lists, [foreach/2, reverse/2]).

-export([start/2]).
```

```
start(C, Nick) ->
    process_flag(trap_exit, true),
    controller(C, self()),
    send(C, ack),
    self() ! {chan, C, {relay, Nick, "I'm starting the group"}},
    group_controller([{C,Nick}]).
```

and the function delete/3 called from the dispatcher loop of the process:

socket_dist/chat_group.erl

```
delete(Pid, [{Pid,Nick}|T], L) -> {Nick, reverse(T, L)};
delete(Pid, [H|T], L)          -> delete(Pid, T, [H|L]);
delete(_, [], L)               -> {"????", L}.
```

11.5 Running the Application

The entire application is stored in the directory pathto/code/socket_dist; it also uses some library modules in the directory pathto/code.

To run the application, obtain the source code from the book's website, and unpack the code to some directory. (We'll assume here that this is in the directory /home/joe/erlbook.) Open a terminal window, and give the following commands:

```
$ cd /home/joe/erlbook/code
/home/joe/erlbook/code $ make
...
/home/joe/erlbook/code $ cd socket_dist
/home/joe/erlbook/code/socket_dist $ make chat_server
...
```

This will start the chat server. Now we have to start a second terminal window and start the client test:

```
$ cd /home/joe/erlbook/code/socket_dist
/home/joe/erlbook/code/socket_dist $ make chat_client
...
```

Running make chat_client runs the function chat_client:test(); this actually creates four windows, all of which connect to the group called "general," which is just for testing purposes. We can see a screen dump showing how the system looks after giving these commands in Figure 11.4, on the next page.

To deploy the system on the Internet, all we need to do is change the password and port to something suitable and enable incoming connections for the port number we have chosen.

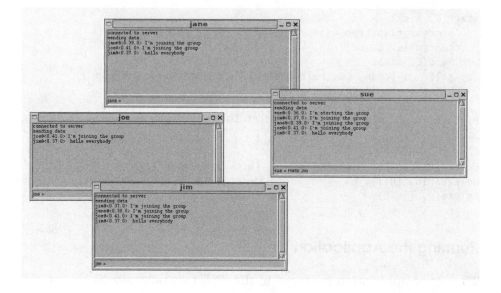

Figure 11.4: SCREEN DUMP SHOWING FOUR TEST WINDOWS CONNECTED
TO THE SAME GROUP

11.6 The Chat Program Source Code

We've now finished the description of the chat program. When describing the program, we broke it into small fragments and missed out on some of the code. This section has all the code in one place, which makes it easier to read. If you have trouble following any of the code, try referring to the descriptions earlier in the chapter.

Chat Client

`socket_dist/chat_client.erl`

```erlang
-module(chat_client).

-import(io_widget,
        [get_state/1, insert_str/2, set_prompt/2, set_state/2,
         set_title/2, set_handler/2, update_state/3]).

-export([start/0, test/0, connect/5]).

start() ->
    connect("localhost", 2223, "AsDT67aQ", "general", "joe").

test() ->
```

```erlang
    connect("localhost", 2223, "AsDT67aQ", "general", "joe"),
    connect("localhost", 2223, "AsDT67aQ", "general", "jane"),
    connect("localhost", 2223, "AsDT67aQ", "general", "jim"),
    connect("localhost", 2223, "AsDT67aQ", "general", "sue").

connect(Host, Port, HostPsw, Group, Nick) ->
    spawn(fun() -> handler(Host, Port, HostPsw, Group, Nick) end).

handler(Host, Port, HostPsw, Group, Nick) ->
    process_flag(trap_exit, true),
    Widget = io_widget:start(self()),
    set_title(Widget, Nick),
    set_state(Widget, Nick),
    set_prompt(Widget, [Nick, " > "]),
    set_handler(Widget, fun parse_command/1),
    start_connector(Host, Port, HostPsw),
    disconnected(Widget, Group, Nick).

disconnected(Widget, Group, Nick) ->
    receive
        {connected, MM} ->
            insert_str(Widget, "connected to server\nsending data\n"),
            lib_chan_mm:send(MM, {login, Group, Nick}),
            wait_login_response(Widget, MM);
        {Widget, destroyed} ->
            exit(died);
        {status, S} ->
            insert_str(Widget, to_str(S)),
            disconnected(Widget, Group, Nick);
        Other ->
            io:format("chat_client disconnected unexpected:~p~n",[Other]),
            disconnected(Widget, Group, Nick)
    end.

wait_login_response(Widget, MM) ->
    receive
        {chan, MM, ack} ->
            active(Widget, MM);
        Other ->
            io:format("chat_client login unexpected:~p~n",[Other]),
            wait_login_response(Widget, MM)
    end.

active(Widget, MM) ->
    receive
        {Widget, Nick, Str} ->
            lib_chan_mm:send(MM, {relay, Nick, Str}),
            active(Widget, MM);
        {chan, MM, {msg, From, Pid, Str}} ->
            insert_str(Widget, [From,"@",pid_to_list(Pid)," ", Str, "\n"]),
            active(Widget, MM);
```

```erlang
                {'EXIT',Widget,windowDestroyed} ->
                    lib_chan_mm:close(MM);
                {close, MM} ->
                    exit(serverDied);
                Other ->
                    io:format("chat_client active unexpected:~p~n",[Other]),
                    active(Widget, MM)
        end.

start_connector(Host, Port, Pwd) ->
    S = self(),
    spawn_link(fun() -> try_to_connect(S, Host, Port, Pwd) end).

try_to_connect(Parent, Host, Port, Pwd) ->
    %% Parent is the Pid of the process that spawned this process
    case lib_chan:connect(Host, Port, chat, Pwd, []) of
        {error, _Why} ->
            Parent ! {status, {cannot, connect, Host, Port}},
            sleep(2000),
            try_to_connect(Parent, Host, Port, Pwd);
        {ok, MM} ->
            lib_chan_mm:controller(MM, Parent),
            Parent ! {connected, MM},
            exit(connectorFinished)
    end.

sleep(T) ->
    receive
    after T -> true
    end.

to_str(Term) ->
    io_lib:format("~p~n",[Term]).

parse_command(Str) -> skip_to_gt(Str).

skip_to_gt(">" ++ T) -> T;
skip_to_gt([_|T])    -> skip_to_gt(T);
skip_to_gt([])       -> exit("no >").
```

lib_chan Configuration

`socket_dist/chat.conf`

```erlang
{port, 2223}.
{service, chat, password,"AsDT67aQ",mfa,mod_chat_controller,start,[]}.
```

Chat Controller

`socket_dist/mod_chat_controller.erl`

```erlang
-module(mod_chat_controller).
-export([start/3]).
-import(lib_chan_mm, [send/2]).
```

```erlang
start(MM, _, _) ->
    process_flag(trap_exit, true),
    io:format("mod_chat_controller off we go ...~p~n",[MM]),
    loop(MM).


loop(MM) ->
    receive
        {chan, MM, Msg} ->
            chat_server ! {mm, MM, Msg},
            loop(MM);
        {'EXIT', MM, _Why} ->
            chat_server ! {mm_closed, MM};
        Other ->
            io:format("mod_chat_controller unexpected message =~p (MM=~p)~n",
                      [Other, MM]),
            loop(MM)
    end.
```

Chat Server

socket_dist/chat_server.erl

```erlang
-module(chat_server).
-import(lib_chan_mm, [send/2, controller/2]).
-import(lists, [delete/2, foreach/2, map/2, member/2,reverse/2]).

-compile(export_all).

start() ->
    start_server(),
    lib_chan:start_server("chat.conf").

start_server() ->
    register(chat_server,
             spawn(fun() ->
                           process_flag(trap_exit, true),
                           Val= (catch server_loop([])),
                           io:format("Server terminated with:~p~n",[Val])
                   end)).

server_loop(L) ->
    receive
        {mm, Channel, {login, Group, Nick}} ->
            case lookup(Group, L) of
                {ok, Pid} ->
                    Pid ! {login, Channel, Nick},
                    server_loop(L);
                error ->
                    Pid = spawn_link(fun() ->
                                             chat_group:start(Channel, Nick)
                                     end),
                    server_loop([{Group,Pid}|L])
            end;
```

```
                    {mm_closed, _} ->
                        server_loop(L);
                    {'EXIT', Pid, allGone} ->
                        L1 = remove_group(Pid, L),
                        server_loop(L1);
                    Msg ->
                        io:format("Server received Msg=~p~n",
                                    [Msg]),
                        server_loop(L)
            end.

lookup(G, [{G,Pid}|_]) -> {ok, Pid};
lookup(G, [_|T])       -> lookup(G, T);
lookup(_,[])           -> error.

remove_group(Pid, [{G,Pid}|T]) -> io:format("~p removed~n",[G]), T;
remove_group(Pid, [H|T])       -> [H|remove_group(Pid, T)];
remove_group(_, [])            -> [].
```

Chat Groups

socket_dist/chat_group.erl

```
-module(chat_group).
-import(lib_chan_mm, [send/2, controller/2]).
-import(lists, [foreach/2, reverse/2]).

-export([start/2]).

start(C, Nick) ->
    process_flag(trap_exit, true),
    controller(C, self()),
    send(C, ack),
    self() ! {chan, C, {relay, Nick, "I'm starting the group"}},
    group_controller([{C,Nick}]).

delete(Pid, [{Pid,Nick}|T], L) -> {Nick, reverse(T, L)};
delete(Pid, [H|T], L)          -> delete(Pid, T, [H|L]);
delete(_, [], L)               -> {"????", L}.

group_controller([]) ->
    exit(allGone);
group_controller(L) ->
    receive
        {chan, C, {relay, Nick, Str}} ->
            foreach(fun({Pid,_}) -> send(Pid, {msg,Nick,C,Str}) end, L),
            group_controller(L);
        {login, C, Nick} ->
            controller(C, self()),
            send(C, ack),
            self() ! {chan, C, {relay, Nick, "I'm joining the group"}},
            group_controller([{C,Nick}|L]);
```

```erlang
        {chan_closed, C} ->
            {Nick, L1} = delete(C, L, []),
            self() ! {chan, C, {relay, Nick, "I'm leaving the group"}},
            group_controller(L1);
        Any ->
            io:format("group controller received Msg=~p~n", [Any]),
            group_controller(L)
    end.
```

The IO Widget

`socket_dist/io_widget.erl`

```erlang
-module(io_widget).

-export([get_state/1,
         start/1, test/0,
         set_handler/2,
         set_prompt/2,
         set_state/2,
         set_title/2, insert_str/2, update_state/3]).

start(Pid) ->
    gs:start(),
    spawn_link(fun() -> widget(Pid) end).

get_state(Pid)          -> rpc(Pid, get_state).
set_title(Pid, Str)     -> Pid ! {title, Str}.
set_handler(Pid, Fun)   -> Pid ! {handler, Fun}.
set_prompt(Pid, Str)    -> Pid ! {prompt, Str}.
set_state(Pid, State)   -> Pid ! {state, State}.
insert_str(Pid, Str)    -> Pid ! {insert, Str}.
update_state(Pid, N, X) -> Pid ! {updateState, N, X}.

rpc(Pid, Q) ->
    Pid ! {self(), Q},
    receive
        {Pid, R} ->
            R
    end.

widget(Pid) ->
    Size = [{width,500},{height,200}],
    Win = gs:window(gs:start(),
                    [{map,true},{configure,true},{title,"window"}|Size]),
    gs:frame(packer, Win,[{packer_x, [{stretch,1,500}]},
                          {packer_y, [{stretch,10,120,100},
                                      {stretch,1,15,15}]}]),
    gs:create(editor,editor,packer, [{pack_x,1},{pack_y,1},{vscroll,right}]),
    gs:create(entry, entry, packer, [{pack_x,1},{pack_y,2},{keypress,true}]),
    gs:config(packer, Size),
    Prompt = " > ",
```

```erlang
            State = nil,
            gs:config(entry, {insert,{0,Prompt}}),
            loop(Win, Pid, Prompt, State, fun parse/1).

loop(Win, Pid, Prompt, State, Parse) ->
    receive
        {From, get_state} ->
            From ! {self(), State},
            loop(Win, Pid, Prompt, State, Parse);
        {handler, Fun} ->
            loop(Win, Pid, Prompt, State, Fun);
        {prompt, Str} ->
            %% this clobbers the line being input ...
            %% this could be fixed - hint
            gs:config(entry, {delete,{0,last}}),
            gs:config(entry, {insert,{0,Str}}),
            loop(Win, Pid, Str, State, Parse);
        {state, S} ->
            loop(Win, Pid, Prompt, S, Parse);
        {title, Str} ->
            gs:config(Win, [{title, Str}]),
            loop(Win, Pid, Prompt, State, Parse);
        {insert, Str} ->
            gs:config(editor, {insert,{'end',Str}}),
            scroll_to_show_last_line(),
            loop(Win, Pid, Prompt, State, Parse);
        {updateState, N, X} ->
            io:format("setelemtn N=~p X=~p Satte=~p~n",[N,X,State]),
            State1 = setelement(N, State, X),
            loop(Win, Pid, Prompt, State1, Parse);
        {gs,_,destroy,_,_} ->
            io:format("Destroyed~n",[]),
            exit(windowDestroyed);
        {gs, entry,keypress,_,['Return'|_]} ->
            Text = gs:read(entry, text),
            %% io:format("Read:~p~n",[Text]),
            gs:config(entry, {delete,{0,last}}),
            gs:config(entry, {insert,{0,Prompt}}),
            try Parse(Text) of
                Term ->
                    Pid ! {self(), State, Term}
            catch
                _:_ ->
                    self() ! {insert, "** bad input**\n** /h for help\n"}
            end,
            loop(Win, Pid, Prompt, State, Parse);
        {gs,_,configure,[],[W,H,_,_]} ->
            gs:config(packer, [{width,W},{height,H}]),
            loop(Win, Pid, Prompt, State, Parse);
        {gs, entry,keypress,_,_} ->
            loop(Win, Pid, Prompt, State, Parse);
```

```
        Any ->
            io:format("Discarded:~p~n",[Any]),
            loop(Win, Pid, Prompt, State, Parse)
    end.

scroll_to_show_last_line() ->
    Size       = gs:read(editor, size),
    Height     = gs:read(editor, height),
    CharHeight = gs:read(editor, char_height),
    TopRow     = Size - Height/CharHeight,
    if  TopRow > 0 -> gs:config(editor, {vscrollpos, TopRow});
        true       -> gs:config(editor, {vscrollpos, 0})
    end.

test() ->
    spawn(fun() -> test1() end).

test1() ->
    W = io_widget:start(self()),
    io_widget:set_title(W, "Test window"),
    loop(W).

loop(W) ->
    receive
        {W, {str, Str}} ->
            Str1 = Str ++ "\n",
            io_widget:insert_str(W, Str1),
            loop(W)
    end.

parse(Str) ->
    {str, Str}.
```

11.7 Exercises

- Improve the graphics widget, adding a side panel to list the names of the people in the current group.
- Add code to show the names of all people in a group.
- Add code to list all the groups.
- Add person-to-person conversations.
- Add code so that the server machine does not run the group controller but so that this functionality is provided by the first user to join the system in a particular group.
- Stare at the message sequence diagram (Figure 11.2, on page 185) to make sure you understand it, and check that you can identify all the messages in the program code.
- Draw your own message sequence diagrams to show how the login phase of the problem is solved.

## Chapter 12

Interfacing Techniques

Suppose we want to interface Erlang to a program written in C or
Python or to run a shell script from Erlang. To do this, we run the
external program in a separate operating system process *outside* the
Erlang runtime system and communicate with this process through a
byte-oriented communication channel. The Erlang side of the communication is controlled by an Erlang *port*. The process that creates a port
is called the *connected process* for that port. The connected process
has a special significance: all messages to the external program must
be tagged with the PID of the connected process, and all messages from
the external program are sent to the connected processes.

We can see the relationship between a connected process (C), a port (P),
and an external operating system process in Figure 12.1.

As far as the programmer is concerned, the port behaves just like an
Erlang process. You can send messages to it, you can register it (just

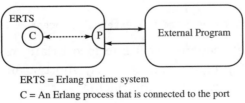

ERTS = Erlang runtime system

C = An Erlang process that is connected to the port

P = A port

Figure 12.1: PORT COMMUNICATION

like a process), and so on. If the external program crashes, then an exit signal will be sent to the connected process, and if the connected process dies, then the external program will be killed.

Perhaps you're wondering why we do things this way. Many programming languages allow code in foreign languages to be linked into the application executable. In Erlang, we don't allow this for reasons of safety.[1] If we were to link an external program into the Erlang executable, then a mistake in the external program could easily crash the Erlang system. For this reason, all foreign language code must be run outside the Erlang system in an external operating system process. The Erlang system and the external process communicate through a byte stream.

12.1 Ports

To create a port, we give the following command:

```
Port = open_port(PortName, PortSettings)
```

This returns a port. The following messages can be sent to a port:[2]

Port ! {PidC, {command, Data}}
>   Send Data (an IO list) to the port.

Port ! {PidC, {connect, Pid1}}
>   Change the PID of the connected process from PidC to Pid1.

Port ! {PidC, close}
>   Close the port.

The connected process can receive message from the external program with this:

```
receive
    {Port, {data, Data}} ->
        ... Data comes from the external process ...
```

In the following sections, we'll interface Erlang with a very simple C program. The C program is deliberately short so as not to distract from the details of how we do the interfacing.

Note: The following example is deliberately simple to highlight the port mechanisms and protocols. Encoding and decoding complex data

---

1. An exception to this is the use of linked-in drivers that we discuss later in this chapter.
2. In all of these messages, PidC is the PID of the connected process.

structures in a portable way is a difficult problem that we won't solve here. At the end of the chapter, we give pointers to a number of libraries that can be used to build interfaces to other programming languages.

12.2 Interfacing an External C Program

We'll start with the C program:

`ports/example1.c`

```c
int twice(int x){
  return 2*x;
}

int sum(int x, int y){
  return x+y;
}
```

Our final goal is to call these routines from Erlang. We'd like to be able to say this (in Erlang):

```erlang
X1 = example1:twice(23),
Y1 = example1:sum(45, 32),
```

As far as the user is concerned, example1 is an Erlang module, and therefore all details of the interface to the C program should be hidden inside the module example1.

Our interface needs a main program that decodes the data sent from the Erlang program. In our example, we first define a protocol between the port and the external C program. We'll use an extremely simple protocol and then show how to implement this in Erlang and C. The protocol is defined as follows:

- All packets start with a 2-byte length code (Len) followed by Len bytes of data.

- To call twice(N), the Erlang program must encode the function call using some convention. We'll assume this is encoded as the 2-byte sequence [1,N]; the 1 means call the function twice, and N is a (1-byte) argument.

- To call sum(N, M), we'll encode the request as the byte sequence [2,N,M].

- Return values are assumed to be a single byte long.

Both the external C program and the Erlang program must follow this protocol. As an example, we'll walk through what happens when an Erlang program wants to compute sum(45,32):

1. The port sends the byte sequence 0,3,2,45,32 to the external program.

   The first two bytes, 0,3, represent the packet length (3); the code 2 means call the external sum function; and 45 and 32 are the arguments to sum (one byte each).

2. The external program reads these five bytes from standard input, calls the sum function, and then writes the byte sequence 0,1,77 to standard output.

   The first two bytes encode the packet length. This is followed by the result, 77 (again 1-byte long).

We now have to write programs on both sides of the interface that strictly follow this protocol. We'll start with the C program.

The C Program

The external C program is made from three files:

- example1.c: This contains the functions that we want to call (we saw this earlier).

- example1_driver.c: This terminates the byte stream protocol and calls the routines in example1.c.

- erl_comm.c: This has routines for reading and writing memory buffers.

example1_driver.c

`ports/example1_driver.c`

```
#include <stdio.h>
typedef unsigned char byte;

int read_cmd(byte *buff);
int write_cmd(byte *buff, int len);

int main() {
  int fn, arg1, arg2, result;
  byte buff[100];

  while (read_cmd(buff) > 0) {
    fn = buff[0];
```

```
  if (fn == 1) {
    arg1 = buff[1];
    result = twice(arg1);
  } else if (fn == 2) {
    arg1 = buff[1];
    arg2 = buff[2];
    /* debug -- you can print to stderr to debug
        fprintf(stderr,"calling sum %i %i\n",arg1,arg2); */
    result = sum(arg1, arg2);
  }

  buff[0] = result;
  write_cmd(buff, 1);
 }
}
```

This code runs an infinite loop reading commands from standard input calling the application routines and writing the results to standard output.

If you want to debug this program, you can write to stderr. An example of a debug statement has been commented out from the code.

erl_comm.c

Finally, here's the code to read and write 2-byte headed packets to and from standard input and output. The code is written this way to allow for possible fragmentation of the IO packets.

ports/erl_comm.c

```
/* erl_comm.c */
#include <unistd.h>

typedef unsigned char byte;

int read_cmd(byte *buf);
int write_cmd(byte *buf, int len);
int read_exact(byte *buf, int len);
int write_exact(byte *buf, int len);

int read_cmd(byte *buf)
{
  int len;

  if (read_exact(buf, 2) != 2)
    return(-1);
  len = (buf[0] << 8) | buf[1];
  return read_exact(buf, len);
}
```

```
int write_cmd(byte *buf, int len)
{
  byte li;

  li = (len >> 8) & 0xff;
  write_exact(&li, 1);

  li = len & 0xff;
  write_exact(&li, 1);

  return write_exact(buf, len);
}

int read_exact(byte *buf, int len)
{
  int i, got=0;

  do {
    if ((i = read(0, buf+got, len-got)) <= 0)
      return(i);
    got += i;
  } while (got<len);

  return(len);
}

int write_exact(byte *buf, int len)
{
  int i, wrote = 0;

  do {
    if ((i = write(1, buf+wrote, len-wrote)) <= 0)
      return (i);
    wrote += i;
  } while (wrote<len);

  return (len);
}
```

This code is specialized for handling packets with a 2-byte length header, so it matches up with the {packet, 2} option given to the port driver program.

The Erlang Program

The Erlang side of the port is driven by the following program:

```
ports/example1.erl
```

```
-module(example1).
-export([start/0, stop/0]).
-export([twice/1, sum/2]).
```

```
start() ->
    spawn(fun() ->
                register(example1, self()),
                process_flag(trap_exit, true),
                Port = open_port({spawn, "./example1"}, [{packet, 2}]),
                loop(Port)
            end).

stop() ->
    example1 ! stop.

twice(X) -> call_port({twice, X}).
sum(X,Y) -> call_port({sum, X, Y}).

call_port(Msg) ->
    example1 ! {call, self(), Msg},
    receive
        {example1, Result} ->
            Result
    end.

loop(Port) ->
    receive
        {call, Caller, Msg} ->
            Port ! {self(), {command, encode(Msg)}},
            receive
                {Port, {data, Data}} ->
                    Caller ! {example1, decode(Data)}
            end,
            loop(Port);
        stop ->
            Port ! {self(), close},
            receive
                {Port, closed} ->
                    exit(normal)
            end;
        {'EXIT', Port, Reason} ->
            exit({port_terminated,Reason})
    end.

encode({twice, X}) -> [1, X];
encode({sum, X, Y}) -> [2, X, Y].

decode([Int]) -> Int.
```

The port is opened with this statement:

```
Port = open_port({spawn, "./example1"}, [{packet, 2}])
```

The {packet,2} option tells the system to automatically add a 2-byte packet length header to all packets sent to the external program. So if we were to send the message {PidC,{command,[2,45,32]}} to the port, the port driver would add a 2-byte packet length header and actually send 0,3,2,45,32 to the external program.

On input the port driver will also assume that each incoming packet is preceded by a 2-byte header and will remove these bytes before sending the data to the Erlang connected process.

That completes the programs; we use the following makefile to build the programs. The command make example1 builds the external program that is used as an argument in the open_port function. Note that the makefile also includes code to make the linked-in driver that is presented later in this chapter.

Makefile

`ports/Makefile`

```
.SUFFIXES: .erl .beam .yrl

.erl.beam:

        erlc -W $<

MODS = example1 example1_lid

all:     ${MODS:%=%.beam} example1 example1_drv.so

example1:  example1.c erl_comm.c example1_driver.c
        gcc -o example1 example1.c erl_comm.c example1_driver.c

example1_drv.so: example1_lid.c example1.c
        gcc -o example1_drv.so -fpic -shared example1.c example1_lid.c

clean:
        rm example1 example1_drv.so *.beam
```

Running the Program

Now we can run the program:

```
1> example1:start().
<0.32.0>
2> example1:sum(45, 32).
77
4> example1:twice(10).
20
...
```

This now completes our first example.

Before passing to the next topic, we should note the following:

- The example program made no attempt to unify Erlang and C's idea of what an integer is. We just assumed that an integer in Erlang and C was a single byte and ignored all problems of precision and signedness. In a realistic application, we would have to think rather carefully about the exact types and precisions of the arguments concerned. This can be difficult, because Erlang happily manages integers of an arbitrary size, whereas languages such as C have fixed ideas about the precision of integers and so on.

- We couldn't just run the Erlang functions without first having started the driver that was responsible for the interface (that is, some program had to evaluate example1:start() *before* we were able to run the program). We would like to be able to do this automatically when the system is started. This is perfectly possible but needs some knowledge of how the system starts and stops. We'll deal with this later in Section 18.7, *The Application*, on page 352.

12.3 open_port

In the previous section we introduced open_port without really saying what the arguments to this function did. We saw one use of open_port, with an argument {packet, 2} that added and removed a 2-byte header to the data sent between Erlang and an external process. open_port takes a relatively large number of arguments.

Some of the more common arguments are as follows:

@spec open_port(PortName, [Opt]) -> Port
    PortName is one of the following:

    {spawn, Command}
        Start an external program. Command is the name of an external program. Command runs outside the Erlang work space unless a linked-in driver with the name Command is found.

    {fd, In, Out}
        Allow an Erlang process to access any currently opened file descriptors used by Erlang. The file descriptor In can be used

for standard input, and the file descriptor Out can be used for standard output.[3]

Opt is one of the following:

{packet, N}

Packets are preceded by an N (1, 2, or 4) byte length count.

stream

Messages are sent without packet lengths. The application must know how to handle these packets.

{line, Max}

Deliver messages on a one-per line basis. If the line is more than Max bytes, then it is split at Max bytes.

{cd, Dir}

Valid only for the {spawn, Command} option. The external program starts in Dir.

{env, Env}

Valid only for the {spawn, Command} option. The environment of external program is extended with the environment variables in the list Env. Env is a list of {VarName, Value} pairs, where VarName and Value are strings.

This is not a complete list of the arguments to open_port. We can find the precise details of the arguments in the manual page for the module erlang.

12.4 Linked-in Drivers

Sometimes, we might want to run a foreign-language program *inside* the Erlang runtime system. In this case, the program is written as a shared library that is dynamically linked into the Erlang runtime system. The linked-in driver appears to the programmer as a port program and obeys exactly the same protocol as for a port program.

Creating a linked-in driver is the most efficient way of interfacing foreign-language code with Erlang, but it is also the most dangerous. Any fatal error in the linked-in driver will crash the Erlang system

---

3. See http://www.erlang.org/examples/examples-2.0.html for an example of connecting to standard input and output.

and affect all processes in the system. For this reason, using linked-in drivers is not recommended; they should be used only when all else fails.

To illustrate this, we'll turn the program we used earlier into a linked-in driver. To do this, we need three files:

- example1_lid.erl: This is the Erlang server.

- example1.c: This contains the C functions that we want to call. These are the same as used earlier.

- example1_lid.c: This is the C program that calls the functions in example1.c.

The Erlang code to manage the interface is as follows:

`ports/example1_lid.erl`

```erlang
-module(example1_lid).
-export([start/0, stop/0]).
-export([twice/1, sum/2]).

start() ->
    start("example1_drv").

start(SharedLib) ->
    case erl_ddll:load_driver(".", SharedLib) of
        ok -> ok;
        {error, already_loaded} -> ok;
        _ -> exit({error, could_not_load_driver})
    end,
    spawn(fun() -> init(SharedLib) end).

init(SharedLib) ->
    register(example1_lid, self()),
    Port = open_port({spawn, SharedLib}, []),
    loop(Port).

stop() ->
    example1_lid ! stop.

twice(X) -> call_port({twice, X}).
sum(X,Y) -> call_port({sum, X, Y}).

call_port(Msg) ->
    example1_lid ! {call, self(), Msg},
    receive
        {example1_lid, Result} ->
            Result
    end.
```

```erlang
loop(Port) ->
    receive
        {call, Caller, Msg} ->
            Port ! {self(), {command, encode(Msg)}},
            receive
                {Port, {data, Data}} ->
                    Caller ! {example1_lid, decode(Data)}
            end,
            loop(Port);
        stop ->
            Port ! {self(), close},
            receive
                {Port, closed} ->
                    exit(normal)
            end;
        {'EXIT', Port, Reason} ->
            io:format("~p ~n", [Reason]),
            exit(port_terminated)
    end.

encode({twice, X})  -> [1, X];
encode({sum, X, Y}) -> [2, X, Y].

decode([Int]) -> Int.
```

If we compare this program to the earlier version that acts as a port interface, we'll see that they are almost identical.

The driver program consists mostly of code to populate elements in the driver struct. The command make example1_drv.so in the makefile given earlier can be used to build the shared library.

`ports/example1_lid.c`

```c
/* example1_lid.c */

#include <stdio.h>
#include "erl_driver.h"

typedef struct {
    ErlDrvPort port;
} example_data;

static ErlDrvData example_drv_start(ErlDrvPort port, char *buff)
{
    example_data* d = (example_data*)driver_alloc(sizeof(example_data));
    d->port = port;
    return (ErlDrvData)d;
}
```

```
static void example_drv_stop(ErlDrvData handle)
{
    driver_free((char*)handle);
}

static void example_drv_output(ErlDrvData handle, char *buff, int bufflen)
{
    example_data* d = (example_data*)handle;
    char fn = buff[0], arg = buff[1], res;
    if (fn == 1) {
      res = twice(arg);
    } else if (fn == 2) {
      res = sum(buff[1], buff[2]);
    }
    driver_output(d->port, &res, 1);
}

ErlDrvEntry example_driver_entry = {
    NULL,                /* F_PTR init, N/A */
    example_drv_start,   /* L_PTR start, called when port is opened */
    example_drv_stop,    /* F_PTR stop, called when port is closed */
    example_drv_output,  /* F_PTR output, called when erlang has sent
                            data to the port */
    NULL,                /* F_PTR ready_input,
                            called when input descriptor ready to read*/
    NULL,                /* F_PTR ready_output,
                            called when output descriptor ready to write */
    "example1_drv",      /* char *driver_name, the argument to open_port */
    NULL,                /* F_PTR finish, called when unloaded */
    NULL,                /* F_PTR control, port_command callback */
    NULL,                /* F_PTR timeout, reserved */
    NULL                 /* F_PTR outputv, reserved */
};

DRIVER_INIT(example_drv) /* must match name in driver_entry */
{
    return &example_driver_entry;
}
```

Here's how we run the program:

```
1> c(example1_lid).
{ok,example1_lid}
2> example1_lid:start().
<0.41.0>
3> example1_lid:twice(50).
100
4> example1_lid:sum(10, 20).
30
```

12.5 Notes

In this chapter, we have looked at the use of ports for interfacing an external program to Erlang. In addition to the port protocol, we can use a number of BIFs to manipulate ports. These are described in the manual page for the erlang module.

At this point you're probably wondering how to pass complex data structures between Erlang and an external program. How can you send strings, tuples, and so on, between Erlang and the outside world? Unfortunately, there is no simple answer to this question; all that ports provide is a low-level mechanism for transferring a sequence of bytes between Erlang and the outside world. This, incidentally, is the same problem as encountered in socket programming. A socket provides a stream of bytes between two applications; how these applications interpret these bytes is up to the application.

However, several libraries included in the Erlang distribution simplify the job of interfacing Erlang to external programs; these include the following:

http://www.erlang.org/doc/pdf/erl_interface.pdf

> Erl interface (ei) is a set of C routines and macros for encoding and decoding the Erlang external format. On the Erlang side, an Erlang program uses term_to_binary to serialize an Erlang term, and on the C side the routines in ei can be used to unpack this binary. ei can also be used to construct a binary, which the Erlang side can unpack with binary_to_term.

http://www.erlang.org/doc/pdf/ic.pdf

> The Erlang IDL Compiler (ic). The ic application is an Erlang implementation of an OMG IDL complier.

http://www.erlang.org/doc/pdf/jinterface.pdf

> Jinteface is a set of tools for interfacing Java to Erlang. It provides a full mapping of Erlang types to Java objects, encoding and decoding Erlang terms, linking to Erlang processes, and so on, as well as a wide range of additional features.

Chapter 13

Programming with Files

In this chapter, we'll look at some of the most commonly used functions for manipulating files. The standard Erlang release has a large number of functions for working with files. We're going to concentrate on the small fraction of these that I use to write most of my programs. We'll also see a few examples of the techniques I use for writing efficient file handling code. In addition, I'll briefly mention some of the more rarely used file operations so you'll know they exist. If you want more details, consult the manual pages.

We'll concentrate on the following areas:

- Organization of the libraries
- Different ways of reading a file
- Different ways of writing to a file
- Directory operations
- Finding information about a file

13.1 Organization of the Libraries

The functions for file manipulation are organized into four modules:

file   This has routines for opening, closing, reading, and writing files; listing directories; and so on. A short summary of some of the more frequently used functions in file is shown in Figure 13.1, on page 221. For full details, consult the manual page for the file module.

filename

> This module has routines that manipulate filenames in a platform-independent manner, so you can run the same code on a number of different operating systems.

filelib

> This module is an extension to file, which contains a number of utilities for listing files, checking file types, and so on. Most of these are written using the functions in file.

io   This module has routines that work on opened files. It contains routines for parsing data in a file and writing formatted data to a file.

13.2   The Different Ways of Reading a File

Let's look at some options when it comes to reading files. We'll start by writing five little programs that open a file and input the data in a number of different ways.

The contents of a file is just sequence of bytes. Whether they mean anything depends upon the interpretation of these bytes.

To demonstrate this, we'll use the same input file for all our examples. It actually contains a sequence of Erlang terms. Depending upon how we open and read the file, we can interpret the contents as a sequence of Erlang terms, as a sequence of text lines, or as raw chunks of binary data with no particular interpretation.

Here's the raw data in the file:

data1.dat
```
{person, "joe", "armstrong",
      [{occupation, programmer},
       {favoriteLanguage, erlang}]}.

{cat, {name, "zorro"},
     {owner, "joe"}}.
```

Now we'll read parts of this file in a number of ways.

Function	Description
change_group	Change group of a file.
change_owner	Change owner of a file.
change_time	Change the modification or last access time of a file.
close	Close a file.
consult	Read Erlang terms from a file.
copy	Copy file contents.
del_dir	Delete a directory.
delete	Delete a file.
eval	Evaluate Erlang expressions in a file.
format_error	Return a descriptive string for an error reason.
get_cwd	Get the current working directory.
list_dir	List files in a directory.
make_dir	Make a directory.
make_link	Make a hard link to a file.
make_symlink	Make a symbolic link to a file or directory.
open	Open a file.
position	Set position in a file.
pread	Read from a file at a certain position.
pwrite	Write to a file at a certain position.
read	Read from a file.
read_file	Read an entire file.
read_file_info	Get information about a file.
read_link	See what a link is pointing to.
read_link_info	Get information about a link or file.
rename	Rename a file.
script	Evaluate and return the value of Erlang expressions in a file.
set_cwd	Set the current working directory.
sync	Synchronize the in-memory state of a file with that on the physical medium.
truncate	Truncate a file.
write	Write to a file.
write_file	Write an entire file.
write_file_info	Change information about a file.

Figure 13.1: SUMMARY OF FILE OPERATIONS (IN MODULE FILE)

Reading All the Terms in the File

data1.dat contains a sequence of Erlang terms; we can read all of these by calling file:consult as follows:

```
1> file:consult("data1.dat").
{ok,[{person,"joe",
            "armstrong",
       [{occupation,programmer},{favoriteLanguage,erlang}]},
     {cat,{name,"zorro"},{owner,"joe"}}]}
```

file:consult(File) assumes that File contains a sequence of Erlang terms. It returns {ok, [Term]} if it can read all the terms in the file; otherwise, it returns {error, Reason}.

Reading the Terms in the File One at a Time

If we want to read the terms in a file one at a time, we first open the file with file:open, then we read the individual terms with io:read until we reach the end of file, and finally we close the file with file:close.

Here's a shell session that shows what happens when we read the terms in a file one at a time:

```
1> {ok, S} = file:open("data1.dat", read).
{ok,<0.36.0>}
2> io:read(S, '').
{ok,{person,"joe",
       "armstrong",
       [{occupation,programmer},{favoriteLanguage,erlang}]}}
3> io:read(S, '').
{ok,{cat,{name,"zorro"},{owner,"joe"}}}
4> io:read(S, '').
eof
5> file:close(S)
```

The functions we've used here are as follows:

@spec file:open(File, read) => {ok, IoDevice} | {error, Why}

Tries to open File for reading. It returns {ok, IoDevice} if it can open the file; otherwise, it returns {error, Reason}. IoDevice is an IO device that is used to access the file.

@spec io:read(IoDevice, Prompt) => {ok, Term} | {error,Why} | eof

Reads an Erlang term Term from IoDevice. Prompt is ignored if IoDevice represents an opened file. Prompt is used only to provide a prompt if we use io:read to read from standard input.

@spec file:close(IoDevice) => ok | {error, Why}

Closes IoDevice.

Using these routines we could have implemented file:consult, which we used in the previous section. Here's how file:consult might have been defined:

`lib_misc.erl`

```
consult(File) ->
    case file:open(File, read) of
        {ok, S} ->
            Val = consult1(S),
            file:close(S),
            {ok, Val};
        {error, Why} ->
            {error, Why}
    end.

consult1(S) ->
    case io:read(S, '') of
        {ok, Term} -> [Term|consult1(S)];
        eof        -> [];
        Error      -> Error
    end.
```

This is *not* how file:consult is actually defined. The standard libraries use an improved version with better error reporting.

Now is a good time to look at the version included in the standard libraries. If you've understood the earlier version, then you should find it easy to follow the code in the libraries. There's only one problem. How can we find the source of the file.erl code? To do this, we use the function code:which, which can locate the object code for any module that has been loaded.

```
1> code:which(file).
"/usr/local/lib/erlang/lib/kernel-2.11.2/ebin/file.beam"
```

In the standard release, each library has two subdirectories. One, called src, contains the source code. The other, called ebin, contains compiled Erlang code. So, the source code for file.erl should be in the following directory:

/usr/local/lib/erlang/lib/kernel-2.11.2/src/file.erl

When all else fails and the manual pages don't provide the answers to all your questions about the code, then a quick peek at the source code can often reveal the answer. Now I know this shouldn't happen, but we're all human, and sometimes the documentation doesn't answer all your questions.

Reading the Lines in a File One at a Time

If we change io:read to io:get_line, we can read the lines in the file one at a time. io:get_line reads characters until it encounters a line-feed character or end-of-file. Here's an example:

```
1> {ok, S} = file:open("data1.dat", read).
{ok,<0.43.0>}
2> io:get_line(S, '').
"{person, \"joe\", \"armstrong\",\n"
3> io:get_line(S, '').
"\t[{occupation, programmer},\n"
4> io:get_line(S, '').
"\t {favoriteLanguage, erlang}]}.\n"
5> io:get_line(S, '').
"\n"
6> io:get_line(S, '').
"{cat, {name, \"zorro\"},\n"
7> io:get_line(S, '').
"      {owner, \"joe\"}}.\n"
8> io:get_line(S, '').
eof
9> file:close(S).
ok
```

Reading the Entire File into a Binary

You can use file:read_file(File) to read an entire file into a binary using a single atomic operation:

```
1> file:read_file("data1.dat").
{ok,<<"{person, \"joe\", \"armstrong\""...>>}
```

file:read_file(File) returns {ok, Bin} if it succeeds and returns {error, Why} otherwise.

This is by far the most efficient way of reading files, and it's a method that I use a lot. For most operations, I read the entire file into memory in one operation, manipulate the contents, and store the file in a single operation (using file:write_file). We'll give an example of this later.

Reading a File with Random Access

If the file we want to read is very large or if it contains binary data in some externally defined format, then we can open the file in raw mode and read any portion of it using file:pread.

Here's an example:

```
1> {ok, S} = file:open("data1.dat", [read,binary,raw]).
{ok,{file_descriptor,prim_file,{#Port<0.106>,5}}}
```

```
2> file:pread(S, 22, 46).
{ok,<<"rong\",\n\t[{occupation, progr...>>}
3> file:pread(S, 1, 10).
{ok,<<"person, \"j">>}
4> file:pread(S, 2, 10).
{ok,<<"erson, \"jo">>}
5> file:close(S).
```

file:pread(IoDevice, Start, Len) reads exactly Len bytes from IoDevice starting at byte Start (the bytes in the file are numbered so that the first byte
in the file is at position 1). It returns {ok, Bin} or {error, Why}.

Finally, we'll use the routines for random file access to write a utility
routine that we'll need in the next chapter. In Section 14.7, *A SHOUT-
cast Server*, on page 259, we'll develop a simple SHOUTcast server (this
is a server for so-called streaming media, in this case for streaming
MP3). Part of this server needs to be able to find the artist and track
names that are embedded in an MP3 file. We'll do this in the next section.

Reading ID3 Tags

MP3 is a binary format used for storing compressed audio data. MP3
files do not themselves contain information about the content of the
file, so, for example, in an MP3 file that contains music, the name of the
artist who recorded the music is not contained in the audio data. This
data (the track name, artist name, and so on) is stored inside the MP3
files in a tagged block format known as ID3. ID3 tags were invented by a
programmer called Eric Kemp to store metadata describing the content
of an audio file. There are actually a number of ID3 formats, but for our
purposes, we'll write code to access only the two simplest forms of ID3
tag, namely, the ID3v1 and ID3v1.1 tags.

The ID3v1 tag has a simple structure—the last 128 bytes of the file contain a fixed-length tag. The first 3 bytes contain the ASCII characters
TAG, followed by a number of fixed-length fields. The entire 128 bytes is
packed as follows:

Length	Contents
3	Header containing the characters *TAG*
30	Title
30	Artist
30	Album
4	Year
30	Comment
1	Genre

In the ID3v1 tag there was no place to add a track number. A method for doing this was suggested by Michael Mutschler, in the ID3v1.1 format. The idea was to change the 30-byte comment field to the following:

Length	Contents
28	Comment
1	0 (a zero)
1	Track number

It's easy to write a program that tries to read the ID3v1 tags in an MP3 file and matches the fields using the binary bit-matching syntax. Here's the program:

`id3_v1.erl`

```erlang
-module(id3_v1).
-import(lists, [filter/2, map/2, reverse/1]).
-export([test/0, dir/1, read_id3_tag/1]).

test() -> dir("/home/joe/music_keep").

dir(Dir) ->
    Files = lib_find:files(Dir, "*.mp3", true),
    L1 = map(fun(I) ->
                     {I, (catch read_id3_tag(I))}
              end,  Files),
    %% L1 = [{File, Parse}] where Parse = error | [{Tag,Val}]
    %% we now have to remove all the entries from L where
    %% Parse = error. We can do this with a filter operation
    L2 = filter(fun({_,error}) -> false;
                   (_) -> true
                end, L1),
    lib_misc:dump("mp3data", L2).

read_id3_tag(File) ->
    case file:open(File, [read,binary,raw]) of
        {ok, S} ->
            Size = filelib:file_size(File),
            {ok, B2} = file:pread(S, Size-128, 128),
            Result = parse_v1_tag(B2),
            file:close(S),
            Result;
        Error ->
            {File, Error}
    end.

parse_v1_tag(<<$T,$A,$G,
              Title:30/binary, Artist:30/binary,
              Album:30/binary, _Year:4/binary,
              _Comment:28/binary, 0:8,Track:8,_Genre:8>>) ->
```

```
    {"ID3v1.1",
     [{track,Track}, {title,trim(Title)},
      {artist,trim(Artist)}, {album, trim(Album)}]};
parse_v1_tag(<<$T,$A,$G,
             Title:30/binary, Artist:30/binary,
             Album:30/binary, _Year:4/binary,
             _Comment:30/binary,_Genre:8>>) ->
    {"ID3v1",
     [{title,trim(Title)},
      {artist,trim(Artist)}, {album, trim(Album)}]};
parse_v1_tag(_) ->
    error.

trim(Bin) ->
    list_to_binary(trim_blanks(binary_to_list(Bin))).

trim_blanks(X) -> reverse(skip_blanks_and_zero(reverse(X))).

skip_blanks_and_zero([$\s|T]) -> skip_blanks_and_zero(T);
skip_blanks_and_zero([0|T])   -> skip_blanks_and_zero(T);
skip_blanks_and_zero(X)       -> X.
```

The main entry point to our program is id3_v1:dir(Dir). The first thing we do is find all our MP3 files by calling lib_find:find(Dir, "*.mp3", true) (shown later in Section 13.8, *A Find Utility*, on page 235), which recursively scans the directories under Dir looking for MP3 files. Having found the file, we parse the tags by calling read_id3_tag. Parsing is greatly simplified because we can merely use the bit-matching syntax to do the parsing for us, and then we can trim the artist and track names by removing trailing whitespace and zero-padding characters, which delimit the character strings. Finally, we dump the results in a file for later use (lib_misc:dump is described in Section E.2, *Debugging Techniques*, on page 423).

Most music files are tagged with ID3v1 tags, even if they also have ID3v2, v3, and v4 tags—the later taggings standards added a differently formatted tag to the beginning of the file (or more rarely in the middle of the file). Tagging programs often appear to add both ID3v1 tags and additional (and more difficult to read) tags at the start of the file. For our purposes, we'll be concerned only with files containing valid ID3v1 and ID3v1.1 tags.

Now that we know how to read a file, we can move to the different ways of writing to a file.

13.3 The Different Ways of Writing to a File

Writing to a file involves pretty much the same operations as reading a file. Let's look at them.

Write a List of Terms to a File

Suppose we want to create a file that we can read with file:consult. The standard libraries don't actually contain a function for this, so we'll write our own. Let's call this function unconsult.[1]

`lib_misc.erl`
```erlang
unconsult(File, L) ->
    {ok, S} = file:open(File, write),
    lists:foreach(fun(X) -> io:format(S, "~p.~n",[X]) end, L),
    file:close(S).
```

We can run this in the shell to create a file called test1.dat:

```erlang
1> lib_misc:unconsult("test1.dat",
                       [{cats,["zorrow","daisy"]},
                        {weather,snowing}]).
ok
```

Let's check it's OK:

```erlang
2> file:consult("test1.dat").
{ok,[{cats,["zorrow","daisy"]},{weather,snowing}]}
```

To implement unconsult, we opened the file in write mode and then used io:format(S, "~p.~n", [X]) to write terms to the file.

io:format is the workhorse for creating formatted output. To produce formatted output, we call the following:

@spec io:format(IoDevice, Format, Args) -> ok

> IoDevice is an IO device (which must have been opened in write mode), Format is a string containing formatting codes, and Args is a list of items to be output.

For each item in Args, there must be a formatting command in the format string. Formatting commands begin with a tilde (~) character. Here are some of the most commonly used formatting commands:

~n   Write a line feed. ~n is smart and writes a line feed in a platform-dependent way. So on a Unix machine, ~n will write ASCII (10)

---

1. The nice thing about writing a book is I can choose any module or function names I want and nobody can argue.

to the output stream, and on a Windows machine it will write carriage-return line-feed ASCII (13, 10) to the output stream.

~p   Pretty-print the argument.

~s   The argument is a string.

~w   Write data with the standard syntax. This is used to output Erlang terms.

The format string has about ten quadzillion arguments that nobody in their right mind can remember. You'll find a complete list in the man page for the module io. I remember only ~p, ~s, and ~n. If you start with these, you won't have many problems.

Aside

I lied—you'll probably need more than just ~p, ~s, and ~n. Here are a few examples:

Format	Result
io:format("|~10s|~n", ["abc"])	|⌴⌴⌴⌴⌴⌴⌴abc|
io:format("|~-10s|~n", ["abc"])	|abc⌴⌴⌴⌴⌴⌴⌴|
io:format("|~10.3.+s|~n",["abc"])	|+++++++abc|
io:format("|~10.10.+s|~n",["abc"])	|abc+++++++|
io:format("|~10.7.+s|~n",["abc"])	|+++abc++++|

Writing Lines to a File

This is similar to the previous example—we just use a different formatting command:

```
1> {ok, S} = file:open("test2.dat", write).
{ok,<0.62.0>}
2> io:format(S, "~s~n", ["Hello readers"]).
ok
3> io:format(S, "~w~n", [123]).
ok
4> io:format(S, "~s~n", ["that's it"]).
ok
5> file:close(S).
```

This created a file called test2.dat with the following contents:

```
Hello readers
123
that's it
```

Writing an Entire File in One Operation

This is the most efficient way of writing to a file. file:write_file(File, IO) writes the data in IO, which is an IO list to File. (An IO list is a list whose elements are IO lists, binaries, or integers from 0 to 255. When an IO list is output, it is automatically "flattened," which means that all the list brackets are removed.) This method is extremely efficient and is one that I often use. The program in the next section illustrates this.

Listing URLs from a File

Let's write a simple function called urls2htmlFile(L, File) that takes a list of URLs, L, and creates an HTML file, where the URLs are presented as clickable links. This lets us play with the technique of creating an entire file in a single IO operation.

We'll write our program in the module scavenge_urls. First here's the program header:

`scavenge_urls.erl`
```erlang
-module(scavenge_urls).
-export([urls2htmlFile/2, bin2urls/1]).
-import(lists, [reverse/1, reverse/2, map/2]).

urls2htmlFile(Urls, File) ->
    file:write_file(File, urls2html(Urls)).

bin2urls(Bin) -> gather_urls(binary_to_list(Bin), []).
```

The program has two entry points. urls2htmlFile(Urls, File) takes a list of URLs and creates an HTML file containing clickable links for each URL, and bin2urls(Bin) searches through a binary and returns a list of all the URLs contained in the binary. urls2htmlFile is as follows:

`scavenge_urls.erl`
```erlang
urls2html(Urls) -> [h1("Urls"),make_list(Urls)].

h1(Title) -> ["<h1>", Title, "</h1>\n"].

make_list(L) ->
    ["<ul>\n",
     map(fun(I) -> ["<li>",I,"</li>\n"] end, L),
     "</ul>\n"].
```

This code returns a deep list of characters. Note we make no attempt to flatten the list (which would be rather inefficient); we make a deep list of characters and just throw it at the output routines. When we write a deep list to a file with file:write_file, the IO system automatically flattens the list (that is, it outputs only the characters embedded in the lists

and not the list brackets themselves). Finally, here's the code to extract
the URLs from a binary:

`scavenge_urls.erl`

```erlang
gather_urls("<a href" ++ T, L) ->
    {Url, T1} = collect_url_body(T, reverse("<a href")),
    gather_urls(T1, [Url|L]);
gather_urls([_|T], L) ->
    gather_urls(T, L);
gather_urls([], L) ->
    L.


collect_url_body("</a>" ++ T, L) -> {reverse(L, "</a>"), T};
collect_url_body([H|T], L)       -> collect_url_body(T, [H|L]);
collect_url_body([], _)          -> {[],[]}.
```

To run this, we need to get some data to parse. The input data (a binary)
is the content of an HTML page, so we need an HTML page to scavenge.
For this we'll use socket_examples:nano_get_url (see Section 14.1, *Fetching Data from a Server*, on page 240):

We'll do this step by step in the shell:

```erlang
1> B = socket_examples:nano_get_url("www.erlang.org"),
   L = scavenge_urls:bin2urls(B),
   scavenge_urls:urls2htmlFile(L, "gathered.html").
ok
```

This produces the file gathered.html:

`gathered.html`

```html
<h1>Urls</h1>
<ul>
<li><a href="old_news.html">Older news.....</a></li>
<li><a href="http://www.erlang-consulting.com/training_fs.html">here</a></li>
<li><a href="project/megaco/">Megaco home</a></li>
<li><a href="EPLICENSE">Erlang Public License (EPL)</a></li>
<li><a href="user.html#smtp_client-1.0">smtp_client-1.0</a></li>
<li><a href="download-stats/">download statistics graphs</a></li>
<li><a href="project/test_server">Erlang/OTP Test
Server</a></li>
<li><a href="http://www.erlang.se/euc/06/">proceedings</a></li>
<li><a href="/doc/doc-5.5.2/doc/highlights.html">
       Read more in the release highlights.
</a></li>
<li><a href="index.html"><img src="images/erlang.gif"
    border="0" alt="Home"></a></li>
</ul>
```

Writing to a Random-Access File

Writing to a file in random-access mode is similar to reading. First, we have to open the file in write mode. Next, we use file:pwrite(Position, Bin) to write to the file.

Here's an example:

```
1> {ok, S} = file:open("...", [raw,write,binary])
{ok, ...}
2> file:pwrite(S, 10, <<"new">>)
ok
3> file:close(S)
ok
```

This writes the characters *new* starting at an offset of 10 in the file, overwriting the original content.

13.4 Directory Operations

Three functions in file are used for directory operations. list_dir(Dir) is used to produce a list of the files in Dir, make_dir(Dir) creates a new directory, and del_dir(Dir) deletes a directory.

If we run list_dir on the code directory that I'm using to write this book, we'll see something like the following:

```
1> cd("/home/joe/book/erlang/Book/code").
/home/joe/book/erlang/Book/code
ok
2> file:list_dir(".").
{ok,["id3_v1.erl~",
     "update_binary_file.beam",
     "benchmark_assoc.beam",
     "id3_v1.erl",
     "scavenge_urls.beam",
     "benchmark_mk_assoc.beam",
     "benchmark_mk_assoc.erl",
     "id3_v1.beam",
     "assoc_bench.beam",
     "lib_misc.beam",
     "benchmark_assoc.erl",
     "update_binary_file.erl",
     "foo.dets",
     "big.tmp",
     ..
```

Observe that there is no particular order to the files and no indication as to whether the files in the directory are files or directories, what the sizes are, and so on.

To find out about the individual files in the directory listing, we'll use file:read_file_info, which is the subject of the next section.

13.5 Finding Information About a File

To find out about a file F, we call file:read_file_info(F). This returns {ok, Info} if F is a valid file or directory name. Info is a record of type #file_info, which is defined as follows:

```
-record(file_info,
        {size,            % Size of file in bytes.
         type,            % Atom: device, directory, regular,
                          % or other.
         access,          % Atom: read, write, read_write, or none.
         atime,           % The local time the file was last read:
                          % {{Year, Mon, Day}, {Hour, Min, Sec}}.
         mtime,           % The local time the file was last written.
         ctime,           % The interpretation of this time field
                          % is dependent on operating system.
                          % On Unix it is the last time the file or
                          % or the inode was changed.  On Windows,
                          % it is the creation time.
         mode,            % Integer: File permissions.  On Windows,
                          % the owner permissions will be duplicated
                          % for group and user.
         links,           % Number of links to the file (1 if the
                          % filesystem doesn't support links).
         major_device,    % Integer: Identifies the file system (Unix),
                          % or the drive number (A: = 0, B: = 1) (Windows).
```

Note: The mode and access fields overlap. You can use mode to set several file attributes in a single operation, whereas you can use access for simpler operations.

To find the size and type of a file, we call read_file_info as in the following example (note we have to include file.hrl, which contains the definition of the #file_info record):

lib_misc.erl
```
-include_lib("kernel/include/file.hrl").
file_size_and_type(File) ->
    case file:read_file_info(File) of
        {ok, Facts} ->
            {Facts#file_info.type, Facts#file_info.size};
        _ ->
            error
    end.
```

Now we can augment the directory listing returned by list_file by adding information about the files in the function ls() as follows:

`lib_misc.erl`

```
ls(Dir) ->
    {ok, L} = file:list_dir(Dir),
    map(fun(I) -> {I, file_size_and_type(I)} end, sort(L)).
```

Now when we list the files, they are ordered and contain additional useful information:

```
1> lib_misc:ls(".").
[{"Makefile",{regular,1244}},
 {"README",{regular,1583}},
 {"abc.erl",{regular,105}},
 {"alloc_test.erl",{regular,303}},
 ...
 {"socket_dist",{directory,4096}},
 ...
```

As a convenience, the module filelib exports a few small routines such as file_size(File) and is_dir(X). These are merely interfaces to file:read_file_info. If we just want to the size of a file, it is more convenient to call filelib:file_size than to call file:read_file_info and unpack the elements of the #file_info record.

13.6 Copying and Deleting Files

file:copy(Source, Destination) copies the file Source to Destination.

file:delete(File) deletes File.

13.7 Bits and Pieces

So far we've mentioned most of the functions that I use on a day-to-day basis for manipulating files. It's actually rare that I need to look up the manual pages to find out more information. So, what have I left out that you might need to know about? I'll give you a brief list of the major omissions. For the details, see the manual pages.

File modes

When we open a file with file:open, we open the file in a particular mode or a combination of modes. There are actually many more modes than we might think; for example, it's possible to read and write gzip-compressed files with the compressed mode flag, and so on. The full list is in the manual pages.

Modification times, groups, symlinks

> We can set all of these with routines in file.

Error codes

> I've rather blandly said that all errors are of the form {error, Why}; in fact, Why is an atom (for example, enoent means a file does not exist, and so on)—there are a large number of error codes, and they are all described in the manual pages.

filename

> The filename module has some useful routines for ripping apart full filenames in directories and finding the file extensions, and so on, as well as for rebuilding filenames for the component parts. All this is done in a platform-independent manner.

filelib

> The filelib module has a small number of routines that can save us some work. For example, filelib:ensure_dir(Name) ensures that all parent directories for the given file or directory name Name exist, trying to create them if necessary.

13.8 A Find Utility

As a final example, we'll use file:list_dir and file:read_file_info to make a general-purpose "find" utility.

The main entry point to this module is as follows:

```
lib_find:files(Dir, RegExp, Recursive, Fun, Acc0)
```

The arguments are as follows:

Dir

> The directory name to start the file search in.

RegExp

> A regular expression[2] to test the files we have found. If the files we encounter match this regular expression, then Fun(File, Acc) will be called, where File is the name of the file that matches the regular expression.

Recursive = true | false

> A flag that determines whether search should recurse into the subdirectories of the current directory in the search path.

---

2. See the man pages for the module regexp for the syntax of regular expressions.

Fun(File, AccIn) -> AccOut

> A function that is applied to the File if regExp matches File. Acc is an accumulator whose initial value is Acc0. Each time Fun is called, it must return a new value of the accumulator that is passed into Fun the next time it is called. The final value of the accumulator is the return value of lib_find:files/5

We can pass any function we want into lib_find:files/5. For example, we can build a list of files using the following function, passing it an empty list initially:

```
fun(File, Acc) -> [File|Acc] end
```

The module entry point lib_find:files(Dir, ShellRegExp, Flag) provides a simplified entry point for a more common usage of the program. Here ShellRegExp is a simplified form of regular expression that is easier to write than the full form of regular expression.

As an example of the short form of calling sequence, the following call:

```
lib_find:files(Dir, "*.erl", true)
```

recursively finds all Erlang files under Dir. If the last argument had been false, then only the Erlang files in the directory Dir would have been found—it would not look in subdirectories.

Finally, here's the code:

`lib_find.erl`

```erlang
-module(lib_find).
-export([files/3, files/5]).
-import(lists, [reverse/1]).

-include_lib("kernel/include/file.hrl").

files(Dir, Re, Flag) ->
    Re1 = regexp:sh_to_awk(Re),
    reverse(files(Dir, Re1, Flag, fun(File, Acc) ->[File|Acc] end, [])).

files(Dir, Reg, Recursive, Fun, Acc) ->
    case file:list_dir(Dir) of
        {ok, Files} -> find_files(Files, Dir, Reg, Recursive, Fun, Acc);
        {error, _}  -> Acc
    end.
```

```erlang
find_files([File|T], Dir, Reg, Recursive, Fun, Acc0) ->
    FullName = filename:join([Dir,File]),
    case file_type(FullName) of
        regular ->
            case regexp:match(FullName, Reg) of
                {match, _, _}  ->
                    Acc = Fun(FullName, Acc0),
                    find_files(T, Dir, Reg, Recursive, Fun, Acc);
                _ ->
                    find_files(T, Dir, Reg, Recursive, Fun, Acc0)
            end;
        directory ->
            case Recursive of
                true ->
                    Acc1 = files(FullName, Reg, Recursive, Fun, Acc0),
                    find_files(T, Dir, Reg, Recursive, Fun, Acc1);
                false ->
                    find_files(T, Dir, Reg, Recursive, Fun, Acc0)
            end;
        error ->
            find_files(T, Dir, Reg, Recursive, Fun, Acc0)
    end;
find_files([], _, _, _, _, A) ->
    A.

file_type(File) ->
    case file:read_file_info(File) of
        {ok, Facts} ->
            case Facts#file_info.type of
                regular   -> regular;
                directory -> directory;
                _         -> error
            end;
        _ ->
            error
    end.
```

Chapter 14

Programming with Sockets

Most of the more interesting programs that I write involve sockets one way or another. A socket is a communication endpoint that allows machines to communicate over the Internet using the Internet Protocol (IP). In this chapter, we'll concentrate on the two core protocols of the Internet: *Transmission Control Protocol* (TCP) and *User Datagram Protocol* (UDP).

UDP lets applications send short messages (called *datagrams*) to each other, but there is no guarantee of delivery for these messages. They can also arrive out of order. TCP, on the other hand, provides a reliable stream of bytes that are delivered in order as long as the connection is established.

Why is programming with sockets fun? Because it allows applications to interact with other machines on the Internet, which has far more potential than just performing local operations.

There are two main libraries for programming with sockets: gen_tcp for programming TCP applications and gen_udp for programming UDP applications.

In this chapter, we'll see how to program client and servers using TCP and UDP sockets. We'll go through the different forms of servers that are possible (parallel, sequential, blocking, and nonblocking) and see how to program traffic-shaping applications that can control the flow of data to the application.

14.1 Using TCP

We'll start our adventures in socket programming by looking at a simple TCP program that fetches data from a server. After this, we'll write a simple sequential TCP server and show how it can be parallelized to handle multiple parallel sessions.

Fetching Data from a Server

Let's start by writing a little function[1] that uses a TCP socket to fetch an HTML page from http://www.google.com:

`socket_examples.erl`

```erlang
nano_get_url() ->
    nano_get_url("www.google.com").

nano_get_url(Host) ->
❶    {ok,Socket} = gen_tcp:connect(Host,80,[binary, {packet, 0}]),
❷    ok = gen_tcp:send(Socket, "GET / HTTP/1.0\r\n\r\n"),
    receive_data(Socket, []).

receive_data(Socket, SoFar) ->
    receive
❸        {tcp,Socket,Bin} ->
            receive_data(Socket, [Bin|SoFar]);
❹        {tcp_closed,Socket} ->
❺            list_to_binary(reverse(SoFar))
    end.
```

How does this work?

❶   We open a TCP socket to port 80 of http://www.google.com by calling gen_tcp:connect. The argument binary in the connect call tells the system to open the socket in "binary" mode and deliver all data to the application as binaries. {packet,0} means the TCP data is delivered directly to the application in an unmodified form.

❷   We call gen_tcp:send and send the message GET / HTTP/1.0\r\n\r\n to the socket. Then we wait for a reply. The reply doesn't come all in one packet but comes fragmented, a bit at a time. These fragments will be received as a sequence of messages that are sent to the process that opened (or controls) the socket.

---

1. The standard library function in the Erlang distribution, http:request(Uri), achieves the same result, but we want to show how this can be done using the library functions in gen_tcp.

❸   We receive a {tcp,Socket,Bin} message. The third argument in this tuple is a binary. This is because we opened the socket in binary mode. This message is one of the data fragments sent to us from the web server. We add it to the list of fragments we have received so far and wait for the next fragment.

❹   We receive a {tcp_closed, Socket} message. This happens when the server has finished sending us data.[2]

❺   When all the fragments have come, we've stored them in the wrong order, so we reverse the order and concatenate all the fragments.

Let's just test that it works:

```
1> B = socket_examples:nano_get_url().
<<"HTTP/1.0 302 Found\r\nLocation: http://www.google.se/\r\n
    Cache-Control: private\r\nSet-Cookie: PREF=ID=b57a2c:TM"...>>
```

Note: When you run nano_get_url, the result is a binary, so you'll see is what a binary looks like when pretty printed in the Erlang shell. When binaries are pretty printed, all control characters are displayed in an escaped format. And the binary is truncated, which is indicated by the three dots (...>>) at the end of the printout. If you want to see all of the binary, you can print it with io:format or break it into pieces with string:tokens:

```
2> io:format("~p~n",[B]).
<<"HTTP/1.0 302 Found\r\nLocation: http://www.google.se/\r\n
    Cache-Control: private\r\nSet-Cookie: PREF=ID=b57a2c:TM"
    TM=176575171639526:LM=1175441639526:S=gkfTrK6AFkybT3;
    expires=Sun, 17-Jan-2038 19:14:07
    ... several lines omitted ...
>>
3>string:tokens(binary_to_list(B),"\r\n").
["HTTP/1.0 302 Found",
"Location: http://www.google.se/",
"Cache-Control: private",
"Set-Cookie: PREF=ID=ec7f0c7234b852dece4:TM=11713424639526:
 LM=1171234639526:S=gsdertTrK6AEybT3;
 expires=Sun, 17-Jan-2038 19:14:07 GMT; path=/; domain=.google.com",
"Content-Type: text/html",
"Server: GWS/2.1",
"Content-Length: 218",
"Date: Fri, 16 Feb 2007 15:25:26 GMT",
"Connection: Keep-Alive",
... lines omitted ...
```

---

2. This is true only for HTTP/1.0; for more modern versions of HTTP, a different strategy is used.

This is more or less how a web client works (with the emphasis on *less*—we would have to do a lot of work to correctly render the resulting data in a web browser). The previous code is, however, a good starting point for your own experiments. You might like to try modifying this code to fetch and store an entire website or automatically go and read your email. The possibilities are boundless.

Note that the code that reassembled the fragments looked like this:

```
receive_data(Socket, SoFar) ->
    receive
        {tcp,Socket,Bin} ->
            receive_data(Socket, [Bin|SoFar]);
        {tcp_closed,Socket} ->
            list_to_binary(reverse(SoFar))
    end.
```

So as the fragments arrive, we just add them to the head of the list SoFar. When all the fragments have arrived and the socket is closed, we reverse the list and concatenate all the fragments.

You might think that it would be better to write the code to accumulate the fragments like this:

```
receive_data(Socket, SoFar) ->
    receive
        {tcp,Socket,Bin} ->
            receive_data(Socket, list_to_binary([SoFar,Bin]));
        {tcp_closed,Socket} ->
            SoFar
    end.
```

This code is correct but less efficient than the original version. The reason is that in the latter version we are continually appending a new binary to the end of the buffer, which involves a lot of copying of data. It's much better to accumulate all the fragments in a list (which will end up in the wrong order) and then reverse the entire list and concatenate all the fragments in one operation.

A Simple TCP Server

In the previous section, we wrote a simple client. Now let's write a server.

This server opens port 2345 and then waits for a single message. This message is a binary that contains an Erlang term. The term is an Erlang string that contains an expression. The server evaluates the expression and sends the result to the client by writing the result to the socket.

How Can We Write a Web Server?

Writing something like a web client or a server is great fun. Sure, other people have already written these things, but if we really want to understand how they work, digging under the surface and finding out exactly how they work is very instructive. Who knows—maybe our web server will be better than the best. So, how can we get started?

To build a web server, or for that matter any software that implements a standard Internet protocol, we need to use the right tools and need to know exactly which protocols to implement.

In our example code that fetched a web page, how did we know that we had to open port 80, and how did we know that we had to send a GET / HTTP/1.0\r\n\r\n command to the server? The answer is easy. All the major protocols for Internet services are defined in *requests for comments* (RFCs). HTTP/1.0 is defined in RFC 1945. The official website for all RFCs is http://www.ietf.org (home of the Internet Engineering Task Force).

The other invaluable source of information is a *packet sniffer*. With a packet sniffer we can capture and analyze all the IP packets coming from and going to our application. Most packet sniffers include software that can decode and analyze the data in the packets and present the data in a meaningful manner. One of the most well-known and possibly the best is Wireshark (previously known as Ethereal), available from http://www.wireshark.org.

Armed with a packet sniffer dump and the appropriate RFCs, we're ready to write our next killer application.

To write this program (and indeed any program that runs over TCP/IP), we have to answer a few simple questions:

- How is the data organized? How do we know how much data makes up a single request or response?
- How is the data within a request or the response encoded and decoded? (Encoding the data is sometimes called *marshaling* and decoding the data is sometimes called *demarshaling*.)

TCP socket data is just an undifferentiated stream of bytes. During transmission, this data can be broken into arbitrary-sized fragments, so we need some convention so that we know how much data represents a single request or response.

In the Erlang case we use the simple convention that every logical request or response will be preceded by an N (1, 2, or 4) byte length count. This is the meaning of the {packet, N}[3] argument in the gen_tcp:connect and gen_tcp:listen functions. Note that the arguments to packet used by the client and the server *must* agree. If the server was opened with {packet,2} and the client with {packet,4}, then nothing would work.

Having opened a socket with the {packet,N} option, we don't need to worry about data fragmentation. The Erlang drivers will make sure that all fragmented data messages are reassembled to the correct lengths before delivering them to the application.

The next concern is data *encoding* and *decoding*. We'll use the simplest possible way of encoding and decoding messages using term_to_binary to encode Erlang terms and using its inverse, binary_to_term, to decode the data.

Note that the packaging convention and encoding rules needed for the client to talk to the server is achieved in two lines of code, by using the {packet,4} option when we open the socket and by using term_to_binary and its inverse to encode and decode the data.

The ease with which we can package and encode Erlang terms gives us a significant advantage over text-based methods such as HTTP or XML. Using the Erlang BIF term_to_binary and its inverse binary_to_term is typically more than an order of magnitude faster than performing

---

3. The word *packet* here refers to the length of an application request or response message, not to the physical packet seen on the wire.

an equivalent operation using XML terms and involves sending far less data. Now to the programs. First, here's a very simple server:

```
socket_examples.erl
```

```
start_nano_server() ->
❶    {ok, Listen} = gen_tcp:listen(2345, [binary, {packet, 4},
                                          {reuseaddr, true},
                                          {active, true}]),
❷    {ok, Socket} = gen_tcp:accept(Listen),
❸    gen_tcp:close(Listen),
     loop(Socket).

loop(Socket) ->
    receive
        {tcp, Socket, Bin} ->
            io:format("Server received binary = ~p~n",[Bin]),
❹            Str = binary_to_term(Bin),
            io:format("Server (unpacked)  ~p~n",[Str]),
❺            Reply = lib_misc:string2value(Str),
            io:format("Server replying = ~p~n",[Reply]),
❻            gen_tcp:send(Socket, term_to_binary(Reply)),
            loop(Socket);
        {tcp_closed, Socket} ->
            io:format("Server socket closed~n")
    end.
```

How does this work?

❶ First we call gen_tcp:listen to listen for a connection on port 2345 and set up the message packaging conventions. {packet, 4} means that each application message will be preceded by a 4-byte length header.

Then gen_tcp:listen(..) returns {ok, Socket} or {error, Why}, but we're interested only in the return case where we were able to open a socket. Therefore, we write the following code:

```
{ok, Listen} = gen_tcp:listen(...),
```

This causes the program to raise a pattern matching exception if gen_tcp:listen returns {error, ...}. In the successful case, this statement binds Listen to the new listening socket. There's only one thing we can do with a listening socket, and that's to use it as an argument to gen_tcp:accept.

❷ Now we call gen_tcp:accept(Listen). At this point the program will suspend and wait for a connection. When we get a connection, this function returns with the variable Socket bound to a socket that can be used to talk to the client that performed the connection.

❸   When accept returns, we immediately call gen_tcp:close(Listen). This closes down the listening socket, so the server will not accept any new connections. This does not affect the existing connection; it just prevents new connections.

❹   We decode the input data (unmarshaling).

❺   Then we evaluate the string.

❻   Then we encode the reply data (marshaling) and send it back to the socket.

Note that this program accepts only a single request; once the program has run to completion, then no more connections will be accepted.

This is the simplest of servers that illustrates how to package and encode the application data. It accepts a request, computes a reply, sends the reply, and terminates.

To test the server, we need a corresponding client:

`socket_examples.erl`

```
nano_client_eval(Str) ->
    {ok, Socket} =
        gen_tcp:connect("localhost", 2345,
                        [binary, {packet, 4}]),
    ok = gen_tcp:send(Socket, term_to_binary(Str)),
    receive
        {tcp,Socket,Bin} ->
            io:format("Client received binary = ~p~n",[Bin]),
            Val = binary_to_term(Bin),
            io:format("Client result = ~p~n",[Val]),
            gen_tcp:close(Socket)
    end.
```

To test our code, we'll run both the client and the server on the same machine, so the hostname in the gen_tcp:connect function is hardwired to localhost.

Note how term_to_binary is called in the client to encode the message and binary_to_term is called in the server to reconstruct the message.

To run this, we need to open two terminal windows and start an Erlang shell in each of the windows.

First we start the server:

```
1> socket_examples:start_nano_server().
```

We won't see any output in the server window, since nothing has happened yet. Then we move to the client window and give the following command:

```
1> socket_examples:nano_client_eval("list_to_tuple([2+3*4,10+20])").
```

In the server window, we should see the following:

```
Server received binary = <<131,107,0,28,108,105,115,116,95,116,
                           111,95,116,117,112,108,101,40,91,50,
                           43,51,42,52,44,49,48,43,50,48,93,41>>
Server (unpacked)  "list_to_tuple([2+3*4,10+20])"
Server replying = {14,30}
```

In the client window, we'll see this:

```
Client received binary = <<131,104,2,97,14,97,30>>
Client result = {14,30}
ok
```

Finally, in the server window, we'll see this:

```
Server socket closed
```

Improving the Server

In the previous section we made a server that accepted only one connection and then terminated. By changing this code slightly, we can make two different types of server:

1. A sequential server—one that accepts one connection at a time.

2. A parallel server—one that accepts multiple parallel connections at the same time.

The original code started like this:

```
start_nano_server() ->
    {ok, Listen} = gen_tcp:listen(...),
    {ok, Socket} = gen_tcp:accept(Listen),
    loop(Socket).
 ...
```

We'll be changing this to make our two server variants.

A Sequential Server

To make a sequential server, we change this code to the following:

```
start_seq_server() ->
    {ok, Listen} = gen_tcp:listen(...),
    seq_loop(Listen).

seq_loop(Listen) ->
    {ok, Socket} = gen_tcp:accept(Listen),
    loop(Socket),
    seq_loop(Listen).

loop(..) -> %% as before
```

This works pretty much as in the previous example, but since we want to serve more than one request, we leave the listening socket open and don't call gen_tcp:close(Listen). The other difference is that after loop(Socket) has finished, we call seq_loop(Listen) again, which waits for the next connection.

If a client tries to connect to the server while the server is busy with an existing connection, then the connection will be queued until the server has finished with the existing connection. If the number of queued connections exceeds the listen backlog, then the connection will be rejected.

We've shown only the code that starts the server. Stopping the server is easy (as is stopping a parallel server); just kill the process that started the server or servers. gen_tcp links itself to the controlling process, and if the controlling process dies, it closes the socket.

A Parallel Server

The trick to making a parallel server is to immediately spawn a new process each time gen_tcp:accept gets a new connection:

```
start_parallel_server() ->
    {ok, Listen} = gen_tcp:listen(...),
    spawn(fun() -> par_connect(Listen) end).

par_connect(Listen) ->
    {ok, Socket} = gen_tcp:accept(Listen),
    spawn(fun() -> par_connect(Listen) end),
    loop(Socket).

loop(..) -> %% as before
```

This code is similar to the sequential server that we saw earlier. The crucial difference is the addition of a spawn, which makes sure that we create a parallel process for each new socket connection. Now is a good chance to compare the two. You should look at the placement of the spawn statements and see how these turned a sequential server into a parallel server.

All three servers call gen_tcp:listen and gen_tcp:accept; the only difference is whether we call these functions in a parallel program or a sequential program.

Notes

Be aware of the following:

- The process that creates a socket (by calling gen_tcp:accept or gen_tcp:connect) is said to be the *controlling process* for that socket. All messages from the socket will be sent to the controlling process; if the controlling process dies, then the socket will be closed. The controlling process for a socket can be changed to NewPid by calling gen_tcp:controlling_process(Socket, NewPid).

- Our parallel server can potentially create many thousands of connections. We might want to limit the maximum number of simultaneous connections. This can be done by maintaining a counter of how many connections are alive at any one time. We increment this counter every time we get a new connection, and we decrement the counter each time a connection finishes. We can use this to limit the total number of simultaneous connections in the system.

- After we have accepted a connection, it's a good idea to explicitly set the required socket options, like this:

```
{ok, Socket} = gen_tcp:accept(Listen),
inet:setopts(Socket, [{packet,4},binary,
                      {nodelay,true},{active, true}]),
loop(Socket)
```

- As of Erlang version R11B-3, several Erlang processes are allowed to call gen_tcp:accept/1 on the same listen socket. This simplifies making a parallel server, because you can have a pool of prespawned processes, all waiting in gen_tcp:accept/1.

14.2 Control Issues

Erlang sockets can be opened in one of three modes: *active, active once,* or *passive.* This is done by including an option {active, true | false | once} in the Options argument to either gen_tcp:connect(Address, Port, Options or gen_tcp:listen(Port, Options).

If {active, true} is specified, then an active socket will be created; {active false} specifies a passive socket. {active, once} creates a socket that is active but only for the reception on one message; after it has received this message, it must be reenabled before it can receive the next message.

We'll go through how these different types of sockets are used in the following sections.

The difference between an active and passive socket has to do with what happens when messages are received by the socket.

- Once an active socket has been created, the controlling process will be sent {tcp, Socket, Data} messages as data is received. There is no way the controlling process can control the flow of these messages. A rogue client could send thousands of messages to the system, and these would all be sent to the controlling process. The controlling process cannot stop this flow of messages.

- If the socket was opened in passive mode, then the controlling process has to call gen_tcp:recv(Socket, N) to receive data from the socket. It will then try to receive exactly N bytes from the socket. If N = 0, then all available bytes are returned. In this case, the server can control the flow of messages from the client by choosing when to call gen_tcp:recv.

Passive sockets are used to control the flow of data to a server. To illustrate this, we can write the message reception loop of a server in three ways:

- Active message reception (nonblocking)
- Passive message reception (blocking)
- Hybrid message reception (partial blocking)

Active Message Reception (Nonblocking)

Our first example opens a socket in active mode and then receives messages from the socket:

```
{ok, Listen} = gen_tcp:listen(Port, [..,{active, true}...]),
{ok, Socket} = gen_tcp:accept(Listen),
loop(Socket).
```

```
loop(Socket) ->
    receive
        {tcp, Socket, Data} ->
            ... do something with the data ...
        {tcp_closed, Socket} ->
            ...
    end.
```

This process cannot control the flow of messages to the server loop. If the client produces data faster than the server can consume this data, then the system can be *flooded* with messages—the message buffers will fill up, and the system might crash or behave strangely.

This type of server is called a *nonblocking* server because it cannot block the client. We should write a nonblocking server only if we can convince ourselves that it can keep up with the demands of the clients.

Passive Message Reception (Blocking)

In this section, we'll write a blocking server. The server opens the socket in passive mode by setting the {active, false} option. This server cannot be crashed by an overactive client that tries to flood it with too much data.

The code in the server loop calls gen_tcp:recv every time it wants to receive data. The client will block until the server has called recv. Note that the OS does some buffering that allows the client to send a small amount of data before it blocks even if recv has not been called.

```
{ok, Listen} = gen_tcp:listen(Port, [..,{active, false}...]),
{ok, Socket} = gen_tcp:accept(Listen),
loop(Socket).

loop(Socket) ->
    case gen_tcp:recv(Socket, N) of
        {ok, B} ->
            ... do something with the data ...
            loop(Socket);
        {error, closed}
            ...
    end.
```

The Hybrid Approach (Partial Blocking)

You might think that using passive mode for all servers is the correct approach. Unfortunately, when we're in passive mode, we can wait for the data from only one socket. This is useless for writing servers that must wait for data from multiple sockets.

Fortunately, we can adopt a hybrid approach, neither blocking nor non-blocking. We open the socket with the option {active, once}. In this mode, the socket is active *but for only one message*. After the controlling processes has been sent a message, it must explicitly call inet:setopts to reenable reception of the next message. The system will block until this happens. This is the best of both worlds. Here's what the code looks like:

```
{ok, Listen} = gen_tcp:listen(Port, [..,{active, once}...]),
{ok, Socket} = gen_tcp:accept(Listen),
loop(Socket).

loop(Socket) ->
    receive
        {tcp, Socket, Data} ->
            ... do something with the data ...
            %% when you're ready enable the next message
            inet:setopts(Sock, [{active, once}]),
            loop(Socket);
        {tcp_closed, Socket} ->
            ...
    end.
```

Using the {active, once} option, the user can implement advanced forms of flow control (sometimes called *traffic shaping*) and thus prevent a server from being flooded by excessive messages.

14.3 Where Did That Connection Come From?

Suppose we write a some kind of online server and find that somebody keeps spamming our site. What can we do about this? The first thing we need to know is where the connection came from. To discover this, we can call inet:peername(Socket).

@spec inet:peername(Socket) -> {ok, {IP_Address, Port}} | {error, Why}

This returns the IP address and port of the other end of the connection so the server can discover who initiated the connection. IP_Address is a tuple of integers {N1,N2,N3,N3} representing the IP address for IPv4 and {K1,K2,K3,K4,K5,K6,K7,K8} for IPv6. Here Ni and Ki are integers in the range 0 to 255.

14.4 Error Handling with Sockets

Error handling with sockets is extremely easy—basically you don't have to do anything. As we said earlier, each socket has a controlling process (that is, the process that created the socket). If the controlling process dies, then the socket will be automatically closed.

This means that if we have, for example, a client and a server and the server dies because of a programming error, the socket owned by the server will be automatically closed, and the client will be sent a {tcp_closed, Socket} message.

We can test this mechanism with the following small program:

`socket_examples.erl`

```erlang
error_test() ->
    spawn(fun() -> error_test_server() end),
    lib_misc:sleep(2000),
    {ok,Socket} = gen_tcp:connect("localhost",4321,[binary, {packet, 2}]),
    io:format("connected to:~p~n",[Socket]),
    gen_tcp:send(Socket, <<"123">>),
    receive
        Any ->
            io:format("Any=~p~n",[Any])
    end.

error_test_server() ->
    {ok, Listen} = gen_tcp:listen(4321, [binary,{packet,2}]),
    {ok, Socket} = gen_tcp:accept(Listen),
    error_test_server_loop(Socket).

error_test_server_loop(Socket) ->
    receive
        {tcp, Socket, Data} ->
            io:format("received:~p~n",[Data]),
            atom_to_list(Data),
            error_test_server_loop(Socket)
    end.
```

When we run it, we see the following:

```
1> socket_examples:error_test().
connected to:#Port<0.152>
received:<<"123">>
=ERROR REPORT==== 9-Feb-2007::15:18:15 ===
Error in process <0.77.0> with exit value:
 {badarg,[{erlang,atom_to_list,[<<3 bytes>>]},
 {socket_examples,error_test_server_loop,1}]}
Any={tcp_closed,#Port<0.152>}
ok
```

We spawn a server, sleep for two seconds to give it a chance to start, and then send it a message containing the binary <<"123">>. When this message arrives at the server, the server tries to compute atom_to_list(Data) where Data is a binary and immediately crashes.[4] Now that the controlling process for the server side of the socket has crashed, the (server-side) socket is automatically closed. The client is then sent a {tcp_closed, Socket} message.

14.5 UDP

Now let's look at the User Datagram Protocol (UDP). Using UDP, machines on the Internet can send each other short messages called *datagrams*. UDP datagrams are unreliable. This means if a client sends a sequence of UDP datagrams to a server, then the datagrams might arrive out of order, not at all, or even more than once, but the individual datagrams, if they arrive, will be undamaged. Large datagrams can get split into smaller fragments, but the IP protocol will reassemble the fragments before delivering them to the application.

UDP is a *connectionless* protocol, which means the client does not have to establish a connection to the server before sending it a message. This means that UDP is well suited for applications where large numbers of clients send small messages to a server.

Writing a UDP client and server in Erlang is much easier than writing in the TCP case since we don't have to worry about maintaining connections to the server.

The Simplest UDP Server and Client

First let's discuss the server. The general form of a UDP server is as follows:

```
server(Port) ->
{ok, Socket} = gen_udp:open(Port, [binary]),
loop(Socket).

loop(Socket) ->
    receive
        {udp, Socket, Host, Port, Bin} ->
            BinReply = ... ,
            gen_udp:send(Socket, Host, Port, BinReply),
            loop(Socket)
    end.
```

---

4. The system monitor prints the diagnostic that you can see in the shell.

This is somewhat easier than the TCP case since we don't need to worry about our process receiving "socket closed" messages. Note that we opened the socket in a *binary* mode, which tells the driver to send all messages to the controlling process as binary data.

Now the client. Here's a very simple client. It merely opens a UDP socket, sends a message to the server, waits for a reply (or timeout), and then closes the socket and returns the value returned by the server.

```erlang
client(Request) ->
    {ok, Socket} = gen_udp:open(0, [binary]),
    ok = gen_udp:send(Socket, "localhost", 4000, Request),
    Value = receive
                {udp, Socket, _, _, Bin} ->
                    {ok, Bin}
            after 2000 ->
                error
            end,
    gen_udp:close(Socket),
    Value
```

We must have a timeout since UDP is unreliable and we might not actually get a reply.

A UDP Factorial Server

We can easily build a UDP server that computes the good ol' factorial of any number that is sent to it. The code is modeled on that in the previous section.

udp_test.erl

```erlang
-module(udp_test).
-export([start_server/0, client/1]).

start_server() ->
    spawn(fun() -> server(4000) end).

%% The server
server(Port) ->
    {ok, Socket} = gen_udp:open(Port, [binary]),
    io:format("server opened socket:~p~n",[Socket]),
    loop(Socket).

loop(Socket) ->
    receive
        {udp, Socket, Host, Port, Bin} = Msg ->
            io:format("server received:~p~n",[Msg]),
            N = binary_to_term(Bin),
            Fac = fac(N),
            gen_udp:send(Socket, Host, Port, term_to_binary(Fac)),
            loop(Socket)
    end.
```

```
fac(0) -> 1;
fac(N) -> N * fac(N-1).

%% The client

client(N) ->
    {ok, Socket} = gen_udp:open(0, [binary]),
    io:format("client opened socket=~p~n",[Socket]),
    ok = gen_udp:send(Socket, "localhost", 4000,
                    term_to_binary(N)),
    Value = receive
                {udp, Socket, _, _, Bin} = Msg ->
                    io:format("client received:~p~n",[Msg]),
                    binary_to_term(Bin)
            after 2000 ->
                    0
            end,
    gen_udp:close(Socket),
    Value.
```

Note that I have added a few print statements so we can see what's happening when we run the program. I always add a few print statements when I develop a program and then edit or comment them out when the program works.

Now let's run this example. First we start the server:

```
1> udp_test:start_server().
server opened socket:#Port<0.106>
<0.34.0>
```

This runs in the background, so we can make a client request:

```
2> udp_test:client(40).
client opened socket=#Port<0.105>
server received:{udp,#Port<0.106>,{127,0,0,1},32785,<<131,97,40>>}
client received:{udp,#Port<0.105>,
                {127,0,0,1}, 4000,
                <<131,110,20,0,0,0,0,0,64,37,5,255,
                  100,222,15,8,126,242,199,132,27,
                  232,234,142>>}
815915283247897734345611269596115894272000000000
```

Additional Notes on UDP

We should note that because UDP is a connectionless protocol, the server has no way to block the client by refusing to read data from it—the server has no idea who the clients are.

Large UDP packets might become fragmented as they pass through the network. Fragmentation occurs when the UDP data size is greater than the maximum transfer unit (MTU) size allowed by the routers that the packet passes though when it travels over the network. The usual advice given in tuning a UDP network is to start with a small packet size (say, about 500 bytes) and then gradually increase it while measuring throughput. If at some point the throughput drops dramatically, then you know the packets are too large.

A UDP packet can be delivered twice (which surprises some people), so you have to be careful writing code for remote procedure calls. It might happen that the reply to a second query was in fact a duplicated answer to the first query. To avoid this, we could modify the client code to include a unique reference and check that this reference is returned by the server. To generate a unique reference, we call the Erlang BIF make_ref, which is guaranteed to return a globally unique reference. The code for a remote procedure call now looks like this:

```
client(Request) ->
    {ok, Socket} = gen_udp:open(0, [binary]),
    Ref = make_ref(), %% make a unique reference
    B1 = term_to_binary({Ref, Request}),
    ok = gen_udp:send(Socket, "localhost", 4000, B1),
    wait_for_ref(Socket, Ref).

wait_for_ref(Socket, Ref) ->
    receive
        {udp, Socket, _, _, Bin} ->
            case binary_to_term(Bin) of
                {Ref, Val} ->
                    %% got the correct value
                    Val;
                {_SomeOtherRef, _} ->
                    %% some other value throw it away
                    wait_for_ref(Socket, Ref)
            end;
    after 1000 ->
        ...
    end.
```

14.6 Broadcasting to Multiple Machines

For completeness, I'll show you how to set up a broadcast channel. This code is rather rare, but one day you might need it.

```
broadcast.erl
-module(broadcast).
-compile(export_all).

send(IoList) ->
    case inet:ifget("eth0", [broadaddr]) of
        {ok, [{broadaddr, Ip}]} ->
            {ok, S} = gen_udp:open(5010, [{broadcast, true}]),
            gen_udp:send(S, Ip, 6000, IoList),
            gen_udp:close(S);
        _ ->
            io:format("Bad interface name, or\n"
                      "broadcasting not supported\n")
    end.

listen() ->
    {ok, S} = gen_udp:open(6000),
    loop(S).

loop(S) ->
    receive
        Any ->
            io:format("received:~p~n", [Any]),
            loop(S)
    end.
```

Here we need two ports, one to send the broadcast and the other to listen for answers. We've chosen port 5010 to send the broadcast request and 6000 to listen for broadcasts (these two numbers have no significance; I just choose two free ports on my system).

Only the process performing a broadcast opens port 5010, but all machines in the network call broadcast:listen(), which opens port 6000 and listens for broadcast messages.

broadcast:send(IoList) broadcasts IoList to all machines on the local area network.

Note: For this to work, the name of the interface must be correct, and broadcasting must be supported. On my iMac, for example, I use the name "en0" instead of "eth0." Note also that if hosts running UDP listeners are on different network subnets, the UDP broadcasts are unlikely to reach them, because by default routers drop such UDP broadcasts.

14.7 A SHOUTcast Server

To finish off this chapter, we'll use our newly acquired skills in socket programming to write a SHOUTcast server. SHOUTcast is a protocol developed by the folks at Nullsoft for streaming audio data.[5] SHOUTcast sends MP3- or AAC-encoded audio data using HTTP as the transport protocol.

To see how things work, we'll first look at the SHOUTcast protocol. Then we'll look at the overall structure of the server. We'll finish with the code.

The SHOUTcast Protocol

The SHOUTcast protocol is simple:

1. First the client (which can be something like XMMS, Winamp, or iTunes) sends an HTTP request to the SHOUTcast server. Here's the request that XMMS generates when I run my SHOUTcast server at home:

```
GET / HTTP/1.1
Host: localhost
User-Agent: xmms/1.2.10
Icy-MetaData:1
```

2. My SHOUTcast server replies with this:

```
ICY 200 OK
icy-notice1: <BR>This stream requires
  <a href=http://www.winamp.com/>;Winamp</a><BR>
icy-notice2: Erlang Shoutcast server<BR>
icy-name: Erlang mix
icy-genre: Pop Top 40 Dance Rock
icy-url: http://localhost:3000
content-type: audio/mpeg
icy-pub: 1
icy-metaint: 24576
icy-br: 96
... data ...
```

3. Now the SHOUTcast servers sends a continuous stream of data. The data has the following structure:

```
F H F H F H F ...
```

---

5. http://www.shoutcast.com/

F is a block of MP3 audio data that must be exactly 24,576 bytes long (the value given in the icy-metaint parameter). H is a header block. The header block consists of a single-byte K followed by exactly 16*K bytes of data. Thus, the smallest header block that can be represented in the binary is <<0>>. The next header block can be represented as follows:

<<1,B1,B2, ..., B16>>

The content of the data part of the header is a string of the form StreamTitle=' ... ';StreamUrl='http:// ...';, which is zero padded to the right to fill up the block.

How the SHOUTcast Server Works

To make a server, we have to attend to the following details:

1. Make a *playlist*. Our server uses a file containing a list of song titles we created in Section 13.2, *Reading ID3 Tags*, on page 225. Audio files are chosen at random from this list.
2. Make a parallel server so we can serve several streams in parallel. We do this using the techniques described in Section 14.1, *A Parallel Server*, on page 248.
3. For each audio file, we want to send only the audio data and *not* the embedded ID3 tags to the client.[6]

   To remove the tags, we use the code in id3_tag_lengths; this code uses the code developed in sections Section 13.2, *Reading ID3 Tags*, on page 225 and Section 5.3, *Finding the Synchronization Frame in MPEG Data*, on page 83. This code is not shown here.

Pseudocode for the SHOUTcast Server

Before we look at the final program, let's look at the overall flow of the code with the details omitted:

```
start_parallel_server(Port) ->
    {ok, Listen} = gen_tcp:listen(Port, ..),
    %% create a song server -- this just knows about all our music
    PidSongServer = spawn(fun() -> songs() end),
    spawn(fun() -> par_connect(Listen, PidSongServer) end).
```

---

6. It is unclear whether this is the correct strategy. Audio encoders are supposed to skip over bad data, so in principle we could send the ID3 tags along with the data. In practice, the program seems to work better if we remove the ID3 tags.

```erlang
%% spawn one of these processes per connection
par_connect(Listen, PidSongServer) ->
    {ok, Socket} = gen_tcp:accept(Listen),
    %% when accept returns spawn a new process to
    %% wait for the next connection
    spawn(fun() -> par_connect(Listen, PidSongServer) end),
    inet:setopts(Socket, [{packet,0},binary, {nodelay,true},
                            {active, true}]),
    %% deal with the request
    get_request(Socket, PidSongServer, []).

%% wait for the TCP request
get_request(Socket, PidSongServer, L) ->
    receive
        {tcp, Socket, Bin} ->
            ... Bin contains the request from the client
            ... if the request is fragmented we call loop again ...
            ... otherwise we call
            .... got_request(Data, Socket, PidSongServer)
        {tcp_closed, Socket} ->
            ... this happens if the client aborts
            ... before it has sent a request (very unlikely)
    end.

%% we got the request -- send a reply
got_request(Data, Socket, PidSongServer) ->
        .. data is the request from the client ...
        .. analayse it ...
        .. we'll always allow the request ..
        gen_tcp:send(Socket, [response()]),
        play_songs(Socket, PidSongServer).

%% play songs forever or until the client quits
play_songs(Socket, PidSongServer) ->
        ... PidSongServer keeps a list of all our MP3 files
        Song = rpc(PidSongServer, random_song),
        ... Song is a random song ...
        Header = make_header(Song),
        ... make the header ...
        {ok, S} = file:open(File, [read,binary,raw]),
        send_file(1, S, Header, 1, Socket),
        file:close(S),
        play_songs(Socket, PidSongServer).

send_file(K, S, Header, OffSet, Socket) ->
    ... send the file in chunks to the client ...
    ... returns when the entire file is sent ...
    ... but exits if we get an error when writing to
    ... the socket -- this happens if the client quits
```

If you look at the real code, you'll see the details differ slightly, but the principles are the same. Here's the full listing:

`shout.erl`

```erlang
-module(shout).

%% In one window > shout:start()
%% in another window xmms http://localhost:3000/stream

-export([start/0]).
-import(lists, [map/2, reverse/1]).

-define(CHUNKSIZE, 24576).

start() ->
    spawn(fun() ->
                  start_parallel_server(3000),
                  %% now go to sleep - otherwise the
                  %% listening socket will be closed
                  lib_misc:sleep(infinity)
          end).

start_parallel_server(Port) ->
    {ok, Listen} = gen_tcp:listen(Port, [binary, {packet, 0},
                                         {reuseaddr, true},
                                         {active, true}]),
    PidSongServer = spawn(fun() -> songs() end),
    spawn(fun() -> par_connect(Listen, PidSongServer) end).

par_connect(Listen, PidSongServer) ->
    {ok, Socket} = gen_tcp:accept(Listen),
    spawn(fun() -> par_connect(Listen, PidSongServer) end),
    inet:setopts(Socket, [{packet,0},binary, {nodelay,true},{active, true}]),
    get_request(Socket, PidSongServer, []).

get_request(Socket, PidSongServer, L) ->
    receive
        {tcp, Socket, Bin} ->
            L1 = L ++ binary_to_list(Bin),
            %% split checks if the header is complete
            case split(L1, []) of
                more ->
                    %% the header is incomplete we need more data
                    get_request(Socket, PidSongServer, L1);
                {Request, _Rest} ->
                    %% header is complete
                    got_request_from_client(Request, Socket, PidSongServer)
            end;
        {tcp_closed, Socket} ->
            void;
```

```erlang
        _Any ->
            %% skip this
            get_request(Socket, PidSongServer, L)
    end.

split("\r\n\r\n" ++ T, L) -> {reverse(L), T};
split([H|T], L)           -> split(T, [H|L]);
split([], _)              -> more.

got_request_from_client(Request, Socket, PidSongServer) ->
    Cmds = string:tokens(Request, "\r\n"),
    Cmds1 = map(fun(I) -> string:tokens(I, " ") end, Cmds),
    is_request_for_stream(Cmds1),
    gen_tcp:send(Socket, [response()]),
    play_songs(Socket, PidSongServer, <<>>).


play_songs(Socket, PidSongServer, SoFar) ->
    Song = rpc(PidSongServer, random_song),
    {File,PrintStr,Header} = unpack_song_descriptor(Song),
    case id3_tag_lengths:file(File) of
        error ->
            play_songs(Socket, PidSongServer, SoFar);
        {Start, Stop} ->
            io:format("Playing:~p~n",[PrintStr]),
            {ok, S} = file:open(File, [read,binary,raw]),
            SoFar1 = send_file(S, {0,Header}, Start, Stop, Socket, SoFar),
            file:close(S),
            play_songs(Socket, PidSongServer, SoFar1)
    end.


send_file(S, Header, OffSet, Stop, Socket, SoFar) ->
    %% OffSet = first byte to play
    %% Stop   = The last byte we can play
    Need = ?CHUNKSIZE - size(SoFar),
    Last = OffSet + Need,
    if
        Last >= Stop ->
            %% not enough data so read as much as possible and return
            Max = Stop - OffSet,
            {ok, Bin} = file:pread(S, OffSet, Max),
            list_to_binary([SoFar, Bin]);
        true ->
            {ok, Bin} = file:pread(S, OffSet, Need),
            write_data(Socket, SoFar, Bin, Header),
            send_file(S, bump(Header),
                      OffSet + Need,  Stop, Socket, <<>>)
    end.
```

```erlang
write_data(Socket, B0, B1, Header) ->
    %% Check that we really have got a block of the right size
    %% this is a very useful check that our program logic is
    %% correct
    case size(B0) + size(B1) of
        ?CHUNKSIZE ->
            case gen_tcp:send(Socket, [B0, B1, the_header(Header)]) of
                ok -> true;
                {error, closed} ->
                    %% this happens if the player
                    %% terminates the connection
                    exit(playerClosed)
            end;
        _Other ->
            %% don't send the block - report an error
            io:format("Block length Error: B0 = ~p b1=~p~n",
                      [size(B0), size(B1)])
    end.

bump({K, H})      -> {K+1, H}.

the_header({K, H}) ->
    case K rem 5 of
        0 -> H;
        _ -> <<0>>
    end.


is_request_for_stream(_) -> true.


response() ->
    ["ICY 200 OK\r\n",
     "icy-notice1: <BR>This stream requires",
     "<a href=\"http://www.winamp.com/\">Winamp</a><BR>\r\n",
     "icy-notice2: Erlang Shoutcast server<BR>\r\n",
     "icy-name: Erlang mix\r\n",
     "icy-genre: Pop Top 40 Dance Rock\r\n",
     "icy-url: http://localhost:3000\r\n",
     "content-type: audio/mpeg\r\n",
     "icy-pub: 1\r\n",
     "icy-metaint: ",integer_to_list(?CHUNKSIZE),"\r\n",
     "icy-br: 96\r\n\r\n"].


songs() ->
    {ok,[SongList]} = file:consult("mp3data"),
    lib_misc:random_seed(),
    songs_loop(SongList).
```

```erlang
songs_loop(SongList) ->
    receive
        {From, random_song} ->
            I = random:uniform(length(SongList)),
            Song = lists:nth(I, SongList),
            From ! {self(), Song},
            songs_loop(SongList)
    end.

rpc(Pid, Q) ->
    Pid ! {self(), Q},
    receive
        {Pid, Reply} ->
            Reply
    end.

unpack_song_descriptor({File, {_Tag,Info}}) ->
    PrintStr = list_to_binary(make_header1(Info)),
    L1 = ["StreamTitle='",PrintStr,
        "';StreamUrl='http://localhost:3000';"],
    %% io:format("L1=~p~n",[L1]),
    Bin = list_to_binary(L1),
    Nblocks = ((size(Bin) - 1) div 16) + 1,
    NPad = Nblocks*16 - size(Bin),
    Extra = lists:duplicate(NPad, 0),
    Header = list_to_binary([Nblocks, Bin, Extra]),
    %% Header is the Shoutcast header
    {File, PrintStr, Header}.

make_header1([{track,_}|T]) ->
    make_header1(T);
make_header1([{Tag,X}|T]) ->
    [atom_to_list(Tag),": ",X," "|make_header1(T)];
make_header1([]) ->
    [].
```

Running the SHOUTcast Server

To run the server and test that it works, we need to perform three steps:

1. Make a playlist.
2. Start the server.
3. Point a client at the server.

Making the Playlist

To make the playlist, follow these steps:

1. Change to the code directory.

2. Edit the path in the function start1 in the file mp3_manager.erl to point to the root of the directories that contain the audio files you want to serve.

3. Compile mp3_manager, and give the command mp3_manager:start1(). You should see something like the following:

```
1> c(mp3_manager).
{ok,mp3_manager}
2> mp3_manager:start1().
Dumping term to mp3data
ok
```

If you're interested, you can now look in the file mp3data to see the results of the analysis.

Starting the SHOUTcast Server

Start the SHOUTcast server with a shell command as follows:

```
1> shout:start().
...
```

Testing the Server

1. Go to another window to start an audio player, and point it to the stream called http://localhost:3000.

   On my system I use XMMS and give the following command:

   xmms http://localhost:3000

   Note: If you want to access the server from another computer, you'll have to give the IP address of the machine where the server is running. So, for example, to access the server from my Windows machine using Winamp, I use the Play > URL menu in Winamp and enter the address http://192.168.1.168:3000 in the Open URL dialog box.

   On my iMac using iTunes I use the Advanced > Open Stream menu and give the previous URL to access the server.

2. You'll see some diagnostic output in the window where you started the server.

3. Enjoy!

14.8 Digging Deeper

In this chapter, we have looked at only the most commonly used functions for manipulating sockets. You can find more information about the socket APIs in the manual pages for gen_tcp, gen_udp, and inet.

## Chapter 15

ETS and DETS: Large Data Storage Mechanisms

ets and dets are two system modules that are used for efficient storage of large numbers of Erlang terms. ETS is short for *Erlang term storage*, and DETS is short for *disk ets*.

ETS and DETS perform basically the same task: they provide large key-value lookup tables. ETS is memory resident, while DETS is disk resident. ETS is highly efficient—using ETS, you can store colossal amounts of data (if you have enough memory) and perform lookups in constant (or in some cases logarithmic) time. DETS provides almost the same interface as ETS but stores the tables on disk. Because DETS uses disk storage, it is far slower than ETS but will have a much smaller memory footprint when running. In addition, ETS and DETS tables can be shared by several processes, making interprocess access to common data highly efficient.

ETS and DETS tables are data structures for associating *keys* with *values*. The most common operations we will perform on tables are *insertions* and *lookups*. An ETS or DETS table is just a collection of Erlang tuples.

Data stored in an ETS table is *transient* and will be deleted when the ETS table concerned is disposed of. Data stored in DETS tables is *persistent* and should survive an entire system crash. When a DETS table is opened, it is checked for consistency. If it is found to be corrupt, then an attempt is made to repair the table (which can take a long time since all the data in the table is checked).

This should recover all data in the table, though the last entry in the table might be lost if it was being made at the time of the system crash.

ETS tables are widely used in applications that have to manipulate large amounts of data in an efficient manner and where it is too costly to program with nondestructive assignment and "pure" Erlang data structures.

ETS tables look as if they were implemented in Erlang, but in fact they are implemented in the underlying runtime system and have different performance characteristics than ordinary Erlang objects. In particular, ETS tables are not garbage collected; this means there are no garbage collection penalties involved in using extremely large ETS tables, though slight penalties are incurred when we create or access ETS objects.

15.1 Basic Operations on Tables

There are four basic operations on ETS and DETS tables:

Create a new table or open an existing table.
> This we do with ets:new or dets:open_file.

Insert a tuple or several tuples into a table.
> Here we call insert(Tablename, X), where X is a tuple or a list of tuples. insert has the same arguments and works the same way in ETS and DETS.

Look up a tuple in a table.
> Here we call lookup(TableName, Key). The result is a list of tuples that match Key. lookup is defined for both ETS and DETS.
>
> (Why is the return value a list of tuples? If the table type is a "bag," then several tuples can have the same key. We'll look at the table types in the next section.)
>
> If no tuples in the table have the required key, then an empty list is returned.

Dispose of a table.
> When we've finished with a table, we can tell the system by calling dets:close(TableId) or ets:delete(TableId).

15.2 Types of Table

ETS and DETS tables store tuples. One of the elements in the tuple (by default, the first) is called the *key* of the table. We insert tuples into the table and extract tuples from the table based on the key. What happens when we insert a tuple into a table depends upon the type of the table and the value of the key. Some tables, called *sets*, require that all the keys in the table are unique. Others, called *bags*, allow several tuples to have the same key.

Choosing the correct type of table has important consequences for the performance of your applications.

Each of the basic set and bag table types has two variants, making for a total of four types of table: sets, ordered sets, bags, and duplicate bags. In a set, all the keys in the different tuples in the table must be unique. In an ordered set, the tuples are sorted. In a bag there can be more than one tuple with the same key, but no two tuples in the bag can be identical. In a duplicate bag several tuples can have the same key, and the same tuple can occur many times in the same table.

We can illustrate how these work with the following little test program:

ets_test.erl

```erlang
-module(ets_test).
-export([start/0]).

start() ->
    lists:foreach(fun test_ets/1,
                  [set, ordered_set, bag, duplicate_bag]).

test_ets(Mode) ->
    TableId = ets:new(test, [Mode]),
    ets:insert(TableId, {a,1}),
    ets:insert(TableId, {b,2}),
    ets:insert(TableId, {a,1}),
    ets:insert(TableId, {a,3}),
    List = ets:tab2list(TableId),
    io:format("~-13w  => ~p~n", [Mode, List]),
    ets:delete(TableId).
```

This program opens an ETS table in one of four modes and inserts the tuples {a,1}, {b,2}, {a,1}, and finally {a,3} into the table. Then we call tab2list, which converts the entire table into a list, and print it.

When we run this, we get the following output:

```
1> ets_test:start().
set            => [{b,2},{a,3}]
ordered_set    => [{a,3},{b,2}]
bag            => [{b,2},{a,1},{a,3}]
duplicate_bag  => [{b,2},{a,1},{a,1},{a,3}]
```

For the set table type, each key occurs only once. If we insert the tuple {a,1} in table followed by {a,3}, then the final value will be {a,3}. The only difference between a set and an ordered set is that the elements in an ordered set are ordered by the key. We can see the order when we convert the table to a list by calling tab2list.

The bag table types can have multiple occurrences of the key. So for example, when we insert {a,1} followed by {a,3}, then the bag will contain both tuples, not just the last. In a duplicate bag multiple identical tuples are allowed in the bag, so when we insert {a,1} followed by {a,1} into the bag, then the resulting table contains two copies of the {a,1} tuple; however, in a regular bag, there would be only one copy of the tuple.

15.3 ETS Table Efficiency Considerations

Internally, ETS tables are represented by hash tables (except ordered sets, which are represented by balanced binary trees). This means there is a slight space penalty for using sets and a time penalty for using ordered sets. Inserting into sets takes place in constant time, but inserting into an ordered set takes place in a time proportional to the log of the number of entries in the table.

When you choose between a set and an ordered set, you should think about what you want to do with the table after it has been constructed—if you want a sorted table, then use an ordered set.

Bags are more expensive to use than duplicate bags, since on each insertion all elements with the same key have to be compared for equality. If there are large numbers of tuples with the same key, this can be rather inefficient.

ETS tables are stored in a separate storage area that is not associated with normal process memory. An ETS table is said to be owned by the process that created it—when that process dies or when ets:delete is called, then the table is deleted. ETS tables are not garbage collected, which means that large amounts of data can be stored in the table without incurring garbage collection penalties.

When a tuple is inserted into an ETS table, all the data structures representing the tuple are copied from the process stack and heap into the ETS table. When a lookup operation is performed on a table, the resultant tuples are copied from the ETS table to the stack and heap of the process.

This is true for all data structures except large binaries. Large binaries are stored in their own off-heap storage area. This area can be shared by several processes and ETS tables, and the individual binaries are managed with a reference-counting garbage collector that keeps track of how many different processes and ETS tables use the binary. When the use count for the number of processes and tables that use a particular binary goes down to zero, then the storage area for the binary can be reclaimed.

All of this might sound rather complicated, but the upshot is that sending messages between processes that contain large binaries is very cheap, and inserting tuples into ETS tables that contain binaries is also very cheap. A good rule is to use binaries as much as possible for representing strings and large blocks of untyped memory.

15.4 Creating an ETS Table

ETS tables are created by calling ets:new. The process that creates the table is called the "owner" of the table. When the table is created, it has a set of options that cannot be changed. If the owner process dies, space for the table is automatically deallocated; otherwise, the table can be deleted by calling ets:delete.

The arguments to ets:new are as follows:

@spec ets:new(Name, [Opt]) -> TableId
> Name is an atom. [Opt] is a list of options, taken from the following:

> set | ordered_set | bag | duplicate_bag
>> Create an ETS table of the given type (we talked about these earlier).

> private
>> Create a private table. Only the owner process can read and write this table.

> ### ETS Tables As Blackboards
>
> Protected tables provide a type of "blackboard system." You can think of an protected ETS table as a kind of named black-board. Anybody who knows the name of the blackboard can read the blackboard, but only the owner can write on the blackboard.
>
> *Note*: An ETS table that has been opened in public mode can be written and read by any process that knows the table name. In this case, the user must ensure that reads and writes to the table are performed in a consistent manner.

public

> Create a public table. Any process that knows the table identifier can read and write this table.

protected

> Create a protected table. Any process that knows the table identifier can read this table, but only the owner process can write to the table.

named_table

> If this is present, then Name can be used for subsequent table operations.

{keypos, K}

> Use K as the key position. Normally position 1 is used for the key. Probably the only time when we would use this option is if we store an Erlang record (which is actually a disguised tuple), where the first element of the record contains the record name.

Note: Opening an ETS table with zero options is the same as opening it with the options [set,protected,{keypos,1}].

All the code in this chapter uses protected ETS tables. Protected tables are particularly useful since they allow data sharing at virtually zero cost. All local processes that know the table identifier can read the data, but only one process can change the data in the table.

15.5 Example Programs with ETS

The examples in this section have to do with trigram generation. This is a nice "show-off" program that demonstrates the power of the ETS tables.

Our goal is to write a heuristic program that tries to predict whether a given string is an English word. We're going to use this when we build a full-text indexing engine in Section 20.4, *mapreduce and Indexing Our Disk*, on page 373.

How can we predict whether a random sequence of letters is an English word? One way is to use *trigrams*. A trigram is a sequence of three letters. Now not all sequences of three letters can occur in a valid English word. For example, there are no English words where the three-letter combinations *akj* or *rwb* occur. So, to test whether a string might be an English word, all we have to do is test all sequences of three consecutive letters in the string against the set of trigrams generated from a large set of English words.

The first thing our program does is to compute all trigrams in the English language from a very large set of words. To do this, we use ETS sets. The decision to use an ETS set is based on a set of measurement of the relative performances of ETS sets and ordered sets and of using "pure" Erlang sets as provided by the sets module.

This is what we're going to do in the next few sections:

1. Make an *iterator* that runs through all the trigrams in the English language. This will greatly simplify writing code to insert the trigrams into different table types.

2. Create ETS tables of type set and ordered_set to represent all these trigrams. Also, build a set containing all these trigrams.

3. Measure the time takes to *build* these different tables.

4. Measure the time to *access* these different tables.

5. Based on the *measurements*, choose the best method and write access routines for the best method.

All the code is in lib_trigrams. We're going to present this in sections, leaving some of the details out. But don't worry, you'll find a complete listing at the end of the chapter. That's the plan, so let's get started.

The Trigram Iterator

We'll define a function for_each_trigram_in_the_english_language(F, A). This function applies the fun F to every trigram in the English language. F is a fun of type fun(Str, A) -> A, Str ranges over all trigrams in the language, and A is an accumulator.

To write our iterator,[1] we need a massive word list. I've used a collection of 354,984 English words[2] to generate the trigrams. Using this word list, we can define the trigram iterator as follows:

`lib_trigrams.erl`

```
for_each_trigram_in_the_english_language(F, A0) ->
    {ok, Bin0} = file:read_file("354984si.ngl.gz"),
    Bin = zlib:gunzip(Bin0),
    scan_word_list(binary_to_list(Bin), F, A0).

scan_word_list([], _, A) ->
    A;
scan_word_list(L, F, A) ->
    {Word, L1} = get_next_word(L, []),
    A1 = scan_trigrams([$\s|Word], F, A),
    scan_word_list(L1, F, A1).

%% scan the word looking for \r\n
%% the second argument is the word (reversed) so it
%% has to be reversed when we find \r\n or run out of characters

get_next_word([$\r,$\n|T], L) -> {reverse([$\s|L]), T};
get_next_word([H|T], L)       -> get_next_word(T, [H|L]);
get_next_word([], L)          -> {reverse([$\s|L]), []}.

scan_trigrams([X,Y,Z], F, A) ->
    F([X,Y,Z], A);
scan_trigrams([X,Y,Z|T], F, A) ->
    A1 = F([X,Y,Z], A),
    scan_trigrams([Y,Z|T], F, A1);
scan_trigrams(_, _, A) ->
    A.
```

Note two points here. First, we used zlib:gunzip(Bin) to unzip the binary in the source file. The word list is rather long, so we prefer to save it on disk as a compressed file rather than as a raw ASCII file. Second, we add a space before and after each word; in our trigram analysis, we want to treat space as if it were a regular letter.

---

1. I've called this an iterator here; to be more strict, it's actually a fold operator very much like lists:foldl.
2. From http://www.dcs.shef.ac.uk/research/ilash/Moby/.

Build the Tables

We build our ETS tables like this:

`lib_trigrams.erl`

```erlang
make_ets_ordered_set() -> make_a_set(ordered_set, "trigramsOS.tab").
make_ets_set()         -> make_a_set(set, "trigramsS.tab").

make_a_set(Type, FileName) ->
    Tab = ets:new(table, [Type]),
    F = fun(Str, _) -> ets:insert(Tab, {list_to_binary(Str)}) end,
    for_each_trigram_in_the_english_language(F, 0),
    ets:tab2file(Tab, FileName),
    Size = ets:info(Tab, size),
    ets:delete(Tab),
    Size.
```

Note how when we have isolated a trigram of three letters, ABC, we actually insert the tuple {<<"ABC">>} into the ETS table representing the trigrams. This looks funny—a tuple with only *one* element. What does that mean? Surely a tuple is a container for several elements, so it doesn't make sense to have a tuple with only one element. But remember that all the entries in an ETS table are tuples, and by default the key in a tuple is the first element in the tuple. So, in our case, the tuple {Key} represents a key with no value.

Now for the code that builds a set of all trigrams (this time with the Erlang module sets and not ETS):

`lib_trigrams.erl`

```erlang
make_mod_set() ->
    D = sets:new(),
    F = fun(Str, Set) -> sets:add_element(list_to_binary(Str),Set) end,
    D1 = for_each_trigram_in_the_english_language(F, D),
    file:write_file("trigrams.set", [term_to_binary(D1)]).
```

How Long Did It Take to Build the Tables?

The function lib_trigrams:make_tables(), shown in the listing at the end of the chapter, builds all the tables. It includes some instrumentation so we can measure the size of our tables and the time taken to build the tables.

```
1> lib_trigrams:make_tables().
Counting - No of trigrams=3357707 time/trigram=0.577938
Ets ordered Set size=19.0200 time/trigram=2.98026
Ets set size=19.0193 time/trigram=1.53711
Module Set size=9.43407 time/trigram=9.32234
ok
```

What do these figures tell us? First there are 3.3 million trigrams, and it took half a microsecond to process each trigram in the word list.

The insertion time per trigram was 2.9 microseconds in an ETS ordered set, 1.5 microseconds in an ETS set, and 9.3 microseconds in an Erlang set. As for storage, ETS sets and ordered sets took 19 bytes per trigram, while the module sets took 9 bytes per trigram.

How Long Does It Take to Access the Tables?

OK, so the tables took some time to build, but in this case *it doesn't matter*. The important question to ask is, How long does it take to access the tables? To answer this, we have to write some code to measure the access times. We'll look up every trigram in our table exactly once and then take the average time per lookup. Here's the code that performs the timings:

`lib_trigrams.erl`

```erlang
timer_tests() ->
    time_lookup_ets_set("Ets ordered Set", "trigramsOS.tab"),
    time_lookup_ets_set("Ets set", "trigramsS.tab"),
    time_lookup_module_sets().

time_lookup_ets_set(Type, File) ->
    {ok, Tab} = ets:file2tab(File),
    L = ets:tab2list(Tab),
    Size = length(L),
    {M, _} = timer:tc(?MODULE, lookup_all_ets, [Tab, L]),
    io:format("~s lookup=~p micro seconds~n",[Type, M/Size]),
    ets:delete(Tab).

lookup_all_ets(Tab, L) ->
    lists:foreach(fun({K}) -> ets:lookup(Tab, K) end, L).

time_lookup_module_sets() ->
    {ok, Bin} = file:read_file("trigrams.set"),
    Set = binary_to_term(Bin),
    Keys = sets:to_list(Set),
    Size = length(Keys),
    {M, _} = timer:tc(?MODULE, lookup_all_set, [Set, Keys]),
    io:format("Module set lookup=~p micro seconds~n",[M/Size]).

lookup_all_set(Set, L) ->
    lists:foreach(fun(Key) -> sets:is_element(Key, Set) end, L).
```

Here we go:

```
1> lib_trigrams:timer_tests().
Ets ordered Set lookup=1.79964 micro seconds
Ets set lookup=0.719279 micro seconds
Module sets lookup=1.35268 micro seconds
ok
```

These timings are in average microseconds per lookup.

And the Winner Is...

Well, it was a walkover. The ETS set won by a large margin. On my machine, sets took about half a microsecond per lookup—that's pretty good!

Note: Performing tests like the previous one and actually measuring how long a particular operation takes is considered good programming practice. We don't need to take this to extremes and time everything, only the most time-consuming operations in our program. The non-time-consuming operations should be programmed in the most *beautiful* way possible. If we are forced to write nonobvious ugly code for efficiency reasons, then it should be well documented.

Now we can write the routines that try to predict whether a string is a proper English word.

To test whether a string might be an English language word, we scan through all the trigrams in the string and check that each trigram occurs in the trigram table that we computed earlier. The function is_word does this.

`lib_trigrams.erl`

```erlang
is_word(Tab, Str) -> is_word1(Tab, "\s" ++ Str ++ "\s").

is_word1(Tab, [_,_,_]=X) -> is_this_a_trigram(Tab, X);
is_word1(Tab, [A,B,C|D]) ->
    case is_this_a_trigram(Tab, [A,B,C]) of
        true  -> is_word1(Tab, [B,C|D]);
        false -> false
    end;
is_word1(_, _) ->
    false.

is_this_a_trigram(Tab, X) ->
    case ets:lookup(Tab, list_to_binary(X)) of
        [] -> false;
        _  -> true
    end.

open() ->
    {ok, I} = ets:file2tab(filename:dirname(code:which(?MODULE))
                           ++ "/trigramsS.tab"),
    I.

close(Tab) -> ets:delete(Tab).
```

The functions open and close open the ETS table we computed earlier and must bracket any call to is_word.

The other trick I used here was the way in which I located the external file containing the trigram table. I store this in the same directory as the directory where the code for the current module is loaded from. code:which(?MODULE) returns the filename where the object code for ?MODULE was located.

15.6 DETS

DETS provides Erlang tuple storage on disk. DETS files have a maximum size of 2GB. DETS files must be opened before they can be used, and they should be properly closed when finished with. If they are not properly closed, then they will be automatically repaired the next time they are opened. Since the repair can take a long time, it's important to close them properly before finishing your application.

DETS tables have different sharing properties to ETS tables. When an DETS table is opened, it must be given a global name. If two or more local processes open a DETS table with the same name and options, then they will share the table. The table will remain open until all processes have closed the table (or crashed).

Example: A Filename Index

We'll start off with an example and yet another utility that we'll need for our full-text indexing engine, which is the subject of Section 20.4, *mapreduce and Indexing Our Disk*, on page 373.

We want to create a disk-based table that maps filenames onto integers, and vice versa. We'll define the function filename2index and its inverse function index2filename.

To implement this, we'll create a DETS table and populate it with three different types of tuple:

{free, N}

> N is the first free index in the table. When we enter a new filename in the table, it will be assigned the index N.

{FileNameBin, K}

> FileNameBin (a binary) has been assigned index K.

{K, FileNameBin}

K (an integer) represents the file FilenameBin.

Note how the addition of every new file adds two entries to the table: a File ↦ Index entry and an inverse Index ↦ Filename. This is for efficiency reasons. When ETS or DETS tables are built, only one item in the tuple acts as a key. Matching on a tuple element that is not the key can be done, but it is very inefficient because it involves searching through the entire table. This is a particularly expensive operation when the entire table resides on disk.

Now let's write the program. We'll start with routines to open and close the DETS table that will store all our filenames.

`lib_filenames_dets.erl`

```erlang
-module(lib_filenames_dets).
-export([open/1, close/0, test/0, filename2index/1, index2filename/1]).

open(File) ->
    io:format("dets opened:~p~n", [File]),
    Bool = filelib:is_file(File),
    case dets:open_file(?MODULE, [{file, File}]) of
        {ok, ?MODULE} ->
            case Bool of
                true  -> void;
                false -> ok = dets:insert(?MODULE, {free,1})
            end,
            true;
        {error,_Reason} ->
            io:format("cannot open dets table~n"),
            exit(eDetsOpen)
    end.

close() -> dets:close(?MODULE).
```

The code for open automatically initializes the DETS table by inserting the tuple {free, 1} if a new table is created. filelib:is_file(File) returns true if File exists; otherwise, it returns false. Note that dets:open_file either creates a new file or opens an exiting file, which is why we have to check whether the file exists before calling dets:open_file.

In this code I've used the macro ?MODULE a lot of times; ?MODULE expands to the current module name (which is lib_filenames_dets). Many of the calls to DETS need a unique atom argument for the table name. To generate a unique table name, we just use the module name. Since there can't be two Erlang modules in the system with the same name, then if we follow this convention everywhere, we'll be reasonably sure that we have a unique name to use for the table name.

I used the macro ?MODULE instead of explicitly writing the module name every time because I have a habit of changing modules names as I write my code. Using macros, if I change the module name, the code will still be correct.

Once we've opened the file, injecting a new filename into the table is easy. This is done as a side effect of calling filename2index. If the filename is in the table, then its index is returned; otherwise, a new index is generated, and the table is updated, this time with three tuples:

`lib_filenames_dets.erl`

```erlang
filename2index(FileName) when is_binary(FileName) ->
    case dets:lookup(?MODULE, FileName) of
        [] ->
            [{_,Free}] = dets:lookup(?MODULE, free),
            ok = dets:insert(?MODULE,
                    [{Free,FileName},{FileName,Free},{free,Free+1}]),
            Free;
        [{_,N}] ->
            N
    end.
```

Note how we store three tuples in the table. The second argument to dets:insert is either a tuple or *a list of tuples*. Note also that the filename is represented by a binary. This is for efficiency reasons. It's a good idea to get into the habit of using binaries to represent strings in ETS and DETS tables.

The observant reader might have noticed that there is a potential race condition in filename2index. If two parallel processes call dets:lookup before dets:insert gets called, then filename2index will return an incorrect value. For this routine to work, we must ensure that it is only ever called by one process at a time.

Converting an index to a filename is easy:

`lib_filenames_dets.erl`

```erlang
index2filename(Index) when is_integer(Index) ->
    case dets:lookup(?MODULE, Index) of
        []       -> error;
        [{_,Bin}] -> Bin
    end.
```

There's a small design decision here. What do we want to happen if we call index2filename(Index) and there is no filename associated with this index? We could crash the caller by calling exit(ebadIndex). We've chosen a gentler alternative: we just return the atom error. The caller can distinguish between a valid filename and incorrect value since all valid returned filenames are of type binary.

Note also the guard tests in filename2index and index2filename. These check that the arguments have the required type. It's a good idea to test these, because entering data of the wrong type into a DETS table can cause situations that are very difficult to debug. We can imagine storing data in a table with the wrong type and reading the table months later, by which time it's too late to do anything about it. It's best to check that all the data is correct before adding it to the table.

15.7 What Haven't We Talked About?

ETS and DETS tables support a number of operations that we haven't talked about in this chapter. These operations fall into the following categories:

- Fetching and deleting objects based on a pattern
- Converting between ETS and DETS tables and between ETS tables and disk files
- Finding resource usage for a table
- Traversing all elements in a table
- Repairing a broken DETS table
- Visualizing a table

You can find more information in the ETS and DETS manual pages available online at http://www.erlang.org/doc/man/ets.html and http://www.erlang.org/doc/man/dets.html.

Finally, ETS and DETS tables were originally designed to be used to implement Mnesia. We haven't talked about Mnesia yet—this is the subject of Chapter 17, *Mnesia: The Erlang Database*, on page 307. Mnesia is a real-time database written in Erlang. Mnesia uses ETS and DETS tables internally, and a lot of the routines exported from the ETS and DETS modules are intended for internal use from Mnesia. Mnesia can do all kinds of operations that are not possible using single ETS and DETS tables. For example, we can index on more than the primary key, so the kind of double insertion trick that we used in the filename2index example is not necessary. Mnesia will actually create several ETS or DETS tables to do this, but this is hidden from the user.

15.8 Code Listings

`lib_trigrams_complete.erl`

```erlang
-module(lib_trigrams).
-export([for_each_trigram_in_the_english_language/2,
        make_tables/0, timer_tests/0,
        open/0, close/1, is_word/2,
        how_many_trigrams/0,
        make_ets_set/0, make_ets_ordered_set/0, make_mod_set/0,
        lookup_all_ets/2, lookup_all_set/2
        ]).
-import(lists, [reverse/1]).

make_tables() ->
    {Micro1, N} = timer:tc(?MODULE, how_many_trigrams, []),
    io:format("Counting - No of trigrams=~p time/trigram=~p~n",[N,Micro1/N]),
    {Micro2, Ntri} = timer:tc(?MODULE, make_ets_ordered_set, []),
    FileSize1 = filelib:file_size("trigramsOS.tab"),
    io:format("Ets ordered Set size=~p time/trigram=~p~n",[FileSize1/Ntri,
                                                           Micro2/N]),
    {Micro3, _} = timer:tc(?MODULE, make_ets_set, []),
    FileSize2 = filelib:file_size("trigramsS.tab"),
    io:format("Ets set size=~p time/trigram=~p~n",[FileSize2/Ntri, Micro3/N]),
    {Micro4, _} = timer:tc(?MODULE, make_mod_set, []),
    FileSize3 = filelib:file_size("trigrams.set"),
    io:format("Module sets size=~p time/trigram=~p~n",[FileSize3/Ntri, Micro4/N]).

make_ets_ordered_set() -> make_a_set(ordered_set, "trigramsOS.tab").
make_ets_set()         -> make_a_set(set, "trigramsS.tab").

make_a_set(Type, FileName) ->
    Tab = ets:new(table, [Type]),
    F = fun(Str, _) -> ets:insert(Tab, {list_to_binary(Str)}) end,
    for_each_trigram_in_the_english_language(F, 0),
    ets:tab2file(Tab, FileName),
    Size = ets:info(Tab, size),
    ets:delete(Tab),
    Size.

make_mod_set() ->
    D = sets:new(),
    F = fun(Str, Set) -> sets:add_element(list_to_binary(Str),Set) end,
    D1 = for_each_trigram_in_the_english_language(F, D),
    file:write_file("trigrams.set", [term_to_binary(D1)]).

timer_tests() ->
    time_lookup_ets_set("Ets ordered Set", "trigramsOS.tab"),
    time_lookup_ets_set("Ets set", "trigramsS.tab"),
    time_lookup_module_sets().
```

```
time_lookup_ets_set(Type, File) ->
    {ok, Tab} = ets:file2tab(File),
    L = ets:tab2list(Tab),
    Size = length(L),
    {M, _} = timer:tc(?MODULE, lookup_all_ets, [Tab, L]),
    io:format("~s lookup=~p micro seconds~n",[Type, M/Size]),
    ets:delete(Tab).

lookup_all_ets(Tab, L) ->
    lists:foreach(fun({K}) -> ets:lookup(Tab, K) end, L).

time_lookup_module_sets() ->
    {ok, Bin} = file:read_file("trigrams.set"),
    Set = binary_to_term(Bin),
    Keys = sets:to_list(Set),
    Size = length(Keys),
    {M, _} = timer:tc(?MODULE, lookup_all_set, [Set, Keys]),
    io:format("Module set lookup=~p micro seconds~n",[M/Size]).

lookup_all_set(Set, L) ->
    lists:foreach(fun(Key) -> sets:is_element(Key, Set) end, L).

how_many_trigrams() ->
    F = fun(_, N) -> 1 + N end,
    for_each_trigram_in_the_english_language(F, 0).

%% An iterator that iterates through all trigrams in the language
for_each_trigram_in_the_english_language(F, A0) ->
    {ok, Bin0} = file:read_file("354984si.ngl.gz"),
    Bin = zlib:gunzip(Bin0),
    scan_word_list(binary_to_list(Bin), F, A0).

scan_word_list([], _, A) ->
    A;
scan_word_list(L, F, A) ->
    {Word, L1} = get_next_word(L, []),
    A1 = scan_trigrams([$\s|Word], F, A),
    scan_word_list(L1, F, A1).

%% scan the word looking for \r\n
%% the second argument is the word (reversed) so it
%% has to be reversed when we find \r\n or run out of characters

get_next_word([$\r,$\n|T], L) -> {reverse([$\s|L]), T};
get_next_word([H|T], L)       -> get_next_word(T, [H|L]);
get_next_word([], L)          -> {reverse([$\s|L]), []}.

scan_trigrams([X,Y,Z], F, A) ->
    F([X,Y,Z], A);
```

```erlang
scan_trigrams([X,Y,Z|T], F, A) ->
    A1 = F([X,Y,Z], A),
    scan_trigrams([Y,Z|T], F, A1);
scan_trigrams(_, _, A) ->
    A.


%% access routines
%%   open() -> Table
%%   close(Table)
%%   is_word(Table, String) -> Bool

is_word(Tab, Str) -> is_word1(Tab, "\s" ++ Str ++ "\s").

is_word1(Tab, [_,_,_]=X) -> is_this_a_trigram(Tab, X);
is_word1(Tab, [A,B,C|D]) ->
    case is_this_a_trigram(Tab, [A,B,C]) of
        true  -> is_word1(Tab, [B,C|D]);
        false -> false
    end;
is_word1(_, _) ->
    false.

is_this_a_trigram(Tab, X) ->
    case ets:lookup(Tab, list_to_binary(X)) of
        [] -> false;
        _  -> true
    end.

open() ->
    {ok, I} = ets:file2tab(filename:dirname(code:which(?MODULE))
                        ++ "/trigramsS.tab"),
    I.

close(Tab) -> ets:delete(Tab).
```

Chapter 16

OTP Introduction

OTP stands for the Open Telecom Platform. The name is actually misleading, because OTP is far more general than you might think. It's an application operating system and a set of libraries and procedures used for building large-scale, fault-tolerant, distributed applications. It was developed at the Swedish telecom company Ericsson and is used within Ericsson for building fault-tolerant systems.[1]

OTP contains a number of powerful tools—such as a complete web server, an FTP server, a CORBA ORB, and so on—all written in Erlang. OTP also contains state-of-the-art tools for building telecom applications with implementations of H248, SNMP, and an ASN.1-to-Erlang cross-compiler. I'm not going to talk about these here; you can find a lot more about these subjects by following the links referred to in Section C.1, *Online Documentation*, on page 395.

If you want to program your own applications using OTP, then the central concept that you will find very useful is the OTP *behavior*. A behavior encapsulates common behavioral patterns—think of it as an application framework that is parameterized by a *callback* module.

The power of OTP comes from the fact that properties such as fault tolerance, scalability, dynamic-code upgrade, and so on, can be provided by the behavior itself. In other words, the writer of the callback does not have to worry about things such as fault tolerance because this is provided by the behavior. For the Java-minded, you can think of a behavior as a J2EE container.

---

1. Ericsson has released OTP subject to the Erlang Public License (EPL). EPL is a derivative of the Mozilla Public License (MPL).

Put simply, the behavior solves the nonfunctional parts of the problem, while the callback solves the functional parts. The nice part about this is that the nonfunctional parts of the problem (for example, how to do live code upgrades) are the same for all applications, whereas the functional parts (as supplied by the callback) are different for every problem.

In this chapter, we'll look at one of these behaviors, the gen_server module, in greater detail. But, before we get down to the nitty-gritty details of how the gen_server works, we'll first start with a simple server (the simplest server we can possibly imagine) and then change it in a number of small steps until we get to the full gen_server module. That way, you should be in a position to really understand how gen_server works and be ready to poke around in the gory details.

Here is the plan of this chapter:

1. Write a small client-server program in Erlang.

2. Slowly generalize this program and add a number of features.

3. Move to the real code.

16.1 The Road to the Generic Server

This is the most important section in the entire book, so read it once, read it twice, read it 100 times—just make sure the message sinks in.

We're going to write four little servers called server1, server2..., each slightly different from the last. The goal is to totally separate the non-functional parts of the problem from the functional parts of the problem. That last sentence probably didn't mean much to you now, but don't worry—it soon will. Take a deep breath....

Server 1: The Basic Server

Here's our first attempt. It's a little server that we can parameterize with a callback module:

server1.erl

```
-module(server1).
-export([start/2, rpc/2]).

start(Name, Mod) ->
    register(Name, spawn(fun() -> loop(Name, Mod, Mod:init()) end)).
```

```
rpc(Name, Request) ->
    Name ! {self(), Request},
    receive
        {Name, Response} -> Response
    end.

loop(Name, Mod, State) ->
    receive
        {From, Request} ->
            {Response, State1} = Mod:handle(Request, State),
            From ! {Name, Response},
            loop(Name, Mod, State1)
    end.
```

This very small amount of code captures the quintessential nature of a
server. Let's write a *callback* for server1. Here's a name server callback:

`name_server.erl`

```
-module(name_server).
-export([init/0, add/2, whereis/1, handle/2]).
-import(server1, [rpc/2]).

%% client routines
add(Name, Place) -> rpc(name_server, {add, Name, Place}).
whereis(Name)    -> rpc(name_server, {whereis, Name}).

%% callback routines
init() -> dict:new().

handle({add, Name, Place}, Dict) -> {ok, dict:store(Name, Place, Dict)};
handle({whereis, Name}, Dict)    -> {dict:find(Name, Dict), Dict}.
```

This code actually performs two tasks. It serves as a callback module
that is called from the server framework code, and at the same time, it
contains the interfacing routines that will be called by the client. The
usual OTP convention is to combine both functions in the same module.

Just to prove that it works, do this:

```
1> server1:start(name_server, name_server).
true
2> name_server:add(joe, "at home").
ok
3> name_server:whereis(joe).
{ok,"at home"}
```

Now *stop and think*. The callback had no code for concurrency, no
spawn, no send, no receive, no register. It is pure sequential code—
nothing else. What does this mean?

*This means we can write client-server models without understanding
anything about the underlying concurrency models.*

This is the *basic* pattern for all servers. Once you understand the basic
structure, it's easy to "roll your own."

Server 2: A Server with Transactions

Here's a server that crashes the client if the query in the server results
in an exception:

`server2.erl`
```erlang
-module(server2).
-export([start/2, rpc/2]).

start(Name, Mod) ->
    register(Name, spawn(fun() -> loop(Name,Mod,Mod:init()) end)).

rpc(Name, Request) ->
    Name ! {self(), Request},
    receive
        {Name, crash} -> exit(rpc);
        {Name, ok, Response} -> Response
    end.

loop(Name, Mod, OldState) ->
    receive
        {From, Request} ->
            try Mod:handle(Request, OldState) of
                {Response, NewState} ->
                    From ! {Name, ok, Response},
                    loop(Name, Mod, NewState)
            catch
                _:Why ->
                    log_the_error(Name, Request, Why),
                    %% send a message to cause the client to crash
                    From ! {Name, crash},
                    %% loop with the *original* state
                    loop(Name, Mod, OldState)
            end
    end.

log_the_error(Name, Request, Why) ->
    io:format("Server ~p request ~p ~n"
              "caused exception ~p~n",
              [Name, Request, Why]).
```

This one gives you "transaction semantics" in the server—it loops with
the *original value* of State if an exception was raised in the handler
function. But if the handler function succeeded, then it loops with the
value of NewState provided by the handler function.

Why does it retain the original state? When the handler function fails, the client that sent the message that caused the failure is sent a message that causes it to crash. The client cannot proceed, because the request it sent to the server caused the handler function to crash. But any other client that wants to use the server will not be affected. Moreover, the state of the server is not changed when an error occurs in the handler.

Note that the callback module for this server is *exactly* the same as the callback module we used for server1. *By changing the server and keeping the callback module constant, we can change the nonfunctional behavior of the callback module.*

Note: The last statement wasn't strictly true. We have to make a very small change to the callback module when we go from server1 to server2, and that is to change the name in the **-import** declaration from server1 to server2. Otherwise, there are no changes.

Server 3: A Server with Hot Code Swapping

Now we'll add hot code swapping:

`server3.erl`
```erlang
-module(server3).
-export([start/2, rpc/2, swap_code/2]).

start(Name, Mod) ->
    register(Name,
             spawn(fun() -> loop(Name,Mod,Mod:init()) end)).

swap_code(Name, Mod) -> rpc(Name, {swap_code, Mod}).

rpc(Name, Request) ->
    Name ! {self(), Request},
    receive
        {Name, Response} -> Response
    end.

loop(Name, Mod, OldState) ->
    receive
        {From, {swap_code, NewCallBackMod}} ->
            From ! {Name, ack},
            loop(Name, NewCallBackMod, OldState);
        {From, Request} ->
            {Response, NewState} = Mod:handle(Request, OldState),
            From ! {Name, Response},
            loop(Name, Mod, NewState)
    end.
```

How does this work?

If we send the server a swap code message, then it will change the callback module to the new module contained in the message.

We can demonstrate this by starting server3 with a callback module and then dynamically swapping the callback module. We can't use name_server as the callback module because we hard-compiled the name of the server into the module. So, we make a copy of this, calling it name_server1 where we change the name of the server:

`name_server1.erl`
```
-module(name_server1).
-export([init/0, add/2, whereis/1, handle/2]).
-import(server3, [rpc/2]).

%% client routines
add(Name, Place) -> rpc(name_server, {add, Name, Place}).
whereis(Name)    -> rpc(name_server, {whereis, Name}).

%% callback routines
init() -> dict:new().

handle({add, Name, Place}, Dict) -> {ok, dict:store(Name, Place, Dict)};
handle({whereis, Name}, Dict)    -> {dict:find(Name, Dict), Dict}.
```

First we'll start server3 with the name_server1 callback module:

```
1> server3:start(name_server, name_server1).
true
2> name_server1:add(joe, "at home").
ok
3> name_server1:add(helen, "at work").
ok
```

Now suppose we want to find all the names that are served by the name server. There is no function in the API that can do this—the module name_server has only add and lookup access routines.

With lightning speed, we fire up our text editor and write a new callback module:

`new_name_server.erl`
```
-module(new_name_server).
-export([init/0, add/2, all_names/0, delete/1, whereis/1, handle/2]).
-import(server3, [rpc/2]).
```

```
%% interface
all_names()        -> rpc(name_server, allNames).
add(Name, Place)  -> rpc(name_server, {add, Name, Place}).
delete(Name)       -> rpc(name_server, {delete, Name}).
whereis(Name)      -> rpc(name_server, {whereis, Name}).

%% callback routines
init() -> dict:new().

handle({add, Name, Place}, Dict) -> {ok, dict:store(Name, Place, Dict)};
handle(allNames, Dict)            -> {dict:fetch_keys(Dict), Dict};
handle({delete, Name}, Dict)      -> {ok, dict:erase(Name, Dict)};
handle({whereis, Name}, Dict)     -> {dict:find(Name, Dict), Dict}.
```

We compile this and tell the server to swap its callback module:

```
4> c(new_name_server).
{ok,new_name_server}
5> server3:swap_code(name_server, new_name_server).
ack
```

Now we can run the new functions in the server:

```
6> new_name_server:all_names().
[joe,helen]
```

Here we *changed the callback module on the fly*—this is dynamic code upgrade, in action before your eyes, with no black magic.

Now stop and think again. The last two tasks we have done are generally considered to be pretty difficult, in fact, very difficult. Servers with "transaction semantics" are difficult to write; servers with dynamic code upgrade are very difficult to write.

This technique is extremely powerful. Traditionally we think of servers as programs with state that change state when we send them messages. The code in the servers is fixed the first time it is called, and if we want to change the code in the server, we have to stop the server and change the code, and then we can restart the server. In the examples we have given, the code in the server can be changed just as easily as we can change the state of the server.[2]

---

2. I use this technique a lot in products that are *never* taken out of service for software maintenance upgrades.

Server 4: Transactions and Hot Code Swapping

In the last two servers, code upgrade and transaction semantics were separate. Let's *combine* them into a single server. Hold onto your hats....

`server4.erl`

```erlang
-module(server4).
-export([start/2, rpc/2, swap_code/2]).

start(Name, Mod) ->
    register(Name, spawn(fun() -> loop(Name,Mod,Mod:init()) end)).

swap_code(Name, Mod) -> rpc(Name, {swap_code, Mod}).

rpc(Name, Request) ->
    Name ! {self(), Request},
    receive
        {Name, crash} -> exit(rpc);
        {Name, ok, Response} -> Response
    end.

loop(Name, Mod, OldState) ->
    receive
        {From, {swap_code, NewCallbackMod}} ->
            From ! {Name, ok, ack},
            loop(Name, NewCallbackMod, OldState);
        {From, Request} ->
            try Mod:handle(Request, OldState) of
                {Response, NewState} ->
                    From ! {Name, ok, Response},
                    loop(Name, Mod, NewState)
            catch
                _: Why ->
                    log_the_error(Name, Request, Why),
                    From ! {Name, crash},
                    loop(Name, Mod, OldState)
            end
    end.

log_the_error(Name, Request, Why) ->
    io:format("Server ~p request ~p ~n"
              "caused exception ~p~n",
              [Name, Request, Why]).
```

This server provides both hot code swapping and transaction semantics. Neat.

Server 5: Even More Fun

Now that we've got the idea of dynamic code change, we can have even more fun. Here's a server that does nothing at all until you tell it to *become* a particular type of server:

`server5.erl`

```erlang
-module(server5).
-export([start/0, rpc/2]).

start() -> spawn(fun() -> wait() end).

wait() ->
    receive
        {become, F} -> F()
    end.

rpc(Pid, Q) ->
    Pid ! {self(), Q},
    receive
        {Pid, Reply} -> Reply
    end.
```

If we start this and then send it a {become, F} message, it will become an F server by evaluating F(). We'll start it:

```erlang
1>  Pid = server5:start().
<0.57.0>
```

Our server does nothing and just waits for a become message.

Let's now define a server function. It's nothing complicated, just something to compute factorial:

`my_fac_server.erl`

```erlang
-module(my_fac_server).
-export([loop/0]).

loop() ->
    receive
        {From, {fac, N}} ->
            From ! {self(), fac(N)},
            loop();
        {become, Something} ->
            Something()
    end.

fac(0) -> 1;
fac(N) -> N * fac(N-1).
```

Erlang on PlanetLab

A few years ago, when I had my research hat on, I was working with PlanetLab. I had access to the PlanetLab* network, so I installed "empty" Erlang servers on all the PlanetLab machines (about 450 of them). I didn't really know what I would do with the machines, so I just set up the server infrastructure to do something later.

Once I had gotten this layer running, it was an easy job to send messages to the empty servers telling them to become real servers.

The usual approach is to start (for example) a web server and then install web server plug-ins. My approach was to back off one step and install an empty server. Later the plug-in turns the empty server into a web server. When we're done with the web server, we might tell it to become something else.

---
*. A planet-wide research network (http://www.planet-lab.org)

Just make sure it's compiled, and then we can tell process <0.57.0> to become a factorial server:

```
2> c(my_fac_server).
{ok,my_fac_server}
3>  Pid ! {become, fun my_fac_server:loop/0}.
{become,#Fun<my_fac_server.loop.0>}
```

Now that our process has become a factorial server, we can call it:

```
4> server5:rpc(Pid, {fac,30}).
265252859812191058636308480000000
```

Our process will remain a factorial server, until we send it a {become, Something} message and tell it to do something else.

As you can see from the previous examples, we can make a range of different types of servers, with different semantics and some quite surprising properties. This technique is almost too powerful. Used to its full potential, it can yield very small programs of quite surprising power and beauty. When we make industrial-scale projects with dozens to hundreds of programmers involved, we might not actually want things to be too dynamic. We have to try to strike a balance between having something general and powerful and having something that is useful for commercial products. Having code that can morph into new versions as it runs is beautiful but terrible to debug if something goes wrong later. If we have made dozens of dynamic changes to our code and it then crashes, finding out exactly what went wrong is not easy.

The server examples in this section are actually not quite correct. They are written this way so as to emphasize the ideas involved, but they do have one or two extremely small and subtle errors. I'm not going to tell you immediately what they are, but I'll give you some hints at the end of the chapter.

The Erlang module gen_server is the kind of logical conclusion of a succession of successively sophisticated servers (just like the ones we've written so far in this chapter).

It has been in use in industrial products since 1998. Hundreds of servers can be part of a single product. These servers have been written by programmers using regular sequential code. All the error handling and all the nonfunctional behavior is factored out in the generic part of the server.

So now we'll take a great leap of imagination and look at the real gen_server.

16.2 Getting Started with gen_server

I'm going to throw you in at the deep end. Here's the simple three-point plan for writing a gen_server callback module:

1. Decide on a callback module name.

2. Write the interface functions.

3. Write the six required callback functions in the callback module.

This is really easy. Don't think—just follow the plan!

Step 1: Decide on the Callback Module Name

We're going to make a very simple payment system. We'll call the module my_bank.[3]

---

3. In case you're wondering, there are actually several online financial services written in Erlang (such as http://kreditor.se/). Now they don't publish their code, but if they did, it might look like ours.

Step 2: Write the Interface Routines

We'll define five interface routines, all in the module my_bank:

start()
> Open the bank.

stop()
> Close the bank.

new_account(Who)
> Create a new account.

deposit(Who, Amount)
> Put money in the bank.

withdraw(Who, Amount)
> Take money out, if in credit.

Each of these results in exactly one call to the routines in gen_server, as follows:

`my_bank.erl`

```
start() -> gen_server:start_link({local, ?MODULE}, ?MODULE, [], []).
stop()  -> gen_server:call(?MODULE, stop).

new_account(Who)      -> gen_server:call(?MODULE, {new, Who}).
deposit(Who, Amount)  -> gen_server:call(?MODULE, {add, Who, Amount}).
withdraw(Who, Amount) -> gen_server:call(?MODULE, {remove, Who, Amount}).
```

gen_server:start_link({local, Name}, Mod, ...) starts a *local* server.[4] The macro ?MODULE expands to the module name my_bank. Mod is the name of the callback module. We'll ignore the other arguments to gen_server:start_link for now.

gen_server:call(?MODULE, Term) is used for a remote procedure call to the server.

Step 3: Write the Callback Routines

Our callback module must export six callback routines: init/1, handle_call/3, handle_cast/2, handle_info/2, terminate/2, and code_change/3.

---

4. With argument global, it would start a global server that could be accessed on a cluster of Erlang nodes.

To make life easy, we can use a number of templates to make a gen_server. Here's the simplest:

```
gen_server_template.mini
```
```erlang
-module().
%% gen_server_mini_template

-behaviour(gen_server).
-export([start_link/0]).
%% gen_server callbacks
-export([init/1, handle_call/3, handle_cast/2, handle_info/2,
         terminate/2, code_change/3]).

start_link() -> gen_server:start_link({local, ?SERVER}, ?MODULE, [], []).

init([]) -> {ok, State}.

handle_call(_Request, _From, State) -> {reply, Reply, State}.
handle_cast(_Msg, State) -> {noreply, State}.
handle_info(_Info, State) -> {noreply, State}.
terminate(_Reason, _State) -> ok.
code_change(_OldVsn, State, Extra) -> {ok, State}.
```

The template contains a simple skeleton that we can fill in to make our server. The keyword -**behaviour** is used by the compiler so that it can generate warning or error messages if we forget to define the appropriate callback functions.

Tip: If you're using emacs, then you can pull in a gen_server template in a few keystrokes. If you edit in erlang-mode, then the Erlang > Skeletons menu offers a tab that creates a gen_server template. If you don't have emacs, don't panic. I've included the template at the end of the chapter.

We'll start with the template and edit it a bit. All we have to do is get the arguments in the interfacing routines to agree with the arguments in the template.

The most important bit is the handle_call/3 function. We have to write code that matches the three query terms defined in the interface routines. That is, we have to fill in the dots in the following:

```erlang
handle_call({new, Who}, From, State} ->
    Reply = ...
    State1 = ...
    {reply, Reply, State1};
```

```
handle_call({add, Who, Amount}, From, State} ->
    Reply = ...
    State1 = ...
    {reply, Reply, State1};
handle_call({remove, Who, Amount}, From, State} ->
    Reply = ...
    State1 = ...
    {reply, Reply, State1};
```

The values of Reply in this code are sent back to the client as the return values of the remote procedure calls.

State is just a variable representing the global state of the server that gets passed around in the server. In our bank module, the state never changes; it's just an ETS table index that is a constant (although the content of the table changes).

When we've filled in the template and edited it a bit, we end up with the following code:

`my_bank.erl`

```
init([]) -> {ok, ets:new(?MODULE,[])}.

handle_call({new,Who}, _From, Tab) ->
    Reply = case ets:lookup(Tab, Who) of
                []  -> ets:insert(Tab, {Who,0}),
                        {welcome, Who};
                [_] -> {Who, you_already_are_a_customer}
            end,
    {reply, Reply, Tab};
handle_call({add,Who,X}, _From, Tab) ->
    Reply = case ets:lookup(Tab, Who) of
                []  -> not_a_customer;
                [{Who,Balance}] ->
                    NewBalance = Balance + X,
                    ets:insert(Tab, {Who, NewBalance}),
                    {thanks, Who, your_balance_is,  NewBalance}
            end,
    {reply, Reply, Tab};
handle_call({remove,Who, X}, _From, Tab) ->
    Reply = case ets:lookup(Tab, Who) of
                []   -> not_a_customer;
                [{Who,Balance}] when X =< Balance ->
                    NewBalance = Balance - X,
                    ets:insert(Tab, {Who, NewBalance}),
                    {thanks, Who, your_balance_is,  NewBalance};
                [{Who,Balance}] ->
                    {sorry,Who,you_only_have,Balance,in_the_bank}
            end,
    {reply, Reply, Tab};
```

```
handle_call(stop, _From, Tab) ->
    {stop, normal, stopped, Tab}.

handle_cast(_Msg, State) -> {noreply, State}.
handle_info(_Info, State) -> {noreply, State}.
terminate(_Reason, _State) -> ok.
code_change(_OldVsn, State, Extra) -> {ok, State}.
```

We start the server by calling gen_server:start_link(Name, CallBackMod, StartArgs, Opts); then the first routine to be called in the callback module is Mod:init(StartArgs), which must return {ok, State}. The value of State reappears as the third argument in handle_call.

Note how we stop the server. handle_call(Stop, From, Tab) returns {stop, normal, stopped, Tab} which stops the server. The second argument (normal) is used as the first argument to my_bank:terminate/2. The third argument (stopped) becomes the return value of my_bank:stop().

That's it, we're done. So let's go visit the bank:

```
1> my_bank:start().
{ok,<0.33.0>}
2> my_bank:deposit("joe", 10).
not_a_customer
3> my_bank:new_account("joe").
{welcome,"joe"}
4> my_bank:deposit("joe", 10).
{thanks,"joe",your_balance_is,10}
5> my_bank:deposit("joe", 30).
{thanks,"joe",your_balance_is,40}
6> my_bank:withdraw("joe", 15).
{thanks,"joe",your_balance_is,25}
7> my_bank:withdraw("joe", 45).
{sorry,"joe",you_only_have,25,in_the_bank}
```

16.3 The gen_server Callback Structure

Now that we've got the idea, we'll take a more detailed look at the gen_server callback structure.

What Happens When We Start the Server?

The call gen_server:start_link(Name, Mod, InitArgs, Opts) starts everything. It creates a generic server called Name. The callback module is Mod. Opts controls the behavior of the generic server. Here we can specify logging of message, debugging functions, and so on. The generic server starts by calling Mod:init(InitArgs).

The template entry for init is as follows:

```
%%-------------------------------------------------------------------
%% Function: init(Args) -> {ok, State}              |
%%                         {ok, State, Timeout}     |
%%                         ignore                    |
%%                         {stop, Reason}
%% Description: Initiates the server
%%-------------------------------------------------------------------
init([]) ->
    {ok, #state{}}.
```

In normal operation, we just return {ok, State}. For the meaning of the other arguments, consult the manual page for gen_server.

If {ok, State} is returned, then we have successfully started the server, and the initial state is State.

What Happens When We Call the Server?

To call the server, the client program calls gen_server:call(Name, Request). This results in handle_call/3 in the callback module being called.

handle_call/3 has the following template entry:

```
%%-------------------------------------------------------------------
%% Function:
%% handle_call(Request, From, State) -> {reply, Reply, State}          |
%%                                      {reply, Reply, State, Timeout} |
%%                                      {noreply, State}               |
%%                                      {noreply, State, Timeout}      |
%%                                      {stop, Reason, Reply, State}   |
%%                                      {stop, Reason, State}
%% Description: Handling call messages
%%-------------------------------------------------------------------
handle_call(_Request, _From, State) ->
    Reply = ok,
    {reply, Reply, State}.
```

Request (the second argument of gen_server:call/2) reappears as the first argument of handle_call/3. From is the PID of the requesting client process, and State is the current state of the client.

Normally we return {reply, Reply, NewState}. When this happens, Reply goes back to the client, where it becomes the return value of gen_server: call. NewState is the next state of the server.

The other return values, {noreply, ..} and {stop, ..}, are used relatively infrequently. no reply causes the server to continue, but the client will wait for a reply so the server will have to delegate the task of replying to some other process. Calling stop with the appropriate arguments will stop the server.

Calls and Casts

We've seen the interplay between gen_server:call and handle_call. This is used for implementing *remote procedure calls*. gen_server:cast(Name, Name) implements a *cast*, which is just a call with no return value (actually just a message, but traditionally it's called a cast to distinguish it from a remote procedure call).

The corresponding callback routine is handle_cast; the template entry is like this:

```
%%--------------------------------------------------------------------
%% Function: handle_cast(Msg, State) -> {noreply, NewState}          |
%%                                      {noreply, NewState, Timeout} |
%%                                      {stop, Reason, NewState}
%% Description: Handling cast messages
%%--------------------------------------------------------------------
handle_cast(_Msg, State) ->
    {noreply, NewState}.
```

The handler usually just returns {noreply, NewState}, which changes the state of the server, or {stop, ...}, which stops the server.

Spontaneous Messages to the Server

The callback function handle_info(Info, State) is used for handling spontaneous messages to the server. So, what's a spontaneous message? If the server is linked to another process and is trapping exits, then it might suddenly receive a unexpected {'EXIT', Pid, What} message. Alternatively, any process in the system that discovers the PID of the generic server can just send it a message. Any message like this ends up at the server as the value of Info.

The template entry for handle_info is as follows:

```
%%--------------------------------------------------------------------
%% Function: handle_info(Info, State) -> {noreply, State}          |
%%                                       {noreply, State, Timeout} |
%%                                       {stop, Reason, State}
%% Description: Handling all non-call/cast messages
%%--------------------------------------------------------------------
handle_info(_Info, State) ->
    {noreply, State}.
```

The return values are the same as for handle_cast.

Hasta la Vista, Baby

The server can terminate for many reasons. One of the handle_Something routines might return a {stop, Reason, NewState}, or the server might crash with {'EXIT', reason}. In all of these circumstances, no matter how they occurred, terminate(Reason, NewState) will be called.

Here's the template:

```
%%-----------------------------------------------------------------
%% Function: terminate(Reason, State) -> void()
%% Description: This function is called by a gen_server when it is
%% about to terminate. It should be the opposite of Module:init/1 and
%% do any necessary
%% cleaning up. When it returns, the gen_server terminates with Reason.
%% The return value is ignored.
%%-----------------------------------------------------------------
terminate(_Reason, State) ->
    ok.
```

This code can't return a new state because we've terminated. So, what can we do with State? Lots of things, it turns out. We could store it on disk, send it in a message to some other process, or discard it depending upon the applications. If you want your server to be restarted in the future, you'll have to write an "I'll be back" function that is triggered by terminate/2.

Code Change

You can dynamically change the state of your server while it is running. This callback function is called by the release handling subsystem when the system performs a software upgrade.

This topic is described in detail in the section on release handling in the OTP design principles documentation.[5]

```
%%-----------------------------------------------------------------
%% Func: code_change(OldVsn, State, Extra) -> {ok, NewState} %%
%% Description: Convert process state when code is changed
%%-----------------------------------------------------------------
code_change(_OldVsn, State, _Extra) -> {ok, State}.
```

---

5. Availiable from http://www.erlang.org/doc/pdf/design_principles.pdf.

16.4 Code and Templates

This is built into emacs-mode:

gen_server template

`gen_server_template.full`

```erlang
%%%-------------------------------------------------------------------
%%% File    : gen_server_template.full
%%% Author  : my name <yourname@localhost.localdomain>
%%% Description :
%%%
%%% Created :  2 Mar 2007 by my name <yourname@localhost.localdomain>
%%%-------------------------------------------------------------------
-module().

-behaviour(gen_server).

%% API
-export([start_link/0]).

%% gen_server callbacks
-export([init/1, handle_call/3, handle_cast/2, handle_info/2,
         terminate/2, code_change/3]).

-record(state, {}).

%%====================================================================
%% API
%%====================================================================
%%--------------------------------------------------------------------
%% Function: start_link() -> {ok,Pid} | ignore | {error,Error}
%% Description: Starts the server
%%--------------------------------------------------------------------
start_link() ->
    gen_server:start_link({local, ?SERVER}, ?MODULE, [], []).


%%====================================================================
%% gen_server callbacks
%%====================================================================


%%--------------------------------------------------------------------
%% Function: init(Args) -> {ok, State} |
%%                         {ok, State, Timeout} |
%%                         ignore               |
%%                         {stop, Reason}
%% Description: Initiates the server
%%--------------------------------------------------------------------
init([]) ->
    {ok, #state{}}.
```

```erlang
%%--------------------------------------------------------------------
%% Function: %% handle_call(Request, From, State) -> {reply, Reply, State} |
%%                                    {reply, Reply, State, Timeout} |
%%                                    {noreply, State} |
%%                                    {noreply, State, Timeout} |
%%                                    {stop, Reason, Reply, State} |
%%                                    {stop, Reason, State}
%% Description: Handling call messages
%%--------------------------------------------------------------------
handle_call(_Request, _From, State) ->
    Reply = ok,
    {reply, Reply, State}.


%%--------------------------------------------------------------------
%% Function: handle_cast(Msg, State) -> {noreply, State} |
%%                                    {noreply, State, Timeout} |
%%                                    {stop, Reason, State}
%% Description: Handling cast messages
%%--------------------------------------------------------------------
handle_cast(_Msg, State) ->
    {noreply, State}.


%%--------------------------------------------------------------------
%% Function: handle_info(Info, State) -> {noreply, State} |
%%                                    {noreply, State, Timeout} |
%%                                    {stop, Reason, State}
%% Description: Handling all non call/cast messages
%%--------------------------------------------------------------------
handle_info(_Info, State) ->
    {noreply, State}.


%%--------------------------------------------------------------------
%% Function: terminate(Reason, State) -> void()
%% Description: This function is called by a gen_server when it is about to
%% terminate. It should be the opposite of Module:init/1 and do any necessary
%% cleaning up. When it returns, the gen_server terminates with Reason.
%% The return value is ignored.
%%--------------------------------------------------------------------
terminate(_Reason, _State) ->
    ok.


%%--------------------------------------------------------------------
%% Func: code_change(OldVsn, State, Extra) -> {ok, NewState}
%% Description: Convert process state when code is changed
%%--------------------------------------------------------------------
code_change(_OldVsn, State, _Extra) ->
    {ok, State}.


%%--------------------------------------------------------------------
%%% Internal functions
%%--------------------------------------------------------------------
```

my_bank

`my_bank.erl`

```erlang
-module(my_bank).

-behaviour(gen_server).
-export([start/0]).
%% gen_server callbacks
-export([init/1, handle_call/3, handle_cast/2, handle_info/2,
         terminate/2, code_change/3]).
-compile(export_all).

start() -> gen_server:start_link({local, ?MODULE}, ?MODULE, [], []).
stop()  -> gen_server:call(?MODULE, stop).

new_account(Who)       -> gen_server:call(?MODULE, {new, Who}).
deposit(Who, Amount)   -> gen_server:call(?MODULE, {add, Who, Amount}).
withdraw(Who, Amount) -> gen_server:call(?MODULE, {remove, Who, Amount}).

init([]) -> {ok, ets:new(?MODULE,[])}.

handle_call({new,Who}, _From, Tab) ->
    Reply = case ets:lookup(Tab, Who) of
                []  -> ets:insert(Tab, {Who,0}),
                       {welcome, Who};
                [_] -> {Who, you_already_are_a_customer}
            end,
    {reply, Reply, Tab};
handle_call({add,Who,X}, _From, Tab) ->
    Reply = case ets:lookup(Tab, Who) of
                []  -> not_a_customer;
                [{Who,Balance}] ->
                    NewBalance = Balance + X,
                    ets:insert(Tab, {Who, NewBalance}),
                    {thanks, Who, your_balance_is,  NewBalance}
            end,
    {reply, Reply, Tab};
handle_call({remove,Who, X}, _From, Tab) ->
    Reply = case ets:lookup(Tab, Who) of
                []  -> not_a_customer;
                [{Who,Balance}] when X =< Balance ->
                    NewBalance = Balance - X,
                    ets:insert(Tab, {Who, NewBalance}),
                    {thanks, Who, your_balance_is,  NewBalance};
                [{Who,Balance}] ->
                    {sorry,Who,you_only_have,Balance,in_the_bank}
            end,
    {reply, Reply, Tab};
handle_call(stop, _From, Tab) ->
    {stop, normal, stopped, Tab}.
```

```
handle_cast(_Msg, State) -> {noreply, State}.
handle_info(_Info, State) -> {noreply, State}.
terminate(_Reason, _State) -> ok.
code_change(_OldVsn, State, Extra) -> {ok, State}.
```

16.5 Digging Deeper

The gen_server is actually rather simple. We haven't been through *all* the interface functions in gen_server, and we haven't talked about all the arguments to all the interface functions. Once you understand the basic ideas, you can look up the details in the manual page for gen_server.

In this chapter, we have looked only at the simplest possible way to use gen_server, but this should be adequate for most purposes. More complex applications often let gen_server reply with a noreply return value and delegate the real reply to another process. For information about this, read the "Design Principles" documentation[6] and the manual pages for the modules sys and proc_lib.

---

6.   http://www.erlang.org/doc/pdf/design_principles.pdf

Chapter 17

Mnesia: The Erlang Database

Suppose you want to write a multiuser game, make a new website, or create an online payment system. You'll probably need a database management system (DBMS).

Hidden in the thousands of files that appear on our disk when we download Erlang is a complete DBMS called Mnesia. It is extremely fast, and it can store any type of Erlang data structure.

It's also highly configurable. Database tables can be stored in RAM (for speed) or on disk (for persistence), and the tables can be replicated on different machines to provide fault-tolerant behavior.

Let's dig deeper.

17.1 Database Queries

Let's start by looking at Mnesia queries. As we look through this, we might be surprised to see that Mnesia queries look a lot like both SQL[1] and list comprehensions, so there's actually very little we need to learn to get started.[2]

---

1. A popular language that is used to query relational databases.
2. In fact, it really isn't that surprising that list comprehensions and SQL look a lot alike. Both are based on mathematical set theory.

In all our examples, I'll assume that we have created a database with two tables called shop and cost. These tables contain the following data.

The shop Table

Item	Quantity	Cost
apple	20	2.3
orange	100	3.8
pear	200	3.6
banana	420	4.5
potato	2456	1.2

The cost Table

Name	Price
apple	1.5
orange	2.4
pear	2.2
banana	1.5
potato	0.6

To represent these tables in Mnesia, we need record definitions that define the columns in the tables. These are as follows:

`test_mnesia.erl`

```erlang
-record(shop, {item, quantity, cost}).
-record(cost, {name, price}).
```

Now comes a little black magic. I want to show you how queries work, and I want you to follow along at home. But to do that I have to create and populate the database for you. So, just for now, trust me. I've written the initialization code in the file test_mnesia.erl. You can just run it from within erl.

```erlang
1> c(test_mnesia).
{ok,test_mnesia}
2> test_mnesia:do_this_once().
=INFO REPORT==== 29-Mar-2007::20:33:12 ===
    application: mnesia
    exited: stopped
    type: temporary
stopped
```

Now we can move on to our examples.

Selecting All Data in a Table

Here's the code to select all the data in the shop table. (For those of you who know SQL, each code fragment starts with a comment showing the equivalent SQL to perform the corresponding operation.)

`test_mnesia.erl`
```
%% SQL equivalent
%%   SELECT * FROM shop;

demo(select_shop) ->
    do(qlc:q([X || X <- mnesia:table(shop)]));
```

The heart of the matter is the call to qlc:q, which compiles the query (its parameter) into an internal form that is used to query the database. We pass the resulting query to a function called do(), which is defined toward the bottom of test_mnesia. It is responsible for running the question and returning the result. To make all this easily callable from erl, we map it to the function demo(select_shop). (The entire listing for mnesia_test appears at the end of this chapter.)

We can run it as follows:

```
1> test_mnesia:start().
ok
2> test_mnesia:reset_tables().
{atomic, ok}
3> test_mnesia:demo(select_shop).
[{shop,orange,100,3.80000},
 {shop,pear,200,3.60000},
 {shop,banana,420,4.50000},
 {shop,potato,2456,1.20000},
 {shop,apple,20,2.30000}]
```

Note: The rows in the table can come out in any order.

The line that sets up the query in this example is as follows:

```
qlc:q([X || X <- mnesia:table(shop)])
```

This looks very much like a list comprehension (see Section 3.6, *List Comprehensions*, on page 51). In fact, qlc stands for *query list comprehensions*. It is one of the modules we can use to access data in an Mnesia database.

[X || X <- mnesia:table(shop)] means "the list of X such that X is taken from the shop Mnesia table." The values of X are Erlang shop records.

Note: The argument of qlc:q/1 must be a list comprehension literal and not something that evaluates to such an expression. So, for example, the following code is *not* equivalent to the code in the example:

```
Var = [X || X <- mnesia:table(shop)],
qlc:q(Var)
```

Projecting Data from a Table

Here's a query that selects the item and quantity columns from the shop table.

```
test_mnesia.erl
```

```
%% SQL equivalent
%%   SELECT item, quantity FROM shop;

demo(select_some) ->
    do(qlc:q([{X#shop.item, X#shop.quantity} || X <- mnesia:table(shop)]));
```

```
4> test_mnesia:demo(select_some).
[{orange,100},{pear,200},{banana,420},{potato,2456},{apple,20}]
```

In the previous query, the values of X are records of type shop. If you recall the record syntax described in Section 3.9, *Records*, on page 59, you'll remember that X#shop.item refers to the item field of the shop record. So, the tuple {X#shop.item, X#shop.quantity} is a tuple of the item and quantity fields of X.

Conditionally Selecting Data from a Table

Here's a query that lists all items in the shop table where the number of items in stock is less than 250. Maybe we'll use this query to decide which items to reorder.

```
test_mnesia.erl
```

```
%% SQL equivalent
%%   SELECT shop.item FROM shop
%%   WHERE  shop.quantity < 250;

demo(reorder) ->
    do(qlc:q([X#shop.item || X <- mnesia:table(shop),
                             X#shop.quantity < 250
                            ]));
```

```
5> test_mnesia:demo(reorder).
[orange,pear,apple]
```

Notice how the condition is described naturally as part of the list comprehension.

Selecting Data from Two Tables (Joins)

Now let's suppose that we want to reorder an item only if there are fewer than 250 items in stock and the item costs less than 2.0 currency units. To do this, we need to access two tables. Here's the query:

`test_mnesia.erl`
```
%% SQL equivalent
%%    SELECT shop.item, shop.quantity, cost.name, cost.price
%%    FROM shop, cost
%%    WHERE shop.item = cost.name
%%      AND cost.price < 2
%%      AND shop.quantity < 250

demo(join) ->
    do(qlc:q([X#shop.item || X <- mnesia:table(shop),
                             X#shop.quantity < 250,
                             Y <- mnesia:table(cost),
                             X#shop.item =:= Y#cost.name,
                             Y#cost.price < 2
                               ])).
```

```
6> test_mnesia:demo(join).
[apple]
```

The key here is the join between the name of the item in the shop table and the name in the cost table:

```
X#shop.item =:= Y#cost.name
```

17.2 Adding and Removing Data in the Database

Again, we'll assume we have created our database and defined a shop table. Now we want to add or remove a row from the table.

Adding a Row

We can add a row to the shop table as follows:

`test_mnesia.erl`
```
add_shop_item(Name, Quantity, Cost) ->
    Row = #shop{item=Name, quantity=Quantity, cost=Cost},
    F = fun() ->
                mnesia:write(Row)
        end,
    mnesia:transaction(F).
```

This creates a shop record and inserts it into the table:

```
1> test_mnesia:start().
ok
```

```
2> test_mnesia:reset_tables().
{atomic, ok}
%% list the shop table
3> test_mnesia:demo(select_shop).
[{shop,orange,100,3.80000},
 {shop,pear,200,3.60000},
 {shop,banana,420,4.50000},
 {shop,potato,2456,1.20000},
 {shop,apple,20,2.30000}]
%% add a new row
4> test_mnesia:add_shop_item(orange, 236, 2.8).
 {atomic,ok}
%% list the shop table again so we can see the change
5> test_mnesia:demo(select_shop).
[{shop,orange,236,2.80000},
 {shop,pear,200,3.60000},
 {shop,banana,420,4.50000},
 {shop,potato,2456,1.20000},
 {shop,apple,20,2.30000}]
```

Note: The *primary key* of the shop table is the first column in the table, that is, the item field in the shop record. The table is of type "set" (see a discussion of the set and bag types in Section 15.2, *Types of Table*, on page 269). If the newly created record has the same primary key as an existing row in the database table, it will overwrite that row; otherwise, a new row will be created.

Removing a Row

To remove a row, we need to know the object ID (OID) of the row. This is formed from the table name and the value of the primary key:

`test_mnesia.erl`
```
remove_shop_item(Item) ->
    Oid = {shop, Item},
    F = fun() ->
                mnesia:delete(Oid)
        end,
    mnesia:transaction(F).
```

```
6> test_mnesia:remove_shop_item(pear).
{atomic,ok}
%% list the table -- the pear has gone
7> test_mnesia:demo(select_shop).
[{shop,orange,236,2.80000},
 {shop,banana,420,4.50000},
 {shop,potato,2456,1.20000},
 {shop,apple,20,2.30000}]
 [{shop,orange,236,2.80000},
8> mnesia:stop().
ok
```

17.3 Mnesia Transactions

When we added or removed data from the database or performed a query, we wrote the code something like this:

```
do_something(...) ->
    F = fun() ->
            % ...
            mnesia:write(Row)
            % ... or ...
            mnesia:delete(Oid)
            % ... or ...
            qlc:e(Q)
        end,
    mnesia:transaction(F)
```

F is a fun with zero arguments. Inside F we called some combination of mnesia:write/1, mnesia:delete/1, or qlc:e(Q) (where Q is a query compiled with qlc:q/1). Having built the fun, we call mnesia:transaction(F), which evaluates the expression sequence in the fun.

Why do we do this? What does the transaction mean? To answer this, suppose we have two processes that try to simultaneously access the same data. For example, suppose I have $10 in my bank account. Now suppose two people try to simultaneously withdraw $8 from that account. What I would like to happen is that one of these transactions succeeds and the other fails.

This is exactly the guarantee that mnesia:transaction/1 provides. Either all the reads and writes to the tables in the database within a particular transaction succeed, or none of them does. If none of them does, the transaction is said to fail. If the transaction fails, no changes will be made to the database.

The strategy that Mnesia uses for this is a form of *pessimistic locking*. Whenever the Mnesia transaction manager accesses a table, it tries to lock the record or the entire table depending upon the context. If it detects that this might lead to deadlock, it immediately aborts the transaction and undoes any changes it has made.

If the transaction initially fails because some other process is accessing the data, the system waits for a short time and retries the transaction. One consequence of this is that the code inside the transaction fun might be evaluated a large number of times.

For this reason, the code inside a transaction fun should not do anything that has any side effects. For example, if we were to write the following:

```
F = fun() ->
    ...
    io:format("reading ..."), %% don't do this
    ...
  end,
mnesia:transaction(F),
```

we might get a lot of output, since the fun might be retried many times.

Note 1: mnesia:write/1 and mnesia:delete/1 should be called only inside a fun that is processed by mnesia:transaction/1.

Note 2: You should never write code to explicitly catch exceptions in the Mnesia access functions (mnesia:write/1, mnesia:delete/1, and so on) since the Mnesia transaction mechanism itself relies upon these functions throwing exceptions on failure. If you catch these exceptions and try to process them yourself, you will break the transaction mechanism.

Aborting a Transaction

Near to our shop, there's a farm. And the farmer grows apples. The farmer loves oranges, and he pays for the oranges with apples. The going rate is two apples for each orange. So, to buy N oranges, the farmer pays 2*N apples.

Here's a function that updates the database when the farmer buys some oranges:

`test_mnesia.erl`

```
farmer(Nwant) ->
    %% Nwant = Number of oranges the farmer wants to buy
    F = fun() ->
            %% find the number of apples
            [Apple] = mnesia:read({shop,apple}),
            Napples = Apple#shop.quantity,
            Apple1  = Apple#shop{quantity = Napples + 2*Nwant},
            %% update the database
            mnesia:write(Apple1),
            %% find the number of oranges
            [Orange] = mnesia:read({shop,orange}),
            NOranges = Orange#shop.quantity,
            if
                NOranges >= Nwant ->
                    N1 = NOranges - Nwant,
                    Orange1 = Orange#shop{quantity=N1},
                    %% update the database
```

```
                        mnesia:write(Orange1);
                true ->
                    %% Oops -- not enough oranges
                    mnesia:abort(oranges)
            end
        end,
    mnesia:transaction(F).
```

This code is written in a pretty stupid way because I want to show how the transaction mechanism works. First, I update the number of apples in the database. This is done *before* I check the number of oranges. The reason I do this is to show that this change gets "undone" if the transaction fails. Normally, I'd delay writing the orange and apple data back to the database until I was sure I had enough oranges.

Let's show this in operation. In the morning, the farmer comes in and buys 50 oranges:

```
1> test_mnesia:start().
ok
2> test_mnesia:reset_tables().
{atomic, ok}
%% List the shop table
3> test_mnesia:demo(select_shop).
[{shop,orange,100,3.80000},
 {shop,pear,200,3.60000},
 {shop,banana,420,4.50000},
 {shop,potato,2456,1.20000},
 {shop,apple,20,2.30000}]
%% The farmer buys 50 oranges
%% paying with 100 apples
4> test_mnesia:farmer(50).
{atomic,ok}
%% Print the shop table again
5> test_mnesia:demo(select_shop).
[{shop,orange,50,3.80000},
 {shop,pear,200,3.60000},
 {shop,banana,420,4.50000},
 {shop,potato,2456,1.20000},
 {shop,apple,120,2.30000}]
```

In the afternoon the farmer wants to buy 100 more oranges (boy, does this guy love oranges):

```
6> test_mnesia:farmer(100).
{aborted,oranges}
7> test_mnesia:demo(select_shop).
[{shop,orange,50,3.80000},
 {shop,pear,200,3.60000},
 {shop,banana,420,4.50000},
 {shop,potato,2456,1.20000},
 {shop,apple,120,2.30000}]
```

> ### Why Is the DBMS Called Mnesia?
>
> The original name was Amnesia. One of our bosses didn't like the name. He said, "You can't possibly call it Amnesia—you can't have a database that forgets things!" So we dropped the A, and the name stuck.

When the transaction failed (when we called mnesia:abort(Reason)), the changes made by mnesia:write were undone. Because of this, the database state was restored to how it was before we entered the transaction.

Loading the Test Data

Now we know how transactions work, so we can look at the code for loading the test data.

The function test_mnesia:example_tables/0 is used to provide data to initialize the database tables. The first element of the tuple is the table name. This is followed by the table data in the order given in the original record definitions.

`test_mnesia.erl`

```erlang
example_tables() ->
    [%% The shop table
     {shop, apple,    20,   2.3},
     {shop, orange,  100,   3.8},
     {shop, pear,    200,   3.6},
     {shop, banana,  420,   4.5},
     {shop, potato, 2456,   1.2},
     %% The cost table
     {cost, apple,    1.5},
     {cost, orange,   2.4},
     {cost, pear,     2.2},
     {cost, banana,   1.5},
     {cost, potato,   0.6}
    ].
```

Here's the code that inserts data into Mnesia from the example tables:

`test_mnesia.erl`

```erlang
reset_tables() ->
    mnesia:clear_table(shop),
    mnesia:clear_table(cost),
    F = fun() ->
                foreach(fun mnesia:write/1, example_tables())
        end,
    mnesia:transaction(F).
```

This just calls mnesia:write for each tuple in the list returned by example_tables/1.

The do() Function

The do function called by demo/1 is slightly more complex:

test_mnesia.erl

```
do(Q) ->
    F = fun() -> qlc:e(Q) end,
    {atomic, Val} = mnesia:transaction(F),
    Val.
```

This calls qlc:e(Q) inside an Mnesia transaction. Q is a compiled QLC query, and qlc:e(Q) evaluates the query and returns all answers to the query in a list. The return value {atomic, Val} means that the transaction succeeded with value Val. Val is the value of the transaction function.

17.4 Storing Complex Data in Tables

If you're a C programmer, how would you store a C struct in a SQL database? Or if you're a Java programmer, how would you store an object in a SQL database? The answer—with great difficulty.

One of the disadvantages of using a conventional DBMS is that there are a limited number of data types you can store in a table column. You can store an integer, a string, a float, and so on. But if you want to store a complex object, then you're in trouble.

Mnesia is designed to store Erlang data structures. In fact, you can store any Erlang data structure you want in an Mnesia table.

To illustrate this, we'll suppose that a number of architects want to store their designs in an Mnesia database. To start with, we must define a record to represent their designs:

test_mnesia.erl

```
-record(design, {id, plan}).
```

Then we can define a function that adds some designs to the database:

test_mnesia.erl

```
add_plans() ->
    D1 = #design{id   = {joe,1},
                 plan = {circle,10}},
    D2 = #design{id   = fred,
                 plan = {rectangle,10,5}},
```

```
         D3 = #design{id    = {jane,{house,23}},
                    plan = {house,
                            [{floor,1,
                              [{doors,3},
                               {windows,12},
                               {rooms,5}]},
                             {floor,2,
                              [{doors,2},
                               {rooms,4},
                               {windows,15}]}]}},
    F = fun() ->
                mnesia:write(D1),
                mnesia:write(D2),
                mnesia:write(D3)
        end,
    mnesia:transaction(F).
```

Now we can add some designs to the database:

```
1> test_mnesia:start().
ok
2> test_mnesia:add_plans().
{atomic,ok}
```

Now we have some plans in the database. We can extract these with the following access function:

test_mnesia.erl

```
get_plan(PlanId) ->
    F = fun() -> mnesia:read({design, PlanId}) end,
    mnesia:transaction(F).
```

```
3> test_mnesia:get_plan(fred).
{atomic,[{design,fred,{rectangle,10,5}}]}
4> test_mnesia:get_plan({jane, {house,23}}).
{atomic,[{design,{jane,{house,23}},
                 {house,[{floor,1,[{doors,3},
                                   {windows,12},
                                   {rooms,5}]},
                         {floor,2,[{doors,2},
                                   {rooms,4},
                                   {windows,15}]}]}}]}
```

As you can see, both the database key and the extracted record can be arbitrary Erlang terms.

In technical terms, we say there is no "impedance mismatch" between the data structures in the database and the data structures in our programming language. This means that inserting and deleting complex data structures into the database is very fast.

> **Fragmented Tables**
>
> Mnesia supports "fragmented tables." (*horizontal partitioning* in database terminology). This is designed for implementing extremely large tables. The tables are split into fragments that are stored on different machines. The fragments are themselves Mnesia tables. The fragments can be replicated, have indexes, and so on, as for any other table.
>
> Refer to the Mnesia User's Guide for more details.

17.5 Table Types and Location

We can configure Mnesia tables in many different ways. First, tables can be in RAM or on disk (or both). Second, tables can be located on a single machine or replicated on several machines.

When we design our tables, we must think about the type of data we want to store in the tables. Here are the properties of the tables:

RAM tables
>   These are very fast. The data in them is *transient* so it will be lost if the machine crashes or when you stop the DBMS.

Disk tables
>   Disk tables should survive a crash (provided the disk is not physically damaged).
>
>   When an Mnesia transaction writes to a table and the table is stored on disk, what actually happens is that the transaction data is first written to a disk log. This disk log grows continuously, and at regular intervals the information in the disk log is consolidated with the other data in the database, and the entry in the disk log is cleared. If the system crashes, then the next time the system is restarted, the disk log is checked for consistency, and any outstanding entries in the log are added to the database before the database is made available. Once a transaction has succeeded, the data should have been properly written to the disk log, and if the system fails after this, then when the system is next restarted, changes made in the transaction should survive the crash.
>
>   If the system crashes during a transaction, then the changes made to the database should be lost.

Before using a RAM table, you need to perform some experiments to see whether the entire table will fit into physical memory. If the RAM tables don't fit into physical memory, the system will page a lot, which will be bad for performance.

Since RAM tables are transient, we need to ask ourselves the question, Does it matter whether all the data in our RAM table is lost? If the answer is yes, we will need to replicate the RAM table on disk or replicate on a second machine (as a RAM or disk table, or both).

Creating Tables

To create a table, we call mnesia:create_table(Name, ArgS), where ArgS is a list of {Key,Val} tuples. create_table returns {atomic, ok} if the table was successfully created; otherwise, it returns {aborted, Reason}.

Some of the most common arguments to create_table are as follows:

Name

> This is the name of the table (an atom). By convention, it is the name of an Erlang record—the table rows will be instances of this record.

{type, Type}

> This specifies the type of the table. Type is one of set, ordered_set, or bag. These types have the same meaning as described in Section 15.2, *Types of Table*, on page 269.

{disc_copies, NodeList}

> NodeList is a list of the Erlang nodes where disk copies of the table will be stored. When we use this option, the system will also create a RAM copy of the table on the node where we performed this operation.

> It is possible to have a replicated table of type disc_copies on one node and to have the same table stored as a different table type on a different node. This is desirable if we want the following:

> 1. Read operations to be very fast and performed from RAM

> 2. Write operations to be performed to persistent storage

{ram_copies, NodeList}

> NodeList is a list of the Erlang nodes where RAM copies of the table will be stored.

{disc_only_copies, NodeList}

> NodeList is a list of the Erlang nodes where disk-only copies of data are stored. These tables have no RAM replicas and are slower to access.

{attributes, AtomList}

> This is a list of the column names of the values in a particular table. Note that to create a table containing the Erlang record xxx, we can use the syntax {attribute, record_info(fields, xxx)} (alternatively we can specify an explicit list of record field names).

Note: There are more options to create_table than I have shown here. Refer to the manual page for mnesia for details of all the options.

Common Combinations of Table Attributes

In all the following, we'll assume that Attrs is an {attributes,...} tuple.

Here are some common table configuration options that cover the most common cases:

```
mnesia:create_table(shop, [Attrs])
```

- RAM resident on a single node.
- If the node crashes, the table will be lost.
- Fastest of all methods.
- Table must fit in memory.

```
mnesia:create_table(shop,[Attrs,{disc_copies,[node()]}])
```

- RAM + disk copy on a single node.
- If the node crashes, the table will be recovered from disk.
- Fast reads, slower writes.
- The table should fit in memory.

```
mnesia:create_table(shop, [Attrs,{disc_only_copies,[node()]}])
```

- Disk-only copy on a single node.
- Large tables don't have to fit in memory.
- Slower than with RAM replicas.

```
mnesia:create_table(shop,
    [Attrs,{ram_copies,[node(),someOtherNode()]}])
```

- RAM resident table on two nodes.
- If both nodes crash, the table will be lost.
- The table must fit into memory.
- The table can be accessed on either node.

```
mnesia:create_table(shop,
  [Attrs, {disc_copies, [node(),someOtherNode()]}])
```

- Disk copies on two nodes.
- Can resume on either node.
- Survives double crash.

Table Behavior

When a table is replicated across several Erlang nodes, it is synchronized as far as possible. If one node crashes, the system will still work, but the number of replicas will be reduced. When the crashed node comes back online, it will resynchronize with the other nodes where the replicas are kept.

Note: Mnesia may become overloaded if the nodes running Mnesia stop functioning. If you are using a laptop that goes to sleep, when it restarts, Mnesia might become temporarily overloaded and produce a number of warning messages. We can ignore these messages.

17.6 Creating the Initial Database

Here is a session that creates an Mnesia database. You need to do this only once.

```
$ erl
1> mnesia:create_schema([node()]).
ok
2> init:stop().
ok
$ ls
Mnesia.nonode@nohost
```

mnesia:create_schema(NodeList) initiates a new Mnesia database on all the nodes in NodeList (which must be a list of valid Erlang nodes). In our case, we gave the node list as [node()], that is, the current node. Mnesia is initialized and creates a directory structure called Mnesia.nonode@nohost to store the database. Then we exit from the Erlang shell and issue the operating system's ls command to verify this.

If we repeat the exercise with a distributed node called joe, we get the following:

```
$ erl -name joe
(joe@doris.myerl.example.com) 1> mnesia:create_schema([node()]).
ok
```

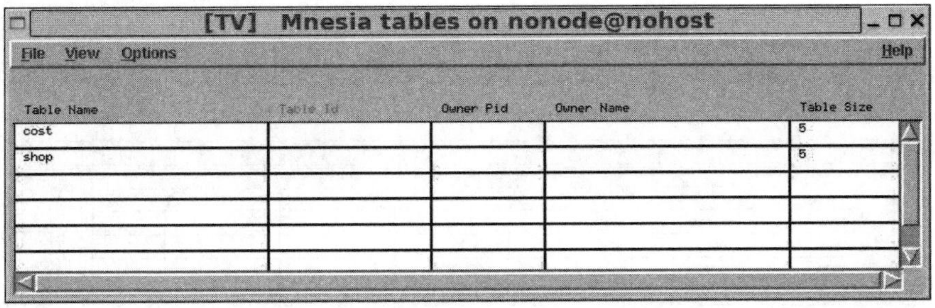

Figure 17.1: TABLE VIEWER INITIAL SCREEN

```
2> init:stop().
ok
$ ls
Mnesia.joe@doris.myerl.example.com
```

Or we can point to a specific database when we start Erlang:

```
$ erl  -mnesia dir '"/home/joe/some/path/to/Mnesia.company"'
1> mnesia:create_schema([node()]).
ok
2> init:stop().
ok
```

/home/joe/some/path/to/Mnesia.company is the name of the directory in which the database will be stored.

17.7 The Table Viewer

The table viewer is a GUI for viewing Mnesia and ETS tables. The command tv:start() starts the table viewer. You'll see the initial display screen similar to Figure 17.1. To see the tables in Mnesia, you have to select View > Tab. We can see the table viewer displaying the shop table in Figure 17.2, on the next page.

17.8 Digging Deeper

I hope I've whetted your appetite for Mnesia. Mnesia is a very powerful DBMS. It has been in production use in a number of demanding telecom applications delivered by Ericsson since 1998.

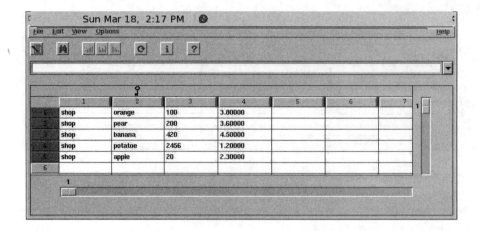

Figure 17.2: TABLE VIEWER

Since this is a book about Erlang and not Mnesia, I can't really do any more than just give a few examples of the most common ways to use Mnesia. The techniques I've shown in this chapter are those I use myself. I don't actually use (or understand) much more than what I've shown you. But with what I've shown you, you can have a lot of fun and build some pretty sophisticated applications.

The main areas I've omitted are as follows:

- *Backup and recovery*: Mnesia has a range of options for configuring backup operations allowing for different types of disaster recovery.
- *Dirty operations*: Mnesia allows a number of *dirty* operations (dirty_read, dirty_write, ...). These are operations that are performed outside a transaction context. These are very dangerous operations that can be used if you know that your application is single-threaded or under other special circumstances. Dirty operations are used for efficiency reasons.
- SNMP tables: Mnesia has a built-in SNMP table type. This makes implementing SNMP management systems very easy.

The definitive reference to Mnesia is the Mnesia User's Guide available from the main Erlang distribution site (see Appendix C, on page 395). In addition, the examples subdirectory in the Mnesia distribution (/usr/local/lib/erlang/lib/mnesia-X.Y.Z/examples on my machine) has some Mnesia examples.

17.9 Listings

test_mnesia.erl

```erlang
-module(test_mnesia).
-import(lists, [foreach/2]).
-compile(export_all).

%% IMPORTANT: The next line must be included
%%            if we want to call qlc:q(...)

-include_lib("stdlib/include/qlc.hrl").

-record(shop, {item, quantity, cost}).
-record(cost, {name, price}).
-record(design, {id, plan}).

do_this_once() ->
    mnesia:create_schema([node()]),
    mnesia:start(),
    mnesia:create_table(shop,   [{attributes, record_info(fields, shop)}]),
    mnesia:create_table(cost,   [{attributes, record_info(fields, cost)}]),
    mnesia:create_table(design, [{attributes, record_info(fields, design)}]),
    mnesia:stop().

start() ->
    mnesia:start(),
    mnesia:wait_for_tables([shop,cost,design], 20000).


%% SQL equivalent
%%   SELECT * FROM shop;

demo(select_shop) ->
    do(qlc:q([X || X <- mnesia:table(shop)])).


%% SQL equivalent
%%   SELECT item, quantity FROM shop;

demo(select_some) ->
    do(qlc:q([{X#shop.item, X#shop.quantity} || X <- mnesia:table(shop)])).


%% SQL equivalent
%%    SELECT shop.item FROM shop
%%    WHERE  shop.quantity < 250;

demo(reorder) ->
    do(qlc:q([X#shop.item || X <- mnesia:table(shop),
                             X#shop.quantity < 250
                                 ])).
```

```erlang
%% SQL equivalent
%%    SELECT shop.item, shop.quantity, cost.name, cost.price
%%    FROM shop, cost
%%    WHERE shop.item = cost.name
%%        AND cost.price < 2
%%        AND shop.quantity < 250

demo(join) ->
    do(qlc:q([X#shop.item || X <- mnesia:table(shop),
                             X#shop.quantity < 250,
                             Y <- mnesia:table(cost),
                             X#shop.item =:= Y#cost.name,
                             Y#cost.price < 2
                                 ])).

do(Q) ->
    F = fun() -> qlc:e(Q) end,
    {atomic, Val} = mnesia:transaction(F),
    Val.


example_tables() ->
    [%% The shop table
     {shop, apple,   20,    2.3},
     {shop, orange,  100,   3.8},
     {shop, pear,    200,   3.6},
     {shop, banana,  420,   4.5},
     {shop, potato,  2456, 1.2},
     %% The cost table
     {cost, apple,   1.5},
     {cost, orange,  2.4},
     {cost, pear,    2.2},
     {cost, banana,  1.5},
     {cost, potato,  0.6}
    ].

add_shop_item(Name, Quantity, Cost) ->
    Row = #shop{item=Name, quantity=Quantity, cost=Cost},
    F = fun() ->
                mnesia:write(Row)
        end,
    mnesia:transaction(F).

remove_shop_item(Item) ->
    Oid = {shop, Item},
    F = fun() ->
                mnesia:delete(Oid)
        end,
    mnesia:transaction(F).
```

```erlang
farmer(Nwant) ->
    %% Nwant = Number of oranges the farmer wants to buy
    F = fun() ->
                %% find the number of apples
                [Apple] = mnesia:read({shop,apple}),
                Napples = Apple#shop.quantity,
                Apple1  = Apple#shop{quantity = Napples + 2*Nwant},
                %% update the database
                mnesia:write(Apple1),
                %% find the number of oranges
                [Orange] = mnesia:read({shop,orange}),
                NOranges = Orange#shop.quantity,
                if
                    NOranges >= Nwant ->
                        N1 =  NOranges - Nwant,
                        Orange1 = Orange#shop{quantity=N1},
                        %% update the database
                        mnesia:write(Orange1);
                    true ->
                        %% Oops -- not enough oranges
                        mnesia:abort(oranges)
                end
        end,
    mnesia:transaction(F).


reset_tables() ->
    mnesia:clear_table(shop),
    mnesia:clear_table(cost),
    F = fun() ->
                foreach(fun mnesia:write/1, example_tables())
        end,
    mnesia:transaction(F).


add_plans() ->
    D1 = #design{id   = {joe,1},
                 plan = {circle,10}},
    D2 = #design{id   = fred,
                 plan = {rectangle,10,5}},
    D3 = #design{id   = {jane,{house,23}},
                 plan = {house,
                            [{floor,1,
                              [{doors,3},
                               {windows,12},
                               {rooms,5}]},
                             {floor,2,
                              [{doors,2},
                               {rooms,4},
                               {windows,15}]}]}},
```

```
        F = fun() ->
                    mnesia:write(D1),
                    mnesia:write(D2),
                    mnesia:write(D3)
            end,
        mnesia:transaction(F).

get_plan(PlanId) ->
    F = fun() -> mnesia:read({design, PlanId}) end,
    mnesia:transaction(F).
```

## Chapter 18

Making a System with OTP

In this chapter, we're going to make a system that could function as the back end of a web-based company. Our company has two items for sale: prime numbers and areas. Customers can buy a prime number from us, or we'll calculate the area of a geometric object for them. I think our company has great potential.

We'll build two servers: one to generate prime numbers and the other to compute areas. To do this, we'll use the gen_server framework that we talked about in Section 16.2, *Getting Started with gen_server*, on page 295.

When we build the system, we have to think about errors. Even though we have thoroughly tested our software, we might not have caught all the bugs. We'll assume that one of our servers has a fatal error that crashes the server. In fact, we'll introduce a *deliberate error* into one of the servers that will cause it to crash.

When the server crashes, we'll need some mechanism to detect the fact that it has crashed and to restart it. For this we'll use the idea of a *supervision tree*. We'll create a supervisor that watches over our servers and restarts them if they crash.

Of course, if a server does crash, we'll want to know why it crashed so that we can fix the problem later. To log all errors, we'll use the OTP error logger. We'll show how to configure the error logger and how to generate error reports from the error logs.

When we're computing prime numbers and, in particular large prime numbers, our CPU might overheat. To prevent this, we'll need to turn on a powerful fan. To do so, we'll need to think about *alarms*. We'll use the OTP event handling framework to generate and handle alarms.

All of these topics (creating a server, supervising a server, logging errors, and detecting alarms) are typical problems that have to be solved in any production system. So even though our company might have a rather uncertain future, we can reuse the architecture here in many systems. In fact, this architecture *is* used in a number of commercially successful companies.

Finally, when everything works, we'll package all our code into an OTP *application*. This is a specialized way of grouping everything that has to do with a particular problem so that it can be started and stopped and managed by the OTP system itself.

The order in which this material is presented is slightly tricky since there are many circular dependencies between the different areas. Error logging is just a special case of event management. Alarms are just events, the error logger is a supervised process, but the process supervisor can call the error logger.

I'll try to impose some order here and present these topics in an order that makes some kind of sense. We'll do the following:

1. We'll look at the ideas used in a generic event handler.
2. We'll see how the error logger works.
3. We'll add alarm management.
4. We'll write two application servers.
5. We'll make a supervision tree and add the servers to it.
6. We'll package everything into an application.

18.1 Generic Event Handling

An *event* is just something that happens—something noteworthy that the programmer thinks somebody should do something about.

When we're programming and something noteworthy happens, we just send an event message to a registered process, like this:

```
RegProcName ! {event, E}
```

E is the event (any Erlang term). RegProcName is the name of a registered process.

We don't know (or care) what happens to the message after we have sent it. We have done our job and told somebody else that something has happened.

Now let's turn our attention to the process that receives the event messages. This is called an *event handler*. The simplest possible event handler is a "do nothing" handler. When it receives an {event, X} message, it does nothing with the event; it just throws it away.

Here's our first attempt at a generic event handler program:

`event_handler.erl`
```
-module(event_handler).
-export([make/1, add_handler/2, event/2]).

%% make a new event handler called Name
%%  the handler function is noOp -- so we do nothing with the event
make(Name) ->
    register(Name, spawn(fun() -> my_handler(fun no_op/1) end)).

add_handler(Name, Fun) -> Name ! {add, Fun}.

%% generate an event
event(Name, X) -> Name ! {event, X}.

my_handler(Fun) ->
    receive
        {add, Fun1} ->
            my_handler(Fun1);
        {event, Any} ->
            (catch Fun(Any)),
            my_handler(Fun)
    end.

no_op(_) -> void.
```

The event handler API is as follows:

event_handler:make(Name)

> Make a "do nothing" event handler called Name (an atom). This provides a place to which to send events.

event_handler:event(Name, X)

> Send the event X to the event handler called Name.

event_handler:add_handler(Name, Fun)

> Add a handler Fun to the event handler called Name. Now when an event X occurs, the event handler will evaluate Fun(X).

Now we'll create an event handler and generate an error:

```
1> event_handler:make(errors).
true
2> event_handler:event(errors, hi).
{event,hi}
```

Nothing special happens, because we haven't installed a callback module in the event handler.

To get the event handler to do something, we have to write a callback module and install it in the event handler. Here's the code for an event handler callback module:

`motor_controller.erl`

```erlang
-module(motor_controller).

-export([add_event_handler/0]).

add_event_handler() ->
    event_handler:add_handler(errors, fun controller/1).

controller(too_hot) ->
    io:format("Turn off the motor~n");
controller(X) ->
    io:format("~w ignored event: ~p~n",[?MODULE, X]).
```

Once this has been compiled, it can be installed:

```
3> c(motor_controller).
{ok,motor_controller}
4> motor_controller:add_event_handler().
{add,#Fun<motor_controller.0.99476749>}
```

Now when we send events to the handler, they are processed by the motor_controller:controller/1 function:

```
5> event_handler:event(errors, cool).
motor_controller ignored event: cool
{event,cool}
6> event_handler:event(errors, too_hot).
Turn off the motor
{event,too_hot}
```

What was the point of this exercise? First we provided a name to which to send events. In this case, it was the registered process called errors. Then we defined a protocol to send events to this registered process. But we did not say what would happen to the message when it got there. In fact, all that happened was that we evaluated noOp(X). Then at a later stage we installed a custom event handler.

Very Late Binding with "Change Your Mind"

Suppose we write a function that hides the event_handler:event routine from the programmer. For example, say we write the following:

lib_misc.erl

```
too_hot() ->
    event_handler:event(errors, too_hot).
```

Then we tell the programmer to call lib_misc:too_hot() in their code when things go wrong. In most programming languages, the call to the function too_hot will be statically or dynamically linked to the code that calls the function. Once it has been linked, it will perform a fixed job depending upon the code. If we change our mind later and decide that we want to do something else, we have no easy way of changing the behavior of the system.

The Erlang way of handling events is completely different. It allows us to decouple the generation of the event from the processing of the event. We can change the processing at any time we want by just sending a new handler function to the event handler. Nothing is statically linked, and the event handlers can be changed whenever you want.

Using this mechanism, we can build systems that *evolve with time* and that never need to be stopped to upgrade the code.

Note: This is not "late binding"—it's "very late binding, and you can change your mind later."

You might be a little puzzled here. Why have we talked about event handlers? The key point to note is that the event handler provides an infrastructure where we can install custom handlers.

The error logger infrastructure follows the event handler pattern. We can install different handlers in the error logger to get it to do different things. The alarm handling infrastructure also follows this pattern.

18.2 The Error Logger

The OTP system comes packaged with a customizable error logger. We can look at the error logger from three points of view. The *programmer view* concerns the function calls that programmers make in their code in order to log an error. The *configuration view* is concerned with where and how the error logger stores its data. The *report view* is concerned with the analysis of errors after they have occurred. We'll look at each of these in turn.

Logging an Error

As far as the programmer is concerned, the API to the error logger is simple. Here's a simple subset of the API:

@spec error_logger:error_msg(String) -> ok

> Send an error message to the error logger.

```
1> error_logger:error_msg("An error has occurred\n").
=ERROR REPORT==== 28-Mar-2007::10:46:28 ===
An error has occurred
ok
```

@spec error_logger:error_msg(Format, Data) -> ok

> Send an error message to the error logger. The arguments are the same as for io:format(Format, Data).

```
2> error_logger:error_msg("~s, an error has occurred\n", ["Joe"]).
=ERROR REPORT==== 28-Mar-2007::10:47:09 ===
Joe, an error has occurred
ok
```

@spec error_logger:error_report(Report) -> ok

> Send a standard error report to the error logger.

- @type Report = [{Tag, Data} | term()] | string() | term()]
- @type Tag = term()
- @type Data = term()

```
3> error_logger:error_report([{tag1,data1},a_term,{tag2,data}]).
=ERROR REPORT==== 28-Mar-2007::10:51:51 ===
tag1: data1
a_term
tag2: data
```

This is only a subset of the available API. Discussing this in detail is not particularly interesting. We'll use only error_msg in our programs anyway. The full details are in the error_logger manual page.

Configuring the Error Logger

We can configure the error logger in many ways. We can see all errors in the Erlang shell (this is the default if we don't do anything special). We can write all errors that are reported in the shell into a single format-ted text file. Finally, we can create a *rotating log*. You can think of the rotating log as a large circular buffer containing messages produced by the error logger. As new messages come, they are appended to the end of the log, and when the log is full, the earliest entries in the log are deleted.

The rotating log is extremely useful. You decide how many files the log should occupy and how big each individual log file should be, and the system takes care of deleting old log files and creating new files in a large circular buffer. You can size the log to keep a record of the last few days of operations, which is usually sufficient for most purposes.

The Standard Error Loggers

When we start Erlang, we can give the system a *boot argument*:

$ erl -boot start_clean

> This creates an environment suited for program development. Only a simple form of error logging is provided. (The command erl with no boot argument is equivalent to erl -boot start_clean.)

$ erl -boot start_sasl

> This creates an environment suitable for running a production system. System Architecture Support Libraries (SASL) takes care of error logging, overload protection, and so on.

Log file configuration is best done from configuration files, because nobody can ever remember all the arguments to the logger. In the following sections, we'll look at how the default system works and then look at four specific configurations that change how the error logger works.

SASL with No Configuration

Here's what happens when we start SASL with no configuration file:

```
$ erl -boot start_sasl
Erlang (BEAM) emulator version 5.5.3 [async-threads:0]  ...

=PROGRESS REPORT==== 27-Mar-2007::11:49:12 ===
supervisor: {local,sasl_safe_sup}
   started: [{pid,<0.32.0>},
             {name,alarm_handler},
             {mfa,{alarm_handler,start_link,[]}},
             {restart_type,permanent},
             {shutdown,2000},
             {child_type,worker}]

... many lines removed ...
Eshell V5.5.3  (abort with ^G)
```

Now we'll call one of the routines in error_logger to report an error:

```
1> error_logger:error_msg("This is an error\n").
=ERROR REPORT==== 27-Mar-2007::11:53:08 ===
This is an error
ok
```

Note the error is reported in the Erlang shell. Where the error is reported depends upon the error logger configuration.

Controlling What Gets Logged

The error logger produces a number of types of report:

Supervisor reports
> These are issued whenever an OTP supervisor starts or stops a supervised process (we'll talk about supervisors in Section 18.5, *The Supervision Tree*, on page 345).

Progress reports
> These are issued whenever an OTP supervisor starts or stops.

Crash reports
> These are issued when a process started by an OTP behavior terminates with an exit reason other than normal or shutdown.

These three reports are produced automatically without the programmer having to do anything.

In addition, we can explicitly call routines in the error_handler module to produce three types of log report. These let us log errors, warnings, and informational messages. These three terms have no semantic meaning; they are merely tags used by the programmer to indicate the nature of the entry in the error log.

Later, when the error log is analyzed, we can use these tags to help us decide which log entry to investigate. When we configure the error logger, we can choose to save only errors and discard all other types of entry. Now we'll write the configuration file elog1.config to configure the error logger:

elog1.config

```
%% no tty
[{sasl, [
        {sasl_error_logger, false}
        ]}].
```

If we start the system with this configuration file, we'll get only error reports and not progress reports and so on. All these error reports are only in the shell.

```
$ erl -boot start_sasl -config elog1
1> error_logger:error_msg("This is an error\n").
=ERROR REPORT==== 27-Mar-2007::11:53:08 ===
This is an error
ok
```

Text File and Shell

The next configuration file lists error reports in the shell, and a copy of everything reported in the shell is also made to a file:

elog2.config

```
%% single text file - minimal tty
[{sasl, [
        %% All reports go to this file
        {sasl_error_logger, {file, "/home/joe/error_logs/THELOG"}}
      ]}].
```

To test this, we start Erlang, generate an error message, and then look in the log file:

```
$ erl -boot start_sasl -config elog2
1> error_logger:error_msg("This is an error\n").
=ERROR REPORT==== 27-Mar-2007::11:53:08 ===
This is an error ok
```

If we now look in /home/joe/error_logs/THELOG, we'll find it starts like this:

```
=PROGRESS REPORT==== 28-Mar-2007::11:30:55 ===
supervisor: {local,sasl_safe_sup}
   started: [{pid,<0.34.0>},
            {name,alarm_handler},
            {mfa,{alarm_handler,start_link,[]}},
            {restart_type,permanent},
            {shutdown,2000},
            {child_type,worker}]
...
```

Rotating Log and Shell

This configuration gives us shell output plus a copy of everything that was written to the shell in a rotating log file. This is a very useful configuration.

elog3.config

```
%% rotating log and minimal tty
[{sasl, [
        {sasl_error_logger, false},
        %% define the parameters of the rotating log
        %% the log file directory
        {error_logger_mf_dir,"/home/joe/error_logs"},
        %% # bytes per logfile
        {error_logger_mf_maxbytes,10485760}, % 10 MB
        %% maximum number of logfiles
        {error_logger_mf_maxfiles, 10}
      ]}].
```

```
$erl -boot start_sasl -config elog3
1> error_logger:error_msg("This is an error\n").
=ERROR REPORT==== 28-Mar-2007::11:36:19 ===
This is an error
false
```

When we run the system, all the errors go into a rotating error log. Later in this chapter we'll see how to extract this error from the log.

Production Environment

In a production environment, we are really interested only in errors and not progress or information reports, so we tell the error logger to report only errors. Without this setting, the system might get swamped with information and progress reports.

elog4.config

```
%% rotating log and errors
[{sasl, [
        %% minimise shell error logging
        {sasl_error_logger, false},
        %% only report errors
        {errlog_type, error},
        %% define the parameters of the rotating log
        %% the log file directory
        {error_logger_mf_dir,"/home/joe/error_logs"},
        %% # bytes per logfile
        {error_logger_mf_maxbytes,10485760}, % 10 MB
        %% maximum number of
        {error_logger_mf_maxfiles, 10}
      ]}].
```

Running this results in a similar output to the previous example. The difference is that only errors are reported in the error log.

Analyzing the Errors

Reading the error logs is the responsibility of the rb module. It has an extremely simple interface.

```
1> rb:help().
Report Browser Tool - usage
============================
rb:start()          - start the rb_server with default options
rb:start(Options)   - where Options is a list of:
                       {start_log, FileName}
                         - default: standard_io
                       {max, MaxNoOfReports}
                         - MaxNoOfReports should be an integer or 'all'
                         - default: all

    ...
    ... many lines omitted ...
    ...
```

We start the report browser by telling it how many log entries to read (in this case the last twenty):

```
2> rb:start([{max,20}]).
rb: reading report...done.
3> rb:list().
No            Type       Process   Date        Time
==            ====       =======   ====        ====
11            progress   <0.29.0>  2007-03-28  11:34:31
10            progress   <0.29.0>  2007-03-28  11:34:31
9             progress   <0.29.0>  2007-03-28  11:34:31
8             progress   <0.29.0>  2007-03-28  11:34:31
7             progress   <0.22.0>  2007-03-28  11:34:31
6             progress   <0.29.0>  2007-03-28  11:35:53
5             progress   <0.29.0>  2007-03-28  11:35:53
4             progress   <0.29.0>  2007-03-28  11:35:53
3             progress   <0.29.0>  2007-03-28  11:35:53
2             progress   <0.22.0>  2007-03-28  11:35:53
1             error      <0.23.0>  2007-03-28  11:36:19
ok
> rb:show(1).

ERROR REPORT  <0.40.0>                       2007-03-28 11:36:19
================================================================

This is an error
ok
```

To isolate a particular error, we can use commands such as rb: grep(RegExp), which will find all reports matching the regular expression RegExp. I don't want to go into all the details of how to analyze the error log. The best thing is to spend some time interacting with rb and seeing what it can do. Note that you never need to actually delete an error report, since the rotation mechanism will eventually delete old error logs.

If you want to keep all the error logs, you'll have to poll the error log at regular intervals and remove the information in which you're interested.

18.3 Alarm Management

When we write our application, we need only one alarm—we'll raise it when the CPU starts melting because we're computing a humongous prime (remember, we were making a company that sells prime numbers). This time we'll use the real OTP alarm handler (and not the simple one we saw at the start of this chapter).

The alarm handler is a callback module for the OTP gen_event behavior. Here's the code:

`my_alarm_handler.erl`

```erlang
-module(my_alarm_handler).
-behaviour(gen_event).

%% gen_event callbacks
-export([init/1, handle_event/2, handle_call/2,
         handle_info/2, terminate/2]).

%% init(Args) must return {ok, State}
init(Args) ->
    io:format("*** my_alarm_handler init:~p~n",[Args]),
    {ok, 0}.

handle_event({set_alarm, tooHot}, N) ->
    error_logger:error_msg("*** Tell the Engineer to turn on the fan~n"),
    {ok, N+1};
handle_event({clear_alarm, tooHot}, N) ->
    error_logger:error_msg("*** Danger over. Turn off the fan~n"),
    {ok, N};
handle_event(Event, N) ->
    io:format("*** unmatched event:~p~n",[Event]),
    {ok, N}.

handle_call(_Request, N) -> Reply = N, {ok, N,  N}.

handle_info(_Info, N)      -> {ok, N}.

terminate(_Reason, _N)     -> ok.
```

This code is pretty similar to the callback code for gen_server, which we saw earlier in Section 16.3, *What Happens When We Call the Server?*, on page 300. The interesting routine is handle_event(Event, State). This should return {ok, NewState}. Event is a tuple of the form {EventType, EventArg}, where EventType is set_event or clear_event and EventArg is a user-supplied argument. We'll see later how these events are generated.

Now we can have some fun. We'll start the system, generate an alarm, install an alarm handler, generate a new alarm, and so on:

```
$ erl -boot start_sasl -config elog3
1> alarm_handler:set_alarm(tooHot).
ok
=INFO REPORT==== 28-Mar-2007::14:20:06 ===
alarm_handler: {set,tooHot}

2> gen_event:swap_handler(alarm_handler,
                          {alarm_handler, swap},
                          {my_alarm_handler, xyz}).

*** my_alarm_handler init:{xyz,{alarm_handler,[tooHot]}}
3> alarm_handler:set_alarm(tooHot).
ok
=ERROR REPORT==== 28-Mar-2007::14:22:19 ===
*** Tell the Engineer to turn on the fan
4> alarm_handler:clear_alarm(tooHot).
ok
=ERROR REPORT==== 28-Mar-2007::14:22:39 ===
*** Danger over. Turn off the fan
```

What happened here?

1. We started Erlang with -boot start_sasl. When we do this, we get a standard alarm handler. When we set or clear an alarm, nothing happens. This is similar to the "do nothing" event handler we discussed earlier.

2. When we set an alarm (line 1), we just get an information report. There is no special handling of the alarm.

3. We install a custom alarm handler (line 2). The argument to my_alarm_handler (xyz) has no particular significance; the syntax requires some value here, but since we don't use the value and we just used the atom xyz, we can identify the argument when it is printed.

   The ** my_alarm_handler_init: ... printout came from our callback module.

4. We set and clear a tooHot alarm (lines 3 and 4). This is processed by our custom alarm handler. We can verify this by reading the shell printout.

Reading the Log

Let's go back to the error logger to see what happened:

```
1> rb:start([{max,20}]).
rb: reading report...done.
2> rb:list().
No              Type      Process   Date        Time
==              ====      =======   ====        ====
...
3          info_report   <0.29.0>  2007-03-28  14:20:06
2                error    <0.29.0>  2007-03-28  14:22:19
1                error    <0.29.0>  2007-03-28  14:22:39
3> rb:show(1).

ERROR REPORT   <0.33.0>              2007-03-28  14:22:39
=========================================================
*** Danger over. Turn off the fan
ok
4> rb:show(2).
ERROR REPORT   <0.33.0>              2007-03-28  14:22:19
=========================================================
*** Tell the Engineer to turn on the fan
```

So, we can see that the error logging mechanism works.

In practice we would make sure the error log was big enough for several days or weeks of operation. Every few days (or weeks) we'd check the error logs and investigate all errors.

Note: The rb module has functions to select specific types of errors and to extract these errors to a file. So, the process of analyzing the error logs can be fully automated.

18.4 The Application Servers

Our application has two servers: a prime number server and an area server. Here's the prime number server. It has been written using the gen_server behavior (see Section 16.2, *Getting Started with gen_server*, on page 295). Note how it includes the alarm handling procedures we developed in the previous section.

The Prime Number Server

`prime_server.erl`

```erlang
-module(prime_server).
-behaviour(gen_server).

-export([new_prime/1, start_link/0]).

%% gen_server callbacks
-export([init/1, handle_call/3, handle_cast/2, handle_info/2,
         terminate/2, code_change/3]).

start_link() ->
    gen_server:start_link({local, ?MODULE}, ?MODULE, [], []).

new_prime(N) ->
    %% 20000 is a timeout (ms)
    gen_server:call(?MODULE, {prime, N}, 20000).

init([]) ->
    %% Note we must set trap_exit = true if we
    %% want terminate/2 to be called when the application
    %% is stopped
    process_flag(trap_exit, true),
    io:format("~p starting~n",[?MODULE]),
    {ok, 0}.

handle_call({prime, K}, _From, N) ->
    {reply, make_new_prime(K), N+1}.

handle_cast(_Msg, N)   -> {noreply, N}.

handle_info(_Info, N)  -> {noreply, N}.

terminate(_Reason, _N) ->
    io:format("~p stopping~n",[?MODULE]),
    ok.

code_change(_OldVsn, N, _Extra) -> {ok, N}.

make_new_prime(K) ->
    if
        K > 100 ->
            alarm_handler:set_alarm(tooHot),
            N = lib_primes:make_prime(K),
            alarm_handler:clear_alarm(tooHot),
            N;
        true ->
            lib_primes:make_prime(K)
    end.
```

The Area Server

And now the area server. This is also written with the gen_server behavior. Note that writing a server this way is extremely quick. When I wrote this example, I cut and pasted the code in the prime server and made it into an area server. This took only a few minutes.

The area server is not the most brilliant program in the world, and it contains a deliberate error (can you find it?). My not-so-cunning plan is to let the server crash and be restarted by the supervisor. And what's more, we'll get a report of all of this in the error log.

area_server.erl

```erlang
-module(area_server).
-behaviour(gen_server).

-export([area/1, start_link/0]).

%% gen_server callbacks
-export([init/1, handle_call/3, handle_cast/2, handle_info/2,
         terminate/2, code_change/3]).

start_link() ->
    gen_server:start_link({local, ?MODULE}, ?MODULE, [], []).

area(Thing) ->
    gen_server:call(?MODULE, {area, Thing}).

init([]) ->
    %% Note we must set trap_exit = true if we
    %% want terminate/2 to be called when the application
    %% is stopped
    process_flag(trap_exit, true),
    io:format("~p starting~n",[?MODULE]),
    {ok, 0}.

handle_call({area, Thing}, _From, N) -> {reply, compute_area(Thing), N+1}.

handle_cast(_Msg, N)   -> {noreply, N}.

handle_info(_Info, N)   -> {noreply, N}.

terminate(_Reason, _N) ->
    io:format("~p stopping~n",[?MODULE]),
    ok.

code_change(_OldVsn, N, _Extra) -> {ok, N}.

compute_area({square, X})       -> X*X;
compute_area({rectangle, X, Y}) -> X*Y.
```

one_for_one supervision

If one process crashes, it is restarted

one_for_all supervision

If one process crashes, all are terminated
and then restarted

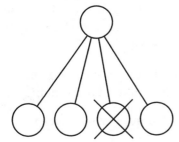 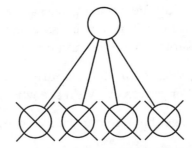

Figure 18.1: TWO TYPES OF SUPERVISION TREE

18.5 The Supervision Tree

A supervision tree is a tree of processes. The upper processes (supervisors) in the tree monitor the lower processes (workers) in the tree and restart the lower processes if they fail. There are two types of supervision tree. You can see them in Figure 18.1.

One-for-one supervision trees

In one-for-one supervision, if a worker fails, it is restarted by the supervisor.

One-for-all supervision trees

In one-for-all supervision, if any worker dies, then all the worker processes are killed (by calling the terminate/2 function in the appropriate callback module). Then all the worker processes are restarted.

Supervisors are created using the OTP *supervisor* behavior. This behavior is parameterized with a callback module that specifies the supervisor strategy and how to start the individual worker processes in the supervision tree. The supervisor tree is specified with a function of this form:

```
init(...) ->
    {ok, {RestartStrategy, MaxRestarts, Time},
        [Worker1, Worker2, ...]}.
```

Here RestartStrategy is one of the atoms one_for_one or one_for_all.
MaxRestarts and Time specify a "restart frequency." If a supervisor performs more than MaxRestarts in Time seconds, then the supervisor will
terminate all the worker processes and then itself. This is to try to stop
the situation where a process crashes, is restarted, and then crashes
for the same reason, on and on, in an endless loop.

Worker1, Worker2, and so on, are tuples describing how to start each of
the worker processes. We'll see what these look like in a moment.

Now let's get back to our company and build a supervision tree.

The first thing we need to do is to choose a name for our company.
Let's call it sellaprime. The job of the sellaprime supervisor is to make
sure the prime and area servers are always running. To do this, we'll
write yet another callback module, this time for gen_supervisor. Here's
the callback module:

`sellaprime_supervisor.erl`

```erlang
-module(sellaprime_supervisor).
-behaviour(supervisor).          % see erl -man supervisor

-export([start/0, start_in_shell_for_testing/0, start_link/1, init/1]).

start() ->
    spawn(fun() ->
                supervisor:start_link({local,?MODULE}, ?MODULE, _Arg = [])
          end).

start_in_shell_for_testing() ->
    {ok, Pid} = supervisor:start_link({local,?MODULE}, ?MODULE, _Arg = []),
    unlink(Pid).

start_link(Args) ->
    supervisor:start_link({local,?MODULE}, ?MODULE, Args).

init([]) ->
    %% Install my personal error handler
      gen_event:swap_handler(alarm_handler,
                                        {alarm_handler, swap},
                                        {my_alarm_handler, xyz}),
    {ok, {{one_for_one, 3, 10},
          [{tag1,
            {area_server, start_link, []},
            permanent,
            10000,
            worker,
            [area_server]},
```

```
        {tag2,
         {prime_server, start_link, []},
         permanent,
         10000,
         worker,
         [prime_server]}
        ]}}.
```

The important part of this is the data structure returned by init/1:

`sellaprime_supervisor.erl`

```
{ok, {{one_for_one, 3, 10},
      [{tag1,
        {area_server, start_link, []},
        permanent,
        10000,
        worker,
        [area_server]},
       {tag2,
        {prime_server, start_link, []},
        permanent,
        10000,
        worker,
        [prime_server]}
      ]}}.
```

This data structure defines a supervision strategy. We talked about the supervision strategy and restart frequency earlier. Now all that remains are the start specifications for the area server and the prime number server.

The Worker specifications are tuples of the following form:

```
{Tag, {Mod, Func, ArgList},
      Restart,
      Shutdown,
      Type,
      [Mod1]}
```

What do these arguments mean?

Tag

This is an atom tag that we can use to refer to the worker process later (if necessary).

{Mod, Func, ArgList}

This defines the function that the supervisor will use to start the worker. It is used as arguments to apply(Mod, Fun, ArgList).

Restart = permanent | transient | temporary

A permanent process will always be restarted. A transient process is restarted only if it terminates with a non-normal exit value. A temporary process is never restarted.

Shutdown

This is a shutdown time. This is the maximum time a worker is allowed to take in terminating. If it takes longer than this, it will be killed. (Other values are possible—see the supervisor manual pages.)

Type = worker | supervisor

This is the type of the supervised process. We can construct tree of supervisors by adding supervisor processes in the place of worker processes.

[Mod1]

This is the name of the callback module if the child process is a supervisor or gen_server behavior callback module. (Other values are possible—see the supervisor manual page.)

These arguments look scarier than they actually are. In practice, you can cut and paste the values from the earlier area server code and insert the name of your module. This will suffice for most purposes.

18.6 Starting the System

Now we're ready for prime time. Let's launch our company. Off we go. Who wants to buy the first prime number?

Let's start the system:

```
$ erl -boot start_sasl -config elog3
1> sellaprime_supervisor:start_in_shell_for_testing().
*** my_alarm_handler init:{xyz,{alarm_handler,[]}}
area_server starting
prime_server starting
```

Now make a valid query:

```
2> area_server:area({square,10}).
100
```

Now make an invalid query:

```
3> area_server:area({rectangle,10,20}).
area_server stopping

=ERROR REPORT==== 28-Mar-2007::15:15:54 ===
** Generic server area_server terminating
** Last message in was {area,{rectangle,10,20}}
```

> ### Does the Supervision Strategy Work?
>
> Erlang was designed for programming fault-tolerant systems. It was originally developed in the Computer Science Laboratory at the Swedish Telecom company Ericsson. Since then, the OTP group at Ericsson took over development aided by dozens of internal users. Using gen_server, gen_supervisor, and so on, Erlang has been used to build systems with 99.9999999% reliability (that's nine nines). Used correctly, the error handling mechanisms can help make your program run forever (well, almost). The error logger described here has been run for years in live products.

```
** When Server state == 1
** Reason for termination ==
** {function_clause,[[{area_server,compute_area,[{rectangle,10,20}]},
                     {area_server,handle_call,3},
                     {gen_server,handle_msg,6},
                     {proc_lib,init_p,5}]]}
  area_server starting
** exited: {{function_clause,
             [{area_server,compute_area,[{rectangle,10,20}]},
              {area_server,handle_call,3},
              {gen_server,handle_msg,6},
              {proc_lib,init_p,5}]},
             {gen_server,call,
               [area_server,{area,{rectangle,10,20}}]}}} **
```

Whoops—what happened here? The area server crashed; we hit the deliberate error. The crash was detected by the supervisor, and the area server was restarted by the supervisor. All of this was logged by the error logger.

After the crash, everything is back to normal, as it should be. Let's make a valid request this time:

```
4> area_server:area({square,25}).
625
```

We're up and running again. Now let's generate a little prime:

```
5> prime_server:new_prime(20).
Generating a 20 digit prime .......
37864328602551726491
```

And let's generate a big prime:

```
6> prime_server:new_prime(120).
Generating a 120 digit prime
=ERROR REPORT==== 28-Mar-2007::15:22:17 ===
*** Tell the Engineer to turn on the fan
.....................................

=ERROR REPORT==== 28-Mar-2007::15:22:20 ===
*** Danger over. Turn off the fan
765525474077993399589034417231006593110007130279318737419683
288059079481951097205184294443332300308877493399942800723107
```

Now we have a working system. If a server crashes, it is automatically restarted, and in the error log there will be information about the error.

Let's now look at the error log:

```
1> rb:start([{max,20}]).
rb: reading report...done.
rb: reading report...done.
{ok,<0.53.0>}
2> rb:list().
No              Type        Process   Date       Time
==              ====        =======   ====       ====
20              progress    <0.29.0>  2007-03-28 15:05:15
19              progress    <0.22.0>  2007-03-28 15:05:15
18              progress    <0.23.0>  2007-03-28 15:05:21
17    supervisor_report    <0.23.0>  2007-03-28 15:05:21
16                 error    <0.23.0>  2007-03-28 15:07:07
15                 error    <0.23.0>  2007-03-28 15:07:23
14                 error    <0.23.0>  2007-03-28 15:07:41
13              progress    <0.29.0>  2007-03-28 15:15:07
12              progress    <0.29.0>  2007-03-28 15:15:07
11              progress    <0.29.0>  2007-03-28 15:15:07
10              progress    <0.29.0>  2007-03-28 15:15:07
9               progress    <0.22.0>  2007-03-28 15:15:07
8               progress    <0.23.0>  2007-03-28 15:15:13
7               progress    <0.23.0>  2007-03-28 15:15:13
6                  error    <0.23.0>  2007-03-28 15:15:54
5           crash_report  area_server 2007-03-28 15:15:54
4    supervisor_report    <0.23.0>  2007-03-28 15:15:54
3               progress    <0.23.0>  2007-03-28 15:15:54
2                  error    <0.29.0>  2007-03-28 15:22:17
1                  error    <0.29.0>  2007-03-28 15:22:20
```

Something is wrong here. We have a crash report for the area server. What happened (as if we didn't know)?

```
9> rb:show(5).
```

```
CRASH REPORT   <0.43.0>                    2007-03-28 15:15:54
==============================================================
Crashing process
pid                                               <0.43.0>
registered_name                                  area_server
error_info
{function_clause,[{area_server,compute_area,[{rectangle,10,20}]},
                 {area_server,handle_call,3},
                    {gen_server,handle_msg,6},
                    {proc_lib,init_p,5}]]}
initial_call
    {gen,init_it,
        [gen_server,
         <0.42.0>,
         <0.42.0>,
         {local,area_server},
         area_server,
         [],
         []]}
ancestors                         [sellaprime_supervisor,<0.40.0>]
messages                                                 []
links                                            [<0.42.0>]
dictionary                                               []
trap_exit                                             false
status                                              running
heap_size                                               233
stack_size                                               21
reductions                                              199
ok
```

The printout {function_clause, compute_area, ...} shows us exactly the point in the program where the server crashed. It should be an easy job to locate and correct this error. Let's move on to the next errors:

```
10> rb:show(2).
```

```
ERROR REPORT   <0.33.0>                    2007-03-28 15:22:17
==============================================================
*** Tell the Engineer to turn on the fan
```

And.

```
10> rb:show(1).
```

```
ERROR REPORT   <0.33.0>                    2007-03-28 15:22:20
==============================================================
*** Danger over. Turn off the fan
```

These were our fan alarms caused by computing too large primes!

18.7 The Application

We're almost through. All we have to do now is write a file with the extension .app that contains information about our application:

`sellaprime.app`

```
%% This is the application resource file (.app file) for the 'base'
%% application.
{application, sellaprime,
 [{description, "The Prime Number Shop"},
  {vsn, "1.0"},
  {modules, [sellaprime_app, sellaprime_supervisor, area_server,
             prime_server, lib_primes, my_alarm_handler]},
  {registered,[area_server, prime_server, sellaprime_super]},
  {applications, [kernel,stdlib]},
  {mod, {sellaprime_app,[]}},
  {start_phases, []}
 ]}.
```

Then we have to write a callback module with the same name as the mod file in the previous file:

`sellaprime_app.erl`

```
-module(sellaprime_app).
-behaviour(application).
-export([start/2, stop/1]).

%%--------------------------------------------------------------------
%% Function: start(Type, StartArgs) -> {ok, Pid} |
%%                                     {ok, Pid, State} |
%%                                     {error, Reason}
%% Description: This function is called whenever an application
%% is started using application:start/1,2, and should start the processes
%% of the application. If the application is structured according to the
%% OTP design principles as a supervision tree, this means starting the
%% top supervisor of the tree.
%%--------------------------------------------------------------------

start(_Type, StartArgs) ->
    sellaprime_supervisor:start_link(StartArgs).

%%--------------------------------------------------------------------
%% Function: stop(State) -> void()
%% Description: This function is called whenever an application
%% has stopped. It is intended to be the opposite of Module:start/2 and
%% should do any necessary cleaning up. The return value is ignored.
%%--------------------------------------------------------------------

stop(_State) ->
    ok.
```

This must export the functions start/2 and stop/1. Once we've done all of this, we can start and stop our application in the shell.

```
$ erl -boot start_sasl -config elog3
1> application:loaded_applications().
[{kernel,"ERTS  CXC 138 10","2.11.3"},
 {stdlib,"ERTS  CXC 138 10","1.14.3"},
 {sasl,"SASL  CXC 138 11","2.1.4"}]
2> application:load(sellaprime).
ok
3> application:loaded_applications().
[{sellaprime,"The Prime Number Shop","1.0"},
 {kernel,"ERTS  CXC 138 10","2.11.3"},
 {stdlib,"ERTS  CXC 138 10","1.14.3"},
 {sasl,"SASL  CXC 138 11","2.1.4"}]
4> application:start(sellaprime).
*** my_alarm_handler init:{xyz,{alarm_handler,[]}}
area_server starting
prime_server starting
ok
5> application:stop(sellaprime).
prime_server stopping
area_server stopping

=INFO REPORT==== 2-Apr-2007::19:34:44 ===
application: sellaprime
exited: stopped
type: temporary
ok
6> application:unload(sellaprime).
ok
7> application:loaded_applications().
[{kernel,"ERTS  CXC 138 10","2.11.4"},
 {stdlib,"ERTS  CXC 138 10","1.14.4"},
 {sasl,"SASL  CXC 138 11","2.1.5"}]
```

This is now a fully fledged OTP application. In line 2 we loaded the application; this loads all the code but does not start the application. Line 4 started the application, and line 5 stopped the application. Note that we can see from the printout that when the applications were started and stopped, the appropriate callback functions in the area server and prime number server were called. In Line 6 we unloaded the application. All the module code for the application is removed.

When we build complex systems using OTP, we package them as applications. This allows us to start, stop, and administer them uniformly.

Note that when we use init:stop() to close down the system, then all running applications will be closed down in an orderly manner.

```
$ erl -boot start_sasl -config elog3
1>  application:start(sellaprime).
*** my_alarm_handler init:{xyz,{alarm_handler,[]}}
area_server starting
prime_server starting
ok
2> init:stop().
ok
prime_server stopping
area_server stopping
$
```

The two lines following command 2 come from the area and prime number servers, which shows that the terminate/2 methods in the gen_server callback modules were called.[1]

18.8 File System Organization

I haven't mentioned anything about the file system organization yet. This is deliberate—my intention is to confuse you with only one thing at a time.

Well-behaved OTP applications usually have the files belonging to different parts of the application in well-defined places. This is not a requirement; as long as all the relevant files can be found at runtime, it doesn't matter how the files are organized.

In this book I have put most of the demonstration files in the same directory. This simplifies the examples and avoids problems with search paths and interactions between the different programs.

The main files used in the sellaprime company are as follows:

File	Content
area_server.erl	Area server—a gen_server callback
prime_server.erl	Prime number server—a gen_server callback
sellaprim_supervisor.erl	Supervisor callback
sellaprim_app.erl	Application callback
my_alam_handler.erl	Event callback for gen_event
sellaprime.app	Application specification
elog4.config	Error logger configuration file

To see how these files and modules are used, we can look at the sequence of events that happens when we start the application:

---

1. He did come back!

1. We start the system with the following commands:

```
$ erl -boot start_sasl -config elog4.config
1> application:start(sellaprime).
...
```

The file sellaprime.app must be in the root directory where Erlang was started or in a subdirectory of this directory.

The application controller then looks for a {mod, ...} declaration in the sellaprime.app. This contains the name of the application controller. In our case, this was the module sellaprime_app.

2. The callback routine sellaprime_app:start/2 is called.

3. sellaprime_app:start/2 calls sellaprime_supervisor:start_link/2, which starts the sellaprime supervisor.

4. The supervisor callback sellaprime_supervisor:init/1 is called. This installs an error handler and returns a supervision specification. The supervision specification says how to start the area server and prime number server.

5. The sellaprime supervisor starts the area server and prime number server. These are both implemented as gen_server callback modules.

Stopping everything is easy. We just call application:stop(sellaprime) or init:stop().

18.9 The Application Monitor

The application monitor is a GUI for viewing applications. The command appmon:start() starts the application viewer. When you give this command, you'll see a window similar to Figure 18.2, on the following page. To see the applications, you have to click one of the applications. The application monitor view of the sellaprime application is shown in Figure 18.3, on the next page.

18.10 Digging Deeper

I've skipped over quite a lot of detail here, explaining just the principles involved. You can find the details in the manual pages for gen_event, error_logger, supervisor, and application.

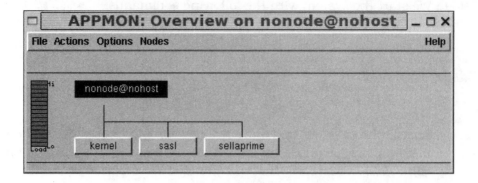

Figure 18.2: APPLICATION MONITOR INITIAL WINDOW

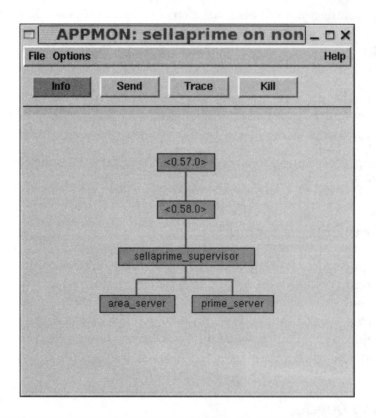

Figure 18.3: THE SELLAPRIME APPLICATION

The following files also have some more details on how to use the OTP behaviors:

http://www.erlang.org/doc/pdf/design_principles.pdf
> (97 pages) Gen servers, gen event, supervisors

http://www.erlang.org/doc/pdf/system_principles.pdf
> (19 pages) How to make a boot file

http://www.erlang.org/doc/pdf/appmon.pdf
> (16 pages) The application monitor

18.11 How Did We Make That Prime?

Easy.

`lib_primes.erl`

```erlang
%% make a prime with at least K decimal digits.
%% Here we use 'Bertrand's postulate.
%% Bertrands postulate is that for every N > 3,
%% there is a prime P satisfying N < P < 2N - 2
%% This was proved by Tchebychef in 1850
%% (Erdos improved this proof in 1932)

make_prime(1) ->
    lists:nth(random:uniform(4), [2,3,5,7]);
make_prime(K) when K > 0 ->
    new_seed(),
    N = make_random_int(K),
    if N > 3 ->
            io:format("Generating a ~w digit prime ",[K]),
            MaxTries = N - 3,
            P1 = make_prime(MaxTries, N+1),
            io:format("~n",[]),
            P1;
       true ->
            make_prime(K)
    end.

make_prime(0, _) ->
    exit(impossible);
make_prime(K, P) ->
    io:format(".",[]),
    case is_prime(P) of
        true  -> P;
        false -> make_prime(K-1, P+1)
    end.
```

```
%% Fermat's little theorem says that if
%% N is a prime and if A < N then
%% A^N mod N = A

is_prime(D) when D < 10 ->
    lists:member(D, [2,3,5,7]);
is_prime(D) ->
    new_seed(),
    is_prime(D, 100).


is_prime(D, Ntests) ->
    N = length(integer_to_list(D)) -1,
    is_prime(Ntests, D, N).


is_prime(0, _, _) -> true;
is_prime(Ntest, N, Len) ->
    K = random:uniform(Len),
    %% A is a random number less than N
    A = make_random_int(K),
    if
        A < N ->
            case lib_lin:pow(A,N,N) of
                A -> is_prime(Ntest-1,N,Len);
                _ -> false
            end;
        true ->
            is_prime(Ntest, N, Len)
    end.
```

```
1> lib_primes:make_prime(500).
Generating a 500 digit prime ............................
79101572698720102790905559711509612690859292134250829726624 39
12592631402855283461324397013307924771094786030944973946964 40
43996967587143749405312224229469667076229261393850020965783 09
06253416678060326101222602345918132555576402830692884411518 13
91107802007557066746476035515105154017421267382367314941956 50
55784744975452526667182809768904015301840652144065085734906 1
21398067893809435266737267269190669316978313361811142362289 04
01868042872198074546193740053777668271056036892838181730070 34
056505784153
```

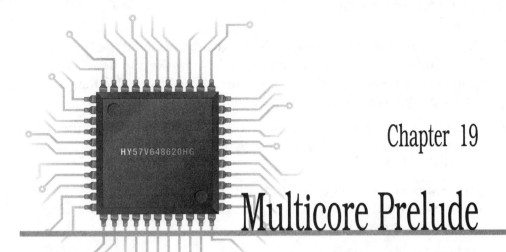

Chapter 19

Multicore Prelude

How can we write programs that run faster on a multicore CPU? It's all about mutable state and concurrency.

Back in the old days (twenty-odd years ago), there were two models of concurrency:

- Shared state concurrency
- Message passing concurrency

The programming world went one way (toward shared state). The Erlang community went the other way. (Few other languages followed the "message passing concurrency" road. Others were Oz and Occam.)

In message passing concurrency, there is no shared state. All computations are done in processes, and the *only* way to exchange data is through asynchronous message passing.

Why is this good?

Shared state concurrency involves the idea of "mutable state" (literally memory that can be changed)—all languages such as C, Java, C++, and so on, have the notion that there is this stuff called "state" and that we can change it.

This is fine as long as you have only *one* process doing the changing.

If you have multiple processes sharing and modifying the *same* memory, you have a recipe for disaster—madness lies here.

To protect against the simultaneous modification of shared memory, we use a locking mechanism. Call this a mutex, a synchronized method, or what you will, but it's still a lock.

If programs crash in the critical region (when they hold the lock), disaster results. All the other programs don't know what to do. If programs corrupt the memory in the shared state, disaster will also happen. The other programs won't know what to do.

How do programmers fix these problems? With great difficulty. On a unicore processor, their program might just work; but on a multicore—disaster.

There are various solutions to this (transactional memory is probably the best), but these are at best kludges. At their worst, they are the stuff of nightmares.

Erlang has no mutable data structures:[1]

- No mutable data structures = No locks
- No mutable data structures = Easy to parallelize

How do we do the parallelization? Easy. The programmer breaks up the solution of the problem into a number of parallel processes.

This style of programming has its own terminology; it's called *concurrency-oriented programming.*

Now on to the final chapter in the book where we'll see how our programs work on a multicore CPU.

---

1. That's not quite true, but it's true enough.

## Chapter 20

Programming Multicore CPUs

Here's the good news for Erlang programmers: your Erlang program might run n times faster on an n core processor—*without any changes to the program.*

But you have to follow a simple set of rules.

If you want your application to run faster on a multicore CPU, you'll have to make sure that it has lots of processes, that the processes don't interfere with each other, and that you have no sequential bottlenecks in your program.

If instead you've written your code in one great monolithic clump of sequential code and never used spawn to create a parallel process, your program might not go any faster.

Don't despair. Even if your program started as a gigantic sequential program, several simple changes to the program will parallelize it.

In this chapter, we'll look at the following topics:

- What we have to do to make our programs run efficiently on a multicore CPU
- How to parallelize a sequential program
- The problem of sequential bottlenecks
- How to avoid side effects

When we've done this, we'll look at the design issues involved in a more complex problem. We'll implement a higher-order function called mapreduce and show how it can be used to program a full-text indexing engine. mapreduce is an abstraction developed by Google for performing parallel computations over sets of processing elements.

> ## Why Should We Care About Multicore CPUs?
>
> You might wonder what all the fuss is about. Do we have to bother parallelizing our program so that it can run on a multicore? The answer is yes. Today, dual-core CPUs are commonplace. In the lab at my workplace, we have some quad cores to play with, and occasionally we get to experiment with a thirty-two core machine.
>
> Making a program go twice as fast on a dual-core machine is not that exciting (but it is a little bit exciting). But let's not delude ourselves. The clock speeds on dual-core processors are slower than on a single-core CPU, so the performance gains can be marginal.
>
> Intel has a project called Keifer aimed at producing at a thirty-two core processor timed for the market in 2009/2010. Sun already has an eight-core (with four hardware threads per core) Niagra machine on the market today.
>
> Now although two times doesn't get me excited, ten times does, and 100 times is really, really exciting. Modern processors are so fast that a single core can run four hyperthreads, so a thirty-two-core CPU might give us an equivalent of 128 threads to play with. This means that 100 times faster is within striking distance.
>
> A factor of 100 does make me excited.
>
> All we have to do is write the code.

20.1 How to Make Programs Run Efficiently on a Multicore CPU

To run efficiently, we have to try to do the following:

1. Use lots of processes.
2. Avoid side effects.
3. Avoid sequential bottlenecks.
4. Write "small messages, big computations" code.

If we do all of these, our Erlang program should run efficiently on a multicore CPU.

Use Lots of Processes

This is important—we have to keep the CPUs busy. All the CPUs should be busy all the time. The easiest way to achieve this is to have lots of processes.

When I say lots of processes, I mean lots in relation to the number of CPUs. If we have lots of processes, then we won't need to worry about keeping the CPUs busy. This appears to be a purely statistical effect. If we have a small number of processes, they might accidentally hog one of the same CPUs; this effect seems to go away if we have a large number of processes. If we want our programs to be future-proof, we should think that even though today's chips might have only a small number of CPUs, in the future we might have thousands of CPUs per chip.

Preferably the processes should do similar amounts of work. It's a bad idea to write programs where one process does a lot of work and the others do very little.

In many applications we get lots of processes "for free." If the application is "intrinsically parallel," then we don't have to worry about parallelizing our code. For example, if we're writing a messaging system that manages some tens of thousands of simultaneous connections, then we get the concurrency from the tens of thousands of connections; the code that handles an individual connection will not have to worry about concurrency.

Avoid Side Effects

Side effects prevent concurrency. Right in the beginning of the book we talked about "variables that do not vary." This is the key to understanding why Erlang programs can run faster on a multicore CPU than programs written in languages that can destructively modify memory.

In a language with shared memory and threads, a disaster might happen if two threads write to common memory at the same time. Systems with shared memory concurrency prevent this by locking the shared memory while the memory is being written to. These locks are hidden from the programmer and appear as mutex or synchronized methods in their programming languages. The main problem with shared memory is that one thread can corrupt the memory used by another thread. So even if my program is correct, another thread can mess up my data structures and cause my program to crash.

Erlang does not have shared memory, so this problem does not exist. Actually, this is not quite true. There are only two ways to share memory, and the problem can be easily avoided. These two ways of sharing memory have to do with shared ETS or DETS tables.

Shared ETS or DETS Tables

ETS tables can be shared by several processes. In Section 15.4, *Creating an ETS Table*, on page 271, we talked about the different ways of creating an ETS table. Using one of the options to ets:new, we could create a public table type. Recall what this did:

Create a public table. Any process that knows the table identifier can read and write this table.

This can be dangerous. It is safe only if

- we can guarantee that only one process at a time writes to the table and that all other processes read from the table, and
- the process that writes to the ETS table is correct and does not write incorrect data into the table.

These properties cannot in general be guaranteed by the system but instead depend upon the program logic.

Note 1: Individual operations on ETS tables are atomic. What is not possible is performing a sequence of ETS operations as one atomic unit. Although we cannot corrupt the data in an ETS table, the tables can become logically inconsistent if several processes try to simultaneously update a shared table without coordinating their activities.

Note 2: The ETS table type protected is far safer. Only one process (the owner) can write to this table, but several processes can read the table. This property *is guaranteed* by the system. But remember, even if only one process can write to an ETS table, if this process corrupts the data in the table, all processes reading the table will be affected.

If you use the ETS table, type private, and then your programs will be safe. Similar observations apply to DETS. We can create a shared DETS table to which several different processes can write. This should be avoided.

Note: ETS and DETS were created in order to implement Mnesia and were not originally intended for stand-alone use. The intention is that application programs should use the Mnesia transaction mechanisms if they want to simulate shared memory between processes.

Sequential Bottlenecks

Once we've parallelized our program and have made sure we have lots of processes and no shared memory operations, the next problem to think about is sequential bottlenecks. Certain things are intrinsically sequential. If the "sequentialness" lies in the problem, we can't make it go away. Certain events happen in a certain sequential order, and no matter how we try, we can't change this order. We are born, we live, we die. We can't change the order. We can't do these things in parallel.

A sequential bottleneck is where several concurrent processes need access to a sequential resource. A typical example is IO. Typically we have a single disk, and all output to the disk is ultimately sequential. The disk has one set of heads, not two, and we can't change that.

Every time we make a registered process, we are creating a potential sequential bottleneck. So try to avoid the use of registered processes. If you do create a registered process and use it as a server, make sure that it responds to all requests as quickly as possible.

Often, the only solution to a sequential bottleneck is to change the algorithm concerned. There is no cheap and easy fix here. We have to change the algorithm from a nondistributed algorithm to a distributed algorithm. This topic (distributed algorithms) has a vast research literature but has had relatively little take-up in conventional programming language libraries. The main reason for this is that the need for such algorithms is not apparent until we try to program networked algorithms or multicore computers.

Programming computers that are permanently connected to the Internet and multicore CPUs will force us to dig into the research literature and implement some of these amazing algorithms.

A Distributed Ticket-Booking System

Suppose we have a single resource, a set of tickets to the next concert of the Strolling Bones. To guarantee that when you buy a ticket you actually get a ticket, we'd conventionally use a single agency that books all the tickets. But this introduces a sequential bottleneck. How can we avoid this?

Easy. Imagine you have two ticket agencies. At the start of sales, the first ticket agency is given all the even-numbered tickets, and the second agency is given all the odd-numbered tickets. This way the agencies are guaranteed not to sell the same ticket twice.

If one of the agencies runs out of tickets, then it can request a bundle of tickets from the other agency.

I'm not saying this is a good method: you might actually want to sit next to your friends when you go to a concert. But it does remove the bottleneck, replacing a single ticket office with two.

Replacing the single booking agency by n distributed agencies where n can vary with time and where the individual agencies can join and leave the network and crash at any time is an area of active research in distributed computing. This research goes under the name of *distributed hash tables*. If you Google this term, you'll find a vast array of literature on the subject.

20.2 Parallelizing Sequential Code

Remember the emphasis we made on list-at-a-time operations and in particular the function lists:map? map is defined like this:

```
map(_, [])    -> [];
map(F, [H|T]) -> [F(H)|map(F, T)].
```

A simple strategy for speeding up our sequential programs would replace all calls to map with a new version of map, which I'll call pmap, which evaluates all its arguments in parallel:

```
lib_misc.erl
```
```
pmap(F, L) ->
    S = self(),
    %% make_ref() returns a unique reference
    %%   we'll match on this later
    Ref = erlang:make_ref(),
    Pids = map(fun(I) ->
                        spawn(fun() -> do_f(S, Ref, F, I) end)
                end, L),
    %% gather the results
    gather(Pids, Ref).

do_f(Parent, Ref, F, I) ->
    Parent ! {self(), Ref, (catch F(I))}.

gather([Pid|T], Ref) ->
    receive
        {Pid, Ref, Ret} -> [Ret|gather(T, Ref)]
    end;
gather([], _) ->
    [].
```

pmap works like map, but when we call pmap(F, L), it creates one parallel process to evaluate each argument in L. Note that the processes that evaluate the arguments of L can complete in any order.

The selective receive in the gather function ensures that the order of the arguments in the return value corresponds to the ordering in the original list.

There is a slight semantic difference between map and pmap. In pmap, we use (catch F(H)) when we map the function over the list. In map we just use F(H). This is because we want to make sure pmap terminates correctly in the case where the computation of F(H) raises an exception. In the case where no exceptions are raised, the behavior of the two functions is identical.

Important: This last statement is not strictly true. map and pmap will not behave the same way if they have side effects. Suppose F(H) has some code that modifies the process dictionary. When we call map, the changes to the process dictionary will be made in the process dictionary of the process that called map.

When we call pmap, each F(H) is evaluated in its own process, so if we use the process dictionary, the changes in the dictionary will not affect the process dictionary in the program that called pmap. *So be warned*: Code that has side effects cannot be simply parallelized by replacing a call to map with pmap.

When Can We Use pmap?

Using pmap instead of map is not a general panacea for speeding up your programs. The following are some things to think about.

Granularity of Concurrency

Don't use pmap if the amount of work done in the function is small. Suppose we say this:

```
map(fun(I) -> 2*I end, L)
```

Here the amount of work done inside the fun is minimal. The overhead of setting up a process and waiting for a reply is greater than the benefit of using parallel processes to do the job.

Don't Create Too Many Processes

Remember that pmap(F, L) creates length(L) parallel processes. If L is very large, you will create a lot of processes. How many processes should we create? The Swedes[1] have a good word for this; we should create a *lagom* number of processes (not too few, not too many, but just the right number).

Think About the Abstractions You Need

pmap might not be the right abstraction. We can think of many different ways of mapping a function over a list in parallel; we chose the simplest possible here.

The pmap version we used cared about the order of the elements in the return value (we used selective receive to do this). If we didn't care about the order of the return values, we could write this:

`lib_misc.erl`

```
pmap1(F, L) ->
    S = self(),
    Ref = erlang:make_ref(),
    foreach(fun(I) ->
                      spawn(fun() -> do_f1(S, Ref, F, I) end)
            end, L),
    %% gather the results
    gather1(length(L), Ref, []).

do_f1(Parent, Ref, F, I) ->
    Parent ! {Ref, (catch F(I))}.

gather1(0, _, L) -> L;
gather1(N, Ref, L) ->
    receive
        {Ref, Ret} -> gather1(N-1, Ref, [Ret|L])
    end.
```

A simple change to this could turn this into a parallel foreach. The code is similar to the previous code, but we don't build any return value. We just note the termination of the program.

Another method would be to implement pmap using at most K processes where K is some fixed constant. This might be useful if we want to use pmap on very large lists.

---

1. Erlang comes from Sweden, where the expression "lagom är bäst" (loosely translated as "just enough is best") is often said to summarize the national character.

Yet another version of pmap could map the computations not only over the processes in a multicore CPU but also over nodes in a distributed network.

I'm not going to show you how to do this here. You can think about this for yourself.

The purpose of this section is to point out that there is a large family of abstractions that can easily be built from the basic **spawn**, **send**, and **receive** primitives. You can use these primitives to create your own parallel control abstractions to increase the concurrency of your program.

As before—the absence of side effects is the key to increasing concurrency. Never forget this.

20.3 Small Messages, Big Computations

We've talked theory; now for some measurements. In this section, we'll perform two experiments. We'll map two functions over a list of 100 elements, and we'll compare the time it takes with a parallel and sequential map.

We'll use two different problem sets. The first computes this:

```
L = [L1, L2, ..., L100],
map(fun lists:sort/1, L)
```

Each of the elements in L is a list of 1,000 random integers.

The second computes this:

```
L = [27,27,..., 27],
map(fun ptests:fib/1, L)
```

Here, L is a list of 100 twenty-sevens, and we compute the list [fib(27), fib(27), ...] 100 times. (fib is the Fibonacci function.)

We'll time both these functions. Then we'll replace map with pmap and repeat the timings.

Using pmap in the first computation (sort) involves sending a relatively large amount of data (a list of 1,000 random numbers) in messages between the different processes. The sorting process is rather quick. The second computation involves sending a small request (to compute fib(27)) to each process, but the work involved in recursively computing fib(27) is relatively large.

Since there is little copying of data between processes in computing fib(27) and a relatively large amount of work involved, we would expect the second problem to perform better than the first on a multicore CPU.

To see how this works in practice, we need a script that automates our tests. But first we'll look at how to start SMP Erlang.

Running SMP Erlang

SMP[2] Erlang runs on a number of different architectures and operating systems. The current system runs with Intel dual- and quad-core processors on motherboards with one or two processors. It also runs with Sun and Cavium processors. This is an area of extremely rapid development, and the number of supported operating systems and processors increases with every release of Erlang. You can find up-to-date information in the release notes of the current Erlang distribution. (Click the title entry for the latest version of Erlang in the download directory at http://www.erlang.org/download.html.)

Note: SMP Erlang has been enabled by default (that is, an SMP virtual machine is built by default) since R11B-0 on all platforms where SMP Erlang is known to work. To force SMP Erlang to be built on other platforms, the --enable-smp-support flag should be given to the configure command.

SMP Erlang has two command-line flags that determine how it runs on a multicore CPU:

```
$erl -smp +S N
```

-smp

Start SMP Erlang.

+S N

Run Erlang with N schedulers. Each Erlang scheduler is a complete virtual machine that knows about all the other virtual machines. If this parameter is omitted, it defaults to the number of logical processors in the SMP machine.

Why would we want to vary this? We would want to for a number of reasons:

---

2. A symmetric multiprocessing (SMP) machine has two or more identical CPUs that are connected to a single shared memory. These CPUs may be on a single multicore chip, spread across several chips, or a combination of both.

- When we do performance measurements, we want to vary the number of the schedulers to see the effect of running with a different number of CPUs.

- On a single-core CPU, we can emulate running on a multicore CPU by varying N.

- We might want to have more schedulers than physical CPUs. This can sometimes increase throughput and make the system behave in a better manner. These effects are not fully understood and are the subject of active research.

To perform our tests, we need a script to run the tests:

`runtests`

```
#!/bin/sh
echo "" >results
for i in 1 2 3 4 5 6 7 8 9 10 11 12 13 14 15 16\
        17 18 19 20 21 22 23 24 25 26 27 28 29 30 31 32
do
    echo $i
    erl -boot start_clean -noshell -smp +S $i \
        -s ptests tests $i >> results
done
```

This just starts Erlang with one to thirty-two different schedulers, runs a timing test, and collects all the timings into a file called results.

Then we need a test program:

`ptests.erl`

```
-module(ptests).
-export([tests/1, fib/1]).
-import(lists, [map/2]).
-import(lib_misc, [pmap/2]).

tests([N]) ->
    Nsched = list_to_integer(atom_to_list(N)),
    run_tests(1, Nsched).

run_tests(N, Nsched) ->
    case test(N) of
        stop ->
            init:stop();
        Val ->
            io:format("~p.~n",[{Nsched, Val}]),
            run_tests(N+1, Nsched)
    end.
```

```erlang
test(1) ->
    %% Make 100 lists
    %%   Each list contains 1000 random integers
    seed(),
    S = lists:seq(1,100),
    L = map(fun(_) -> mkList(1000) end, S),
    {Time1, S1} = timer:tc(lists,    map, [fun lists:sort/1, L]),
    {Time2, S2} = timer:tc(lib_misc, pmap, [fun lists:sort/1, L]),
    {sort, Time1, Time2, equal(S1, S2)};
test(2) ->
    %% L = [27,27,27,..] 100 times
    L = lists:duplicate(100, 27),
    {Time1, S1} = timer:tc(lists,    map, [fun ptests:fib/1, L]),
    {Time2, S2} = timer:tc(lib_misc, pmap, [fun ptests:fib/1, L]),
    {fib, Time1, Time2, equal(S1, S2)};
test(3) ->
    stop.

%% Equal is used to test that map and pmap compute the same thing
equal(S,S)   -> true;
equal(S1,S2) ->  {differ, S1, S2}.

%% recursive (inefficent) fibonacci
fib(0) -> 1;
fib(1) -> 1;
fib(N) -> fib(N-1) + fib(N-2).

%% Reset the random number generator. This is so we
%% get the same sequence of random numbers each time we run
%% the program

seed() -> random:seed(44,55,66).

%% Make a list of K random numbers
%%    Each random number in the range 1..1000000
mkList(K) -> mkList(K, []).

mkList(0, L) -> L;
mkList(N, L) -> mkList(N-1, [random:uniform(1000000)|L]).
```

This runs map and pmap in the two different test cases. You can see the results in Figure 20.1, on the next page, where we have plotted the ratio of times taken by pmap and map. As we can see, CPU-bound computations with little message passing have linear speed-up, whereas lighter-weight computations with more message passing scale less well.

As a final note, we shouldn't read too much into these figures. SMP Erlang is undergoing daily changes, so what is true today may not be true tomorrow. All we can say is that we are very encouraged by our results. Ericsson is building commercial products that run almost twice as fast on dual-core processors, so we are very happy.

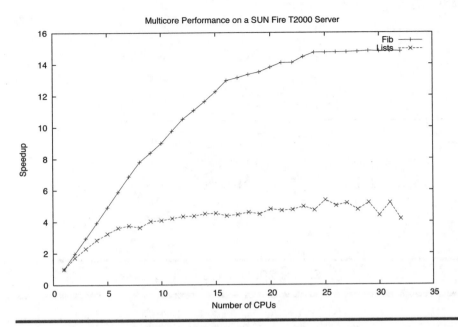

Figure 20.1: SPEED-UP ON MULTICORE CPU

20.4 mapreduce and Indexing Our Disk

Now we're going to turn theory in practice. First we'll look at the higher-order function mapreduce; then we'll use mapreduce to make a simple indexing engine. The goal here is not actually to make the world's fastest and best indexing engine but to address the design issues that are involved in constructing such a program.

mapreduce

In Figure 20.2, on the following page, we can see the basic idea of mapreduce. We have a number of *mapping* processes, which produce streams of {Key, Value} pairs. The mapping processes send these pairs to a *reduce* process that merges the pairs, combining pairs with the same key.

Warning: The word *map*, used in the context of mapreduce, is completely different from the map function that occurs elsewhere in this book.

mapreduce is a *parallel higher-order function*. Proposed by Jeffrey Dean and Sanjay Ghemawat of Google, it is said to be in daily use on Google clusters.

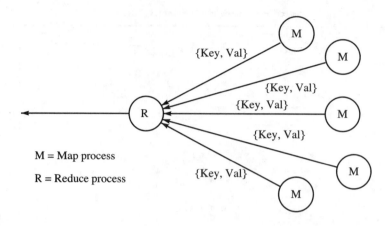

Figure 20.2: MAPREDUCE

We can implement mapreduce in lots of different ways and with lots of different semantics—it's actually more a family of algorithms than one particular algorithm.

mapreduce is defined as follows:

```
@spec mapreduce(F1, F2, Acc0, L) -> Acc
    F1 = fun(Pid, X) -> void,
    F2 = fun(Key, [Value], Acc0) -> Acc
    L  = [X]
    Acc = X = term()
```

F1(Pid, X) is the mapping function.

> The job of F1 is to send a stream of {Key, Value} messages to the process Pid and then to terminate. mapreduce will spawn a fresh process for each value of X in the list L.

F2(Key, [Value], Acc0) -> Acc is the reduction function.

> When all the mapping processes have terminated, the reduce process will have merged all the values for a particular key together. mapreduce then calls F2(Key, [Value], Acc) for each of the {Key, [Value]} pairs it has collected. Acc is an accumulator whose initial value is Acc0. F2 returns a new accumulator. (Another way of describing this is to say that F2 performs a *fold* over the {Key, [Value]} pairs that it has collected.)

Acc0 is the initial value of the accumulator, used when calling F2.

L is a list of X values.

F1(Pid, X) will be called for each value of X in L.Pid is a process identifier of the reduce process; this is created by mapreduce.

mapreduce is defined in the module phofs (short for *parallel higher-order functions*):

`phofs.erl`

```erlang
-module(phofs).
-export([mapreduce/4]).

-import(lists, [foreach/2]).

%% F1(Pid, X) -> sends {Key,Val} messages to Pid
%% F2(Key, [Val], AccIn) -> AccOut

mapreduce(F1, F2, Acc0, L) ->
    S = self(),
    Pid = spawn(fun() -> reduce(S, F1, F2, Acc0, L) end),
    receive
        {Pid, Result} ->
            Result
    end.

reduce(Parent, F1, F2, Acc0, L) ->
    process_flag(trap_exit, true),
    ReducePid = self(),
    %% Create the Map processes
    %%    One for each element X in L
    foreach(fun(X) ->
                    spawn_link(fun() -> do_job(ReducePid, F1, X) end)
            end, L),
    N = length(L),
    %% make a dictionary to store the Keys
    Dict0 = dict:new(),
    %% Wait for N Map processes to terminate
    Dict1 = collect_replies(N, Dict0),
    Acc = dict:fold(F2, Acc0, Dict1),
    Parent ! {self(), Acc}.

%% collect_replies(N, Dict)
%%     collect and merge {Key, Value} messages from N processes.
%%     When N processes have terminated return a dictionary
%%     of {Key, [Value]} pairs

collect_replies(0, Dict) ->
    Dict;
```

```
collect_replies(N, Dict) ->
    receive
        {Key, Val} ->
            case dict:is_key(Key, Dict) of
                true ->
                    Dict1 = dict:append(Key, Val, Dict),
                    collect_replies(N, Dict1);
                false ->
                    Dict1 = dict:store(Key,[Val], Dict),
                    collect_replies(N, Dict1)
            end;
        {'EXIT', _,  Why} ->
            collect_replies(N-1, Dict)
    end.

%% Call F(Pid, X)
%%    F must send {Key, Value} messsages to Pid
%%       and then terminate

do_job(ReducePid, F, X) ->
    F(ReducePid, X).
```

Before we go any further, we'll test mapreduce so as to be really clear about what it does.

We'll write a little program to count the frequencies of all words in the code directory that accompanies this book. Here is the program:

`test_mapreduce.erl`

```
-module(test_mapreduce).
-compile(export_all).
-import(lists, [reverse/1, sort/1]).

test() ->
    wc_dir(".").

wc_dir(Dir) ->
    F1 = fun generate_words/2,
    F2 = fun count_words/3,
    Files = lib_find:files(Dir, "*.erl", false),
    L1 = phofs:mapreduce(F1, F2, [], Files),
    reverse(sort(L1)).

generate_words(Pid, File) ->
    F = fun(Word) -> Pid ! {Word, 1} end,
    lib_misc:foreachWordInFile(File, F).

count_words(Key, Vals, A) ->
    [{length(Vals), Key}|A].
```

```
5> test_mapreduce:test().
[{341,"1"},
 {330,"end"},
 {318,"0"},
 {265,"N"},
 {235,"X"},
 {214,"T"},
 {213,"2"},
 {205,"start"},
 {196,"L"},
 {194,"is"},
 {185,"file"},
 {177,"Pid"},
 ...
```

When I ran this, there were 102 Erlang modules in the code directory; mapreduce created 102 parallel processes, each sending a stream of pairs to the reduce process. This should run nicely on a 100-core processor (if the disk can keep up).

Now that we understand how mapreduce works, we can go back to our indexing engine.

Full-Text Indexing

When we build an index, one of the things we need to do is find all the words in a file. This is going to be used in the "map" phase of a mapreduce operation.

Before we do this, we'll look at the data structures needed to make a full-text index.

The Inverted Index

Our full-text index is implemented using an *inverted index*—in this section, we'll review the idea of an inverted index and see how this is stored in our system.

To illustrate this, we'll start with a simple example. Suppose we have a file system with three files and each file contains a small number of words.

Our files and their contents might look like this:

Filename	Contents
/home/dogs	rover jack buster winston
/home/animals/cats	zorro daisy jaguar
/home/cars	rover jaguar ford

To compute our inverted index, we first number all the files, like this:

Index	Filename
1	/home/dogs
2	/home/animals/cats
3	/home/cars

And then we make a table of the words in the files against the indexes of the files where these words occur:

Word	File Index
rover	1, 3
jack	1
buster	1
winston	1
zorro	2
daisy	2
jaguar	2, 3
ford	3

Querying the Inverted Index

Once we have built an inverted index, querying the index is easy. Suppose we want to look up the term *buster*. This occurs in file 1, namely, /home/dogs. To query *rover AND jaguar*, we look up *rover* (answer, files 1 and 3) and then *jaguar* (answer, files 2 and 3), and then we take the intersection of the two answers (file 3), which is the file /home/cars.

Data Structures for the Inverted Index

We need two persistent data structures:

- *The filename-to-index table*: Filenames are represented by integers in the inverted index. This is to save space. A common word will occur in thousands of files, so we want a compact representation of the filename. We'll use a DETS table to represent this information. Earlier in Section 15.6, *Example: A Filename Index*, on page 278, we developed a program to do this.

- *The word-to-file index table*: For each word in our files, we need to keep a record of the indexes of the files where this word is contained. To do this, we use the file system. In our example, we create files called rover, buster, and so on. The indexer program stores these words in some index directory. For example, if the index directory was /usr/index, we'd expect to find files called /usr/index/buster, and so on, in this directory containing the indexes of the files.

The Operation of the Indexer

We start everything by calling indexer:start(). This is defined as follows:

`indexer-1.1/indexer.erl`

```
start() ->
    indexer_server:start(output_dir()),
    spawn_link(fun() -> worker() end).
```

This does two things. First, it starts a server called indexer_server (which was written using gen_server). Second, it spawns a worker process to do the indexing.

`indexer-1.1/indexer.erl`

```
worker() ->
    possibly_stop(),
    case indexer_server:next_dir() of
        {ok, Dir} ->
            Files = indexer_misc:files_in_dir(Dir),
            index_these_files(Files),
            indexer_server:checkpoint(),
            possibly_stop(),
            sleep(10000),
            worker();
        done ->
            true
    end.
```

The worker process does the following:

1. Calls indexer_server:next_dir(), which returns the next directory to index.

2. Calls indexer_misc:files_in_dir to find the files in the directory that should be indexed.

3. Calls index_these_files(Files) to compute the inverted index for Files.

4. Calls indexer_server:checkpoint(). This has to do with crash recovery. Once we have indexed a new directory, we tell the server that we have indexed this directory. If the program crashes or is stopped and subsequently restarted, the next call to indexer_server:next_dir() will resume from the next directory.

After each cycle of indexing, the worker calls possibly_stop() to see whether a stop has been scheduled. If not, it sleeps for a while and continues.

The actual indexing takes place in index_these_files. This is where we go parallel and use mapreduce.

`indexer-1.1/indexer.erl`

```erlang
index_these_files(Files) ->
    Ets = indexer_server:ets_table(),
    OutDir = filename:join(indexer_server:outdir(), "index"),
    F1 = fun(Pid, File) -> indexer_words:words_in_file(Pid, File, Ets) end,
    F2 = fun(Key, Val, Acc) -> handle_result(Key, Val, OutDir, Acc) end,
    indexer_misc:mapreduce(F1, F2, 0, Files).

handle_result(Key, Vals, OutDir, Acc) ->
    add_to_file(OutDir, Key, Vals),
    Acc + 1.
```

add_to_file(OutDir, Word, Is) appends a list of indexes in Is to the file Word in OutDir.

`indexer-1.1/indexer.erl`

```erlang
add_to_file(OutDir, Word, Is) ->
    L1 = map(fun(I) -> <<I:32>> end, Is),
    OutFile = filename:join(OutDir, Word),
    case file:open(OutFile, [write,binary,raw,append]) of
        {ok, S} ->
            file:pwrite(S, 0, L1),
            file:close(S);
        {error, E} ->
            exit({ebadFileOp, OutFile, E})
    end.
```

Running the Indexer

```erlang
1> indexer:cold_start().
2> indexer:start().
...
N> indexer:stop().
Scheduling a stop
ack
Stopping
```

Comments

This is a complex program (the most complex one in this book), and it is by no means complete. Even though it is complex, it has a structure that is simple and understandable.

It has a strategy for starting and stopping the program and recovering from errors. This is a achieved with indexer_checkpoint. It parallelizes the search using mapreduce, and it makes a brave attempt at isolating words from a file.

What would we have to do to turn this toy indexer into a full-featured indexer? We would have to make a number of improvements:

- Improve the word extraction. This is probably the single area that needs some major effort. The problem is not particularly difficult, but the problem has no generic solution. Each file type (Erlang, PDF, TXT, C, Java, and so on) requires a separate (and different) analysis technique to extract what might be relevant words. This has to be repeated for all major natural languages (and spellings).

- mapreduce must be improved to handle extremely large data sets. The key-value merge steps that I used in mapreduce shown here ran in memory and without backing disk store. We must give some careful thought to the problem of how to represent sets of values where the numbers of elements are extremely large.

- The data structures for the inverted index just used the file system as a data store and a single DETS table for storing the filename-to-index map. This technique doesn't scale well to encompass, for example, all the filenames of all machines on the planet. For this, a distributed hash table seems appropriate.

Let's disregard these problems for a moment and step back to think about the solution. On the positive side, we have learned a number of techniques for programming multicore CPUs based on the use of simple higher-order functions that are free from side effects.

The Indexer Code

All the code for the indexer is in the indexer directory in the code download. It consists of nine files. These files total about 1,200 lines of code, so we won't kill trees by including them here.

indexer.erl
> The main program. This exports start(), stop(), and cold_start(). These are the only routines that a user of the indexer is supposed to know about.

indexer_porter.erl
> Stemming algorithm. To reduce the number of words in the index, we try to reduce words to the same base or root form. So, for example, all the words *fishing*, *fished*, and *fisher* have the same root (*fish*). This process is called *stemming*. The algorithm we use is the Porter algorithm (because of Martin Porter) and is implemented in the module indexer_porter.

indexer_server.erl

> A server built with gen_server. This owns the DETS table used by indexer_filenames_dets. It keeps track of global data, like the name of the directories to index and the progress of indexing, and so on.

indexer_filenames_dets.erl

> The filename to index code. This is a copy of lib_filenames_dets.

indexer_checkpoint.erl

> The checkpointing mechanism. This stores a data structure on disk that allows the application to recover if it crashes.

indexer_trigrams.erl

> This is similar to lib_trigrams.erl. This performs trigram analysis of words (see Section 15.5, *Example Programs with ETS*, on page 273).

indexer_misc.erl

> Miscellaneous routines, including a copy of mapreduce.

indexer_words.erl

> Extracts words from a file and calls routines to perform trigram analysis and stemming on a word.

indexer_dir_crawler.erl

> Reentrant directory listing program called by indexer_server.

You'll notice something about these filenames. There is one file called indexer.erl and then a number of files called indexer_XXXX.erl. This follows the usual convention used for distributing complex Erlang applications. When we have the application working, we choose an application name (in this case indexer). Then we make a "main module" (in indexer.erl) and a number of "submodules" (indexer_XXXX).

In doing so, we copy, rename, and possibly modify code from other modules. This method has a number of advantages and disadvantages. The main advantage is that using these namespace conventions we can independently develop code without worrying about how it is shared. The disadvantage is that common library code can end up with several different names and in several different versions when in fact it should be merged.

The code in the Erlang distribution follows this convention. So, for example, the code in /usr/local/lib/erlang/lib/mnesia-4.3.4/src follows this convention. The main exceptions to this rule are the modules in the libraries kernel and stdlib, which follow no naming conventions but try to use short intuitive names.

20.5 Growing Into the Future

The landscape of computing is changing. Large, monolithic processors are slowly becoming dinosaurs, eclipsed by the idea that we can put processing power where we need it. The future has multiple cores, and the future has distributed processors.

The techniques that we grew up with for writing programs are struggling in this new world. Erlang is a solution for this. In this book, I've shown you how a few basic concepts in Erlang lead to code that is reliable, maintainable, and that scales well on today's (and tomorrow's) architectures.

Enjoy writing these new style programs.

Documenting Our Program

Erlang has strong ideas about types, but much of what it knows is implicit. To make it more explicit in documentation, and when talking about functions, the Erlang community has developed a notation for talking about types. This notation isn't part of a program's source code. Instead, it's a documentation device—a way of talking about Erlang source. Using it, we can specify unambiguously what kinds of parameters a function may accept and what types it returns.

More recently, this same notation has been adopted by a range of tools that work with Erlang source (which we'll talk about later).

The type notation is used only for documentation purposes. Type declarations are *not* Erlang code and cannot be typed into the shell. Type declarations in Erlang modules are written as part of comments and are totally ignored by the Erlang compiler. For example, we might write this:

```
-module(math).
-export([fac/1]).

%% @spec fac(int()) -> int().

fac(0) -> 1;
fac(N) -> N * fac(N-1).
```

The type notation is used in the Erlang manual pages and in the API descriptions that you can find in this book. The notation is informal, in that we often don't fully specify the types, but it is formal enough that we can capture the essence of what a function does.

A.1 Erlang Type Notation

We need to define two things: *types* and function *specifications*.

Defining a Type

The type named "typeName" is written as typeName(). Types are either predefined or user-defined. The predefined types are any(), atom(), binary(), bool(), char(), cons(), deep_string(), float(), function(), integer(), iolist(), list(), nil(), none(), number(), pid(), port(), reference(), string(), term(), and tuple().

They have the following meanings:

- any() means "any Erlang data type." term() is an alias for any().

- atom(), binary(), float(), function(), integer(), pid(), port(), and reference() are the primitive data types of the Erlang programming language.

- bool() is one of the atoms true or false.

- char() is a subset of integer() representing a character.

- iolist() is recursively defined as [char() | binary() | iolist()]. A binary is also allowed as the tail of the list. This is commonly used as an efficient way of generating character output. See Section 13.3, *Listing URLs from a File*, on page 230 for an example of a function that produces an IO list.

- tuple() is a tuple.

- list(L) is an alias for [L].

- nil() is an alias for the empty list [].

- string() is an alias for list(char()).

- deep_string() is recursively defined as [char()|deep_string()].

- none() means "no data type." This is used for a function that never returns (an infinite receive loop, for example). Strictly, it's not a type but a way of documenting the fact that the function never returns.

We can construct new types (user-defined types) by writing this:

```
@type newType() = TypeExpression.
```

We'll give some examples first and then give a more formal definition of the rules defining a type expression:

```
@type onOff() = on | off.
@type person() = {person, name(), age()}.
@type people() = [person()].
@type name() = {firstname, string()}.
@type age() = integer().
...
```

These rules say that, for example, {firstname, "dave"} is of type name(), [{person, {firstname,"john"}, 35}, {person, {firstname,"mary"}, 26}] is of type people(), and so on.

TypeExpression is defined inductively as follows:

- {T1, T2, ..., Tn} is a type expression (called a *tuple type*) if T1, T2, ... Tn are type expressions. We say that {X1, X2, ..., Xn} is of type {T1, T2, ..., Tn} if X1 is of type T1, X2 is of type T2, ... and Xn is of type Tn.

- [T] is a type expression (called a *list type*) if T is a type expression. We say that the list [X1, X2, ..., Xn] is of type [T] if all the Xis are of type T.

- T1 | T2 is a type expression (called the *alternation type*) if T1 is a type and T2 is a type. We say that X is of type T1 | T2 if X is of type T1 or type T2.

- fun(T1, T2, ..., Tn) -> T is a type expression (called the *function type*) if all the Tis are type expressions and if T is a type expression. We say that fun(X1, X2, ..., Xn) -> X is of type fun(T1, T2, ..., Tn) -> T if X1 is of type T1, X2 is of type T2, ..., and X is of type T.

- A predefined type, a user-defined type, or an instance of a predefined type is a type expression.

Now that we know how to define types, we can move on to function specifications.

Specifying the Input and Output Types of a Function

Function specifications say what the types of the arguments to a function are and what the type of the return value of the function is. A function specification is written like this:

```
@spec functionName(T1, T2, ..., Tn) -> Tret.
```

Here T1, T2, ..., Tn describe the types of the arguments to a function, and Tret describes the type of the return value of the function.

Each of the Tis can have one of three possible forms:

- TypeVar: A type variable. A *type variable* is a variable used in a type declaration that represents an unknown type (and incidentally has nothing to do with an Erlang variable). If we use the same type variable more than once in a type specification, then all instances of the type variable must have the same type.
- TypeVar::Type: A type variable followed by a type. This means that TypeVar has type Type (a type expression).
- Type: A type expression.

We'll start with an example, and then I'll explain the details:

```
@spec file:open(FileName, Mode) -> {ok, Handle} | {error, Why}.
@spec file:read_line(Handle) -> {ok, Line} | eof.
```

The specification of file:open/2 says that if we open the file FileName, we should get a return value that is either {ok, Handle} or {error, Why}. The vertical bar | means OR.

Note: Often the module part of a function is implied by the context. For example, if we're talking only about the file module, I'll write @spec open(...) instead of @spec file:open(...).

FileName and Mode are type variables, but what types are they? Is FileName an atom, a string, or something else? We can't actually see this from the definition—this is why the definition is informal. Sometimes we don't need to know what the data type of an argument is; for example, we don't need to know what data type Handle (one of the return values of file:open) is because all we do is pass it unmodified into file:read_line/1.

We can also use function types as in the following examples:

```
@spec lists:map(fun(A) -> B, [A]) -> [B].
@spec lists:filter(fun(X) -> bool(), [X]) -> [X].
```

Often we don't need to go into great detail about what type a function argument has; we represent it by a descriptive name, and we can guess from the context what this means.

If we wanted to remove the guesswork, we could refine our specification in a number of different ways, which are all equivalent. Here's an example:

```
@spec file:open(FileName::string(), [mode()]) ->
    {ok, Handle::file_handle()} | {error, Why::string()}.
@type mode() = read | write | compressed | raw | binary | ...
```

Here's another example:

```
@spec file:open(string(), Modes) -> {ok, Handle} | {error, string()}
    Handle = file_handle(),
    Modes = [Mode],
    Mode = read | write | compressed | raw | binary | ...
```

Or here's even another example:

```
@spec file:open(string(), [mode()]) -> {ok, file_handle()} | error().
@type error() = {error, string()}.
@type mode() = read | write | compressed | raw | binary | ...
```

Type Definitions in APIs

When we define APIs in manual pages or in this book, we'll often use descriptive lists for function type definitions. In this case we omit the **@spec** keyword and write the definition directly. Often we'll just use type variables and describe them in the text that follows the description.

Here's an example, showing part of the file manual page:

file:open(File, [Mode]) -> {ok, Handle} | {error, Why}

> Open File (a string) according to Mode. Mode is one of read, write, and so on. It returns {ok, Handle} if the file could be opened or {error, Why} where Why is a string describing the error. Once the file has been successfully opened, it can be accessed through Handle.

file:read_line(Handle) -> {ok, Line} | eof

> Read a line from the file opened with Handle. It returns Line (a string) or eof at end-of-file.

and so on....

A.2 Tools That Use Types

Here are some tools that use types:

EDoc

> EDoc is the Erlang program documentation generator. Inspired by the Javadoc tool for the Java programming language, EDoc is adapted to the conventions of the Erlang world.

> EDoc lets you write the documentation of an Erlang program as annotations that are embedded in comments in the source code. These annotations are introduced using tags such as **@name**, **@doc**, **@type**, **@author**, and so on.

The module `edoc` exports a large number of functions that can be used to manipulate Erlang source code files containing Edoc annotations.

The Dialyzer

The Dialyzer is a static analysis tool that identifies software discrepancies such as type errors, unreachable code, unnecessary tests, and so on. It works for single Erlang modules or entire (sets of) applications.

Both these tools are distributed as part of the standard Erlang distribution.

Erlang on Microsoft Windows

I run Erlang on many different platforms, and I like the development environment to be almost the same on all of them. For Windows I have found the following setup to be useful. (You might need to change some of the directory names to match those on your own system.)

Step B.1 is essential for all Windows users. You can follow steps B.2 to B.4 if you want to have a Unix-like development environment on Windows. You can follow step B.5 if you want to install emacs on Windows (this is useful since emacs has an advanced mode for editing Erlang programs).

B.1 Erlang

Go to http://www.erlang.org/download.html, and get the latest Windows binary (37MB), called otp_win32-R11B-3.exe. When you click the file icon, Erlang is installed in the default directory. When I did this on my machine, Erlang was installed in C:\Program Files\erl.5.4.12\.

B.2 Fetch and Install MinGW

MinGW[1] stands for Minimalist GNU for Windows.

1. Fetch the MinGW installer. This is a small program (about 130KB) that talks you through the installation procedure. I used MinGW-5.0.2.exefrom the download area at http://www.mingw.org/download. shtml.

---

1. http://www.mingw.org

2. Run the install procedure. Make sure the checkboxes for "MinGW base tools" and "MinGW make" are selected.

3. Answer Yes to everything. This will install about 44MB of stuff in the directory C:\MinGW.

B.3 Fetch and Install MSYS

1. Go to http://www.mingw.org/download.shtml, and fetch the latest version of MSYS. Look for the current system in the section marked MSYS, and download the file MSYS-1.0.10.exe (2742KB).

2. Install MSYS-1.0.10.exe by clicking the file icon.

3. Go to the download area of http://sourceforge.net/projects/mingw.

4. Answer the questions. You'll be asked one question—the location of MinGW. Reply c:\MinGW.

After this step, you should have a function shell. Selecting Start > Programs > MinGW > MSYS > msys starts a shell. You should also have a blue desktop icon that you can click to start the shell.

If you click the icon with a large *M* on it, you'll get a shell window where a lot of your favorite Unix commands will work.

B.4 Install the MSYS Developer Toolkit (Optional)

I do this so I get ssh, and so on. These are "nice to have" but not essential.

1. Find the file MsysDTK-1.0.1.exe.

2. Use the one-click installer.

B.5 Emacs

1. Go to ftp://ftp.gnu.org/gnu/emacs/windows/, and download the file emacs-21.3-fullbin-i386.tar.gz.

2. Use WinZip to unpack this into a suitable directory.

3. To complete the installation, navigate to the emacs bin directory, and click addpm. (This adds a shortcut to emacs in the Start > Programs tab.) I also make a shortcut to runemacs from my desktop.

Customizing emacs

To customize emacs, copy the contents of the file emacs.setup (shown here) into a file called .emacs in your home directory. On my system this is the file C:/.emacs.

`emacs.setup`

```
(setq default-frame-alist
      '((top . 10) (left . 10)
        (width . 80) (height . 43)
        (cursor-color . "blue")
        (cursor-type . box)
        (foreground-color . "black")
        (background-color . "white")
        (font . "-*-Courier New-bold-r-*-*-18-108-120-120-c-*-iso8859-8")))

(show-paren-mode)

(global-font-lock-mode t)
(setq font-lock-maximum-decoration t)


;; Erlang stuff this is the path to erlang

;; windows path below -- change to match your environment
(setq load-path (cons  "c:/Program Files/er15.5.3/lib/tools-2.5.3/emacs"
                       load-path))

(require 'erlang-start)

;; (if window-system
;;    (add-hook 'erlang-mode-hook 'erlang-font-lock-level-3))

(add-hook 'erlang-mode-hook 'erlang-font-lock-level-3)
```

Appendix C

Resources

C.1 Online Documentation

The Main Erlang Documentation..............http://www.erlang.org/doc/
All the Erlang documentation at the main distribution site.

The Erlang Manual Page..........http://www.erlang.org/doc/man/erlang.html
All the missing details not talked about in this book.

The Erlang Style Guide....http://www.erlang.se/doc/programming_rules.shtml
This is a set of rules defining what we think good Erlang programming is. These
rules are used in several commercial projects.[1]

The Erlang FAQ............................http://www.erlang.org/faq/t1.html
Every good project deserves answers to frequently asked questions.

The Manual Pages.................http://www.erlang.org/doc/man/index.html
All the latest manual pages for all documented Erlang modules and all OS
commands (such as erl, erlc, escript, and so on). Individual manual pages have
names like erlang.org/doc/man/lists.html.

PDF Manuals........................http://www.erlang.org/doc/pdf/index.html
Top-level index of the latest version of all PDF manuals in the system.
Individual manuals (for example, the Mnesia manual) have a names like
erlang.org/doc/pdf/mnesia.pdf.

Application Documentation..........http://www.erlang.org/doc/apps/Name
Documentation for individual applications. For example, we can find all documentation for Mnesia at http://www.erlang.org/doc/apps/mnesia.

---

1. Also at http://www.erlang.se/doc/programming_rules.pdf.

C.2 Books and Theses

Concurrent Programming in Erlang [VWWA96]

> The first Erlang book has two sections: Part I is about the language, and Part II is about applications. Part I is freely available as a PDF file.[2]

Erlang Programmation [Rém03] (French)

> Mickaël Rémond's book for French readers.

"Making Reliable Systems in the Presence of Software Errors"

> This is my doctoral thesis.[3] It contains the theory and partial history of Erlang. This is a more formal treatment than in this book. You'll find some more OTP behaviors described and some case studies of the use of Erlang.

The Erlang 4.7 Specification

> Not for the faint of heart, this was an attempt to precisely specify Erlang version 4.7.[4] Although this is rather out-of-date, it still has the best available description of those parts of the language that have not changed since version 4.7. In fact, much of it is still relevant to the current Erlang 5.5.

C.3 Link Collections

http://www.it.uu.se/research/group/hipe/publications.shtml

> High-Performance Erlang (HIPE) is a group at the University of Uppsala that has been involved with the development of Erlang for many years. This page has pointers to a large number of Erlang papers and research reports.

http://dmoz.org/Computers/Programming/Languages/Erlang/

> Open Directory Erlang listings.

C.4 Blogs

http://armstrongonsoftware.blogspot.com/

> My musings on software.

---

2. http://www.erlang.org/download/erlang-book-part1.pdf
3. http://www.erlang.org/download/armstrong_thesis_2003.pdf
4. http://www.erlang.org/download/erl_spec47.ps.gz

http://yarivsblog.com/
> Yariv Sadan blogs about Erlang and about ErlyWeb, which is a WEB framework written in Erlang.

http://www.process-one.net/en/blogs/
> Blogs by Mickaël Rémond and friends.

C.5 Forums, Online Communities, and Social Sites

http://www.erlang.org/mailman/listinfo
> The main Erlang lists. This is mirrored at many sites.

http://www.trapexit.org/
> Large Erlang community, including forums, a wiki, and how-tos. The how-to section[5] and the cookbook[6] are pretty useful.

Erlounges
> Erlounges are held at irregular times and places all over the world. Erlounges are social events where Erlang users get together (usually in Pubs or Restaurants) and talk about the joys of programming in Erlang. They are advertised on the Erlang mailing list.

IRC Channels
> #erlang on irc.freenode.net.

C.6 Conferences

ACM SIGPLAN Workshop
> Annual event. One day.

Erlang User Conference
> Annual event.[7] Two days.

C.7 Projects

http://jungerl.sourceforge.net/
> A large repository of Erlang projects at SourceForge.

---

5. http://wiki.trapexit.org/index.php/Category:HowTo
6. http://wiki.trapexit.org/index.php/Category:CookBook
7. http://www.erlang.se/euc.

http://cean.process-one.net/
>   The Comprehensive Erlang Archive Network. An attempt to merge all ongoing Erlang projects.

http://yaws.hyber.org/
>   Yet Another Web Server. This is a web server in Erlang that is used in many commercial products.

http://ejabberd.jabber.ru/
>   Instant messaging server for the Jabber protocol, written in Erlang.

C.8 Bibliography

[Rém03]   Mickaël Rémond. *Erlang Programmation*. Eyrolles, Paris, 2003.

[VWWA96] Robert Virding, Claes Wikstrom, Mike Williams, and Joe Armstrong. *Concurrent Programming in Erlang*. Prentice Hall, Englewood Cliffs, NJ, second edition, 1996.

A Socket Application

This appendix is devoted to the implementation of the library lib_chan. We introduced this library in Section 10.5, *lib_chan*, on page 179, and we used it Chapter 11, *IRC Lite*, on page 183.

The code for lib_chan implements an entire layer of networking on top of TCP/IP, providing both authentication and streams of Erlang terms. Once we understand the principles used in lib_chan, we should be able to tailor-make our own communication infrastructure and layer it on top of TCP/IP.

In its own right, lib_chan is a useful component for building distributed systems.

To make the appendix self-contained, there is a considerable amount of overlap with the material in Section 10.5, *lib_chan*, on page 179.

The code in this appendix is some of the most complex code I've introduced so far, so don't worry if you don't understand it all on the first reading. If you just want to use lib_chan and don't care about how it works, read the first section and skip the rest.

D.1 An Example

We'll start with a simple example that shows how to use lib_chan. We're going to create a simple server that can compute factorials and Fibonacci numbers. We'll protect it with a password.

The server will operate on port 2233.

We'll take four steps to create this server:

1. Write a configuration file.

2. Write the code for the server.

3. Start the server.

4. Access the server over the network.

Step 1: Write a Configuration File

Here's the configuration file for our example:

`socket_dist/config1`

```
{port, 2233}.
{service, math, password, "qwerty", mfa, mod_math, run, []}.
```

The configuration file has a number of service tuples of this form:

```
{service, <Name>, password, <P>, mfa, <Mod>, <Func>, <ArgList>}
```

The arguments are delimited by the atoms service, password, and mfa. mfa is short for *module, function, args*, meaning that the next three arguments are to be interpreted as a module name, a function name, and a list of arguments to some function call.

In our example, the configuration file specifies a service called *math* that will be available on port 2233. The service is protected by the password *qwerty*. It is implemented in a module called mod_math and will be started by calling mod_math:run/3. The third argument of run/3 will be [].

Step 2: Write the Code for the Server

The math server code looks like this:

`socket_dist/mod_math.erl`

```
-module(mod_math).
-export([run/3]).

run(MM, ArgC, ArgS) ->
    io:format("mod_math:run starting~n"
              "ArgC = ~p ArgS=~p~n",[ArgC, ArgS]),
    loop(MM).

loop(MM) ->
    receive
        {chan, MM, {factorial, N}} ->
            MM ! {send, fac(N)},
            loop(MM);
```

```
            {chan, MM, {fibonacci, N}} ->
                MM ! {send, fib(N)},
                loop(MM);
            {chan_closed, MM} ->
                io:format("mod_math stopping~n"),
                exit(normal)
    end.

fac(0) -> 1;
fac(N) -> N*fac(N-1).

fib(1) -> 1;
fib(2) -> 1;
fib(N) -> fib(N-1) + fib(N-2).
```

When a client connects to port 2233 and requests the service called *math*, lib_auth will authenticate the client and, if the password is correct, spawn a handler process by spawning the function mod_math:run(MM, ArgC, ArgS). MM is the PID of a *middle man*. ArgC comes from the client, and ArgS comes from the configuration file.

When the client sends to a message X to the server, it will arrive as a {chan, MM, X} message. If the client dies or something goes wrong with the connection, the server will be sent a {chan_closed, MM} message. To send a message Y to the client, the server evaluated MM ! {send, Y}, and to close the communication channel, it evaluated MM ! close.

The math server is simple; it just waits for a {chan, MM, {factorial, N}} message and then sends the result to the client by evaluating MM ! {send, fac(N)}.

Step 3: Starting the Server

We start the server as follows:

```
1> lib_chan:start_server("./config1").
lib_chan starting:"./config1"
Terms=[{port,2233},
       {service,math,password,"qwerty",
        mfa,mod_math,run,[]}]
true
```

Step 4: Accessing the Server Over the Network

We can test this code on a single machine:

```
2> {ok, S} = lib_chan:connect("localhost",2233,math,
                              "qwerty",{yes,go}).

{ok,<0.47.0>}
```

```
3> lib_chan:rpc(S, {factorial,20}).
2432902008176640000
4> lib_chan:rpc(S, {fibonacci,15}).
610
4> lib_chan:disconnect(S).
close
mod_math stopping
```

D.2 How lib_chan Works

lib_chan is built using code in four modules:

- lib_chan acts as a "main module." The only routines that the programmer needs to know about are the routines that are exported from lib_chan. The other three modules (discussed next) are used internally in the implementation of lib_chan.

- lib_chan_mm encodes and decodes Erlang messages and manages the socket communication.

- lib_chan_cs sets up the server and manages client connections. One of its main jobs is to limit the maximum number of simultaneous client connections.

- lib_chan_auth has code for simple challenge/response authentication.

lib_chan

lib_chan has the following structure:

```
-module(lib_chan).

start_server(ConfigFile) ->
    %% read configuration file - check syntax
    %% call start_port_server(Port, ConfigData)
    %% where Port is the required Port and ConfigData
    %% contines the configuration data

start_port_server(Port, ConfigData) ->
    lib_chan_cs:start_raw_server( ..
            fun(Socket) ->
                start_port_instance(Socket, ConfigData),
            end, ... )
    %% lib_chan_cs manages the connection
    %% when a new connection comes the fun which is an
    %% argument to start_raw_server will be called
```

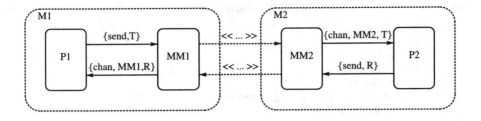

Figure D.1: SOCKET COMMUNICATION WITH A MIDDLE MAN

```
start_port_instance(Socket, ConfigData) ->
    %% this is spawned when the client connects
    %% to the server. Here we setup a middle man,
    %% then perform authentication. If everything works call
    %% really_start(MM, ArgC, {Mod, Func, ArgS})
    %% (the last three arguments come from the configuration file

really_start(MM, ArgC, {Mod, Func, ArgS}) ->
    apply(Mod, Func, [MM, ArgC, ArgS]).

connect(Host, Port, Service, Password, ArgC) ->
    %% client side code
```

lib_chan_mm: The Middle Man

lib_chan_mm implements a middle man. It hides the socket communication from the applications, turning streams of data on TCP sockets into Erlang messages. The middle man is responsible for assembling the message (which might have become fragmented) and for encoding and decoding Erlang terms into streams of bytes that can be sent to and received from a socket.

Now is a good time to take a quick look at Figure D.1, which shows our middle-man architecture. When a process P1 on a machine M1 wants to send a message T to a process P2 on a machine M2, it evaluates MM1 ! {send, T}. MM1 acts as a *proxy* for P2. Anything sent to MM1 is encoded and written to a socket and sent to MM2. MM2 decodes anything it receives on a socket and sends the message {chan, MM2, T} to P2.

On the machine M1 the process MM1 behaves as a proxy for P2, and on M2 the process MM2 behaves as a proxy for P1.

MM1 and MM2 are PIDs of middle-men processes. The middle-man process code looks something like this:

```erlang
loop(Socket, Pid) ->
    receive
        {tcp, Socket, Bin} ->
            Pid ! {chan, self(), binary_to_term(Bin)},
            loop(Socket, Pid);
        {tcp_closed, Socket} ->
            Pid ! {chan_closed, self()};
        close ->
            gen_tcp:close(Socket);
        {send, T} ->
            gen_tcp:send(Socket, [term_to_binary(T)]),
            loop(Socket, Pid)
    end.
```

This loop is used as an interface between the world of socket data and the world of Erlang message passing. You can find the complete code for lib_chan_mm in Section D.3, *lib_chan_mm*, on page 412. This is slightly more complex than the code shown here, but the principle is the same. The only difference is that we've added some code for tracing messages and some interfacing routines.

lib_chan_cs

lib_chan_cs is responsible for setting up client and server communication. The two important routines that it exports are as follows:

start_raw_server(Port, Max, Fun, PacketLength)
> This starts a listener that listens for a connection on Port. At most, Max simultaneous sessions are allowed. Fun is a fun of arity 1; when a connection starts, Fun(Socket) is evaluated. The socket communication assumes a packet length of PacketLength.

start:raw_client(Host, Port, PacketLength) => {ok, Socket} | {error, Why}
> This tries to connect to a port opened with start_raw_server.

The code for lib_chan_cs follows the pattern described in Section 14.1, *A Parallel Server*, on page 248, but in addition it keeps track of the maximum number of simultaneously open connections. This small detail, though conceptually simple, adds twenty-odd lines of rather strange-looking code that traps exits and so on. Code like this is a mess, but don't worry: it does its job and hides the complexity from the user of the module.

lib_chan_auth

This module implements a simple form of challenge/response authentication. Challenge/response authentication is based on the idea of a shared secret that is associated with the service name. To show how it works, we'll assume there is a service called math that has a shared secret qwerty.

If a client wants to use the service math, then the client has to prove to the server that they know the shared secret. This works as follows:

1. The client sends a request to the server saying it wants to use the math service.

2. The server computes a random string C and sends it to the client. This is the *challenge*. The string is computed by the function lib_chan_auth:make_challenge(). We can use it interactively to see what it does:

   ```
   1> C = lib_chan_auth:make_challenge().
   "qnyrgzqefvnjdombanrsmxikc"
   ```

3. The client receives this string (C) and computes a response (R) where R = MD5(C ++ Secret). R is computed using lib_chan_auth: make_response. For example:

   ```
   2> R = lib_chan_auth:make_response(Challenge, "qwerty").
   "e759ef3778228beae988d91a67253873"
   ```

4. The response is sent back to the server. The server receives the response and checks whether it is correct by computing the expected value of the response. This is done in lib_chan_auth: is_response_correct:

   ```
   3> lib_chan_auth:is_response_correct(C, R, "qwerty").
   true
   ```

D.3 The lib_chan Code

Now for the code.

lib_chan

`socket_dist/lib_chan.erl`

```
-module(lib_chan).
-export([cast/2, start_server/0, start_server/1,
         connect/5, disconnect/1, rpc/2]).
-import(lists, [map/2, member/2, foreach/2]).
-import(lib_chan_mm, [send/2, close/1]).
```

```erlang
%%----------------------------------------------------------------------
%% Server code

start_server() ->
    case os:getenv("HOME") of
        false ->
            exit({ebadEnv, "HOME"});
        Home ->
            start_server(Home ++ "/.erlang_config/lib_chan.conf")
    end.

start_server(ConfigFile) ->
    io:format("lib_chan starting:~p~n",[ConfigFile]),
    case file:consult(ConfigFile) of
        {ok, ConfigData} ->
            io:format("ConfigData=~p~n",[ConfigData]),
            case check_terms(ConfigData) of
                [] ->
                    start_server1(ConfigData);
                Errors ->
                    exit({eDeaemonConfig, Errors})
            end;
        {error, Why} ->
            exit({eDaemonConfig, Why})
    end.

%% check_terms() -> [Error]

check_terms(ConfigData) ->
    L = map(fun check_term/1, ConfigData),
    [X || {error, X} <- L].

check_term({port, P}) when is_integer(P)       -> ok;
check_term({service,_,password,_,mfa,_,_,_}) -> ok;
check_term(X) -> {error, {badTerm, X}}.

start_server1(ConfigData) ->
    register(lib_chan, spawn(fun() -> start_server2(ConfigData) end)).

start_server2(ConfigData) ->
    [Port] = [ P || {port,P} <- ConfigData],
    start_port_server(Port, ConfigData).

start_port_server(Port, ConfigData) ->
    lib_chan_cs:start_raw_server(Port,
                                  fun(Socket) ->
                                          start_port_instance(Socket,
                                                              ConfigData) end,
                    100,
                    4).
```

```erlang
start_port_instance(Socket, ConfigData) ->
    %% This is where the low-level connection is handled
    %% We must become a middle man
    %% But first we spawn a connection handler
    S = self(),
    Controller = spawn_link(fun() -> start_erl_port_server(S, ConfigData) end),
    lib_chan_mm:loop(Socket, Controller).

start_erl_port_server(MM, ConfigData) ->
    receive
        {chan, MM, {startService, Mod, ArgC}} ->
            case get_service_definition(Mod, ConfigData) of
                {yes, Pwd, MFA} ->
                    case Pwd of
                        none ->
                            send(MM, ack),
                            really_start(MM, ArgC, MFA);
                        _ ->
                            do_authentication(Pwd, MM, ArgC, MFA)
                    end;
                no ->
                    io:format("sending bad service~n"),
                    send(MM, badService),
                    close(MM)
            end;
        Any ->
            io:format("*** ErL port server got:~p ~p~n",[MM, Any]),
            exit({protocolViolation, Any})
    end.

do_authentication(Pwd, MM, ArgC, MFA) ->
    C = lib_chan_auth:make_challenge(),
    send(MM, {challenge, C}),
    receive
        {chan, MM, {response, R}} ->
            case lib_chan_auth:is_response_correct(C, R, Pwd) of
                true ->
                    send(MM, ack),
                    really_start(MM, ArgC, MFA);
                false ->
                    send(MM, authFail),
                    close(MM)
            end
    end.


%% MM is the middle man
%% Mod is the Module we want to execute ArgC and ArgS come from the client and
%% server respectively
```

```erlang
really_start(MM, ArgC, {Mod, Func, ArgS}) ->
    %% authentication worked so now we're off
    case (catch apply(Mod,Func,[MM,ArgC,ArgS])) of
        {'EXIT', normal} ->
            true;
        {'EXIT', Why} ->
            io:format("server error:~p~n",[Why]);
        Why ->
            io:format("server error should die with exit(normal) was:~p~n",
                      [Why])
    end.

%% get_service_definition(Name, ConfigData)

get_service_definition(Mod, [{service, Mod, password, Pwd, mfa, M, F, A}|_]) ->
    {yes, Pwd, {M, F, A}};
get_service_definition(Name, [_|T]) ->
    get_service_definition(Name, T);
get_service_definition(_, []) ->
    no.

%%-------------------------------------------------------------------------
%% Client connection code
%% connect(...) -> {ok, MM} | Error

connect(Host, Port, Service, Secret, ArgC) ->
    S = self(),
    MM = spawn(fun() -> connect(S, Host, Port) end),
    receive
        {MM, ok} ->
            case authenticate(MM, Service, Secret, ArgC) of
                ok    -> {ok, MM};
                Error -> Error
            end;
        {MM, Error} ->
            Error
    end.

connect(Parent, Host, Port) ->
    case lib_chan_cs:start_raw_client(Host, Port, 4) of
        {ok, Socket} ->
            Parent ! {self(), ok},
            lib_chan_mm:loop(Socket, Parent);
        Error ->
            Parent ! {self(),  Error}
    end.

authenticate(MM, Service, Secret, ArgC) ->
    send(MM, {startService, Service, ArgC}),
    %% we should get back a challenge or a ack or closed socket
    receive
```

```
            {chan, MM, ack} ->
                ok;
            {chan, MM, {challenge, C}} ->
                R = lib_chan_auth:make_response(C, Secret),
                send(MM, {response, R}),
                receive
                    {chan, MM, ack} ->
                        ok;
                    {chan, MM, authFail} ->
                        wait_close(MM),
                        {error, authFail};
                    Other ->
                        {error, Other}
                end;
            {chan, MM, badService} ->
                wait_close(MM),
                {error, badService};
            Other ->
                {error, Other}
    end.

wait_close(MM) ->
    receive
        {chan_closed, MM} ->
            true
    after 5000 ->
            io:format("**errror lib_chan~n"),
            true
    end.

disconnect(MM) -> close(MM).

rpc(MM, Q) ->
    send(MM, Q),
    receive
        {chan, MM, Reply} ->
            Reply
    end.

cast(MM, Q) ->
    send(MM, Q).
```

lib_chan_cs

`socket_dist/lib_chan_cs.erl`

```
-module(lib_chan_cs).
%% cs stands for client_server

-export([start_raw_server/4, start_raw_client/3]).
-export([stop/1]).
-export([children/1]).
```

```erlang
%% start_raw_server(Port, Fun, Max)
%%    This server accepts up to Max connections on Port
%%    The *first* time a connection is made to Port
%%    Then Fun(Socket) is called.
%%    Thereafter messages to the socket result in messages to the handler.

%% tcp_is typically used as follows:
%% To setup a listener
%%    start_agent(Port) ->
%%       process_flag(trap_exit, true),
%%       lib_chan_server:start_raw_server(Port,
%%                                        fun(Socket) -> input_handler(Socket) end,
%%                                        15,
%%                                        0).

start_raw_client(Host, Port, PacketLength) ->
    gen_tcp:connect(Host, Port,
                    [binary, {active, true}, {packet, PacketLength}]).

%% Note when start_raw_server returns it should be ready to
%% Immediately accept connections

start_raw_server(Port, Fun, Max, PacketLength) ->
    Name = port_name(Port),
    case whereis(Name) of
        undefined ->
            Self = self(),
            Pid = spawn_link(fun() ->
                                 cold_start(Self,Port,Fun,Max,PacketLength)
                             end),
            receive
                {Pid, ok} ->
                    register(Name, Pid),
                    {ok, self()};
                {Pid, Error} ->
                    Error
            end;
        _Pid ->
            {error, already_started}
    end.

stop(Port) when integer(Port) ->
    Name = port_name(Port),
    case whereis(Name) of
        undefined ->
            not_started;
        Pid ->
            exit(Pid, kill),
            (catch unregister(Name)),
            stopped
    end.
```

```erlang
children(Port) when integer(Port) ->
    port_name(Port) ! {children, self()},
    receive
        {session_server, Reply} -> Reply
    end.


port_name(Port) when integer(Port) ->
    list_to_atom("portServer" ++ integer_to_list(Port)).


cold_start(Master, Port, Fun, Max, PacketLength) ->
    process_flag(trap_exit, true),
    %% io:format("Starting a port server on ~p...~n",[Port]),
    case gen_tcp:listen(Port, [binary,
                                %% {dontroute, true},
                                {nodelay,true},
                                {packet, PacketLength},
                                {reuseaddr, true},
                                {active, true}]) of
        {ok, Listen} ->
            %% io:format("Listening to:~p~n",[Listen]),
            Master ! {self(), ok},
            New = start_accept(Listen, Fun),
            %% Now we're ready to run
            socket_loop(Listen, New, [], Fun, Max);
        Error ->
            Master ! {self(), Error}
    end.


socket_loop(Listen, New, Active, Fun, Max) ->
    receive
        {istarted, New} ->
            Active1 = [New|Active],
            possibly_start_another(false,Listen,Active1,Fun,Max);
        {'EXIT', New, _Why} ->
            %% io:format("Child exit=~p~n",[Why]),
            possibly_start_another(false,Listen,Active,Fun,Max);
        {'EXIT', Pid, _Why} ->
            %% io:format("Child exit=~p~n",[Why]),
            Active1 = lists:delete(Pid, Active),
            possibly_start_another(New,Listen,Active1,Fun,Max);
        {children, From} ->
            From ! {session_server, Active},
            socket_loop(Listen,New,Active,Fun,Max);
        _Other ->
            socket_loop(Listen,New,Active,Fun,Max)
    end.
```

```erlang
possibly_start_another(New, Listen, Active, Fun, Max)
  when pid(New) ->
    socket_loop(Listen, New, Active, Fun, Max);
possibly_start_another(false, Listen, Active, Fun, Max) ->
    case length(Active) of
        N when N < Max ->
            New = start_accept(Listen, Fun),
            socket_loop(Listen, New, Active, Fun,Max);
        _ ->
            socket_loop(Listen, false, Active, Fun, Max)
    end.

start_accept(Listen, Fun) ->
    S = self(),
    spawn_link(fun() -> start_child(S, Listen, Fun) end).

start_child(Parent, Listen, Fun) ->
    case gen_tcp:accept(Listen) of
        {ok, Socket} ->
            Parent ! {istarted,self()},                % tell the controller
            inet:setopts(Socket, [{packet,4},
                                   binary,
                                   {nodelay,true},
                                   {active, true}]),
            %% before we activate socket
            %% io:format("running the child:~p Fun=~p~n", [Socket, Fun]),
            process_flag(trap_exit, true),
            case (catch Fun(Socket)) of
                {'EXIT', normal} ->
                    true;
                {'EXIT', Why} ->
                    io:format("Port process dies with exit:~p~n",[Why]),
                    true;
                _ ->
                    %% not an exit so everything's ok
                    true
            end
    end.
```

lib_chan_mm

`socket_dist/lib_chan_mm.erl`

```erlang
%% Protocol
%%    To the controlling process
%%        {chan, MM, Term}
%%        {chan_closed, MM}
%%    From any process
%%        {send, Term}
%%        close

-module(lib_chan_mm).
```

```erlang
%% TCP Middle man
%%    Models the interface to gen_tcp

-export([loop/2, send/2, close/1, controller/2, set_trace/2, trace_with_tag/2]).

send(Pid, Term)        -> Pid ! {send, Term}.
close(Pid)             -> Pid ! close.
controller(Pid, Pid1)  -> Pid ! {setController, Pid1}.
set_trace(Pid, X)      -> Pid ! {trace, X}.

trace_with_tag(Pid, Tag) ->
    set_trace(Pid, {true,
                    fun(Msg) ->
                            io:format("MM:~p ~p~n",[Tag, Msg])
                    end}).

loop(Socket, Pid) ->
    %% trace_with_tag(self(), trace),
    process_flag(trap_exit, true),
    loop1(Socket, Pid, false).

loop1(Socket, Pid, Trace) ->
    receive
        {tcp, Socket, Bin} ->
            Term = binary_to_term(Bin),
            trace_it(Trace,{socketReceived, Term}),
            Pid ! {chan, self(), Term},
            loop1(Socket, Pid, Trace);
        {tcp_closed, Socket} ->
            trace_it(Trace, socketClosed),
            Pid ! {chan_closed, self()};
        {'EXIT', Pid, Why} ->
            trace_it(Trace,{controllingProcessExit, Why}),
            gen_tcp:close(Socket);
        {setController, Pid1} ->
            trace_it(Trace, {changedController, Pid}),
            loop1(Socket, Pid1, Trace);
        {trace, Trace1} ->
            trace_it(Trace, {setTrace, Trace1}),
            loop1(Socket, Pid, Trace1);
        close ->
            trace_it(Trace, closedByClient),
            gen_tcp:close(Socket);
        {send, Term}  ->
            trace_it(Trace, {sendingMessage, Term}),
            gen_tcp:send(Socket, term_to_binary(Term)),
            loop1(Socket, Pid, Trace);
        UUg ->
            io:format("lib_chan_mm: protocol error:~p~n",[UUg]),
            loop1(Socket, Pid, Trace)
    end.
```

```erlang
trace_it(false, _)       -> void;
trace_it({true, F}, M) -> F(M).
```

lib_chan_auth

socket_dist/lib_chan_auth.erl

```erlang
-module(lib_chan_auth).

-export([make_challenge/0, make_response/2, is_response_correct/3]).

make_challenge() ->
    random_string(25).

make_response(Challenge, Secret) ->
    lib_md5:string(Challenge ++ Secret).

is_response_correct(Challenge, Response, Secret) ->
    case lib_md5:string(Challenge ++ Secret) of
        Response -> true;
        _        -> false
    end.

%% random_string(N) -> a random string with N characters.

random_string(N) -> random_seed(), random_string(N, []).

random_string(0, D) -> D;
random_string(N, D) ->
    random_string(N-1, [random:uniform(26)-1+$a|D]).

random_seed() ->
    {_,_,X} = erlang:now(),
    {H,M,S} = time(),
    H1 = H * X rem 32767,
    M1 = M * X rem 32767,
    S1 = S * X rem 32767,
    put(random_seed, {H1,M1,S1}).
```

Miscellaneous

This appendix presents material about analyzing and debugging code, and it describes how dynamic code loading works.

E.1 Analysis and Profiling Tools

How can we look into our running program? How can we look for potential problem code, investigate performance problems, and check for dead code or the use of deprecated functions? That's what this section is all about.

Coverage

When we're testing our code, it's often nice to see not only which lines of code are executed a lot but also which lines are never executed. Lines of code that are never executed are a potential source of error, so it's really good to find out where these are. To do this, we use the program coverage analyzer.

Here's an example:

```
1> cover:start().          %% start the coverage analyser
{ok,<0.34.0>}
2> cover:compile(shout).   %% compile shout.erl for coverage
{ok,shout}
3> shout:start().          %% run the program
<0.41.0>
Playing:<<"title: track018 performer: .. ">>
4> %% let the program run for a bit
4>  cover:analyse_to_file(shout).  %% analyse the results
{ok,"shout.COVER.out"}            %% this is the results file
```


The Best of All Test Methods?

Performing a coverage analysis of our code answers the question, Which lines of code are never executed? Once we know which lines of code are never executed, we can design test cases that force these lines of code to be executed.

Doing this is a surefire way to find unexpected and obscure bugs in your program. Every line of code that has never been executed might contain an error. Forcing these lines to be executed is the best way I know to test a program.

I did this to the original Erlang JAM* compiler. I think we got three bug reports in two years. After this, there were no reported bugs.

---

*. Joe's Abstract Machine (the first Erlang compiler)

The results of this are printed to a file:

```
      ...
    |   send_file(S, Header, OffSet, Stop, Socket, SoFar) ->
    |       %% OffSet = first byte to play
    |       %% Stop   = The last byte we can play
131..|      Need = ?CHUNKSIZE - size(SoFar),
131..|      Last = OffSet + Need,
131..|      if
    |       Last >= Stop ->
    |           %% not enough data so read as much as possible and return
  0..|           Max = Stop - OffSet,
  0..|           {ok, Bin} = file:pread(S, OffSet, Max),
  0..|           list_to_binary([SoFar, Bin]);
    |         true ->
131..|           {ok, Bin} = file:pread(S, OffSet, Need),
131..|           write_data(Socket, SoFar, Bin, Header),
131..|           send_file(S, bump(Header),
    |                       OffSet + Need,  Stop, Socket, <<>>)
    |       end.
      ...
```

On the left side of the file, we see the number of times each statement has been executed. The lines marked with a zero are particularly interesting. Since this code has never been executed, we can't really say whether our program is correct.

Designing test cases that cause all the coverage counts to be greater than zero is a valuable method of systematically finding hidden faults in our programs.

Profiling

The standard Erlang distribution comes with three profiling tools:

- cprof counts the number of times each function is called. This is a lightweight profiler. Running this on a live system adds from 5% to 10% to the system load.

- fprof displays the time for calling and called functions. Output is to a file. This is suitable for large system profiling in a lab or simulated system. It adds significant load to the system.

- eprof measures how time is used in Erlang programs. This is a predecessor of fprof, which is suitable for small-scale profiling.

Here's how you run cprof:

```
1> cprof:start().        %% start the profiler
4501
2> shout:start().        %% run the application
<0.35.0>
3> cprof:pause().        %% pause the profiler
4844
4> cprof:analyse(shout). %% analyse function calls
{shout,232,
    [{{shout,split,2},73},
     {{shout,write_data,4},33},
     {{shout,the_header,1},33},
     {{shout,send_file,6},33},
     {{shout,bump,1},32},
     {{shout,make_header1,1},5},
     {{shout,'-got_request_from_client/3-fun-0-',1},4},
     {{shout,songs_loop,1},2},
     {{shout,par_connect,2},2},
     {{shout,unpack_song_descriptor,1},1},
     ...
5> cprof:stop().         %% stop the profiler
4865
```

In addition, cprof:analyse() analyzes all the modules for which statistics have been collected.

See http://www.erlang.org/doc/man/cprof.html for more details of cprof.

xref

Cross-references can be generated using the xref module. xref works only if your code has been compiled with the debug_info flag set.

Running an occasional cross-reference check on your code when you are developing a program is a good idea. I can't show you the output of xref on the code accompanying this book, because the development is complete and there aren't any missing functions. Instead, I'll show you what happens when I run a cross-reference check on the code in one of my hobby projects.

vsg is a simple graphics program that I might release one day. We'll do an analysis of the code in the vsg directory where I'm developing the program:

```
$ cd /home/joe/2007/vsg-1.6
$ rm *.beam
$ erlc +debug_info *.erl
$ erl
1> xref:d('.')
[{deprecated,[]},
 {undefined,[{{new,win1,0},{wish_manager,on_destroy,2}},
              {{vsg,alpha_tag,0},{wish_manager,new_index,0}},
              {{vsg,call,1},{wish,cmd,1}},
              {{vsg,cast,1},{wish,cast,1}},
              {{vsg,mkWindow,7},{wish,start,0}},
              {{vsg,new_tag,0},{wish_manager,new_index,0}},
              {{vsg,new_win_name,0},{wish_manager,new_index,0}},
              {{vsg,on_click,2},{wish_manager,bind_event,2}},
              {{vsg,on_move,2},{wish_manager,bind_event,2}},
              {{vsg,on_move,2},{wish_manager,bind_tag,2}},
              {{vsg,on_move,2},{wish_manager,new_index,0}}]},
 {unused,[{vsg,new_tag,0},
          {vsg_indicator_box,theValue,1},
          {vsg_indicator_box,theValue,1}]}]
```

xref:d('.') performs a cross-reference analysis of all the code in the current directory that has been compiled with the debug flag. It produces lists of depreciated, undefined, and unused functions.

Like most tools, xref has a large number of options, so reading the manual is necessary if you want to use the more powerful features that this program has.

E.2 Debugging

Debugging Erlang is pretty easy. That might surprise you, but this is a consequence of having single-assignment variables. Since Erlang has no pointers and no mutable state (with the exception of ETS tables and process dictionaries), finding out where things have gone wrong is rarely a problem. Once we have observed that a variable has an incorrect value, it's relatively easy to find out when and where this happened.

I find a debugger is a very helpful tool when I write C programs, because I can tell it to watch variables and tell me when their value changes. This is often important because memory in C can be changed indirectly, via pointers. It can be hard to know just *where* a change to some chunk of memory came from. I don't feel the same need for a debugger in Erlang because we can't modify state through pointers.

In the following sections, we'll look at Erlang's compiler diagnostics, followed by the different ways of debugging a program. They are in order of difficulty. Debugging using print statements is the easiest way to debug your program. Tracing a process is the most complex. We have concentrated on the easiest methods here.

Compiler Diagnostics

When we compile a program, the compiler provides us with helpful error messages if our source code is syntactically incorrect. Most of these are self-evident: if we omit a bracket, a comma, or a keyword, the compiler will give an error message with the filename and line number of the offending statement. The following are some errors we could see.

Head Mismatch

We'll get this error if the clauses that make up a function definition do not have the same name and arity:

`bad.erl`

```
Line 1   foo(1,2) ->
    -        a;
    -    foo(2,3,a) ->
    -        b.

         1> c(bad).
         ./bad.erl:3: head mismatch
```

Unbound Variables

Here's some code containing unbound variables:

`bad.erl`

```
Line 1   foo(A, B) ->
    -        bar(A, dothis(X), B),
    -        baz(Y, X).

         1> c(bad).
         ./bad.erl:2: variable 'X' is unbound
         ./bad.erl:3: variable 'Y' is unbound
```

This means that in line 2 the variable X has no value. The error isn't actually on line 2 but is detected at line 2, which is the first occurrence of the unbound variable X. (X is also used on line 3, but the compiler reports only the first line where the error occurs.)

Unterminated String

unterminated string starting with "..."

If we forget a quote mark in a string or atom, we'll get this error message. Sometimes finding the missing quote mark can be pretty tricky. If you get this message and really can't see where the missing quote is, then try placing a quote mark anywhere in your program (or, better, near to where you think the problem might be). If you recompile the program, you might get a more precise diagnostic that will help you pinpoint the error.

Unsafe Variables

If we compile the following code:

```
bad.erl
Line 1   foo() ->
    -        case bar() of
    -            1 ->
    -                X = 1,
    5                Y = 2;
    -            2 ->
    -                X = 3
    -        end,
    -        b(X).
```

we'll get a warning:

```
1> c(bad).
./bad.erl:5: Warning: variable 'Y' is unused
{ok,bad}
```

This is just a warning, since Y is defined but not used. If we now change the program to the following:

```
bad.erl
Line 1   foo() ->
    -        case bar() of
    -            1 ->
    -                X = 1,
    5                Y = 2;
    -            2 ->
    -                X = 3
    -        end,
    -        b(X, Y).
```

we'll get an error:

```
> c(bad).
./bad.erl:9: variable 'Y' unsafe in 'case' (line 2)
{ok,bad}
```

The compiler reasons that the program might take the second branch through the **case** expression (in which event the variable Y will be undefined), so it produces an "unsafe variable" error message.

Shadowed Variables

bad.erl

Line 1
```
foo(X, L) ->
    lists:map(fun(X) -> 2*X end, L).
```

```
1> c(bad).
./bad.erl:1: Warning: variable 'X' is unused
./bad.erl:2: Warning: variable 'X' shadowed in 'fun'
{ok,bad}
```

Here, the compiler is worried that we might have made a mistake in our program. Inside the fun we compute 2*X, but which X are we talking about: the X that is the argument to the fun or the X that is the argument to foo?

If this happens, the best thing to do is to rename one of the Xs to make the warning go away. We could rewrite this as follows:

bad.erl
```
foo(X, L) ->
    lists:map(fun(Z) -> 2*Z end, L).
```

Now there is no problem if we want to use X inside the fun definition.

Runtime Diagnostics

If an Erlang process crashes, we might get an error message. To see the error message, some other process has to monitor the crashing process and print an error message when the monitored process dies. If we just create a process with spawn and the process dies, we won't get any error message. The best thing to do if we want to see all the error messages is always to use spawn_link.

The Stack Trace

Every time a process crashes that is linked to the shell, a stack trace will be printed.

To see what's in the stack trace, we'll write a simple function with a deliberate error and call this function from the shell:

lib_misc.erl

```
deliberate_error(A) ->
    bad_function(A, 12),
    lists:reverse(A).

bad_function(A, _) ->
    {ok, Bin} = file:open({abc,123}, A),
    binary_to_list(Bin).
```

```
1> lib_misc:deliberate_error("file.erl").
** exited: {{badmatch,{error,einval}},
            [{lib_misc,bad_function,2},
             {lib_misc,deliberate_error,1},
             {erl_eval,do_apply,5},
             {shell,exprs,6},
             {shell,eval_loop,3}]} **
```

When we called lib_misc:deliberate_error("file.erl"), an error occurred, and we got a stack trace. Starting at the top of the stack trace, we see the following line:

```
{badmatch,{error,einval}}
```

This comes from the line:

```
{ok, Bin} = file:open({abc,123}, A),
```

Calling file:open/2 returned {error, einval}.[1] This was because {abc,123} is not a valid input value to file:open. When we try to match the return value with {ok, Bin}, we get a badmatch error, and the runtime system prints {badmatch, {error, einval}}, which is the value that could not be matched. Following this is a stack trace. The stack trace starts with the name of the function where the error occurred. This is followed by a list of the names of the functions that the current function will return to when it completes. Thus, the error occurred in lib_misc:bad_function/2, which would have returned to lib_misc:deliberate_error/1, and so on.

Note that it is really only the top entries in the stack trace that are interesting. If the call sequence to the erroneous function involves a tail call, then the call won't be in the stack trace. To see this, we'll rename the function deliberate_error and change it the following:

lib_misc.erl

```
deliberate_error1(A) ->
    bad_function(A, 12).
```

---

1. einval is a POSIX error code short for *invalid value*.

When we call this and get an error, the function deliberate_error1 will be missing from the stack trace:

```
2> lib_misc:deliberate_error1("file.erl").
** exited: {{badmatch,{error,einval}},
            [{lib_misc,bad_function,2},
             {erl_eval,do_apply,5},
             {shell,exprs,6},
             {shell,eval_loop,3}]} **
```

The call to deliberate_error1 is not in the trace since bad_function was called as the last statement in deliberate_error1 and will not return to deliberate_error1 when it completes but will return to the caller of deliberate_error1.

(This is because Erlang applies *last-call* optimization; if the last thing executed in a function is a function call, that call is effectively replaced with a jump. Without this optimization, the *infinite loop* style of programming we use to code message reception loops would not work. However, because of this optimization, the calling function is effectively replaced in the call stack by the called function and hence becomes invisible in stack traces.)

Debugging Techniques

Erlang programmers use a variety of techniques for debugging their programs. By far the most common technique is to just add print statements to the incorrect programs. This techniques fails if the data structures you are interested in become very large, in which case they can be dumped to a file for later inspection.

Some folks use the error logger to save error messages, and others write them in a file. Failing this we can use the Erlang debugger or trace the execution of the program. Let's look at each of these techniques.

io:format Debugging

Adding print statements to the program is the most common form of debugging. You simply add io:format(...) statements to print the values of variables you are interested in at critical points in your program.

When debugging parallel programs, it's often a good idea to print message immediately *before* you send a message to another process and immediately *after* you have received a message.

When I'm writing a concurrent program, I almost always start writing a receive loop like this:

```
loop(...) ->
    receive
        Any ->
            io:format("*** warning unexpected message:~p~n",[Any])
            loop(...)
    end
```

Then, as I add patterns to the receive loop, I get warning messages printed if my process gets any message it doesn't understand. I also use **spawn_link** instead of **spawn** to make sure error messages are printed if my process exits abnormally.

I often use a macro NYI (not yet implemented), which I define like this:

`lib_misc.erl`

```
-define(NYI(X),(begin
                    io:format("*** NYI ~p ~p ~p~n",[?MODULE, ?LINE, X]),
                    exit(nyi)
                end)).
```

Then I might use this macro as follows:

`lib_misc.erl`

```
glurk(X, Y) ->
    ?NYI({glurk, X, Y}).
```

The body of the function glurk is not yet written, so when I call glurk, the program crashes:

```
> lib_misc:glurk(1,2).
*** NYI lib_misc 83 {glurk,1,2}
** exited: nyi *
```

The program exits and an error message is displayed, so I know it's time to complete the implementation of my function.

Dumping to a File

If the data structure we're interested in is large, then we can write it to a file using a function such as dump/2:

`lib_misc.erl`

```
dump(File, Term) ->
    Out = File ++ ".tmp",
    io:format("** dumping to ~s~n",[Out]),
    {ok, S} = file:open(Out, [write]),
    io:format(S, "~p.~n",[Term]),
    file:close(S).
```

This prints a warning message to remind us that we have created a new file. It then adds a .tmp file extension to the filename (so we can easily delete all the temporary files later). Then it pretty-prints the term we are interested in to a file. We can examine the file in a text editor at a later stage. This technique is simple and particularly useful when examining large data structures.

Using the Error Logger

We can use the error logger and create a text file with debugging output. To do so, we create a configuration file such as the following:

`elog5.config`

```
%% text error log
[ {kernel,
  [{error_logger,
    {file, "/home/joe/error_logs/debug.log"}}]}].
```

Then we start Erlang with the following command:

```
erl -config elog5.config
```

Any error messages created by calling routines in the error_logger module, along with any error messages printed in the shell, will end up in the file specified in the configuration file.

The Debugger

The standard Erlang distribution contains a debugger. I'm not going to say a lot about it here, other than to tell you how to start it and to give you pointers to the documentation. Using the debugger once it has been started is pretty easy. You can inspect variables, single-step the code, set breakpoints, and so on. Because we'll often want to debug several processes, the debugger can also spawn copies of itself, so we can have several debug windows, one for each process we are debugging.

The only tricky thing is getting the debugger started:

```
1> %% recompile lib_misc so we can debug it
1> c(lib_misc, [debug_info]).
{ok, lib_misc}
2> im().  %% A window will pop up. Ignore it for now
<0.42.0>
3> ii(lib_misc).
{module,lib_misc}
4> iaa([init]).
true.
5> lib_misc:
...
```

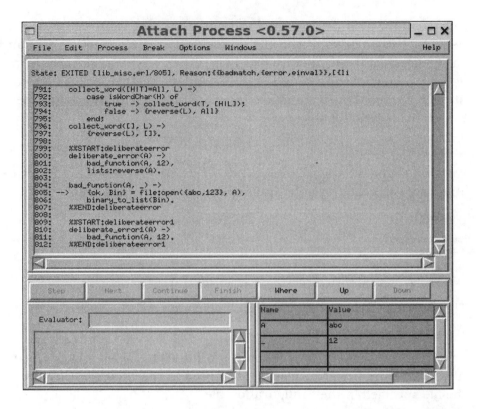

Figure E.1: TABLE VIEWER INITIAL SCREEN

Running this opens the window shown in Figure E.1.

All the commands without a module prefix (ii/1, iaa/1, and so on) are exported from the module i. This is the debugger/interpreter interface module. These routines are accessible from the shell without giving the module prefix.

The functions we called to get the debugger running do the following:

im()

> Start a new graphical monitor. This is the main window of the debugger. It displays the state of all the processes that the debugger is monitoring.

ii(Mod)
> Interpret the code in the module Mod.

iaa([init])
> Attach the debugger to any process executing interpreted code when that process is started.

Digging Deeper

To learn more about debugging, try these resources:

http://www.erlang.org/doc/pdf/debugger.pdf
> The debugger reference manual (a 46-page PDF file) is an introduction to the debugger, with screen dumps, API documentation, and more. It's a must-read for serious users of the debugger.

http://www.erlang.org/doc/man/i.html
> Here you can find the debugger commands that are available in the shell.

E.3 Tracing

You can always trace a process without having to compile your code in a special way. Tracing a process (or processes) provides a powerful way of understanding how your system behaves and can be used to test complex systems without modifying the code. This is particularly useful in embedded systems or where you cannot modify the code being tested.

At a low-level, we can set up a trace by calling a number of Erlang BIFs. Using these BIFs for setting up complex traces is difficult, so several libraries are designed to make this task easier.

We'll start by looking at the low-level Erlang BIFs for tracing and see how to set up a simple tracer; then we'll review the libraries that can provide a higher-level interface to the trace BIFs.

For low-level tracing, two BIFs are particularly important. erlang:trace/3 says, basically, "I want to monitor this process, so please send me a message if something interesting happens." erlang:trace_pattern defines what counts as being "interesting."

erlang:trace(PidSpec, How, FlagList)

> This starts tracing. PidSpec tells the system what to trace. How is a boolean that can turn the trace on or off. FlagList governs what is to be traced (for example, we can trace all function calls, all messages being sent, when garbage collections occur, and so on).
>
> Once we have called erlang:trace/3, the process that called this BIF will be sent trace message when trace events occur. The trace events themselves are determined by calling erlang:trace_pattern/3.

erlang:trace_pattern(MFA, MatchSpec, FlagList)

> This is used to set up a *trace pattern*. If the pattern is matched, then the actions requested are performed. Here MFA is a {Module, Function, Args} tuple that says to which code the trace pattern applies. MatchSpec is a pattern that is tested every time the function specified by MFA is entered, and FlagList tells what to do if the tracing conditions are satisfied.

Writing match specifications for MatchSpec is complicated and doesn't really add much to our understanding of tracing. Fortunately, some libraries[2] make this easier.

Using the previous two BIFs, we can write a simple tracer. trace_module(Mod, Fun) sets up tracing on the module Mod and then evaluates Fun(). We want to trace all function calls and return values in the module Mod.

`tracer_test.erl`

```erlang
trace_module(Mod, StartFun) ->
    %% We'll spawn a process to do the tracing
    spawn(fun() -> trace_module1(Mod, StartFun) end).

trace_module1(Mod, StartFun) ->
    %% The next line says: trace all function calls and return
    %%                      values in Mod
    erlang:trace_pattern({Mod, '_','_'},
                         [{'_',[],[{return_trace}]}],
                         [local]),
    %% spawn a function to do the tracing
    S = self(),
    Pid = spawn(fun() -> do_trace(S, StartFun) end),
    %% setup the trace. Tell the system to start tracing
    %% the process Pid
    erlang:trace(Pid, true, [call,procs]),
```

---

2. http://www.erlang.org/doc/man/ms_transform.html

```erlang
    %% Now tell Pid to start
    Pid ! {self(), start},
    trace_loop().

%% do_trace evaluates StartFun()
%%     when it is told to do so by Parent
do_trace(Parent, StartFun) ->
    receive
        {Parent, start} ->
            StartFun()
    end.

%% trace_loop displays the function call and return values
trace_loop() ->
    receive
        {trace,_,call, X} ->
            io:format("Call: ~p~n",[X]),
            trace_loop();
        {trace,_,return_from, Call, Ret} ->
            io:format("Return From: ~p => ~p~n",[Call, Ret]),
            trace_loop();
        Other ->
            %% we get some other message - print them
            io:format("Other = ~p~n",[Other]),
            trace_loop()
    end.
```

Now we define a test case like this:

`tracer_test.erl`

```erlang
test2() ->
    trace_module(tracer_test, fun() -> fib(4) end).

fib(0) -> 1;
fib(1) -> 1;
fib(N) -> fib(N-1) + fib(N-2).
```

Then we can trace our code:

```erlang
1> c(tracer_test).
{ok,tracer_test}
2> tracer_test:test2().
<0.42.0>Call: {tracer_test,'-trace_module1/2-fun-0-',
             [<0.42.0>,#Fun<tracer_test.0.36786085>]}
Call: {tracer_test,do_trace,[<0.42.0>,#Fun<tracer_test.0.36786085>]}
Call: {tracer_test,'-test2/0-fun-0-',[]}
Call: {tracer_test,fib,[4]}
Call: {tracer_test,fib,[3]}
Call: {tracer_test,fib,[2]}
Call: {tracer_test,fib,[1]}
Return From: {tracer_test,fib,1} => 1
Call: {tracer_test,fib,[0]}
```

```
Return From: {tracer_test,fib,1} => 1
Return From: {tracer_test,fib,1} => 2
Call: {tracer_test,fib,[1]}
Return From: {tracer_test,fib,1} => 1
Return From: {tracer_test,fib,1} => 3
Call: {tracer_test,fib,[2]}
Call: {tracer_test,fib,[1]}
Return From: {tracer_test,fib,1} => 1
Call: {tracer_test,fib,[0]}
Return From: {tracer_test,fib,1} => 1
Return From: {tracer_test,fib,1} => 2
Return From: {tracer_test,fib,1} => 5
Return From: {tracer_test,'-test2/0-fun-0-',0} => 5
Return From: {tracer_test,do_trace,2} => 5
Return From: {tracer_test,'-trace_module1/2-fun-0-',2} => 5
Other = {trace,<0.43.0>,exit,normal}
```

Using the Libraries

We can perform the same trace as the previous one using the library
module dbg. This hides all the details of the low-level Erlang BIFs.

`tracer_test.erl`

```
test1() ->
    dbg:tracer(),
    dbg:tpl(tracer_test,fib,'_',
            dbg:fun2ms(fun(_) -> return_trace() end)),
    dbg:p(all,[c]),
    tracer_test:fib(4).
```

Running this, we get the following:

```
1> tracer_test:test1().
(<0.34.0>) call tracer_test:fib(4)
(<0.34.0>) call tracer_test:fib(3)
(<0.34.0>) call tracer_test:fib(2)
(<0.34.0>) call tracer_test:fib(1)
(<0.34.0>) returned from tracer_test:fib/1 -> 1
(<0.34.0>) call tracer_test:fib(0)
(<0.34.0>) returned from tracer_test:fib/1 -> 1
(<0.34.0>) returned from tracer_test:fib/1 -> 2
(<0.34.0>) call tracer_test:fib(1)
(<0.34.0>) returned from tracer_test:fib/1 -> 1
(<0.34.0>) returned from tracer_test:fib/1 -> 3
(<0.34.0>) call tracer_test:fib(2)
(<0.34.0>) call tracer_test:fib(1)
(<0.34.0>) returned from tracer_test:fib/1 -> 1
(<0.34.0>) call tracer_test:fib(0)
(<0.34.0>) returned from tracer_test:fib/1 -> 1
(<0.34.0>) returned from tracer_test:fib/1 -> 2
(<0.34.0>) returned from tracer_test:fib/1 -> 5
```

Digging Deeper

To learn more about tracing, you need to read three manual pages for the following modules:

- dbg provides a simplified interface to the Erlang trace BIFs.
- ttb is yet another interface to the trace BIFs. It is higher level than dbg.
- ms_transform makes match specifications for use in the tracer software.

E.4 Dynamic Code Loading

Dynamic code loading is one of the most surprising features built into the heart of Erlang. The nice part is that it just works without you really being aware of what's happening in the background.

The idea is simple: every time we call someModule:someFunction(...), we'll always call the latest version of the function in the latest version of the module, *even if we recompile the module while code is running in this module.*

If a calls b in a loop and we recompile b, then a will automatically call the new version of b the next time b is called.

If many different processes are running and all of them call b, then all of them will call the new version of b if b is recompiled. To see how this works, we'll write two little modules: a and b. b is very simple:

`b.erl`
```
-module(b).
-export([x/0]).

x() -> 1.
```

Now we'll write a:

`a.erl`
```
-module(a).
-compile(export_all).

start(Tag) ->
    spawn(fun() -> loop(Tag) end).

loop(Tag) ->
    sleep(),
    Val = b:x(),
    io:format("Vsn1 (~p) b:x() = ~p~n",[Tag, Val]),
    loop(Tag).
```

```
sleep() ->
    receive
        after 3000 -> true
    end.
```

Now we can compile a and start a couple of a processes:

```
1> c(b).
{ok, b}
2> c(a).
{ok, a}
3> a:start(one).
<0.41.0>
Vsn1 (one) b:x() = 1
4> a:start(two).
<0.43.0>
Vsn1 (one) b:x() = 1
Vsn1 (two) b:x() = 1
Vsn1 (one) b:x() = 1
Vsn1 (two) b:x() = 1
```

The a processes sleep for three seconds, wake up and call b:x(), and then print the result. Now we'll go into the editor and change the module b to the following:

```
-module(b).
-export([x/0]).

x() -> 2.
```

Then we recompile b in the shell. This is what happens:

```
4> c(b).
{ok,b}
Vsn1 (one) b:x() = 2
Vsn1 (two) b:x() = 2
Vsn1 (one) b:x() = 2
Vsn1 (two) b:x() = 2
...
```

The two original versions of a are still running, but now they call the *new* version of b. So when we call b:x() from within the module a, we really call "the latest version of b." We can change and recompile b as many times as we want, and all the modules that call it will automatically call the new version of b without having to do anything special.

Now we've recompiled b, but what happens if we change and recompile a? We'll do an experiment and change a to the following:

```
-module(a).
-compile(export_all).
```

```
start(Tag) ->
    spawn(fun() -> loop(Tag) end).

loop(Tag) ->
    sleep(),
    Val = b:x(),
    io:format("Vsn2 (~p) b:x() = ~p~n",[Tag, Val]),
    loop(Tag).

sleep() ->
    receive
        after 3000 -> true
    end.
```

Now we compile and start a:

```
5> c(a).
{ok,a}
Vsn1 (one) b:x() = 2
Vsn1 (two) b:x() = 2
...
6> a:start(three).
<0.53.0>
Vsn1 (one) b:x() = 2
Vsn1 (two) b:x() = 2
Vsn2 (three) b:x() = 2
Vsn1 (one) b:x() = 2
Vsn1 (two) b:x() = 2
Vsn2 (three) b:x() = 2
...
```

Something funny is going on here. When we start the new version of a, we see that new version running. However, the existing processes running the first version of a are still running that old version of a without any problems.

Now we could try changing b yet again:

```
-module(b).
-export([x/0]).

x() -> 3.
```

We'll recompile b in the shell. Watch what happens:

```
7> c(b).
{ok,b}
Vsn1 (one) b:x() = 3
Vsn1 (two) b:x() = 3
Vsn2 (three) b:x() = 3
...
```

Now both the old and new versions of a call the latest version of b.

Finally, we'll change a again (this is the third change to a):

```erlang
-module(a).
-compile(export_all).

start(Tag) ->
    spawn(fun() -> loop(Tag) end).

loop(Tag) ->
    sleep(),
    Val = b:x(),
    io:format("Vsn3 (~p) b:x() = ~p~n",[Tag, Val]),
    loop(Tag).

sleep() ->
    receive
        after 3000 -> true
    end.
```

Now when we recompile a and start a new version of a, we see the following:

```erlang
8> c(a).
{ok,a}
Vsn2 (three) b:x() = 3
...
9> a:start(four).
<0.106.0>
Vsn2 (three) b:x() = 3
Vsn3 (four) b:x() = 3
Vsn2 (three) b:x() = 3
Vsn3 (four) b:x() = 3
...
```

The output contains strings generated by the last two versions of a (versions 2 and 3); the process running version 1 of a's code has died.

Erlang can have two versions of a module running at any one time, the current version and an old version. When you recompile a module, any process running code in the old version is killed, the current version becomes the old version, and the newly compiled module becomes the current version. Think of this as a shift register with two versions of the code. As we add new code, the oldest version is junked. Processes can simultaneously run old and new versions of the code.

Read the purge_module documentation[3] for more details.

---

3. http://www.erlang.org/doc/man/erlang.html#purge_module/1

Module and Function Reference

This appendix contains one-line summaries for most of the modules in the kernel and stdlib libraries in the standard Erlang distribution. (I've omitted some of the more obscure modules in order to keep the weight of this book below the point where you'd need mechanical assistance to pick it up.)

Note: The modules ordsets and orddict are not included in this appendix. ordsets exports the same functions as sets; the only difference is that an ordered list is used to represent the elements of the set. orddict exports the same functions as dict, but a list of pairs is used to represent the dictionary. The list is ordered by the keys in the dictionary.

F.1 Module: application

Generic OTP application functions.

Module:config_change(Changed, New, Removed) -> ok
Update the configuration parameters for an application.

Module:prep_stop(State) -> NewState
Prepare an application for termination.

Module:start(StartType, StartArgs) -> {ok, Pid} | {ok, Pid, State} | {error, Reason}
Start an application.

Module:start_phase(Phase, StartType, PhaseArgs) -> ok | {error, Reason}
Extended start of an application.

Module:stop(State)
Clean up after termination of an application.

get_all_env(Application) -> Env
Get the configuration parameters for an application.

get_all_key(Application) -> {ok, Keys} | undefined
Get the application specification keys.

get_application(Pid | Module) -> {ok, Application} | undefined
Get the name of an application containing a certain process or module.

get_env(Application, Par) -> {ok, Val} | undefined
Get the value of a configuration parameter.

get_key(Application, Key) -> {ok, Val} | undefined
Get the value of an application specification key.

load(AppDescr, Distributed) -> ok | {error, Reason}
Load an application.

loaded_applications() -> ({Application, Description, Vsn})
Get the currently loaded applications.

permit(Application, Bool) -> ok | {error, Reason}
Change an application's permission to run on a node.

set_env(Application, Par, Val, Timeout) -> ok
Set the value of a configuration parameter.

start(Application, Type) -> ok | {error, Reason}
Load and start an application.

start_type() -> StartType | local | undefined
Get the start type of an ongoing application start-up.

stop(Application) -> ok | {error, Reason}
Stop an application.

takeover(Application, Type) -> ok | {error, Reason}
Take over a distributed application.

unload(Application) -> ok | {error, Reason}
Unload an application.

unset_env(Application, Par, Timeout) -> ok
Unset the value of a configuration parameter.

which_applications(Timeout) -> ({Application, Description, Vsn})
Get the currently running applications.

F.2   Module: base64

Implements base 64 encode and decode; see RFC 2045.

encode_to_string(Data) -> Base64String
Encode data into base 64.

mime_decode_string(Base64) -> DataString
Decode a base 64–encoded string to data.

F.3   Module: beam_lib

An interface to the BEAM file format.

chunks(Beam, (ChunkRef)) -> {ok, {Module, (ChunkData)}} | {error, beam_lib, Reason}
    Read selected chunks from a BEAM file or binary.

chunks(Beam, (ChunkRef), (Option)) -> {ok, {Module, (ChunkResult)}} | {error, beam_lib, Reason}
    Read selected chunks from a BEAM file or binary.

clear_crypto_key_fun() -> {ok, Result}
    Unregister the current crypto key fun.

cmp(Beam1, Beam2) -> ok | {error, beam_lib, Reason}
    Compare two BEAM files.

cmp_dirs(Dir1, Dir2) -> {Only1, Only2, Different} | {error, beam_lib, Reason1}
    Compare the BEAM files in two directories.

crypto_key_fun(CryptoKeyFun) -> ok | {error, Reason}
    Register a fun that provides a crypto key.

diff_dirs(Dir1, Dir2) -> ok | {error, beam_lib, Reason1}
    Compare the BEAM files in two directories.

format_error(Reason) -> Chars
    Return an English description of a BEAM read error reply.

info(Beam) -> ({Item, Info}) | {error, beam_lib, Reason1}
    Information about a BEAM file.

md5(Beam) -> {ok, {Module, MD5}} | {error, beam_lib, Reason}
    Read the BEAM file's module version.

strip(Beam1) -> {ok, {Module, Beam2}} | {error, beam_lib, Reason1}
    Remove chunks not needed by the loader from a BEAM file.

strip_files(Files) -> {ok, ({Module, Beam2})} | {error, beam_lib, Reason1}
    Remove chunks not needed by the loader from BEAM files.

strip_release(Dir) -> {ok, ({Module, Filename})} | {error, beam_lib, Reason1}
    Remove chunks not needed by the loader from all BEAM files of a release.

version(Beam) -> {ok, {Module, (Version)}} | {error, beam_lib, Reason}
    Read the BEAM file's module version.

F.4   Module: c

Command interface module.

bt(Pid) -> void()
    Stack backtrace for a process.

c(File, Options) -> {ok, Module} | error
    Compile and load code in a file.

cd(Dir) -> void()
> Change working directory.

flush() -> void()
> Flush any messages sent to the shell.

help() -> void()
> Help information.

i(X, Y, Z) -> void()
> Information about pid <X.Y.Z>.

l(Module) -> void()
> Load or reload module.

lc(Files) -> ok
> Compile a list of files.

ls() -> void()
> List files in the current directory.

ls(Dir) -> void()
> List files in a directory.

m() -> void()
> Which modules are loaded.

m(Module) -> void()
> Information about a module.

memory() -> ({Type, Size})
> Memory allocation information.

memory((Type)) -> ({Type, Size})
> Memory allocation information.

nc(File, Options) -> {ok, Module} | error
> Compile and load code in a file on all nodes.

ni() -> void()
> Information about the system.

nl(Module) -> void()
> Load module on all nodes.

nregs() -> void()
> Information about registered processes.

pid(X, Y, Z) -> pid()
> Convert X,Y,Z to a PID.

pwd() -> void()
> Print working directory.

q() -> void()
> Quit; shorthand for init:stop().

xm(ModSpec) -> void()
> Cross-reference check a module.

y(File) -> YeccRet
> Generate an LALR-1 parser.

y(File, Options) -> YeccRet
> Generate an LALR-1 parser.

F.5 Module: calendar

Local and universal time, day-of-the-week, date and time conversions.

date_to_gregorian_days(Year, Month, Day) -> Days
> Compute the number of days from year 0 up to the given date.

datetime_to_gregorian_seconds({Date, Time}) -> Seconds
> Compute the number of seconds from year 0 up to the given date and time.

day_of_the_week(Year, Month, Day) -> DayNumber
> Compute the day of the week.

gregorian_days_to_date(Days) -> Date
> Compute the date given the number of Gregorian days.

gregorian_seconds_to_datetime(Seconds) -> {Date, Time}
> Compute the date given the number of Gregorian days.

is_leap_year(Year) -> bool()
> Check whether a year is a leap year.

last_day_of_the_month(Year, Month) -> int()
> Compute the number of days in a month.

local_time() -> {Date, Time}
> Compute local time.

local_time_to_universal_time({Date1, Time1}) -> {Date2, Time2}
> Convert from local time to universal time (deprecated).

local_time_to_universal_time_dst({Date1, Time1}) -> ({Date, Time})
> Convert from local time to universal time(s).

now_to_datetime(Now) -> {Date, Time}
> Convert now to date and time.

now_to_local_time(Now) -> {Date, Time}
> Convert now to local date and time.

seconds_to_daystime(Seconds) -> {Days, Time}
> Compute days and time from seconds.

seconds_to_time(Seconds) -> Time
> Compute time from seconds.

time_difference(T1, T2) -> {Days, Time}
> Compute the difference between two times (deprecated).

time_to_seconds(Time) -> Seconds
> Compute the number of seconds since midnight up to the given time.

universal_time() -> {Date, Time}
    Compute universal time.

universal_time_to_local_time({Date1, Time1}) -> {Date2, Time2}
    Convert from universal time to local time.

valid_date(Year, Month, Day) -> bool()
    Check whether a date is valid.

F.6 Module: code

Erlang code server.

add_patha(Dir) -> true | {error, What}
    Add a directory to the beginning of the code path.

add_pathsa(Dirs) -> ok
    Add directories to the beginning of the code path.

add_pathsz(Dirs) -> ok
    Add directories to the end of the code path.

add_pathz(Dir) -> true | {error, What}
    Add a directory to the end of the code path.

all_loaded() -> ({Module, Loaded})
    Get all loaded modules.

clash() -> ok
    Search for modules with identical names.

compiler_dir() -> string()
    Library directory for the compiler.

del_path(Name | Dir) -> true | false | {error, What}
    Delete a directory from the code path.

delete(Module) -> true | false
    Remove current code for a module.

ensure_loaded(Module) -> {module, Module} | {error, What}
    Ensure that a module is loaded.

get_object_code(Module) -> {Module, Binary, Filename} | error
    Get the object code for a module.

get_path() -> Path
    Return the code server search path.

is_loaded(Module) -> {file, Loaded} | false
    Check whether a module is loaded.

lib_dir() -> string()
    Library directory of Erlang/OTP.

lib_dir(Name) -> string() | {error, bad_name}
    Library directory for an application.

load_abs(Filename) -> {module, Module} | {error, What}
> Load a module, residing in a given file.

load_binary(Module, Filename, Binary) -> {module, Module} | {error, What}
> Load object code for a module.

load_file(Module) -> {module, Module} | {error, What}
> Load a module.

objfile_extension() -> ".beam"
> Object code file extension.

priv_dir(Name) -> string() | {error, bad_name}
> Priv directory for an application.

purge(Module) -> true | false
> Remove old code for a module.

rehash() -> ok
> Rehash or create code path cache.

replace_path(Name, Dir) -> true | {error, What}
> Replace a directory with another in the code path.

root_dir() -> string()
> Root directory of Erlang/OTP.

set_path(Path) -> true | {error, What}
> Set the code server search path.

soft_purge(Module) -> true | false
> Remove old code for a module, unless no process uses it.

stick_dir(Dir) -> ok | {error, What}
> Mark a directory as sticky.

unstick_dir(Dir) -> ok | {error, What}
> Remove a sticky directory mark.

where_is_file(Filename) -> Absname | non_existing
> Full name of a file located in the code path.

which(Module) -> Which
> The object code file of a module.

F.7 Module: dets

A disk-based term storage.

all() -> (Name)
> Return a list of the names of all open DETS tables on this node.

bchunk(Name, Continuation) -> {Continuation2, Data} | '$end_of_table' | {error, Reason}
> Return a chunk of objects stored in a DETS table.

close(Name) -> ok | {error, Reason}
> Close a DETS table.

delete(Name, Key) -> ok | {error, Reason}
Delete all objects with a given key from a DETS table.

delete_all_objects(Name) -> ok | {error, Reason}
Delete all objects from a DETS table.

delete_object(Name, Object) -> ok | {error, Reason}
Delete a given object from a DETS table.

first(Name) -> Key | '$end_of_table'
Return the first key stored in a DETS table.

foldl(Function, Acc0, Name) -> Acc1 | {error, Reason}
Fold a function over a DETS table.

foldr(Function, Acc0, Name) -> Acc1 | {error, Reason}
Fold a function over a DETS table.

from_ets(Name, EtsTab) -> ok | {error, Reason}
Replace the objects of a DETS table with the objects of an ETS table.

info(Name) -> InfoList | undefined
Return information about a DETS table.

info(Name, Item) -> Value | undefined
Return the information associated with a given item for a DETS table.

init_table(Name, InitFun (, Options)) -> ok | {error, Reason}
Replace all objects of a DETS table.

insert(Name, Objects) -> ok | {error, Reason}
Insert one or more objects into a DETS table.

insert_new(Name, Objects) -> Bool
Insert one or more objects into a DETS table.

is_compatible_bchunk_format(Name, BchunkFormat) -> Bool
Test the compatibility of a table's chunk data.

is_dets_file(FileName) -> Bool | {error, Reason}
Test for a DETS table.

lookup(Name, Key) -> (Object) | {error, Reason}
Return all objects with a given key stored in a DETS table.

match(Continuation) -> {(Match), Continuation2 | '$end_of_table' | {error, Reason}
Match a chunk of objects stored in a DETS table, and return a list of variable bindings.

match(Name, Pattern) -> (Match) | {error, Reason}
Match the objects stored in a DETS table, and return a list of variable bindings.

match(Name, Pattern, N) -> {(Match), Continuation} | '$end_of_table' | {error, Reason}
Match the first chunk of objects stored in a DETS table, and return a list of variable bindings.

match_delete(Name, Pattern) -> N | {error, Reason}
Delete all objects that match a given pattern from a DETS table.

match_object(Continuation) -> {(Object), Continuation2} | '$end_of_table' | {error, Reason}
Match a chunk of objects stored in a DETS table and return a list of objects.

match_object(Name, Pattern) -> (Object) | {error, Reason}
Match the objects stored in a DETS table and return a list of objects.

match_object(Name, Pattern, N) -> {(Object), Continuation} | '$end_of_table' | {error, Reason}
Match the first chunk of objects stored in a DETS table and return a list of objects.

member(Name, Key) -> Bool | {error, Reason}
Test for occurrence of a key in a DETS table.

next(Name, Key1) -> Key2 | '$end_of_table'
Return the next key in a DETS table.

open_file(Filename) -> {ok, Reference} | {error, Reason}
Open an existing DETS table.

open_file(Name, Args) -> {ok, Name} | {error, Reason}
Open a DETS table.

pid2name(Pid) -> {ok, Name} | undefined
Return the name of the DETS table handled by a PID.

repair_continuation(Continuation, MatchSpec) -> Continuation2
Repair a continuation from select/1 or select/3.

safe_fixtable(Name, Fix)
Fix a DETS table for safe traversal.

select(Continuation) -> {Selection, Continuation2} | '$end_of_table' | {error, Reason}
Apply a match specification to some objects stored in a DETS table.

select(Name, MatchSpec) -> Selection | {error, Reason}
Apply a match specification to all objects stored in a DETS table.

select(Name, MatchSpec, N) -> {Selection, Continuation} | '$end_of_table' | {error, Reason}
Apply a match specification to the first chunk of objects stored in a DETS table.

select_delete(Name, MatchSpec) -> N | {error, Reason}
Delete all objects that match a given pattern from a DETS table.

slot(Name, I) -> '$end_of_table' | (Object) | {error, Reason}
Return the list of objects associated with a slot of a DETS table.

sync(Name) -> ok | {error, Reason}
Ensure that all updates made to a DETS table are written to disk.

table(Name (, Options)) -> QueryHandle
Return a QLC query handle.

to_ets(Name, EtsTab) -> EtsTab | {error, Reason}
Insert all objects of a DETS table into an ETS table.

traverse(Name, Fun) -> Return | {error, Reason}
Apply a function to all or some objects stored in a DETS table.

update_counter(Name, Key, Increment) -> Result
> Update a counter object stored in a DETS table.

F.8 Module: dict

Key-value dictionary.

append(Key, Value, Dict1) -> Dict2
> Append a value to keys in a dictionary.

append_list(Key, ValList, Dict1) -> Dict2
> Append new values to keys in a dictionary.

erase(Key, Dict1) -> Dict2
> Erase a key from a dictionary.

fetch(Key, Dict) -> Value
> Look up values in a dictionary.

fetch_keys(Dict) -> Keys
> Return all keys in a dictionary.

filter(Pred, Dict1) -> Dict2
> Choose elements which satisfy a predicate.

find(Key, Dict) -> {ok, Value} | error
> Search for a key in a dictionary.

fold(Fun, Acc0, Dict) -> Acc1
> Fold a function over a dictionary.

from_list(List) -> Dict
> Convert a list of pairs to a dictionary.

is_key(Key, Dict) -> bool()
> Test whether a key is in a dictionary.

map(Fun, Dict1) -> Dict2
> Map a function over a dictionary.

merge(Fun, Dict1, Dict2) -> Dict3
> Merge two dictionaries.

new() -> dictionary()
> Create a dictionary.

store(Key, Value, Dict1) -> Dict2
> Store a value in a dictionary.

to_list(Dict) -> List
> Convert a dictionary to a list of pairs.

update(Key, Fun, Dict1) -> Dict2
> Update a value in a dictionary.

update(Key, Fun, Initial, Dict1) -> Dict2
> Update a value in a dictionary.

update_counter(Key, Increment, Dict1) -> Dict2
> Increment a value in a dictionary.

F.9 Module: digraph

Directed graphs.

add_edge(G, V1, V2) -> edge() | {error, Reason}
> Add an edge to a digraph.

add_vertex(G) -> vertex()
> Add or modify a vertex of a digraph.

del_edge(G, E) -> true
> Delete an edge from a digraph.

del_edges(G, Edges) -> true
> Delete edges from a digraph.

del_path(G, V1, V2) -> true
> Delete paths from a digraph.

del_vertex(G, V) -> true
> Delete a vertex from a digraph.

del_vertices(G, Vertices) -> true
> Delete vertices from a digraph.

delete(G) -> true
> Delete a digraph.

edge(G, E) -> {E, V1, V2, Label} | false
> Return the vertices and the label of an edge of a digraph.

edges(G) -> Edges
> Return all edges of a digraph.

edges(G, V) -> Edges
> Return the edges emanating from or incident on a vertex of a digraph.

get_cycle(G, V) -> Vertices | false
> Find one cycle in a digraph.

get_path(G, V1, V2) -> Vertices | false
> Find one path in a digraph.

get_short_cycle(G, V) -> Vertices | false
> Find one short cycle in a digraph.

get_short_path(G, V1, V2) -> Vertices | false
> Find one short path in a digraph.

in_degree(G, V) -> integer()
> Return the in-degree of a vertex of a digraph.

in_edges(G, V) -> Edges
> Return all edges incident on a vertex of a digraph.

in_neighbours(G, V) -> Vertices
> Return all in-neighbors of a vertex of a digraph.

info(G) -> InfoList
> Return information about a digraph.

new() -> digraph()
> Return a protected empty digraph, where cycles are allowed.

new(Type) -> digraph() | {error, Reason}
> Create a new empty digraph.

no_edges(G) -> integer() >= 0
> Return the number of edges of a digraph.

no_vertices(G) -> integer() >= 0
> Return the number of vertices of a digraph.

out_degree(G, V) -> integer()
> Return the out-degree of a vertex of a digraph.

out_edges(G, V) -> Edges
> Return all edges emanating from a vertex of a digraph.

out_neighbours(G, V) -> Vertices
> Return all out-neighbors of a vertex of a digraph.

vertex(G, V) -> {V, Label} | false
> Return the label of a vertex of a digraph.

vertices(G) -> Vertices
> Return all vertices of a digraph.

F.10 Module: digraph_utils

Algorithms for directed graphs.

components(Digraph) -> (Component)
> Return the components of a digraph.

condensation(Digraph) -> CondensedDigraph
> Return a condensed graph of a digraph.

cyclic_strong_components(Digraph) -> (StrongComponent)
> Return the cyclic strong components of a digraph.

is_acyclic(Digraph) -> bool()
> Check whether a digraph is acyclic.

loop_vertices(Digraph) -> Vertices
> Return the vertices of a digraph included in some loop.

postorder(Digraph) -> Vertices
> Return the vertices of a digraph in post-order.

preorder(Digraph) -> Vertices
> Return the vertices of a digraph in pre-order.

reachable(Vertices, Digraph) -> Vertices
> Return the vertices reachable from some vertices of a digraph.

reachable_neighbours(Vertices, Digraph) -> Vertices
> Return the neighbours reachable from some vertices of a digraph.

reaching(Vertices, Digraph) -> Vertices
> Return the vertices that reach some vertices of a digraph.

reaching_neighbours(Vertices, Digraph) -> Vertices
> Return the neighbours that reach some vertices of a digraph.

strong_components(Digraph) -> (StrongComponent)
> Return the strong components of a digraph.

subgraph(Digraph, Vertices (, Options)) -> Subgraph | {error, Reason}
> Return a subgraph of a digraph.

topsort(Digraph) -> Vertices | false
> Return a topological sorting of the vertices of a digraph.

F.11   Module: disk_log

A disk-based term logging facility.

accessible_logs() -> {(LocalLog), (DistributedLog)}
> Return the accessible disk logs on the current node.

balog(Log, Bytes) -> ok | {error, Reason}
> Asynchronously log an item onto a disk log.

balog_terms(Log, BytesList) -> ok | {error, Reason}
> Asynchronously log several items onto a disk log.

bchunk(Log, Continuation, N) -> {Continuation2, Binaries} | {Continuation2, Binaries, Badbytes} | eof | {error, Reason}
> Read a chunk of items written to a disk log.

block(Log, QueueLogRecords) -> ok | {error, Reason}
> Block a disk log.

blog(Log, Bytes) -> ok | {error, Reason}
> Log an item onto a disk log.

blog_terms(Log, BytesList) -> ok | {error, Reason}
> Log several items onto a disk log.

breopen(Log, File, BHead) -> ok | {error, Reason}
> Reopen a disk log and save the old log.

btruncate(Log, BHead) -> ok | {error, Reason}
> Truncate a disk log.

change_header(Log, Header) -> ok | {error, Reason}
> Change the head or head_func option for an owner of a disk log.

change_notify(Log, Owner, Notify) -> ok | {error, Reason}
> Change the notify option for an owner of a disk log.

change_size(Log, Size) -> ok | {error, Reason}
> Change the size of an open disk log.

chunk_info(Continuation) -> InfoList | {error, Reason}
> Return information about a chunk continuation of a disk log.

chunk_step(Log, Continuation, Step) -> {ok, Continuation2} | {error, Reason}
> Step forward or backward among the wrap log files of a disk log.

close(Log) -> ok | {error, Reason}
> Close a disk log.

format_error(Error) -> Chars
> Return an English description of a disk log error reply.

inc_wrap_file(Log) -> ok | {error, Reason}
> Change to the next wrap log file of a disk log.

info(Log) -> InfoList | {error, no_such_log}
> Return information about a disk log.

lclose(Log, Node) -> ok | {error, Reason}
> Close a disk log on one node.

open(ArgL) -> OpenRet | DistOpenRet
> Open a disk log file.

pid2name(Pid) -> {ok, Log} | undefined
> Return the name of the disk log handled by a PID.

sync(Log) -> ok | {error, Reason}
> Flush the contents of a disk log to the disk.

unblock(Log) -> ok | {error, Reason}
> Unblock a disk log.

F.12 Module: epp

An Erlang code preprocessor.

close(Epp) -> ok
> Close the preprocessing of the file associated withEpp.

open(FileName, IncludePath, PredefMacros) -> {ok,Epp} | {error, ErrorDescriptor}
> Open a file for preprocessing.

parse_erl_form(Epp) -> {ok, AbsForm} | {eof, Line} | {error, ErrorInfo}
> Return the next Erlang form from the opened Erlang source file.

parse_file(FileName,IncludePath,PredefMacro) -> {ok,(Form)} | {error,OpenError}
> Preprocess and parse an Erlang source file.

F.13 Module: erl_eval

The Erlang meta interpreter.

add_binding(Name, Value, Bindings) -> BindingStruct
Add a binding.

binding(Name, BindingStruct) -> Binding
Return bindings.

bindings(BindingStruct) -> Bindings
Return bindings.

del_binding(Name, Bindings) -> BindingStruct
Delete a binding.

expr(Expression, Bindings, LocalFunctionHandler, NonlocalFunctionHandler) -> {value, Value, NewBindings}
Evaluate the expression.

expr_list(ExpressionList, Bindings, LocalFunctionHandler, NonlocalFunctionHandler) -> {ValueList, NewBindings}
Evaluate a list of expressions.

exprs(Expressions, Bindings, LocalFunctionHandler, NonlocalFunctionHandler) -> {value, Value, NewBindings}
Evaluate expressions.

new_bindings() -> BindingStruct
Return a bindings structure.

F.14 Module: erl_parse

The Erlang parser.

abstract(Data) -> AbsTerm
Convert an Erlang term into an abstract form.

format_error(ErrorDescriptor) -> Chars
Format an error descriptor.

normalise(AbsTerm) -> Data
Convert abstract form to an Erlang term.

parse_exprs(Tokens) -> {ok, Expr_list} | {error, ErrorInfo}
Parse Erlang expressions.

parse_form(Tokens) -> {ok, AbsForm} | {error, ErrorInfo}
Parse an Erlang form.

parse_term(Tokens) -> {ok, Term} | {error, ErrorInfo}
Parse an Erlang term.

tokens(AbsTerm, MoreTokens) -> Tokens
Generate a list of tokens for an expression.

F.15 Module: erl_pp

The Erlang pretty printer.

attribute(Attribute, HookFunction) -> DeepCharList
Pretty-print an attribute.

expr(Expression, Indent, Precedence, HookFunction) ->-> DeepCharList
Pretty-print one Expression.

exprs(Expressions, Indent, HookFunction) -> DeepCharList
Pretty-print Expressions.

form(Form, HookFunction) -> DeepCharList
Pretty-print a form.

function(Function, HookFunction) -> DeepCharList
Pretty-print a function.

guard(Guard, HookFunction) -> DeepCharList
Pretty-print a guard.

F.16 Module: erl_scan

The Erlang token scanner.

format_error(ErrorDescriptor) -> string()
Format an error descriptor.

reserved_word(Atom) -> bool()
Test for a reserved word.

string(CharList) -> {ok, Tokens, EndLine} | Error
Scan a string, and return the Erlang tokens.

tokens(Continuation, CharList, StartLine) ->Return
Re-entrant scanner.

F.17 Module: erl_tar

Unix TAR utility for reading and writing TAR archives.

add(TarDescriptor, Filename, Options) -> RetValue
Add a file to an open TAR file.

add(TarDescriptor, Filename, NameInArchive, Options) -> RetValue
Add a file to an open TAR file.

close(TarDescriptor)
Close an open TAR file.

create(Name, FileList) ->RetValue
Create a TAR archive.

create(Name, FileList, OptionList)
Create a TAR archive with options.

extract(Name) -> RetValue
>   Extract all files from a TAR file.

extract(Name, OptionList)
>   Extract files from a TAR file.

format_error(Reason) -> string()
>   Convert error term to a readable string.

open(Name, OpenModeList) -> RetValue
>   Open a TAR file.

t(Name)
>   Print the name of each file in a TAR file.

table(Name) -> RetValue
>   Retrieve the name of all files in a TAR file.

table(Name, Options)
>   Retrieve name and information of all files in a TAR file.

tt(Name)
>   Print name and information for each file in a TAR file.

F.18   Module: erlang

The Erlang BIFs.

abs(Number) -> int() | float()
>   Arithmetical absolute value.

apply(Fun, Args) -> term() | empty()
>   Apply a function to an argument list.

apply(Module, Function, Args) -> term() | empty()
>   Apply a function to an argument list.

atom_to_list(Atom) -> string()
>   Text representation of an atom.

binary_to_list(Binary) -> (char())
>   Convert a binary to a list.

binary_to_list(Binary, Start, Stop) -> (char())
>   Convert part of a binary to a list.

binary_to_term(Binary) -> term()
>   Decode an Erlang external term format binary.

check_process_code(Pid, Module) -> bool()
>   Check whether a process is executing old code for a module.

concat_binary(ListOfBinaries)
>   Concatenate a list of binaries (deprecated).

date() -> {Year, Month, Day}
>   Current date.

delete_module(Module) -> true | undefined
Make the current code for a module old.

disconnect_node(Node) -> bool() | ignored
Force the disconnection of a node.

element(N, Tuple) -> term()
Get Nth element of a tuple.

erase() -> ({Key, Val})
Return and delete the process dictionary.

erase(Key) -> Val | undefined
Return and delete a value from the process dictionary.

erlang:append_element(Tuple1, Term) -> Tuple2
Append an extra element to a tuple.

erlang:bump_reductions(Reductions) -> void()
Increment the reduction counter.

erlang:cancel_timer(TimerRef) -> Time | false
Cancel a timer.

erlang:demonitor(MonitorRef) -> true
Stop monitoring.

erlang:demonitor(MonitorRef, OptionList) -> true
Stop monitoring.

erlang:display(Term) -> true
Print a term on standard output.

erlang:error(Reason)
Stop execution with a given reason.

erlang:error(Reason, Args)
Stop execution with a given reason.

erlang:fault(Reason)
Stop execution with a given reason.

erlang:fault(Reason, Args)
Stop execution with a given reason.

erlang:fun_info(Fun) -> ({Item, Info})
Information about a fun.

erlang:fun_info(Fun, Item) -> {Item, Info}
Information about a fun.

erlang:fun_to_list(Fun) -> string()
Text representation of a fun.

erlang:function_exported(Module, Function, Arity) -> bool()
Check whether a function is exported and loaded.

erlang:get_cookie() -> Cookie | nocookie
Get the magic cookie of the local node.

erlang:get_stacktrace() -> ({Module, Function, Arity | Args})
Get the call stack backtrace of the last exception.

erlang:hash(Term, Range) -> Hash
Hash function (deprecated).

erlang:hibernate(Module, Function, Args)
Hibernate a process until a message is sent to it.

erlang:info(Type) -> Res
Information about the system (deprecated).

erlang:integer_to_list(Integer, Base) -> string()
Text representation of an integer.

erlang:is_builtin(Module, Function, Arity) -> bool()
Check whether a function is a BIF implemented in C.

erlang:list_to_integer(String, Base) -> int()
Convert from text representation to an integer.

erlang:loaded() -> (Module)
List of all loaded modules.

erlang:localtime() -> {Date, Time}
Current local date and time.

erlang:localtime_to_universaltime({Date1, Time1}) -> {Date2, Time2}
Convert from local to Universal Time Coordinated (UTC) date and time.

erlang:localtime_to_universaltime({Date1, Time1}, IsDst) -> {Date2, Time2}
Convert from local to Universal Time Coordinated (UTC) date and time.

erlang:make_tuple(Arity, InitialValue) -> tuple()
Create a new tuple of a given arity.

erlang:md5(Data) -> Digest
Compute an MD5 message digest.

erlang:md5_final(Context) -> Digest
Finish the update of an MD5 context, and return the computed MD5 message digest.

erlang:md5_init() -> Context
Create an MD5 context.

erlang:md5_update(Context, Data) -> NewContext
Update an MD5 context with data, and return a new context.

erlang:memory() -> ({Type, Size})
Information about dynamically allocated memory.

erlang:memory(Type | (Type)) -> Size | ({Type, Size})
Information about dynamically allocated memory.

erlang:monitor(Type, Item) -> MonitorRef
Start monitoring.

erlang:monitor_node(Node, Flag, Options) -> true
Monitor the status of a node.

erlang:phash(Term, Range) -> Hash
Portable hash function.

erlang:phash2(Term (, Range)) -> Hash
Portable hash function.

erlang:port_call(Port, Operation, Data) -> term()
Synchronous call to a port with term data.

erlang:port_info(Port) -> ({Item, Info}) | undefined
Information about a port.

erlang:port_info(Port, Item) -> {Item, Info} | undefined | ()
Information about a port.

erlang:port_to_list(Port) -> string()
Text representation of a port identifier.

erlang:ports() -> (port())
All open ports.

erlang:process_display(Pid, Type) -> void()
Write information about a local process on standard error.

erlang:raise(Class, Reason, Stacktrace)
Stop execution with an exception of given class, reason, and call stack backtrace.

erlang:read_timer(TimerRef) -> int() | false
Number of milliseconds remaining for a timer.

erlang:ref_to_list(Ref) -> string()
Text representation of a reference.

erlang:resume_process(Pid) -> true
Resume a suspended process.

erlang:send(Dest, Msg) -> Msg
Send a message.

erlang:send(Dest, Msg, (Option)) -> Res
Send a message conditionally.

erlang:send_after(Time, Dest, Msg) -> TimerRef
Start a timer.

erlang:send_nosuspend(Dest, Msg) -> bool()
Try to send a message without ever blocking.

erlang:send_nosuspend(Dest, Msg, Options) -> bool()
Try to send a message without ever blocking.

erlang:set_cookie(Node, Cookie) -> true
Set the magic cookie of a node.

erlang:spawn_monitor(Fun) -> {pid(),reference()}
Create and monitor a new process with a fun as entry point.

erlang:spawn_monitor(Module, Function, Args) -> {pid(),reference()}
Create and monitor a new process with a function as entry point.

erlang:start_timer(Time, Dest, Msg) -> TimerRef
> Start a timer.

erlang:suspend_process(Pid) -> true
> Suspend a process.

erlang:system_flag(Flag, Value) -> OldValue
> Set system flags.

erlang:system_info(Type) -> Res
> Information about the system.

erlang:system_monitor() -> MonSettings
> Current system performance monitoring settings.

erlang:system_monitor(undefined | {MonitorPid, Options}) -> MonSettings
> Set or clear system performance monitoring options.

erlang:system_monitor(MonitorPid, (Option)) -> MonSettings
> Set system performance monitoring options.

erlang:trace(PidSpec, How, FlagList) -> int()
> Set trace flags for a process or processes.

erlang:trace_delivered(Tracee) -> Ref
> Notification when trace has been delivered.

erlang:trace_info(PidOrFunc, Item) -> Res
> Trace information about a process or function.

erlang:trace_pattern(MFA, MatchSpec) -> int()
> Set trace patterns for global call tracing.

erlang:trace_pattern(MFA, MatchSpec, FlagList) -> int()
> Set trace patterns for tracing of function calls.

erlang:universaltime() -> {Date, Time}
> Current date and time according to Universal Time Coordinated (UTC).

erlang:universaltime_to_localtime({Date1, Time1}) -> {Date2, Time2}
> Convert from Universal Time Coordinated (UTC) to local date and time.

erlang:yield() -> true
> Let other processes get a chance to execute.

exit(Reason)
> Stop execution with a given reason.

exit(Pid, Reason) -> true
> Send an exit signal to a process.

float(Number) -> float()
> Convert a number to a float.

float_to_list(Float) -> string()
> Text representation of a float.

garbage_collect() -> true
> Force an immediate garbage collection of the calling process.

garbage_collect(Pid) -> bool()

Force an immediate garbage collection of a process.

get() -> ({Key, Val})

Return the process dictionary.

get(Key) -> Val | undefined

Return a value from the process dictionary.

get_keys(Val) -> (Key)

Return a list of keys from the process dictionary.

group_leader() -> GroupLeader

Get the group leader for the calling process.

group_leader(GroupLeader, Pid) -> true

Set the group leader for a process.

halt()

Halt the Erlang runtime system, and indicate normal exit to the calling environment.

halt(Status)

Halt the Erlang runtime system.

hd(List) -> term()

Head of a list.

integer_to_list(Integer) -> string()

Text representation of an integer.

iolist_size(Item) -> int()

Size of an iolist.

iolist_to_binary(IoListOrBinary) -> binary()

Convert an iolist to a binary.

is_alive() -> bool()

Check whether the local node is alive.

is_atom(Term) -> bool()

Check whether a term is an atom.

is_binary(Term) -> bool()

Check whether a term is a binary.

is_boolean(Term) -> bool()

Check whether a term is a boolean.

is_float(Term) -> bool()

Check whether a term is a float.

is_function(Term) -> bool()

Check whether a term is a fun.

is_function(Term, Arity) -> bool()

Check whether a term is a fun with a given arity.

is_integer(Term) -> bool()

Check whether a term is an integer.

is_list(Term) -> bool()
> Check whether a term is a list.

is_number(Term) -> bool()
> Check whether a term is a number.

is_pid(Term) -> bool()
> Check whether a term is a PID.

is_port(Term) -> bool()
> Check whether a term is a port.

is_process_alive(Pid) -> bool()
> Check whether a process is alive.

is_record(Term, RecordTag) -> bool()
> Check whether a term appears to be a record.

is_record(Term, RecordTag, Size) -> bool()
> Check whether a term appears to be a record.

is_reference(Term) -> bool()
> Check whether a term is a reference.

is_tuple(Term) -> bool()
> Check whether a term is a tuple.

length(List) -> int()
> Length of a list.

link(Pid) -> true
> Create a link to another process (or port).

list_to_atom(String) -> atom()
> Convert from a text representation to an atom.

list_to_binary(IoList) -> binary()
> Convert a list to a binary.

list_to_existing_atom(String) -> atom()
> Convert from a text representation to an atom.

list_to_float(String) -> float()
> Convert from a text representation to a float.

list_to_integer(String) -> int()
> Convert from a text representation to an integer.

list_to_pid(String) -> pid()
> Convert from text representation to a PID.

list_to_tuple(List) -> tuple()
> Convert a list to a tuple.

load_module(Module, Binary) -> {module, Module} | {error, Reason}
> Load object code for a module.

make_ref() -> ref()
> Return an almost unique reference.

module_loaded(Module) -> bool()
Check whether a module is loaded.

monitor_node(Node, Flag) -> true
Monitor the status of a node.

node() -> Node
Name of the local node.

node(Arg) -> Node
At which node is a PID, port, or reference located.

nodes() -> Nodes
All visible nodes in the system.

nodes(Arg | (Arg)) -> Nodes
All nodes of a certain type in the system.

now() -> {MegaSecs, Secs, MicroSecs}
Elapsed time since 00:00 GMT.

open_port(PortName, PortSettings) -> port()
Open a port.

pid_to_list(Pid) -> string()
Text representation of a PID.

port_close(Port) -> true
Close an open port.

port_command(Port, Data) -> true
Send data to a port.

port_connect(Port, Pid) -> true
Set the owner of a port.

port_control(Port, Operation, Data) -> Res
Perform a synchronous control operation on a port.

pre_loaded() -> (Module)
List of all preloaded modules.

process_flag(Flag, Value) -> OldValue
Set process flags for the calling process.

process_flag(Pid, Flag, Value) -> OldValue
Set process flags for a process.

process_info(Pid) -> ({Item, Info}) | undefined
Information about a process.

process_info(Pid, Item) -> {Item, Info} | undefined | ()
Information about a process.

processes() -> (pid())
All processes.

purge_module(Module) -> void()
Remove old code for a module.

put(Key, Val) -> OldVal | undefined
Add a new value to the process dictionary.

register(RegName, Pid | Port) -> true
Register a name for a PID (or port).

registered() -> (RegName)
All registered names.

round(Number) -> int()
Return an integer by rounding a number.

self() -> pid()
Pid of the calling process.

setelement(Index, Tuple1, Value) -> Tuple2
Set Nth element of a tuple.

size(Item) -> int()
Size of a tuple or binary.

spawn(Fun) -> pid()
Create a new process with a fun as entry point.

spawn(Node, Fun) -> pid()
Create a new process with a fun as entry point on a given node.

spawn(Module, Function, Args) -> pid()
Create a new process with a function as entry point.

spawn(Node, Module, Function, ArgumentList) -> pid()
Create a new process with a function as entry point on a given node.

spawn_link(Fun) -> pid()
Create and link to a new process with a fun as entry point.

spawn_link(Node, Fun) ->
Create and link to a new process with a fun as entry point on a specified node.

spawn_link(Module, Function, Args) -> pid()
Create and link to a new process with a function as entry point.

spawn_link(Node, Module, Function, Args) -> pid()
Create and link to a new process with a function as entry point on a given node.

spawn_opt(Fun, (Option)) -> pid() | {pid(),reference()}
Create a new process with a fun as entry point.

spawn_opt(Node, Fun, (Option)) -> pid()
Create a new process with a fun as entry point on a given node.

spawn_opt(Module, Function, Args, (Option)) -> pid() | {pid(),reference()}
Create a new process with a function as entry point.

spawn_opt(Node, Module, Function, Args, (Option)) -> pid()
Create a new process with a function as entry point on a given node.

split_binary(Bin, Pos) -> {Bin1, Bin2}
Split a binary into two.

statistics(Type) -> Res
Information about the system.

term_to_binary(Term) -> ext_binary()
Encode a term to an Erlang external term format binary.

term_to_binary(Term, (Option)) -> ext_binary()
Encode a term to en Erlang external term format binary.

throw(Any)
Throw an exception.

time() -> {Hour, Minute, Second}
Current time.

tl(List1) -> List2
Tail of a list.

trunc(Number) -> int()
Return an integer by the truncating a number.

tuple_to_list(Tuple) -> (term())
Convert a tuple to a list.

unlink(Id) -> true
Remove a link, if there is one, to another process or port.

unregister(RegName) -> true
Remove the registered name for a process (or port).

whereis(RegName) -> pid() | port() | undefined
Get the PID (or port) with a given registered name.

F.19 Module: error_handler

Default system error handler.

undefined_function(Module, Function, Args) -> term()
Called when an undefined function is encountered.

undefined_lambda(Module, Fun, Args) -> term()
Called when an undefined lambda (fun) is encountered.

F.20 Module: error_logger

Erlang error logger.

add_report_handler(Handler, Args) -> Result
Add an event handler to the error logger.

delete_report_handler(Handler) -> Result
Delete an event handler from the error logger.

error_report(Report) -> ok
> Send a standard error report event to the error logger.

error_report(Type, Report) -> ok
> Send a user defined error report event to the error logger.

format(Format, Data) -> ok
> Send an standard error event to the error logger.

info_msg(Format, Data) -> ok
> Send a standard information event to the error logger.

info_report(Report) -> ok
> Send a standard information report event to the error logger.

info_report(Type, Report) -> ok
> Send a user defined information report event to the error logger.

logfile(Request) -> ok | Filename | {error, What}
> Enable or disable error printouts to a file.

tty(Flag) -> ok
> Enable or disable printouts to the tty.

warning_map() -> Tag
> Return the current mapping for warning events.

warning_msg(Format, Data) -> ok
> Send a standard warning event to the error logger.

warning_report(Report) -> ok
> Send a standard warning report event to the error logger.

warning_report(Type, Report) -> ok
> Send a user defined warning report event to the error logger.

F.21 Module: ets

Built-in term storage.

all() -> (Tab)
> Return a list of all ETS tables.

delete(Tab) -> true
> Delete an entire ETS table.

delete(Tab, Key) -> true
> Delete all objects with a given key from an ETS table.

delete_all_objects(Tab) -> true
> Delete all objects in an ETS table.

delete_object(Tab,Object) -> true
> Delete a specific from an ETS table.

file2tab(Filename) -> {ok,Tab} | {error,Reason}
> Read an ETS table from a file.

first(Tab) -> Key | '$end_of_table'
Return the first key in an ETS table.

fixtable(Tab, true|false) -> true | false
Fix an ETS table for safe traversal (obsolete).

foldl(Function, Acc0, Tab) -> Acc1
Fold a function over an ETS table.

foldr(Function, Acc0, Tab) -> Acc1
Fold a function over an ETS table.

from_dets(Tab, DetsTab) -> Tab
Fill an ETS table with objects from a DETS table.

fun2ms(LiteralFun) -> MatchSpec
Pseudofunction that transforms fun syntax to a match_spec.

i() -> void()
Display information about all ETS tables on tty.

i(Tab) -> void()
Browse an ETS table on tty.

info(Tab) -> ({Item, Value}) | undefined
Return information about an ETS table.

info(Tab, Item) -> Value | undefined
Return the information associated with given item for an ETS table.

init_table(Name, InitFun) -> true
Replace all objects of an ETS table.

insert(Tab, ObjectOrObjects) -> true
Insert an object into an ETS table.

insert_new(Tab, ObjectOrObjects) -> bool()
Insert an object into an ETS table if the key is not already present.

is_compiled_ms(Term) -> bool()
Checks whether an Erlang term is the result ofets:match_spec_compile.

last(Tab) -> Key | '$end_of_table'
Return the last key in an ETS table of typeordered_set.

lookup(Tab, Key) -> (Object)
Return all objects with a given key in an ETS table.

lookup_element(Tab, Key, Pos) -> Elem
Return the Pos :th element of all objects with a given key in an ETS table.

match(Continuation) -> {(Match),Continuation} | '$end_of_table'
Continue matching objects in an ETS table.

match(Tab, Pattern) -> (Match)
Match the objects in an ETS table against a pattern.

match(Tab, Pattern, Limit) -> {(Match),Continuation} | '$end_of_table'
Match the objects in an ETS table against a pattern, and return part of the answers.

match_delete(Tab, Pattern) -> true
> Delete all objects which match a given pattern from an ETS table.

match_object(Continuation) -> {(Match),Continuation} | '$end_of_table'
> Continue matching objects in an ETS table.

match_object(Tab, Pattern) -> (Object)
> Match the objects in an ETS table against a pattern.

match_object(Tab, Pattern, Limit) -> {(Match),Continuation} | '$end_of_table'
> Match the objects in an ETS table against a pattern, and return part of the answers.

match_spec_compile(MatchSpec) -> CompiledMatchSpec
> Compile a match specification into its internal representation.

match_spec_run(List,CompiledMatchSpec) -> list()
> Perform matching, using a compiledmatch_spec, on a list of tuples.

member(Tab, Key) -> true | false
> Test for occurrence of a key in an ETS table.

new(Name, Options) -> tid()
> Create a new ETS table.

next(Tab, Key1) -> Key2 | '$end_of_table'
> Return the next key in an ETS table.

prev(Tab, Key1) -> Key2 | '$end_of_table'
> Return the previous key in an ETS table of typeordered_set.

rename(Tab, Name) -> Name
> Rename a named ETS table.

repair_continuation(Continuation, MatchSpec) -> Continuation
> Repair a continuation fromets:select/1orets:select/3that has passed through external representation.

safe_fixtable(Tab, true|false) -> true
> Fix an ETS table for safe traversal.

select(Continuation) -> {(Match),Continuation} | '$end_of_table'
> Continue matching objects in an ETS table.

select(Tab, MatchSpec) -> (Match)
> Match the objects in an ETS table against amatch_spec.

select(Tab, MatchSpec, Limit) -> {(Match),Continuation} | '$end_of_table'
> Match the objects in an ETS table against amatch_spec, and return part of the answers.

select_count(Tab, MatchSpec) -> NumMatched
> Match the objects in an ETS table against amatch_spec, and return the number of objects for which thematch_specreturnstrue.

select_delete(Tab, MatchSpec) -> NumDeleted
> Match the objects in an ETS table against amatch_spec, and delete objects where thematch_specreturnstrue.

slot(Tab, I) -> (Object) | '$end_of_table'
> Return all objects in a given slot of an ETS table.

tab2file(Tab, Filename) -> ok | {error,Reason}
Dump an ETS table to a file.

tab2list(Tab) -> (Object)
Return a list of all objects in an ETS table.

table(Tab (, Options)) -> QueryHandle
Return a QLC query handle.

test_ms(Tuple, MatchSpec) -> {ok, Result} | {error, Errors}
Test a match_spec for use in ets:select/2.

to_dets(Tab, DetsTab) -> Tab
Fill a DETS table with objects from an ETS table.

update_counter(Tab, Key, Incr) -> Result
Update a counter object in an ETS table.

F.22 Module: file

File interface module.

change_group(Filename, Gid) -> ok | {error, Reason}
Change group of a file.

change_owner(Filename, Uid) -> ok | {error, Reason}
Change owner of a file.

change_owner(Filename, Uid, Gid) -> ok | {error, Reason}
Change owner and group of a file.

change_time(Filename, Mtime) -> ok | {error, Reason}
Change the modification time of a file.

change_time(Filename, Mtime, Atime) -> ok | {error, Reason}
Change the modification and last access time of a file.

close(IoDevice) -> ok | {error, Reason}
Close a file.

consult(Filename) -> {ok, Terms} | {error, Reason}
Read Erlang terms from a file.

copy(Source, Destination, ByteCount) -> {ok, BytesCopied} | {error, Reason}
Copy file contents.

del_dir(Dir) -> ok | {error, Reason}
Delete a directory.

delete(Filename) -> ok | {error, Reason}
Delete a file.

eval(Filename) -> ok | {error, Reason}
Evaluate Erlang expressions in a file.

eval(Filename, Bindings) -> ok | {error, Reason}
Evaluate Erlang expressions in a file.

file_info(Filename) -> {ok, FileInfo} | {error, Reason}
Get information about a file (deprecated).

format_error(Reason) -> Chars
Return a descriptive string for an error reason.

get_cwd() -> {ok, Dir} | {error, Reason}
Get the current working directory.

get_cwd(Drive) -> {ok, Dir} | {error, Reason}
Get the current working directory for the drive specified.

list_dir(Dir) -> {ok, Filenames} | {error, Reason}
List files in a directory.

make_dir(Dir) -> ok | {error, Reason}
Make a directory.

make_link(Existing, New) -> ok | {error, Reason}
Make a hard link to a file.

make_symlink(Name1, Name2) -> ok | {error, Reason}
Make a symbolic link to a file or directory.

open(Filename, Modes) -> {ok, IoDevice} | {error, Reason}
Open a file.

path_consult(Path, Filename) -> {ok, Terms, FullName} | {error, Reason}
Read Erlang terms from a file.

path_eval(Path, Filename) -> {ok, FullName} | {error, Reason}
Evaluate Erlang expressions in a file.

path_open(Path, Filename, Modes) -> {ok, IoDevice, FullName} | {error, Reason}
Open a file.

path_script(Path, Filename) -> {ok, Value, FullName} | {error, Reason}
Evaluate and return the value of Erlang expressions in a file.

path_script(Path, Filename, Bindings) -> {ok, Value, FullName} | {error, Reason}
Evaluate and return the value of Erlang expressions in a file.

pid2name(Pid) -> string() | undefined
Return the name of the file handled by a PID.

position(IoDevice, Location) -> {ok, NewPosition} | {error, Reason}
Set a position in a file.

pread(IoDevice, LocNums) -> {ok, DataL} | {error, Reason}
Read from a file at certain positions.

pread(IoDevice, Location, Number) -> {ok, Data} | {error, Reason}
Read from a file at a certain position.

pwrite(IoDevice, LocBytes) -> ok | {error, {N, Reason}}
Write to a file at certain positions.

pwrite(IoDevice, Location, Bytes) -> ok | {error, Reason}
Write to a file at a certain position.

read(IoDevice, Number) -> {ok, Data} | eof | {error, Reason}
    Read from a file.

read_file(Filename) -> {ok, Binary} | {error, Reason}
    Read a file.

read_file_info(Filename) -> {ok, FileInfo} | {error, Reason}
    Get information about a file.

read_link(Name) -> {ok, Filename} | {error, Reason}
    See what a link is pointing to.

read_link_info(Name) -> {ok, FileInfo} | {error, Reason}
    Get information about a link or file.

rename(Source, Destination) -> ok | {error, Reason}
    Rename a file.

script(Filename) -> {ok, Value} | {error, Reason}
    Evaluate and return the value of Erlang expressions in a file.

script(Filename, Bindings) -> {ok, Value} | {error, Reason}
    Evaluate and return the value of Erlang expressions in a file.

set_cwd(Dir) -> ok | {error,Reason}
    Set the current working directory.

sync(IoDevice) -> ok | {error, Reason}
    Synchronize the in-memory state of a file with that on the physical
    medium.

truncate(IoDevice) -> ok | {error, Reason}
    Truncate a file.

write(IoDevice, Bytes) -> ok | {error, Reason}
    Write to a file.

write_file(Filename, Binary) -> ok | {error, Reason}
    Write a file.

write_file(Filename, Binary, Modes) -> ok | {error, Reason}
    Write a file.

write_file_info(Filename, FileInfo) -> ok | {error, Reason}
    Change information about a file.

F.23 Module: file_sorter

File sorter.

check(FileNames, Options) -> Reply
    Check whether terms on files are sorted.

keycheck(KeyPos, FileNames, Options) -> Reply
    Check whether terms on files are sorted by key.

keymerge(KeyPos, FileNames, Output, Options) -> Reply
    Merge terms on files by key.

keysort(KeyPos, Input, Output, Options) -> Reply
> Sort terms on files by key.

merge(FileNames, Output, Options) -> Reply
> Merge terms on files.

sort(Input, Output, Options) -> Reply
> Sort terms on files.

F.24 Module: filelib

File utilities, such as wildcard matching of filenames.

ensure_dir(Name) -> ok | {error, Reason}
> Ensure that all parent directories for a file or directory exist.

file_size(Filename) -> integer()
> Return the size in bytes of the file.

fold_files(Dir, RegExp, Recursive, Fun, AccIn) -> AccOut
> Fold over all files matching a regular expression.

is_dir(Name) -> true | false
> Test whetherNamerefers to a directory.

is_file(Name) -> true | false
> Test whetherNamerefers to a file or directory.

is_regular(Name) -> true | false
> Test whetherNamerefers to a (regular) file.

last_modified(Name) -> {{Year,Month,Day},{Hour,Min,Sec}}
> Return the local date and time when a file was last modified.

wildcard(Wildcard) -> list()
> Match filenames using Unix-style wildcards.

wildcard(Wildcard, Cwd) -> list()
> Match filenames using Unix-style wildcards starting at a specified directory.

F.25 Module: filename

Filename manipulation functions.

absname(Filename) -> string()
> Convert a filename to an absolute name, relative the working directory.

absname(Filename, Dir) -> string()
> Convert a filename to an absolute name, relative a specified directory.

absname_join(Dir, Filename) -> string()
> Join an absolute directory with a relative filename.

basename(Filename) -> string()
> Return the last component of a filename.

basename(Filename, Ext) -> string()
> Return the last component of a filename, stripped of the specified extension.

dirname(Filename) -> string()
> Return the directory part of a path name.

extension(Filename) -> string()
> Return the file extension.

find_src(Beam, Rules) -> {SourceFile, Options}
> Find the filename and compiler options for a module.

flatten(Filename) -> string()
> Convert a filename to a flat string.

join(Components) -> string()
> Join a list of filename components with directory separators.

join(Name1, Name2) -> string()
> Join two filename components with directory separators.

nativename(Path) -> string()
> Return the native form of a file path.

pathtype(Path) -> absolute | relative | volumerelative
> Return the type of a path.

rootname(Filename, Ext) -> string()
> Remove a filename extension.

split(Filename) -> Components
> Split a filename into its path components.

F.26 Module: gb_sets

General balanced trees.

add_element(Element, Set1) -> Set2
> Add an (possibly existing) element to agb_set.

balance(Set1) -> Set2
> Rebalance tree representation of agb_set.

del_element(Element, Set1) -> Set2
> Remove a (possibly nonexisting) element from agb_set.

delete(Element, Set1) -> Set2
> Remove an element from agb_set.

filter(Pred, Set1) -> Set2
> Filtergb_setelements.

fold(Function, Acc0, Set) -> Acc1
> Fold overgb_setelements.

from_list(List) -> Set
> Convert a list into agb_set.

from_ordset(List) -> Set
> Make agb_setfrom an ordset list.

insert(Element, Set1) -> Set2
> Add a new element to agb_set.

intersection(SetList) -> Set
> Return the intersection of a list ofgb_sets.

intersection(Set1, Set2) -> Set3
> Return the intersection of twogb_sets.

is_element(Element, Set) -> bool()
> Test for membership of agb_set.

is_empty(Set) -> bool()
> Test for emptygb_set.

is_set(Set) -> bool()
> Test for agb_set.

is_subset(Set1, Set2) -> bool()
> Test for subset.

iterator(Set) -> Iter
> Return an iterator for agb_set.

largest(Set) -> term()
> Return largest element.

new() -> Set
> Return an emptygb_set.

next(Iter1) -> {Element, Iter2 | none}
> Traverse agb_setwith an iterator.

singleton(Element) -> gb_set()
> Return agb_setwith one element.

size(Set) -> int()
> Return the number of elements in agb_set.

smallest(Set) -> term()
> Return the smallest element.

subtract(Set1, Set2) -> Set3
> Return the difference of twogb_sets.

take_largest(Set1) -> {Element, Set2}
> Extract the largest element.

take_smallest(Set1) -> {Element, Set2}
> Extract the smallest element.

to_list(Set) -> List
> Convert agb_setinto a list.

union(SetList) -> Set
> Return the union of a list ofgb_sets.

union(Set1, Set2) -> Set3
> Return the union of twogb_sets.

F.27 Module: gb_trees

General balanced trees.

balance(Tree1) -> Tree2
> Rebalance a tree.

delete(Key, Tree1) -> Tree2
> Remove a node from a tree.

delete_any(Key, Tree1) -> Tree2
> Remove a (possibly nonexisting) node from a tree.

empty() -> Tree
> Return an empty tree.

enter(Key, Val, Tree1) -> Tree2
> Insert or update key with value in a tree.

from_orddict(List) -> Tree
> Make a tree from an orddict.

get(Key, Tree) -> Val
> Look up a key in a tree, if present.

insert(Key, Val, Tree1) -> Tree2
> Insert a new key and value in a tree.

is_defined(Key, Tree) -> bool()
> Test for membership of a tree.

is_empty(Tree) -> bool()
> Test for empty tree.

iterator(Tree) -> Iter
> Return an iterator for a tree.

keys(Tree) -> (Key)
> Return a list of the keys in a tree.

largest(Tree) -> {Key, Val}
> Return largest key and value.

lookup(Key, Tree) -> {value, Val} | none
> Look up a key in a tree.

next(Iter1) -> {Key, Val, Iter2
> Traverse a tree with an iterator.

size(Tree) -> int()
> Return the number of nodes in a tree.

smallest(Tree) -> {Key, Val}
> Return the smallest key and value.

take_largest(Tree1) -> {Key, Val, Tree2}
> Extract largest key and value.

take_smallest(Tree1) -> {Key, Val, Tree2}
> Extract smallest key and value.

to_list(Tree) -> ({Key, Val})
> Convert a tree into a list.

update(Key, Val, Tree1) -> Tree2
> Update a key to new value in a tree.

values(Tree) -> (Val)
> Return a list of the values in a tree.

F.28 Module: gen_event

Generic event handling behavior.g

Module:code_change(OldVsn, State, Extra) -> {ok, NewState}
> Update the internal state during upgrade/downgrade.

Module:handle_call(Request, State) -> Result
> Handle a synchronous request.

Module:handle_event(Event, State) -> Result
> Handle an event.

Module:handle_info(Info, State) -> Result
> Handle an incoming message.

Module:init(InitArgs) -> {ok,State}
> Initialize an event handler.

Module:terminate(Arg, State) -> term()
> Clean up before deletion.

add_handler(EventMgrRef, Handler, Args) -> Result
> Add an event handler to a generic event manager.

add_sup_handler(EventMgrRef, Handler, Args) -> Result
> Add a supervised event handler to a generic event manager.

call(EventMgrRef, Handler, Request, Timeout) -> Result
> Make a synchronous call to a generic event manager.

delete_handler(EventMgrRef, Handler, Args) -> Result
> Delete an event handler from a generic event manager.

start(EventMgrName) -> Result
> Create a stand-alone event manager process.

start_link(EventMgrName) -> Result
> Create a generic event manager process in a supervision tree.

stop(EventMgrRef) -> ok
> Terminate a generic event manager.

swap_handler(EventMgrRef, {Handler1,Args1}, {Handler2,Args2}) -> Result
Replace an event handler in a generic event manager.

swap_sup_handler(EventMgrRef, {Handler1,Args1}, {Handler2,Args2}) -> Result
Replace an event handler in a generic event manager.

sync_notify(EventMgrRef, Event) -> ok
Notify an event manager about an event.

which_handlers(EventMgrRef) -> (Handler)
Return all event handlers installed in a generic event manager.

F.29 Module: gen_fsm

Generic finite state machine behavior.

Module:StateName(Event, StateData) -> Result
Handle an asynchronous event.

Module:StateName(Event, From, StateData) -> Result
Handle a synchronous event.

Module:code_change(OldVsn, StateName, StateData, Extra) ->
{ok, NextStateName, NewStateData}
Update the internal state data during upgrade/downgrade.

Module:handle_event(Event, StateName, StateData) -> Result
Handle an asynchronous event.

Module:handle_info(Info, StateName, StateData) -> Result
Handle an incoming message.

Module:handle_sync_event(Event, From, StateName, StateData) -> Result
Handle a synchronous event.

Module:init(Args) -> Result
Initialize process and internal state name and state data.

Module:terminate(Reason, StateName, StateData)
Clean up before termination.

cancel_timer(Ref) -> RemainingTime | false
Cancel an internal timer in a generic FSM.

enter_loop(Module, Options, StateName, StateData, FsmName, Timeout)
Enter thegen_fsmreceive loop.

reply(Caller, Reply) -> true
Send a reply to a caller.

send_all_state_event(FsmRef, Event) -> ok
Send an event asynchronously to a generic FSM.

send_event(FsmRef, Event) -> ok
Send an event asynchronously to a generic FSM.

send_event_after(Time, Event) -> Ref
Send a delayed event internally in a generic FSM.

start(FsmName, Module, Args, Options) -> Result
> Create a stand-alone gen_fsm process.

start_link(FsmName, Module, Args, Options) -> Result
> Create a gen_fsm process in a supervision tree.

start_timer(Time, Msg) -> Ref
> Send a timeout event internally in a generic FSM.

sync_send_all_state_event(FsmRef, Event, Timeout) -> Reply
> Send an event syncronously to a generic FSM.

sync_send_event(FsmRef, Event, Timeout) -> Reply
> Send an event synchronously to a generic FSM.

F.30 Module: gen_sctp

The gen_sctp module provides functions for communicating with sockets using the SCTP protocol.

abort(sctp_socket(), Assoc) -> ok | {error, posix()}
> Abnormally terminate the association given byAssoc, without flushing of unsent data.

close(sctp_socket()) -> ok | {error, posix()}
> Completely close the socket and all associations on it.

connect(Socket, IP, Port, Opts) -> {ok,Assoc} | {error, posix()}
> Same asconnect(Socket, IP, Port, Opts, infinity).

connect(Socket, IP, Port, (Opt), Timeout) -> {ok, Assoc} | {error, posix()}
> Establish a new association for the socketSocket, with a peer (SCTP server socket).

controlling_process(sctp_socket(), pid()) -> ok
> Assign a new controlling process PID to the socket.

eof(Socket, Assoc) -> ok | {error, Reason}
> Gracefully terminate the association given byAssoc, with flushing of all unsent data.

error_string(integer()) -> ok | string() | undefined
> Translate an SCTP error number into a string.

listen(Socket, IsServer) -> ok | {error, Reason}
> Set up a socket to listen.

open((Opt)) -> {ok, Socket} | {error, posix()}
> Create an SCTP socket and bind it to local addresses.

recv(sctp_socket(), timeout()) -> {ok, {FromIP, FromPort, AncData, Data}} | {error, Reason}
> Receive a message from a socket.

send(Socket, SndRcvInfo, Data) -> ok | {error, Reason}
> Send a message using an#sctp_sndrcvinfo{}record.

send(Socket, Assoc, Stream, Data) -> ok | {error, Reason}
> Send a message over an existing association and given stream.

F.31 Module: gen_server

Generic server behavior.

Module:code_change(OldVsn, State, Extra) -> {ok, NewState}
Update the internal state during upgrade/downgrade.

Module:handle_call(Request, From, State) -> Result
Handle a synchronous request.

Module:handle_cast(Request, State) -> Result
Handle an asynchronous request.

Module:handle_info(Info, State) -> Result
Handle an incoming message.

Module:init(Args) -> Result
Initialize process and internal state.

Module:terminate(Reason, State)
Clean up before termination.

abcast(Nodes, Name, Request) -> abcast
Send an asynchronous request to several generic servers.

call(ServerRef, Request, Timeout) -> Reply
Make a synchronous call to a generic server.

cast(ServerRef, Request) -> ok
Send an asynchronous request to a generic server.

enter_loop(Module, Options, State, ServerName, Timeout)
Enter thegen_serverreceive loop.

multi_call(Nodes, Name, Request, Timeout) -> Result
Make a synchronous call to several generic servers.

reply(Client, Reply) -> true
Send a reply to a client.

start(ServerName, Module, Args, Options) -> Result
Create a stand-alonegen_serverprocess.

start_link(ServerName, Module, Args, Options) -> Result
Create agen_serverprocess in a supervision tree.

F.32 Module: gen_tcp

Interface to TCP/IP sockets.

accept(ListenSocket, Timeout) -> {ok, Socket} | {error, Reason}
Accept an incoming connection request on a listen socket.

close(Socket) -> ok | {error, Reason}
Close a TCP socket.

connect(Address, Port, Options, Timeout) -> {ok, Socket} | {error, Reason}
Connect to a TCP port.

controlling_process(Socket, Pid) -> ok | {error, eperm}
   Change controlling process of a socket.

listen(Port, Options) -> {ok, ListenSocket} | {error, Reason}
   Set up a socket to listen on a port.

recv(Socket, Length, Timeout) -> {ok, Packet} | {error, Reason}
   Receive a packet from a passive socket.

send(Socket, Packet) -> ok | {error, Reason}
   Send a packet.

shutdown(Socket, How) -> ok | {error, Reason}
   Immediately close a socket.

F.33 Module: gen_udp

Interface to UDP sockets.

close(Socket) -> ok | {error, Reason}
   Close a UDP socket.

controlling_process(Socket, Pid) -> ok
   Change controlling process of a socket.

open(Port, Options) -> {ok, Socket} | {error, Reason}
   Associate a UDP port number with the process calling it.

recv(Socket, Length, Timeout) -> {ok, {Address, Port, Packet}} | {error, Reason}
   Receive a packet from a passive socket.

send(Socket, Address, Port, Packet) -> ok | {error, Reason}
   Send a packet.

F.34 Module: global

A global name registration facility.

del_lock(Id, Nodes) -> void()
   Delete a lock.

notify_all_name(Name, Pid1, Pid2) -> none
   Name resolving function that notifies both PIDs.

random_exit_name(Name, Pid1, Pid2) -> Pid1 | Pid2
   Name resolving function that kills one PID.

random_notify_name(Name, Pid1, Pid2) -> Pid1 | Pid2
   Name resolving function that notifies one PID.

re_register_name(Name, Pid, Resolve) -> void()
   Atomically reregister a name.

register_name(Name, Pid, Resolve) -> yes | no
   Globally register a name for a PID.

registered_names() -> (Name)
> All globally registered names.

send(Name, Msg) -> Pid
> Send a message to a globally registered PID.

set_lock(Id, Nodes, Retries) -> boolean()
> Set a lock on the specified nodes.

sync() -> void()
> Synchronize the global name server.

trans(Id, Fun, Nodes, Retries) -> Res | aborted
> Micro transaction facility.

unregister_name(Name) -> void()
> Remove a globally registered name for a PID.

whereis_name(Name) -> pid() | undefined
> Get the PID with a given globally registered name.

F.35 Module: inet

Access to TCP/IP protocols.

close(Socket) -> ok
> Close a socket of any type.

format_error(Posix) -> string()
> Return a descriptive string for an error reason.

get_rc() -> ({Par, Val})
> Return a list of IP configuration parameters.

getaddr(Host, Family) -> {ok, Address} | {error, posix()}
> Return the IP address for a host.

getaddrs(Host, Family) -> {ok, Addresses} | {error, posix()}
> Return the IP addresses for a host.

gethostbyaddr(Address) -> {ok, Hostent} | {error, posix()}
> Return a hostent record for the host with the given address.

gethostbyname(Name) -> {ok, Hostent} | {error, posix()}
> Return a hostent record for the host with the given name.

gethostbyname(Name, Family) -> {ok, Hostent} | {error, posix()}
> Return a hostent record for the host with the given name.

gethostname() -> {ok, Hostname} | {error, posix()}
> Return the local hostname.

getopts(Socket, Options) -> OptionValues | {error, posix()}
> Get one or more options for a socket.

peername(Socket) -> {ok, {Address, Port}} | {error, posix()}
> Return the address and port for the other end of a connection.

port(Socket) -> {ok, Port}
> Return the local port number for a socket.

setopts(Socket, Options) -> ok | {error, posix()}
> Set one or more options for a socket.

sockname(Socket) -> {ok, {Address, Port}} | {error, posix()}
> Return the local address and port number for a socket.

F.36 Module: init

Coordination of system start-up.

boot(BootArgs) -> void()
> Start the Erlang runtime system.

get_args() -> (Arg)
> Get all nonflag command-line arguments.

get_argument(Flag) -> {ok, Arg} | error
> Get the values associated with a command-line user flag.

get_arguments() -> Flags
> Get all command-line user flags.

get_plain_arguments() -> (Arg)
> Get all nonflag command-line arguments.

get_status() -> {InternalStatus, ProvidedStatus}
> Get system status information.

reboot() -> void()
> Take down an Erlang node smoothly.

restart() -> void()
> Restart the running Erlang node.

script_id() -> Id
> Get the identity of the used boot script.

stop() -> void()
> Take down an Erlang node smoothly.

F.37 Module: io

Standard IO server interface functions.

format((IoDevice,) Format, Data) -> ok
> Write formatted output.

fread((IoDevice,) Prompt, Format) -> Result
> Read formatted input.

get_chars((IoDevice,) Prompt, Count) -> string() | eof
> Read a specified number of characters.

get_line((IoDevice,) Prompt) -> string() | eof
> Read a line.

nl((IoDevice)) -> ok
> Write a newline.

parse_erl_exprs((IoDevice,) Prompt, StartLine) -> Result
> Read, tokenize and parse Erlang expressions.

parse_erl_form((IoDevice,) Prompt, StartLine) -> Result
> Read, tokenize and parse an Erlang form.

put_chars((IoDevice,) IoData) -> ok
> Write a list of characters.

read((IoDevice,) Prompt) -> Result
> Read a term.

read(IoDevice, Prompt, StartLine) -> Result
> Read a term.

scan_erl_exprs((IoDevice,) Prompt, StartLine) -> Result
> Read and tokenize Erlang expressions.

scan_erl_form((IoDevice,) Prompt, StartLine) -> Result
> Read and tokenize an Erlang form.

setopts((IoDevice,) Opts) -> ok | {error, Reason}
> Set options.

write((IoDevice,) Term) -> ok
> Write a term.

F.38 Module: io_lib

IO library functions.

char_list(Term) -> bool()
> Test for a list of characters.

deep_char_list(Term) -> bool()
> Test for a deep list of characters.

format(Format, Data) -> chars()
> Write formatted output.

fread(Format, String) -> Result
> Read formatted input.

fread(Continuation, String, Format) -> Return
> Reentrant formatted reader.

indentation(String, StartIndent) -> int()
> Indentation after printing string.

nl() -> chars()
> Write a newline.

print(Term, Column, LineLength, Depth) -> chars()
> Pretty-print a term.

printable_list(Term) -> bool()
> Test for a list of printable characters.

write(Term, Depth) -> chars()
> Write a term.

write_atom(Atom) -> chars()
> Write an atom.

write_char(Integer) -> chars()
> Write a character.

write_string(String) -> chars()
> Write a string.

F.39 Module: lib

A number of useful library functions.

error_message(Format, Args) -> ok
> Print error message.

flush_receive() -> void()
> Flush messages.

nonl(String1) -> String2
> Remove last newline.

progname() -> atom()
> Return name of Erlang start script.

send(To, Msg)
> Send a message.

sendw(To, Msg)
> Send a message, and wait for an answer.

F.40 Module: lists

List-processing functions.

all(Pred, List) -> bool()
> Return true if all elements in the list satisfyPred.

any(Pred, List) -> bool()
> Return true if any of the elements in the list satisfiesPred.

append(ListOfLists) -> List1
> Append a list of lists.

append(List1, List2) -> List3
> Append two lists.

concat(Things) -> string()
> Concatenate a list of atoms.

delete(Elem, List1) -> List2
> Delete an element from a list.

dropwhile(Pred, List1) -> List2
> Drop elements from a list while a predicate is true.

duplicate(N, Elem) -> List
> Make N copies of element.

filter(Pred, List1) -> List2
> Choose elements that satisfy a predicate.

flatlength(DeepList) -> int()
> Length of flattened deep list.

flatmap(Fun, List1) -> List2
> Map and flatten in one pass.

flatten(DeepList) -> List
> Flatten a deep list.

flatten(DeepList, Tail) -> List
> Flatten a deep list.

foldl(Fun, Acc0, List) -> Acc1
> Fold a function over a list.

foldr(Fun, Acc0, List) -> Acc1
> Fold a function over a list.

foreach(Fun, List) -> void()
> Apply a function to each element of a list.

keydelete(Key, N, TupleList1) -> TupleList2
> Delete an element from a list of tuples.

keymap(Fun, N, TupleList1) -> TupleList2
> Map a function over a list of tuples.

keymember(Key, N, TupleList) -> bool()
> Test for membership of a list of tuples.

keymerge(N, TupleList1, TupleList2) -> TupleList3
> Merge two key-sorted lists of tuples.

keyreplace(Key, N, TupleList1, NewTuple) -> TupleList2
> Replace an element in a list of tuples.

keysearch(Key, N, TupleList) -> {value, Tuple} | false
> Search for an element in a list of tuples.

keysort(N, TupleList1) -> TupleList2
> Sort a list of tuples.

last(List) -> Last
> Return last element in a list.

map(Fun, List1) -> List2
    Map a function over a list.

mapfoldl(Fun, Acc0, List1) -> {List2, Acc1}
    Map and fold in one pass.

mapfoldr(Fun, Acc0, List1) -> {List2, Acc1}
    Map and fold in one pass.

max(List) -> Max
    Return maximum element of a list.

member(Elem, List) -> bool()
    Test for membership of a list.

merge(ListOfLists) -> List1
    Merge a list of sorted lists.

merge(List1, List2) -> List3
    Merge two sorted lists.

merge(Fun, List1, List2) -> List3
    Merge two sorted list.

merge3(List1, List2, List3) -> List4
    Merge three sorted lists.

min(List) -> Min
    Return minimum element of a list.

nth(N, List) -> Elem
    Return the Nth element of a list.

nthtail(N, List1) -> Tail
    Return the Nth tail of a list.

partition(Pred, List) -> {Satisfying, NonSatisfying}
    Partition a list into two lists based on a predicate.

prefix(List1, List2) -> bool()
    Test for list prefix.

reverse(List1) -> List2
    Reverse a list.

reverse(List1, Tail) -> List2
    Reverse a list appending a tail.

seq(From, To, Incr) -> Seq
    Generate a sequence of integers.

sort(List1) -> List2
    Sort a list.

sort(Fun, List1) -> List2
    Sort a list.

split(N, List1) -> {List2, List3}
    Split a list into two lists.

splitwith(Pred, List) -> {List1, List2}
> Split a list into two lists based on a predicate.

sublist(List1, Len) -> List2
> Return a sublist of a certain length, starting at the first position.

sublist(List1, Start, Len) -> List2
> Return a sublist starting at a given position and with a given number of elements.

subtract(List1, List2) -> List3
> Subtract the element in one list from another list.

suffix(List1, List2) -> bool()
> Test for list suffix.

sum(List) -> number()
> Return sum of elements in a list.

takewhile(Pred, List1) -> List2
> Take elements from a list while a predicate is true.

ukeymerge(N, TupleList1, TupleList2) -> TupleList3
> Merge two key-sorted lists of tuples, removing duplicates.

ukeysort(N, TupleList1) -> TupleList2
> Sort a list of tuples, removing duplicates.

umerge(ListOfLists) -> List1
> Merge a list of sorted lists, removing duplicates.

umerge(List1, List2) -> List3
> Merge two sorted lists, removing duplicates.

umerge(Fun, List1, List2) -> List3
> Merge two sorted lists, removing duplicates.

umerge3(List1, List2, List3) -> List4
> Merge three sorted lists, removing duplicates.

unzip(List1) -> {List2, List3}
> Unzip a list of two tuples into two lists.

unzip3(List1) -> {List2, List3, List4}
> Unzip a list of three tuples into three lists.

usort(List1) -> List2
> Sort a list, removing duplicates.

usort(Fun, List1) -> List2
> Sort a list, removing duplicates.

zip(List1, List2) -> List3
> Zip two lists into a list of two tuples.

zip3(List1, List2, List3) -> List4
> Zip three lists into a list of three tuples.

zipwith(Combine, List1, List2) -> List3
> Zip two lists into one list according to a fun.

zipwith3(Combine, List1, List2, List3) -> List4
> Zip three lists into one list according to a fun.

F.41   Module: math

Mathematical functions.

erf(X) -> float()
> Error function.

erfc(X) -> float()
> Another error function.

pi() -> float()
> A useful number.

sqrt(X)
> Diverse math functions.

F.42   Module: ms_transform

Parse_transform that translates fun syntax into match specifications.

format_error(Errcode) -> ErrMessage
> Error formatting function as required by theparse_transforminterface.

parse_transform(Forms,_Options) -> Forms
> Transforms Erlang abstract format containing calls toets/dbg:fun2msinto literal match specifications.

transform_from_shell(Dialect,Clauses,BoundEnvironment) -> term()
> Used when transforming fun's created in the shell intomatch_specifications.

F.43   Module: net_adm

Various Erlang net administration routines.

dns_hostname(Host) -> {ok, Name} | {error, Host}
> Official name of a host.

host_file() -> Hosts | {error, Reason}
> Read the.hosts.erlangfile.

localhost() -> Name
> Name of the local host.

names(Host) -> {ok, ({Name, Port})} | {error, Reason}
> Names of Erlang nodes at a host.

ping(Node) -> pong | pang
> Set up a connection to a node.

world(Arg) -> (node())
> Lookup and connect to all nodes at all hosts in.hosts.erlang.

world_list(Hosts, Arg) -> (node())
> Lookup and connect to all nodes at specified hosts.

F.44 Module: net_kernel

Erlang networking kernel.

allow(Nodes) -> ok | error
> Limit access to a specified set of nodes.

connect_node(Node) -> true | false | ignored
> Establish a connection to a node.

get_net_ticktime() -> Res
> Get net_ticktime.

monitor_nodes(Flag, Options) -> ok | Error
> Subscribe to node status change messages.

set_net_ticktime(NetTicktime, TransitionPeriod) -> Res
> Setnet_ticktime.

start((Name, NameType, Ticktime)) -> {ok, pid()} | {error, Reason}
> Turn an Erlang runtime system into a distributed node.

stop() -> ok | {error, not_allowed | not_found}
> Turn a node into a nondistributed Erlang runtime system.

F.45 Module: os

Operating system–specific functions.

cmd(Command) -> string()
> Execute a command in a shell of the target OS.

find_executable(Name, Path) -> Filename | false
> Absolute filename of a program.

getenv() -> (string())
> List all environment variables.

getenv(VarName) -> Value | false
> Get the value of an environment variable.

getpid() -> Value
> Return the process identifier of the emulator process.

putenv(VarName, Value) -> true
> Set a new value for an environment variable.

type() -> {Osfamily, Osname} | Osfamily
> Return the OS family and, in some cases, the OS name of the current operating system.

version() -> {Major, Minor, Release} | VersionString
> Return the operating system version.

F.46 Module: proc_lib

Functions for asynchronous and synchronous start of processes adhering to the OTP design principles.

format(CrashReport) -> string()
> Format a crash report.

hibernate(Module, Function, Args)
> Hibernate a process until a message is sent to it.

init_ack(Ret) -> void()
> Used by a process when it has started.

initial_call(Process) -> {Module,Function,Args} | Fun | false
> Extract the initial call of aproc_libspawned process.

spawn(Node, Module, Function, Args) -> pid()
> Spawn a new process.

spawn_link(Node, Module, Function, Args) -> pid()
> Spawn and link to a new process.

spawn_opt(Node, Module, Func, Args, SpawnOpts) -> pid()
> Spawn a new process with given options.

start_link(Module, Function, Args, Time, SpawnOpts) -> Ret
> Start a new process synchronously.

translate_initial_call(Process) -> {Module,Function,Arity} | Fun
> Extract and translate the initial call of a proc_lib spawned process.

F.47 Module: qlc

Query interface to Mnesia, ETS, DETS, and so on.

append(QHL) -> QH
> Return a query handle.

append(QH1, QH2) -> QH3
> Return a query handle.

cursor(QueryHandleOrList (, Options)) -> QueryCursor
> Create a query cursor.

delete_cursor(QueryCursor) -> ok
> Delete a query cursor.

e(QueryHandleOrList (, Options)) -> Answers
> Return all answers to a query.

fold(Function, Acc0, QueryHandleOrList (, Options)) -> Acc1 | Error
> Fold a function over the answers to a query.

format_error(Error) -> Chars
> Return an English description of a an error tuple.

info(QueryHandleOrList (, Options)) -> Info
>   Return code describing a query handle.

keysort(KeyPos, QH1 (, SortOptions)) -> QH2
>   Return a query handle.

next_answers(QueryCursor (, NumberOfAnswers)) -> Answers | Error
>   Return some or all answers to a query.

q(QueryListComprehension (, Options)) -> QueryHandle
>   Return a handle for a query list comprehension.

sort(QH1 (, SortOptions)) -> QH2
>   Return a query handle.

string_to_handle(QueryString (, Options (, Bindings))) -> QueryHandle | Error
>   Return a handle for a query list comprehension.

table(TraverseFun, Options) -> QueryHandle
>   Return a query handle for a table.

F.48 Module: queue

Abstract data type for FIFO queues.

cons(Item, Q1) -> Q2
>   Insert an item at the head of a queue.

daeh(Q) -> Item
>   Return the last item of a queue.

from_list(L) -> queue()
>   Convert a list to a queue.

head(Q) -> Item
>   Return the item at the head of a queue.

in(Item, Q1) -> Q2
>   Insert an item at the tail of a queue.

in_r(Item, Q1) -> Q2
>   Insert an item at the head of a queue.

init(Q1) -> Q2
>   Remove the last item from a queue.

is_empty(Q) -> true | false
>   Test whether a queue is empty.

join(Q1, Q2) -> Q3
>   Join two queues.

lait(Q1) -> Q2
>   Remove the last item from a queue.

last(Q) -> Item
>   Return the last item of a queue.

len(Q) -> N
> Get the length of a queue.

new() -> Q
> Create a new empty FIFO queue.

out(Q1) -> Result
> Remove the head item from a queue.

out_r(Q1) -> Result
> Remove the last item from a queue.

reverse(Q1) -> Q2
> Reverse a queue.

snoc(Q1, Item) -> Q2
> Insert an item at the end of a queue.

split(N, Q1) -> {Q2,Q3}
> Split a queue in two.

tail(Q1) -> Q2
> Remove the head item from a queue.

to_list(Q) -> list()
> Convert a queue to a list.

F.49 Module: random

Pseudorandom number generation.

seed() -> ran()
> Seeds random number generation with default values.

seed(A1, A2, A3) -> ran()
> Seeds random number generator.

seed0() -> ran()
> Return default state for random number generation.

uniform()-> float()
> Return a random float.

uniform(N) -> int()
> Return a random integer.

uniform_s(State0) -> {float(), State1}
> Return a random float.

uniform_s(N, State0) -> {int(), State1}
> Return a random integer.

F.50 Module: regexp

Regular expression functions for strings.

first_match(String, RegExp) -> MatchRes
Match a regular expression.

format_error(ErrorDescriptor) -> Chars
Format an error descriptor.

gsub(String, RegExp, New) -> SubRes
Substitute all occurrences of a regular expression.

match(String, RegExp) -> MatchRes
Match a regular expression.

matches(String, RegExp) -> MatchRes
Match a regular expression.

parse(RegExp) -> ParseRes
Parse a regular expression.

sh_to_awk(ShRegExp) -> AwkRegExp
Convert an sh regular expression into an AWK one.

split(String, RegExp) -> SplitRes
Split a string into fields.

sub(String, RegExp, New) -> SubRes
Substitute the first occurrence of a regular expression.

F.51 Module: rpc

Remote procedure call services.

abcast(Name, Msg) -> void()
Broadcast a message asynchronously to a registered process on all nodes.

abcast(Nodes, Name, Msg) -> void()
Broadcast a message asynchronously to a registered process on specific nodes.

async_call(Node, Module, Function, Args) -> Key
Evaluate a function call on a node, asynchrous version.

block_call(Node, Module, Function, Args) -> Res | {badrpc, Reason}
Evaluate a function call on a node in the RPC server's context.

block_call(Node, Module, Function, Args, Timeout) -> Res | {badrpc, Reason}
Evaluate a function call on a node in the RPC server's context.

call(Node, Module, Function, Args) -> Res | {badrpc, Reason}
Evaluate a function call on a node.

call(Node, Module, Function, Args, Timeout) -> Res | {badrpc, Reason}
Evaluate a function call on a node.

cast(Node, Module, Function, Args) -> void()
 Run a function on a node ignoring the result.

eval_everywhere(Module, Funtion, Args) -> void()
 Run a function on all nodes, ignoring the result.

eval_everywhere(Nodes, Module, Function, Args) -> void()
 Run a function on specific nodes, ignoring the result.

multi_server_call(Name, Msg) -> {Replies, BadNodes}
 Interact with the servers on a number of nodes.

multi_server_call(Nodes, Name, Msg) -> {Replies, BadNodes}
 Interact with the servers on a number of nodes.

multicall(Module, Function, Args) -> {ResL, BadNodes}
 Evaluate a function call on a number of nodes.

multicall(Module, Function, Args, Timeout) -> {ResL, BadNodes}
 Evaluate a function call on a number of nodes.

multicall(Nodes, Module, Function, Args) -> {ResL, BadNodes}
 Evaluate a function call on a number of nodes.

multicall(Nodes, Module, Function, Args, Timeout) -> {ResL, BadNodes}
 Evaluate a function call on a number of nodes.

nb_yield(Key) -> {value, Val} | timeout
 Deliver the result of evaluating a function call on a node (nonblocking).

nb_yield(Key, Timeout) -> {value, Val} | timeout
 Deliver the result of evaluating a function call on a node (nonblocking).

parallel_eval(FuncCalls) -> ResL
 Evaluate several function calls on all nodes in parallel.

pinfo(Pid) -> ({Item, Info}) | undefined
 Information about a process.

pinfo(Pid, Item) -> {Item, Info} | undefined | ()
 Information about a process.

pmap({Module, Function}, ExtraArgs, List2) -> List1
 Parallell evaluation of mapping a function over a list.

safe_multi_server_call(Nodes, Name, Msg) -> {Replies, BadNodes}
 Interact with the servers on a number of nodes (deprecated).

sbcast(Name, Msg) -> {GoodNodes, BadNodes}
 Broadcast a message synchronously to a registered process on all nodes.

sbcast(Nodes, Name, Msg) -> {GoodNodes, BadNodes}
 Broadcast a message synchronously to a registered process on specific nodes.

server_call(Node, Name, ReplyWrapper, Msg) -> Reply | {error, Reason}
 Interact with a server on a node.

yield(Key) -> Res | {badrpc, Reason}
 Deliver the result of evaluating a function call on a node (blocking).

F.52 Module: seq_trace

Sequential tracing of messages.

get_system_tracer() -> Tracer
Return thepid()orport()of the current system tracer.

get_token() -> TraceToken
Return the value of the trace token.

get_token(Component) -> {Component, Val}
Return the value of a trace token component.

print(TraceInfo) -> void()
Put the Erlang termTraceInfointo the sequential trace output.

print(Label, TraceInfo) -> void()
Put the Erlang termTraceInfointo the sequential trace output.

reset_trace() -> void()
Stop all sequential tracing on the local node.

set_system_tracer(Tracer) -> OldTracer
Set the system tracer.

set_token(Token) -> PreviousToken
Set the trace token.

set_token(Component, Val) -> {Component, OldVal}
Set a component of the trace token.

F.53 Module: sets

Functions for set manipulation.

add_element(Element, Set1) -> Set2
Add an element to aSet.

del_element(Element, Set1) -> Set2
Remove an element from aSet.

filter(Pred, Set1) -> Set2
Filter set elements.

fold(Function, Acc0, Set) -> Acc1
Fold over set elements.

from_list(List) -> Set
Convert a list into aSet.

intersection(SetList) -> Set
Return the intersection of a list ofSets.

intersection(Set1, Set2) -> Set3
Return the intersection of two Sets.

is_element(Element, Set) -> bool()
Test for membership of aSet.

is_set(Set) -> bool()
> Test for aSet.

is_subset(Set1, Set2) -> bool()
> Test for subset.

new() -> Set
> Return an empty set.

size(Set) -> int()
> Return the number of elements in a set.

subtract(Set1, Set2) -> Set3
> Return the difference of two Sets.

to_list(Set) -> List
> Convert aSetinto a list.

union(SetList) -> Set
> Return the union of a list of Sets.

union(Set1, Set2) -> Set3
> Return the union of two Sets.

F.54 Module: shell

The Erlang shell.

history(N) -> integer()
> Sets the number of previous commands to keep.

results(N) -> integer()
> Sets the number of previous commands to keep.

start_restricted(Module) -> ok
> Exits a normal shell and starts a restricted shell.

stop_restricted() -> ok
> Exits a restricted shell and starts a normal shell.

F.55 Module: slave

Functions to starting and controlling slave nodes.

pseudo((Master | ServerList)) -> ok
> Start a number of pseudoservers.

pseudo(Master, ServerList) -> ok
> Start a number of pseudoservers.

relay(Pid)
> Run a pseudoserver.

start(Host, Name, Args) -> {ok, Node} | {error, Reason}
> Start a slave node on a host.

start_link(Host, Name, Args) -> {ok, Node} | {error, Reason}
> Start and link to a slave node on a host.

stop(Node) -> ok
> Stop (kill) a node.

F.56 Module: sofs

Functions for manipulating sets of sets.

a_function(Tuples (, Type)) -> Function
> Create a function.

canonical_relation(SetOfSets) -> BinRel
> Return the canonical map.

composite(Function1, Function2) -> Function3
> Return the composite of two functions.

constant_function(Set, AnySet) -> Function
> Create the function that maps each element of a set onto another set.

converse(BinRel1) -> BinRel2
> Return the converse of a binary relation.

difference(Set1, Set2) -> Set3
> Return the difference of two sets.

digraph_to_family(Graph (, Type)) -> Family
> Create a family from a directed graph.

domain(BinRel) -> Set
> Return the domain of a binary relation.

drestriction(BinRel1, Set) -> BinRel2
> Return a restriction of a binary relation.

drestriction(SetFun, Set1, Set2) -> Set3
> Return a restriction of a relation.

empty_set() -> Set
> Return the untyped empty set.

extension(BinRel1, Set, AnySet) -> BinRel2
> Extend the domain of a binary relation.

family(Tuples (, Type)) -> Family
> Create a family of subsets.

family_difference(Family1, Family2) -> Family3
> Return the difference of two families.

family_domain(Family1) -> Family2
> Return a family of domains.

family_field(Family1) -> Family2
> Return a family of fields.

family_intersection(Family1) -> Family2
> Return the intersection of a family of sets of sets.

family_intersection(Family1, Family2) -> Family3
> Return the intersection of two families.

family_projection(SetFun, Family1) -> Family2
> Return a family of modified subsets.

family_range(Family1) -> Family2
> Return a family of ranges.

family_specification(Fun, Family1) -> Family2
> Select a subset of a family using a predicate.

family_to_digraph(Family (, GraphType)) -> Graph
> Create a directed graph from a family.

family_to_relation(Family) -> BinRel
> Create a binary relation from a family.

family_union(Family1) -> Family2
> Return the union of a family of sets of sets.

family_union(Family1, Family2) -> Family3
> Return the union of two families.

field(BinRel) -> Set
> Return the field of a binary relation.

from_external(ExternalSet, Type) -> AnySet
> Create a set.

from_sets(ListOfSets) -> Set
> Create a set out of a list of sets.

from_sets(TupleOfSets) -> Ordset
> Create an ordered set out of a tuple of sets.

from_term(Term (, Type)) -> AnySet
> Create a set.

image(BinRel, Set1) -> Set2
> Return the image of a set under a binary relation.

intersection(SetOfSets) -> Set
> Return the intersection of a set of sets.

intersection(Set1, Set2) -> Set3
> Return the intersection of two sets.

intersection_of_family(Family) -> Set
> Return the intersection of a family.

inverse(Function1) -> Function2
> Return the inverse of a function.

inverse_image(BinRel, Set1) -> Set2
> Return the inverse image of a set under a binary relation.

is_a_function(BinRel) -> Bool
Test for a function.

is_disjoint(Set1, Set2) -> Bool
Test for disjoint sets.

is_empty_set(AnySet) -> Bool
Test for an empty set.

is_equal(AnySet1, AnySet2) -> Bool
Test two sets for equality.

is_set(AnySet) -> Bool
Test for an unordered set.

is_sofs_set(Term) -> Bool
Test for an unordered set.

is_subset(Set1, Set2) -> Bool
Test two sets for subset.

is_type(Term) -> Bool
Test for a type.

join(Relation1, I, Relation2, J) -> Relation3
Return the join of two relations.

multiple_relative_product(TupleOfBinRels, BinRel1) -> BinRel2
Return the multiple relative product of a tuple of binary relations and a relation.

no_elements(ASet) -> NoElements
Return the number of elements of a set.

partition(SetOfSets) -> Partition
Return the coarsest partition given a set of sets.

partition(SetFun, Set) -> Partition
Return a partition of a set.

partition(SetFun, Set1, Set2) -> {Set3, Set4}
Return a partition of a set.

partition_family(SetFun, Set) -> Family
Return a family indexing a partition.

product(TupleOfSets) -> Relation
Return the Cartesian product of a tuple of sets.

product(Set1, Set2) -> BinRel
Return the Cartesian product of two sets.

projection(SetFun, Set1) -> Set2
Return a set of substituted elements.

range(BinRel) -> Set
Return the range of a binary relation.

relation(Tuples (, Type)) -> Relation
Create a relation.

relation_to_family(BinRel) -> Family

Create a family from a binary relation.

relative_product(TupleOfBinRels (, BinRel1)) -> BinRel2

Return the relative product of a tuple of binary relations and a binary relation.

relative_product(BinRel1, BinRel2) -> BinRel3

Return the relative product of two binary relations.

relative_product1(BinRel1, BinRel2) -> BinRel3

Return the relative_product of two binary relations.

restriction(BinRel1, Set) -> BinRel2

Return a restriction of a binary relation.

restriction(SetFun, Set1, Set2) -> Set3

Return a restriction of a set.

set(Terms (, Type)) -> Set

Create a set of atoms or any type of sets.

specification(Fun, Set1) -> Set2

Select a subset using a predicate.

strict_relation(BinRel1) -> BinRel2

Return the strict relation corresponding to a given relation.

substitution(SetFun, Set1) -> Set2

Return a function with a given set as domain.

symdiff(Set1, Set2) -> Set3

Return the symmetric difference of two sets.

symmetric_partition(Set1, Set2) -> {Set3, Set4, Set5}

Return a partition of two sets.

to_external(AnySet) -> ExternalSet

Return the elements of a set.

to_sets(ASet) -> Sets

Return a list or a tuple of the elements of set.

type(AnySet) -> Type

Return the type of a set.

union(SetOfSets) -> Set

Return the union of a set of sets.

union(Set1, Set2) -> Set3

Return the union of two sets.

union_of_family(Family) -> Set

Return the union of a family.

weak_relation(BinRel1) -> BinRel2

Return the weak relation corresponding to a given relation.

F.57 Module: string

String-processing functions.

centre(String, Number, Character) -> Centered
> Center a string.

chars(Character, Number, Tail) -> String
> Return a string consisting of numbers of characters.

concat(String1, String2) -> String3
> Concatenate two strings.

copies(String, Number) -> Copies
> Copy a string.

cspan(String, Chars) -> Length
> Span characters at start of string.

equal(String1, String2) -> bool()
> Test string equality.

left(String, Number, Character) -> Left
> Adjust left end of string.

len(String) -> Length
> Return the length of a string.

rchr(String, Character) -> Index
> Return the index of the first/last occurrence ofCharacterinString.

right(String, Number, Character) -> Right
> Adjust right end of string.

rstr(String, SubString) -> Index
> Find the index of a substring.

strip(String, Direction, Character) -> Stripped
> Strip leading or trailing characters.

sub_string(String, Start, Stop) -> SubString
> Extract a substring.

sub_word(String, Number, Character) -> Word
> Extract subword.

substr(String, Start, Length) -> Substring
> Return a substring of String.

to_float(String) -> {Float,Rest} | {error,Reason}
> Return a float whose text representation is the integers (ASCII values) in String.

to_integer(String) -> {Int,Rest} | {error,Reason}
> Return an integer whose text representation is the integers (ASCII values) in String.

to_upper(Char) -> CharResult
> Convert case of string (ISO/IEC 8859-1).

tokens(String, SeparatorList) -> Tokens
Split string into tokens.

words(String, Character) -> Count
Count blank separated words.

F.58 Module: supervisor

Generic supervisor behavior.

Module:init(Args) -> Result
Return a supervisor specification.

check_childspecs((ChildSpec)) -> Result
Check whether child specifications are syntactically correct.

delete_child(SupRef, Id) -> Result
Delete a child specification from a supervisor.

restart_child(SupRef, Id) -> Result
Restart a terminated child process belonging to a supervisor.

start_child(SupRef, ChildSpec) -> Result
Dynamically add a child process to a supervisor.

start_link(SupName, Module, Args) -> Result
Create a supervisor process.

terminate_child(SupRef, Id) -> Result
Terminate a child process belonging to a supervisor.

which_children(SupRef) -> ({Id,Child,Type,Modules})
Return information about all children specifications and child processes belonging to a supervisor.

F.59 Module: sys

A functional interface to system messages.

Mod:system_code_change(Misc, Module, OldVsn, Extra) -> {ok, NMisc}
Called when the process should perform a code change.

Mod:system_continue(Parent, Debug, Misc)
Called when the process should continue its execution.

Mod:system_terminate(Reason, Parent, Debug, Misc)
Called when the process should terminate.

change_code(Name, Module, OldVsn, Extra, Timeout) -> ok | {error, Reason}
Send the code change system message to the process.

debug_options(Options) -> (dbg_opt())
Convert a list of options to a debug structure.

get_debug(Item,Debug,Default) -> term()
Get the data associated with a debug option.

get_status(Name,Timeout) -> {status, Pid, {module, Mod}, (PDict, SysState, Parent, Dbg, Misc)}
>   Get the status of the process.

handle_debug((dbg_opt()),FormFunc,Extra,Event) -> (dbg_opt())
>   Generate a system event.

handle_system_msg(Msg,From,Parent,Module,Debug,Misc)
>   Take care of system messages.

install(Name,{Func,FuncState},Timeout)
>   Install a debug function in the process.

log(Name,Flag,Timeout) -> ok | {ok, (system_event())}
>   Log system events in memory.

log_to_file(Name,Flag,Timeout) -> ok | {error, open_file}
>   Log system events to the specified file.

no_debug(Name,Timeout) -> void()
>   Turn off debugging.

print_log(Debug) -> void()
>   Print the logged events in the debug structure.

remove(Name,Func,Timeout) -> void()
>   Remove a debug function from the process.

resume(Name,Timeout) -> void()
>   Resume a suspended process.

statistics(Name,Flag,Timeout) -> ok | {ok, Statistics}
>   Enable or disable the collections of statistics.

suspend(Name,Timeout) -> void()
>   Suspend the process.

trace(Name,Flag,Timeout) -> void()
>   Print all system events on standard_io.

F.60   Module: timer

Timer functions.

apply_after(Time, Module, Function, Arguments) -> {ok, Tref} | {error, Reason}
>   ApplyModule:Function(Arguments)after a specifiedTime.

apply_interval(Time, Module, Function, Arguments) -> {ok, TRef} | {error, Reason}
>   EvaluateModule:Function(Arguments)repeatedly at intervals ofTime.

cancel(TRef) -> {ok, cancel} | {error, Reason}
>   Cancel a previously requested timeout identified byTRef.

hms(Hours, Minutes, Seconds) -> Milliseconds
>   Convert Hours + Minutes + Seconds to Milliseconds.

hours(Hours) -> Milliseconds
>   Convert Hours to Milliseconds.

kill_after(Time) -> {ok, TRef} | {error,Reason2}
Send an exit signal with Reason after a specifiedTime.

minutes(Minutes) -> Milliseconds
Converts Minutes to Milliseconds.

now_diff(T2, T1) -> Tdiff
Calculate time difference between now/0 timestamps.

seconds(Seconds) -> Milliseconds
Convert Seconds to Milliseconds.

send_after(Time, Message) -> {ok, TRef} | {error,Reason}
SendMessageto the PID after a specifiedTime.

send_interval(Time, Message) -> {ok, TRef} | {error, Reason}
Send Message repeatedly at intervals ofTime.

sleep(Time) -> ok
Suspend the calling process forTimeamount of milliseconds.

start() -> ok
Start a global timer server (namedtimer_server).

tc(Module, Function, Arguments) -> {Time, Value}
Measure the real time it takes to evaluate apply(Module, Function, Arguments).

F.61 Module: win32reg

Provides access to the registry on Windows.

change_key(RegHandle, Key) -> ReturnValue
Move to a key in the registry.

change_key_create(RegHandle, Key) -> ReturnValue
Move to a key, and create it if it is not there.

close(RegHandle)-> ReturnValue
Close the registry.

current_key(RegHandle) -> ReturnValue
Return the path to the current key.

delete_key(RegHandle) -> ReturnValue
Delete the current key.

delete_value(RegHandle, Name) -> ReturnValue
Delete the named value on the current key.

expand(String) -> ExpandedString
Expand a string with environment variables.

format_error(ErrorId) -> ErrorString
Convert an POSIX error code to a string.

open(OpenModeList)-> ReturnValue
Open the registry for reading or writing.

set_value(RegHandle, Name, Value) -> ReturnValue
> Set value at the current registry key with specified name.

sub_keys(RegHandle) -> ReturnValue
> Get subkeys to the current key.

value(RegHandle, Name) -> ReturnValue
> Get the named value on the current key.

values(RegHandle) -> ReturnValue
> Get all values on the current key.

F.62 Module: zip

Utility for reading and creating ZIP archives.

create(Name, FileList, Options) -> RetValue
> Create a ZIP archive with options.

extract(Archive, Options) -> RetValue
> Extract files from a ZIP archive.

t(Archive)
> Print the name of each file in a ZIP archive.

table(Archive, Options)
> Retrieve the name of all files in a ZIP archive.

tt(Archive)
> Print name and information for each file in a ZIP archive.

zip_close(ZipHandle) -> ok | {error, einval}
> Close an open archive.

zip_get(FileName, ZipHandle) -> {ok, Result} | {error, Reason}
> Extract files from an open archive.

zip_list_dir(ZipHandle) -> Result | {error, Reason}
> Return a table of files in open ZIP archive.

zip_open(Archive, Options) -> {ok, ZipHandle} | {error, Reason}
> Open an archive and return a handle to it.

F.63 Module: zlib

Zlib compression interface.

adler32(Z, Binary) -> Checksum
> Calculate the adler checksum.

adler32(Z, PrevAdler, Binary) -> Checksum
> Calculate the adler checksum.

close(Z) -> ok
> Close a stream.

compress(Binary) -> Compressed
>   Compress a binary with standard zlib functionality.

crc32(Z) -> CRC
>   Get current CRC.

crc32(Z, Binary) -> CRC
>   Calculate CRC.

crc32(Z, PrevCRC, Binary) -> CRC
>   Calculate CRC.

deflate(Z, Data) -> Compressed
>   Compress data.

deflate(Z, Data, Flush) ->
>   Compress data.

deflateEnd(Z) -> ok
>   End deflate session.

deflateInit(Z) -> ok
>   Initialize a session for compression.

deflateInit(Z, Level) -> ok
>   Initialize a session for compression.

deflateInit(Z, Level, Method, WindowBits, MemLevel, Strategy) -> ok
>   Initialize a session for compression.

deflateParams(Z, Level, Strategy) -> ok
>   Dynamicly update deflate parameters.

deflateReset(Z) -> ok
>   Reset the deflate session.

deflateSetDictionary(Z, Dictionary) -> Adler32
>   Initialize the compression dictionary.

getBufSize(Z) -> Size
>   Get buffer size.

gunzip(Bin) -> Decompressed
>   Uncompress a binary with gz header.

gzip(Data) -> Compressed
>   Compress a binary with gz header.

inflate(Z, Data) -> DeCompressed
>   Decompress data.

inflateEnd(Z) -> ok
>   End inflate session.

inflateInit(Z) -> ok
>   Initialize a session for decompression.

inflateInit(Z, WindowBits) -> ok
>   Initialize a session for decompression.

inflateReset(Z) -> ok
>Reset the inflate session.

inflateSetDictionary(Z, Dictionary) -> ok
Initialize the decompression dictionary.

open() -> Z
Open a stream and return a stream reference.

setBufSize(Z, Size) -> ok
Set buffer size.

uncompress(Binary) -> Decompressed
Uncompress a binary with standard zlib functionality.

unzip(Binary) -> Decompressed
Uncompress a binary without the zlib headers.

zip(Binary) -> Compressed
Compress a binary without the zlib headers.

Index

Pragmatic Projects

Release It!

Whether it's in Java, .NET, or Ruby on Rails, getting your application ready to ship is only half the battle. Did you design your system to survive a sudden rush of visitors from Digg or Slashdot? Or an influx of real world customers from 100 different countries? Are you ready for a world filled with flakey networks, tangled databases, and impatient users?

If you're a developer and don't want to be on call at 3AM for the rest of your life, this book will help.

Design and Deploy Production-Ready Software
Michael T. Nygard
(368 pages) ISBN: 0-9787392-1-3. $34.95
http://pragmaticprogrammer.com/titles/mnee

Manage It!

Manage It! is a risk-based guide to making good decisions about how to plan and guide your projects. Author Johanna Rothman shows you how to beg, borrow, and steal from the best methodologies to fit your particular project. You'll find what works best for *you.*

• Learn all about different project lifecycles • See how to organize a project • Compare sample project dashboards • See how to staff a project • Know when you're done—and what that means.

Your Guide to Modern, Pragmatic Project Management
Johanna Rothman
(360 pages) ISBN: 0-9787392-4-8. $34.95
http://pragmaticprogrammer.com/titles/jrpm

Technology

The Definitive ANTLR Reference

This book is the essential reference guide to ANTLR v3, the most powerful, easy-to-use parser generator built to date. Learn all about its amazing new LL(*) parsing technology, tree construction facilities, StringTemplate code generation template engine, and sophisticated ANTLRWorks GUI development environment. Learn to use ANTLR directly from its author!

The Definitive ANTLR Reference: Building Domain-Specific Languages
Terence Parr
(384 pages) ISBN: 0-9787392-5-6. $36.95
http://pragmaticprogrammer.com/titles/tpantlr

Pragmatic Ajax

AJAX redefines the user experience for web applications, providing compelling user interfaces. Now you can dig deeper into AJAX itself as this book shows you how to make AJAX magic. Explore both the fundamental technologies and the emerging frameworks that make it easy.

From Google Maps to Ajaxified Java, .NET, and Ruby on Rails applications, this Pragmatic guide strips away the mystery and shows you the easy way to make Ajax work for you.

Pragmatic Ajax: A Web 2.0 Primer
Justin Gehtland, Ben Galbraith, Dion Almaer
(296 pages) ISBN: 0-9766940-8-5. $29.95
http://pragmaticprogrammer.com/titles/ajax

Agile Methods

Agile Retrospectives

Mine the experience of your software development team continually throughout the life of the project. Rather than waiting until the end of the project—as with a traditional retrospective, when it's too late to help—agile retrospectives help you adjust to change *today*.

The tools and recipes in this book will help you uncover and solve hidden (and not-so-hidden) problems with your technology, your methodology, and those difficult "people issues" on your team.

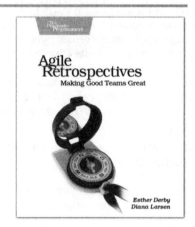

Agile Retrospectives: Making Good Teams Great
Esther Derby and Diana Larsen
(170 pages) ISBN: 0-9776166-4-9. $29.95
http://pragmaticprogrammer.com/titles/dlret

Practices of an Agile Developer

Agility is all about using feedback to respond to change. Learn how to apply the principles of agility throughout the software development process • Establish and maintain an agile working environment • Deliver what users really want • Use personal agile techniques for better coding and debugging • Use effective collaborative techniques for better teamwork • Move to an agile approach

Practices of an Agile Developer: Working in the Real World
Venkat Subramaniam and Andy Hunt
(189 pages) ISBN: 0-9745140-8-X. $29.95
http://pragmaticprogrammer.com/titles/pad

Ruby on Rails

Agile Web Development with Rails

Rails is a full-stack, open-source web framework, with integrated support for unit, functional, and integration testing. It enforces good design principles, consistency of code across your team (and across your organization), and proper release management. This is newly updated Second Edition, which goes beyond the Jolt-award winning first edition with new material on:

• Migrations • RJS templates • Respond_to
• Integration Tests • Additional ActiveRecord features • Another year's worth of Rails best practices

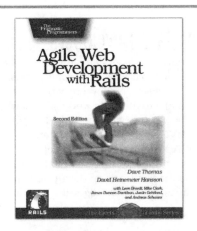

Agile Web Development with Rails: Second Edition
Dave Thomas, and David Heinemeier Hansson with Leon Breedt, Mike Clark, James Duncan Davidson, Justin Gehtland, and Andreas Schwarz
(750 pages) ISBN: 0-9776166-3-0. $39.95
http://pragmaticprogrammer.com/titles/rails2

Rails Recipes

Owning Rails Recipes is like having the best Rails programmers sitting next to you when you code. You'll see seventy in-depth, ready-to-use recipes that you can use right away, including recipes for

• User interface • Database • Controller
• Testing • E-Mail • and big-picture recipes
• Complete worked solutions to common problems.
• Unique Rails productivity tips • See how the pros write their Rails applications. • Includes contributions from Rails core team.

Rails Recipes
Chad Fowler
(368 pages) ISBN: 0-9776166-0-6. $32.95
http://pragmaticprogrammer.com/titles/fr_rr

Rails and More

Rails for Java Developers

Enterprise Java developers already have most of the skills needed to create Rails applications. They just need a guide which shows how their Java knowledge maps to the Rails world. That's what this book does. It covers: • The Ruby language • Building MVC Applications • Unit and Functional Testing • Security • Project Automation • Configuration • Web Services This book is the fast track for Java programmers who are learning or evaluating Ruby on Rails.

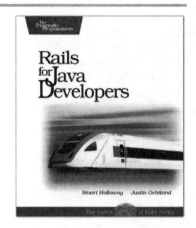

Rails for Java Developers
Stuart Halloway and Justin Gehtland
(300 pages) ISBN: 0-9776166-9-X. $34.95
http://pragmaticprogrammer.com/titles/fr_r4j

TextMate

If you're coding Ruby or Rails on a Mac, then you owe it to yourself to get the TextMate editor. And, once you're using TextMate, you owe it to yourself to pick up this book. It's packed with information which will help you automate all your editing tasks, saving you time to concentrate on the important stuff. Use snippets to insert boilerplate code and refactorings to move stuff around. Learn how to write your own extensions to customize it to the way you work.

TextMate: Power Editing for the Mac
James Edward Gray II
(200 pages) ISBN: 0-9787392-3-X. $29.95
http://pragmaticprogrammer.com/titles/textmate

Pragmatic Career

My Job Went to India

The job market is shifting. Your current job may be outsourced, perhaps to India or eastern Europe. But you can save your job and improve your career by following these practical and timely tips. See how to: • treat your career as a business • build your own brand as a software developer • develop a structured plan for keeping your skills up to date • market yourself to your company and rest of the industry • keep your job!

My Job Went to India: 52 Ways to Save Your Job
Chad Fowler
(185 pages) ISBN: 0-9766940-1-8. $19.95
http://pragmaticprogrammer.com/titles/mjwti

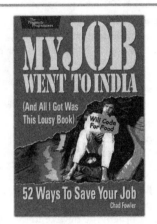

Behind Closed Doors

You can learn to be a better manager—even a great manager—with this guide. You'll find powerful tips covering:

• Delegating effectively • Using feedback and goal-setting • Developing influence • Handling one-on-one meetings • Coaching and mentoring • Deciding what work to do-and what not to do • . . . and more!

Behind Closed Doors Secrets of Great Management
Johanna Rothman and Esther Derby
(192 pages) ISBN: 0-9766940-2-6. $24.95
http://pragmaticprogrammer.com/titles/rdbcd

The Pragmatic Bookshelf

The Pragmatic Bookshelf features books written by developers for developers. The titles continue the well-known Pragmatic Programmer style, and continue to garner awards and rave reviews. As development gets more and more difficult, the Pragmatic Programmers will be there with more titles and products to help you stay on top of your game.

Visit Us Online

Programming Erlang
http://pragmaticprogrammer.com/titles/jaerlang
Source code from this book, errata, and other resources. Come give us feedback, too!

Register for Updates
http://pragmaticprogrammer.com/updates
Be notified when updates and new books become available.

Join the Community
http://pragmaticprogrammer.com/community
Read our weblogs, join our online discussions, participate in our mailing list, interact with our wiki, and benefit from the experience of other Pragmatic Programmers.

New and Noteworthy
http://pragmaticprogrammer.com/news
Check out the latest pragmatic developments in the news.

Save on the PDF

Save on the PDF version of this book. Owning the paper version of this book entitles you to purchase the PDF version at a terrific discount. The PDF is great for carrying around on your laptop. It's hyperlinked, has color, and is fully searchable.

Buy it now at pragmaticprogrammer.com/coupon.

Contact Us

Phone Orders:	1-800-699-PROG (+1 919 847 3884)
Online Orders:	www.pragmaticprogrammer.com/catalog
Customer Service:	orders@pragmaticprogrammer.com
Non-English Versions:	translations@pragmaticprogrammer.com
Pragmatic Teaching:	academic@pragmaticprogrammer.com
Author Proposals:	proposals@pragmaticprogrammer.com